ISIS IS US

The Shocking Truth
Behind the
Army of
Terror

ProgRESSive
Independent Media.
ProgressivePress.com

2016

ISIS IS US
The Shocking Truth
Behind the Army of Terror

© 2016 All rights reserved
ProgressivePress.com, San Diego, Calif.
SECOND EDITION, OCTOBER 10, 2016
Length: 118,000 words.
Paperback List Price: $19.95.
ISBN: 1-61577-152-2, EAN: 978-1-61577-152-3
E-book ISBN 1-61577-515-3

Contributor credits:

"Unmasking ISIS" by George Washington's Blog
"Born of the USA" by Wayne Madsen
"The Truth About ISIS" by Syrian Girl Partisan
"It's the Military-Monetary-Media Complex," etc., by John-Paul Leonard
Citations from Michel Chossudovsky, Webster Griffin Tarpley, Jonathan Mowat, F. Wm. Engdahl, Thierry Meyssan, Vladimir Putin, Tony Cartalucci, Ken O'Keefe, Seymour Hersh, Chris Brennan, The Saker, Deepa Kunar, Tim Anderson and many other thinkers and researchers of our time.

Library of Congress Subject Heading
ISIS/Daesh, LC: HV6433.I722

BISAC Subject Area Codes
POL037000 POLITICAL SCIENCE / Terrorism
POL036000 POLITICAL SCIENCE / Intelligence & Espionage
POL061000 POLITICAL SCIENCE / Genocide & War Crimes
POL045000 POLITICAL SCIENCE / Colonialism & Post-Colonialism
HIS027170 HISTORY / Military / Iraq War (2003-2011)
SOC058000 / POL506000 Conspiracy Investigations

The "US" in "ISIS IS US" has multiple possible meanings. 1). USA. 2). USA and allies. 3). The book or its cover is a portrait of ISIS. 4). We have met the enemy and it is us. It is the USA and it is us – We are responsible for what the US is doing (Ken O'Keefe). 5). We are all one human race, all in the same boat, we can't just make war over there and have peace at home. 6). Anyone could be programmed to act like ISIS

The circular logo on the cover, instead of the Arabic motto on the ISIS flag ("Mohamed is the Prophet of God") says, "There is no God but Money." The letters I, S and U are from the ISIS flag's motto "La ilaha illa-Llah" ("No gods besides God"). The two mottos form the Islamic profession of faith, which figures on both the ISIS and Saudi flags.

Once a ruler becomes religious, it becomes impossible for you to debate with him. Once someone rules in the name of religion, your lives become hell.

– Muammar Gaddafi

We believe America is practicing all kinds of terrorism against Libya. Even the accusation that we are involved in terrorism is in itself an act of terrorism.

– Gaddafi

We came, we saw, he died.

– Hillary Clinton
(laughs, pleased with herself)

Former CIA Contractor Steven Kelley Told *Russia Today*...

"The US has always been the main sponsor and creator of Daesh [Arabic acronym for ISIS], so this charade that they are having anything to do with fighting Daesh in Syria is completely a farce, and I think the rest of the world is smart enough to realize that...

" If I had anything to advise Mr. Putin, I would say get the job done, stop participating in any of these peace agreements and destroy Daesh and get the job over with...

"The US is not going to do anything to help remove Daesh and is going to do everything possible to reconstruct, rearm, and resupply, and put more personnel into the field. So everything they say is a lie, and Putin really needs to stop playing games with the US State Department and get the job done."

Kelley went on to credit Russia for getting involved in Syria when it did, stating that the country would have been "completely overrun" by now if it didn't.

https://www.rt.com/op-edge/361033-syria-russia-us-kerry/ 9/29/16

Note to the Second Edition:

Sore Losers in the Pentagon Threaten WWIII

October, 2016. A year after Russian intervention against ISIS caught the US red-handed in support of terrorism, US hawks are running out of options in Syria. They try to play the Kurdish card to carve up Syria, jeopardizing the relationship with their ally Turkey. They pretend to fight ISIS, while arming ISIS clones by other names. As many as 5,000 US advisers help their "transvestite terrorists" try to stop Assad from retaking Aleppo. Yet the Pentagon neocons are losing this war.

Now they have taken to playing the madman, lashing out with airstrikes on Syrian troops battling ISIS near Deir Ezzor, Syria's oil center. When Russian general Konashenkov reminded the USA about the SAM S-400 missiles in place, US army spokesman Kirby warned Russia of "more body bags" and "attacks on Russian cities" if they don't play along. Gen. Milley raved, "We will destroy you! We'll beat you anywhere, anytime," if Russia defends its positions. The two sides are now warning they could target each other's troops on the ground.

Some say the risk of WWIII is greater now than during the Cuban Missile Crisis. Why all the fuss?

Geopolitics. The USA is the heir to the British empire, the great sea power which aimed to straddle the planet. The greatest obstacle was always the great land power Russia, which stretches almost halfway around the earth, from Europe to the Pacific. Should Russia become closely allied with the Muslim world, its reach would span the Black Sea, Red Sea, and Mediterranean, across Africa to the Atlantic, and south through Afghanistan and Pakistan to the Indian Ocean.

The putsch against the Ukraine, the subversive "Arab Spring," the wars on Iraq, Libya and Syria, are all meant to box in Russia, subdue Africa and Asia, and cement total domination by the "military-monetary-media complex" of the "Anglo-Zionist empire" over the entire globe.

TABLE OF CONTENTS

The ISIS-Contra Affair

Did the "Islamic State" spring full-blown into spontaneous being as the fanatical scourge of the Middle East, or was it helped along by state sponsors?

There are uncanny parallels with Iran-Contra. In the 1980's, the Reagan team wanted to topple the government of Nicaragua, using right-wing mercenaries, or death squads, based in Honduras. But Congress passed a law against it. So they went around, by financing the Contras via Iran.

Thirty years later, the hawks in Washington wanted to topple the elected governments of Libya and Syria, crush the popular resistance in Iraq, and split up those countries on ethnic lines. Once again, they wanted to do this using death squads. So they got around Congress by having Qatar and the Saudis finance it.

To set up the "Sunni" (Al-Qaida) and "Shiite" (regime) death squads to cut up Iraq, they sent John Negroponte as Ambassador to Baghdad in 2004. The same guy they sent to Honduras as Ambassador from 1981 to 1985. In 2011 they sent some of those killers from Iraq to Libya to overthrow Qaddafi, with NATO air cover. From Libya, they were sent to Syria to start the killing there – the dirty war directed by Negroponte's right-hand man, US Ambassador Ford.

The US embedded media perversely pinned these killings on Assad, following the script for another NATO invasion. Only Russia's UN veto spared Syria. So the sheikhs kept financing the "rebels" – and the US pretended to fight them – until they grew into the ISIS terror army. They and their backers have still not quit.

Even Fox News is saying the US coalition against ISIS is a myth.[1] In a recent US poll, just 18% think we have the upper hand in the "war on terror."[2] In a poll by an international firm in Syria, 82% said the US and its allies created ISIS.[3]

The wave of refugees, attacks in Paris and San Bernardino, and early reception to this book, tell me people want an end to the "war on terror," and they want to know what's really going on. So I'm putting the spoiler right here on the first page.

European efforts to subjugate the Middle East go back to the British, Napoleon, the Crusades, the Romans, and Alexander the Great. The British knew the best way to permanently hold a territory was to settle it; this is how they beat the French in North America. The Old World was already well settled, though. So to capture the Near East prize, England joined forces with Herzl's Zionists. In 1917, their Balfour Declaration announced the plan for Jewish settlement in Palestine.

Another way to hold vast domains is divide and chaos, to smash them up into quarreling fiefdoms. And the cheapest way to get people to fight each other is with religion. British, French, Israeli and US strategists have all written up plans to rule the Muslim world, by breaking up the Arab states *along sectarian lines*. That goal is what "ethnic cleansing," Al Qaida, ISIS death squads, "Islamic jihad" terrorism, the Bushes' wars on Iraq and even 9/11 are really all about.

I still hope you'll read the whole book, though. There's a lot more good stuff!

And if you like it, it would be *so* nice if you'd give it a little online review too. :-)

---

[1] http://video.foxbusiness.com/v/4661253273001/obamas-coalition-against-isis-a-myth/
[2] http://www.cnn.com/2015/12/28/politics/american-terrorists-poll-winning-cnn-orc/
[3] www.washingtonsblog.com/2015/09/polls-show-syrians-overwhelmingly-blame-u-s-for-isis.html

Ambassadors of Terror

The world has never seen anything quite like ISIS[4] before. Where in the world did it come from? Many pundits say this unique terrorist army would not exist if we had not crushed Saddam Hussein's regime in Bush's war on Iraq. Politicians like Donald Trump or Rand Paul are saying that Iraq, Libya and Syria were better off under Saddam, Qaddafi and Assad than they are now.

Americans had supported the war on Iraq "to make the world safe for democracy" – to stop a dangerous dictator from oppressing his people and using weapons of mass destruction – not to plunge the Middle East into the hands of savage extremists who seem set on demolishing modern civilization.

The world was shocked by the ISIS blitz of June 2014 that captured huge areas of Iraq, oil fields and the second largest city, Mosul, nearly bringing the government in Baghdad to collapse. NBC News headlined, "Huge Majority Regret Iraq War."[5] A poll showed that only 22% of Americans still thought the Iraq war had been a good idea. This was a new low, down from 32% in 2013 and 62% in March 2003, when Secretary of State Colin Powell told the big lie at the UN about Saddam Hussein's "threat" to our security.

Apparently, many Americans make the link between the war on Iraq, and the rise of terrorism in the region.

Few critics, however, have gone so far as to accuse the US or its allies of the unthinkable madness of *intentionally* creating ISIS.[6] For us in the US this would be difficult to accept. We cherish the faith that our nation is a force for good in the world, or at least tries to be; we want to share the good things about America with the rest of the world when we can.

Yet we have also heard of a dark side, that sometimes bubbles to the surface – for example, the Iran-Contra scandal. And therein lies a tale, a biography of deeds you won't read on Wikipedia for a very long time, at the end of this preface.

A Lot of Blackwater Under the Bridge

It's a basic historical fact that the US has shored up many Latin American dictatorships, but few details are generally known about how they do it. One practitioner who knows is Ambassador John Dimitri Negroponte, a veteran counter-insurgency expert going back to Operation Phoenix in the Vietnam War. He has held many high posts. Including Ambassador to Honduras 1981-1985, and US Ambassador to Iraq, 2004-2005...

---

[4] "Islamic State in Iraq and Shams (Syria)" or "the Levant" (ISIL), or "Islamic Emirate," or Daesh (Arabic initials). "Shams" means "sun" and is the old name for Syria, corresponding to "Levant," meaning "Rising" or "sunrise." (Viz. German *Morgenland und Abendland*.) An "L" could also be there for Libya. As for something new under the sun, the 18th and 19th century Wahhabi-Saudi conquest of Arabia is a precedent with parallels to the ISIS campaign of today; see the entry "A Word on Wahhabism" in the section on "Who Needs a Clash of Civilizations?").

[5] "Not Worth It: Huge Majority Regret Iraq War, Exclusive Poll Shows," June 24, 2014, http://www.nbcnews.com

[6] Vladimir Putin is the best-known such critic. He let diplomatic niceties drop in a speech at the Valdai Club in Sochi, Oct. 15, 2015. See "Statements by Statesmen."

Prof. Michel Chossudovsky of Global Research reveals how Negroponte fulfilled his assignment to defeat the Iraqi insurgency – and nearly managed to destroy Iraq as a nation as well.

> The recruitment of death squads is part of a well-established US military-intelligence agenda. There is a long and gruesome US history of covert funding and support of terror brigades and targeted assassinations going back to the Vietnam war...

> The recruitment and training of terror brigades in both Iraq and Syria was modeled on the "Salvador Option", a "terrorist model" of mass killings by US-sponsored death squads in Central America. It was first applied in El Salvador, in the heyday of resistance against the military dictatorship, resulting in an estimated 75,000 deaths.[7]

As Ambassador to Honduras in the 1980's, Negroponte was the lynch pin between Washington and the US-sponsored death squads in Honduras, El Salvador and Nicaragua.

In April 2004, G.W. Bush hired him as "the man for the job" to bring the "Salvador Option" to Iraq and Syria. In the same month, Al-Qaida in Iraq, the precursor to ISIS, was formed.[8]

Chossudovsky cites a report in *The Times Online*, in Jan. 2005, that the Pentagon was looking at

> forming hit squads of Kurdish and Shia fighters to target leaders of the Iraqi insurgency [Resistance] in a strategic shift borrowed from the American struggle against left-wing guerrillas in Central America 20 years ago.

> Under the so-called "El Salvador option", Iraqi and American forces would be sent to kill or kidnap insurgency leaders, even in Syria, where some are thought to shelter.

> Hit squads would be controversial and would probably be kept secret...

> The Reagan Administration funded and trained teams of nationalist forces to neutralise Salvadorean rebel leaders and sympathisers. ...

> John Negroponte, the US Ambassador in Baghdad, had a front-row seat at the time as Ambassador to Honduras from 1981-85.

> In the early 1980s, President Reagan's Administration funded and helped to train Nicaraguan contras based in Honduras, with the aim of ousting Nicaragua's Sandinista regime. The Contras were equipped using money from illegal American arms sales to Iran, a scandal that could have toppled Mr Reagan.

> The thrust of the Pentagon proposal in Iraq ... is to follow that model ...[9]

But it gets worse. A lot worse. Chossudovsky notes:

---

[7] *The Globalization of War: America's Long War against Humanity*, p. 151, Global Research Publishers, Montreal, 2015; "Terrorism with a 'Human Face': The History of America's Death Squads," Jan. 2013, http://www.globalresearch.ca; "'The Salvador Option For Syria': US-NATO Sponsored Death Squads Integrate 'Opposition Forces'", May 2012, http://www.globalresearch.ca. "Private security contractors" are paid approximately five times as much as ordinary soldiers.

[8] The National Counterterrorism Center's AQI page, http://www.nctc.gov/site/groups/aqi.html

[9] *The Globalization of War*, p. 152

While the stated objective of the "Iraq Salvador Option" was to "take out the insurgency," in practice the US-sponsored terror brigades were involved in routine killings of civilians, with a view to fomenting sectarian violence. In turn, the CIA and MI6 were overseeing "Al Qaeda in Iraq" units involved in targeted assassinations directed against the Shiite population... advised by undercover US Special Forces.

Robert Stephen Ford – subsequently appointed US Ambassador to Syria – was part of Negroponte's team in Baghdad in 2004-2005. In January 2004, he was dispatched as U.S. representative to the Shiite city of Najaf, which was the stronghold of the Mahdi army [an important volunteer force loyal to the charismatic Shiite imam Muqtada al-Sadr], with which he made preliminary contacts.[10]

So they were stoking violence from both sides of the street. The Salvador Option is El Salvador squared, El Salvador on steroids. The primary objective is not just quelling the insurgency to seal a US victory; it is to take that violence and ramp it up into internecine warfare that will rip the country into three parts. This is divide and conquer with a vengeance, following a plan to subjugate Iraq that the Israeli strategist Oded Yinon laid out in the 1980's, of which more later.

Supposedly the war on Iraq was part of the US "war on terror." Bush even made a lame attempt to link Saddam and Al Qaida to justify his war on Iraq (of course, Saddam's regime was naturally trying to eradicate fundamentalist terrorism). Yet now the US was going to put Al Qaida into mass production.

The policy design was devastatingly simple. The Sunnis were to be punished because Saddam and much of his administration had been Sunni. This decapitated the country and gutted its military. A Shiite-leaning government was set up. The Sunni insurgency would direct its ire against this weak center. "Sunni" terrorists of Al Qaida in Iraq (AQI) were unleashed against Shiite civilians, and regime gangs against Sunni civilians. Ethnic cleansing would result, beginning the dissolution into three separate territories, Sunni, Shiite and Kurdish.

John Negroponte and Robert Stephen Ford were put in charge of recruiting the Iraqi death squads. While Negroponte coordinated the operation from his office at the US Embassy, Robert S. Ford, who was fluent in both Arabic and Turkish, was entrusted with the task of establishing strategic contacts with Shiite and Kurdish militia groups outside the "Green Zone".[11]

Chossudovsky quotes Dahr Jamail, the courageous, award-winning American journalist cited by Wikipedia as "one of the few unembedded journalists to report extensively from Iraq during the 2003 Iraq invasion:"

Negroponte had assistance from his colleague from his days in Central America during the 1980's, Ret. Col James Steele. Steele, whose title in Baghdad was Counselor for Iraqi Security Forces, supervised the selection and training of members of the Badr Organization [Badr Brigade] and Mehdi Army, the two largest Shi'ite militias in Iraq, in order to target the leadership and support networks of a primarily Sunni resistance. Planned or not, these death squads promptly spiraled out of control to become the leading cause of death in Iraq.

---

[10] Ibid., p. 153
[11] Ibid.

Intentional or not, the scores of tortured, mutilated bodies which turn up on the streets of Baghdad each day are generated by the death squads whose impetus was John Negroponte. And it is this U.S.-backed sectarian violence which largely led to the hell-disaster that Iraq is today.[12]

Demographic warfare. This was the era when Shiite and Sunni mosques and neighborhoods were rocked by terror bombings, until the residents were forced to flee to areas where their sect was in the majority. This was when the famous incident occurred with the two British SAS special forces mercenaries, dressed in mufti and driving around Basra with detonators in their car, apparently planning to bomb a mosque or a market.[13] They were arrested by the Iraqi police. The British liberated them by driving an assault group of tanks through the walls of the jail. Interesting parallel: during "the troubles" in Northern Ireland, the SAS was caught carrying out terror bombing provocations to stoke sectarian strife there, giving Great Britain its excuse to hold onto the territory.

"On May 4, 2006, Congressman Dennis Kucinich gave a speech on the floor of the House which linked the Bush administration to the death squads in Iraq." Kucinich had written to Defense Secretary Rumsfeld, citing copious references to newspaper articles. "News reports over the past 10 months," Kucinich told Congress, "strongly suggest that the U.S. has trained and supported highly organized Iraqi commando brigades, and that some of those brigades have operated as death squads, abducting and assassinating thousands of Iraqis."[14]

Here are a few of the congressman's news highlights:

July 28, 2005 – *Los Angeles Times* reports that members of a California Army National Guard company, the Alpha Company, who were implicated in a detainee abuse scandal, trained and conducted joint operations with the Wolf Brigade, a commando unit criticized for human rights abuses. In an online Alpha Company newsletter, Captain Haviland wrote, "We have assigned 2nd Platoon to help them transition, and install some of our 'Killer Company' aggressive tactical spirit in them.' The article further states that despite the Wolf Brigade's controversial reputation for human rights violations, it is regarded as the gold standard for Iraqi security forces by U.S. military officials."

August 31, 2005 – BBC reports that on the night of August 24, a large force of the Volcano Brigade raided homes in Al-Hurriyah city in the Baghdad, kidnapping and then executing 76 citizens. The victims were all shot in the head after their hands and feet had been tied up. They suffered the harshest forms of torture, deformation and burning.

November 17, 2005 – *Newsday* reports that in the past year, the U.S. military has helped build up Iraqi commandos under guidance from James Steele, a former Army Special Forces officer who led U.S. counterinsurgency efforts in El Salvador

---

[12] Ibid, p. 154. Dahr Jamail, Managing Escalation: Negroponte and Bush's New Iraq Team, Antiwar.com, January 7, 2007.

[13] "Were British Special Forces Soldiers Planting Bombs in Basra?" www.globalresearch.ca/were-british-special-forces-soldiers-planting-bombs-in-basra/994 . The photo of their car is at http://www.globalresearch.ca/british-uncover-operation-in-basra-agents-provocateurs/990 . Some reports are that the car was already booby-trapped as a car bomb when they were arrested.

[14] "Impunity," Mike Whitney, June 9, 2006, http://www.informationclearinghouse.info/article13558.htm

in the 1980s. The brigades built up over the past year include the Lion Brigade, Scorpion Brigade and Volcano Brigade [the killers cited in the previous article].

February 26, 2006 – *The Independent* reports that outgoing United Nations' human rights chief in Iraq, John Pace, revealed that hundreds of Iraqis are being tortured to death or summarily executed every month in Baghdad alone by the death squads working from the Ministry of Interior. He said that up to three-quarters of the corpses stacked in the Baghdad mortuary show evidence of gunshot wounds to the head or injuries caused by drill-bits or burning cigarettes.

March 9, 2006 – *Los Angeles Times* reports that ... U.S. trainers have also given extensive support to 27 brigades of heavily armed commandos accused of a series of abuses, including the death of 14 Sunni Arabs who were locked in an airtight van last summer.

March 10, 2006 – *Sydney Morning Herald* reports that men wearing the uniforms of U.S.-trained security forces, which are controlled by the Interior Ministry, abducted 50 people in a daylight raid on a security agency. Masked men who are driving what appear to be new government-owned vehicles are carrying out many of the raids.

March 27, 2006 – *The Independent* reports that while U.S. authorities have begun criticizing the Iraqi government over the "death squads," many of the paramilitary groups accused of the abuse, such as the Wolf Brigade, the Scorpion Brigade and the Special Police Commandos were set up with the help of the American military. Furthermore, the militiamen were provided with U.S. advisers some of whom were veterans of Latin American counter-insurgency which also had led to allegations of death squads at the time.[15]

Author Mike Whitney notes that "the appearance of Colonel James Steele, as counselor for the Iraqi Security Forces, should remove any doubt about the real nature of America's involvement... Steele's 'stock in trade' is 'spreading terror through the application of extreme violence' – Max Fuller's apt description of US counterinsurgency campaigns in Latin America."

About 160,000 US troops occupied Iraq; the cost to Iraq has been anywhere from 160,000 to over a million civilian lives. The troops were gradually replaced with mercenaries from Blackwater and other "private security firms." By the end of 2011, the US Army withdrew. It lost 4,400 men, cost $1 trillion,[16] and released thousands of veterans disabled by trauma into US society. They leave behind them a fractured, instable and radioactive Iraq. By 2013, civilian casualties were already on the rise again.[17]

Negroponte understudy Robert S. Ford, the No. 2 "genius of genocide" who helped set up the Iraqi death squads, stayed in Baghdad until 2006. He was then assigned as ambassador to Algeria (another target for regime change) until 2008, when he returned to the Baghdad embassy as Deputy Head of Mission.[18] Ford

---

[15] Ibid.

[16] http://www.infoplease.com/spot/iraq-timeline-2010.html

[17] https://www.iraqbodycount.org/ ; http://www.commondreams.org/news/2015/03/26/body-count-report-reveals-least-13-million-lives-lost-us-led-war-terror

[18] http://www.globalresearch.ca/who-is-ambassador-robert-stephen-ford-the-architect-of-us-sponsored-terrorism-in-syria/5385973

was by then well prepared for his appointment as US Ambassador to Syria in January 2011, coinciding with the "Arab Spring" disturbances by the Muslim Brotherhood in Cairo. In a scarce two months thereafter, the armed insurgency started in Syria. The "military-industrial-media complex" was all geared up to present it as a spree of insane violence by President Assad against his own people.

From the very start, fighters, weapons and supplies were funneled over the border from Iraq and Turkey into Syria – including the vicious and extremist death squads of the LIFG, or Libyan Islamic Fighting group: fresh veterans of the Libya campaign, US mercenaries going back to Afghanistan.[19] The US-trained veteran terrorist brigades began to commit atrocities against civilians, then post footage of the carnage on YouTube, and fix the blame on imaginary pro-government gangs – as if Assad himself had learned the tactics of counter-insurgency terror at the School of the Americas. Each time, the mass media would then join in a chorus of hysteria about the US "responsibility to protect" civilians (so-called R2P) – the trick that had just worked to mobilize the extreme violence of NATO firepower to bring down Qaddafi and smash Libya. Russia and China learned their lesson,[20] and vetoed NATO intervention in Syria at the UN.

Our lying, embedded media are acting as the purveyors of fakery, and the enablers of genocide. They are just as guilty as those who do the actual killing, because these war crimes could never happen without their protection.

***

Damascus holds a place of honor as the world's oldest continuously inhabited city, and the third holiest city in Islam. Religious tolerance has deep roots in Syria. When the city surrendered peacefully to the Muslim siege in 634, the Orthodox Christians were treated benevolently by the new masters. The Koran considers Islam to be a continuation of the Judeo-Christian tradition, and ordains respect towards Christians and Jews as peoples with a holy scripture.[21] "Prior to the conflict, Syria was a regional beacon of religious tolerance... The Sunni/Shia dimension of the Syrian conflict has a greater basis in international rivalries than on-the-ground realities... Hardline Islamist agendas likely have only a narrow base of support."[22]

When the Allies parceled out the Turkish empire after World War I, and the French got their mandate over Syria, they tried to divide and conquer the land by splitting it up into six ethno-religious enclaves. The Syrians, who are three-quarters Sunni, would have none of it. They have an ingrained suspicion of foreign conspiracies attempting to divide them along religious lines.[23] Some critics believe the imperialist aim is not regime change or balkanization, but "merely" the destruction of a non-compliant nation. However, the Kurds, who are Sunni but not Arab, do have aspirations for more autonomy. It was easy enough

---

[19] See my YouTube video, "The Big Lie & Dirty War on Syria: the Foreign Subversive Army Massacres its Human Shields in Daraya" for a profile of the Libyan death squads, and an account of a false flag attack on civilians near Damascus.
https://www.youtube.com/watch?v=_6YAOJ35yMk

[20] http://foreignpolicy.com/2011/03/24/did-russias-libya-ambassador-call-medvedev-a-traitor/

[21] *Islam and the West*, ZDF-Smithsonian TV miniseries, www.archive.org

[22] https://www.onfaith.co/onfaith/2013/09/25/5-faith-facts-on-religion-in-syria/11007

[23] http://progressivepress.com/blog/dirty-war-syria

to get them to cooperate with ISIS, at least to seize Syria's oil fields and smuggle out the oil. So as we will see, the "French option" is not off the table.

Terror attacks have been concentrated against Syria's minorities, especially the Christians and the Alawites, Assad's sect. The effect is to force them to flee as refugees, leaving a Sunni state that will be more susceptible to takeover by extremists, and to join the Sunni bloc of Gulf states allied with the US. In Iraq, the Christian population has now decreased by 80% or 90% from a figure of about 1.5 million in 2003.[24] As to who benefits, well, "three's a crowd." Friendship between Muslims and Christians is the nemesis of Zionism, just as the world alliance between Christendom and Zionism is so fatal to the Muslim peoples.

According to Chossudovsky in *The Globalization of War*,[25] the thesis of a "Sunni belt" or bloc was spawned by Condoleeza Rice in 2006, ostensibly as a strategy to contain Iran. It was implemented by Prince Bandar "Bush," the Saudi spymaster, who went right to work creating the Jabhat al Nusra and ISIL / ISIS terror brigades. Saudi Arabia bankrolled the early years of the death squad campaign against Syria, providing financing and plausible deniability for the US effort.

Within days after Bandar organized a terror bombing against the high command of the Syrian military, in July 2012, he too was nearly killed by a bomb; many believe this was a revenge blow by Syrian military intelligence. That is one reason PM Erdogan of Turkey took the lead role in supporting the insurgency, but there is also the important logistical advantage: Turkey's long border with Syria and Iraq. The bandits financed themselves and made Erdogan's family rich by stealing Syria's oil, which the Turks then sold to Israel. It is widely believed ISIS was able to loot $400 million from the central bank of Mosul, but Iraq has denied it. The UK *Daily Mail* reported on Iraq's claim that ISIS is selling organs harvested from its victims to supplement its $2 million-a-day income from oil, ransom payments, and smuggled antiques.[26]

Takeaways

• Terrorist death squads in Iraq were created using the "El Salvador Option" under cover of US Army counter-insurgency operations in the Iraq War. Ambassador Negroponte and Col. Steele, veterans of the Central American "Contras" project, set up secret police death squads and freelance terror brigades on both sides of the Sunni-Shiite divide. The aim was to instigate a civil war along sectarian lines, as a divide-and-conquer strategy. The Al Qaida or "Sunni" terror brigades were later renamed ISIS (the "Islamic State in Iraq and Syria"). In 2014, ISIS captured huge areas of Iraq, thanks to a stand-down by Iraqi army officers.

• In the "Arab Spring" of March 2011, US "human rights" NGO's organized protests against the Syrian government, which worked as a screen for the death

---

[24] https://en.wikipedia.org/wiki/Religion_in_Iraq

[25] p. 157, citing "The Fiction of 'Fighting the Islamic State', An Entity Created and Financed by the U.S. and Saudi Arabia," by Prof. Mohssen Massarrat, Sept. 2, 2014, http://www.globalresearch.ca/the-fiction-of-fighting-the-islamic-state-an-entity-created-and-financed-by-the-u-s-and-saudi-arabia/5398833 . The article includes a valuable analysis of the Kurdish question.

[26] http://www.dailymail.co.uk/news/article-2958220/UN-urged-investigate-ISIS-s-bloody-trade-human-organs-Iraqi-ambassador-reveals-doctors-executed-not-harvesting-body-parts.html

squad operations organized by Ambassador Ford. Terror brigades brought in from Iraq and Libya committed atrocities which were blamed on the government. Western nations supported them, claiming they were "moderate" pro-democracy rebels. To fight the Syrian Army, a huge army of mercenaries and extremists was recruited, paid for by the Saudis and the theft of Syrian oil. While the US and its allies pretended to fight their own terrorists, ISIS and its ilk grew stronger in Syria. On Sept. 30, 2015, Vladimir Putin changed the game by calling their bluff and carrying out massive airstrikes on ISIS, in coordination with the Syrian Army.

> Eric King: Russia is dominating in Syria... and there's really nothing Washington can do.
>
> Paul Craig Roberts: No, except make a fool of itself by supporting ISIS. We brought ISIS in there — everybody knows that. Just the other day the former head of the Pentagon's Defense Intelligence Agency said on television that 'Yes, we created ISIS and we used them as henchmen to overthrow governments.' (Laughter).[27]

***

It's no fun for anyone to have to admit, "My country: wrong and wrong!" However, the flip side of the freedoms we enjoy, is that burden of responsibility.

This short preface can't tell very much of the story. It can only hope to help the sincere reader set aside natural skepticism, long enough to consider the unfamiliar evidence in the book. It is a strange tale indeed, and unfortunately, there is no way to expose monstrous deceptions without risking being thought a liar oneself.

I have tried here to open one fairly clear window, one reasonably straight thread of the narrative, leading from known points in our history ("our" Central American death squad "rebels" or "Contras"), to the unfamiliar and frightening territory of today's terror bloodbath in the Middle East, in Paris, and beyond.

In this book are contributions from an array of authors, each with a unique perspective, yet arriving at similar conclusions: that ISIS was created *intentionally*, not by accidental "blowback"[28] from misguided policies. Whether or not we convince you, I hope you will find our selections in some measure thought-provoking, stimulating and enlightening.

It's a minority viewpoint, but we should remember – One good reason we have freedom of speech, is that truth always starts from a minority viewpoint.

> – John-Paul Leonard,
> San Diego, Calif.,
> December 2015

---

[27] http://kingworldnews.com/paul-craig-roberts-putin-and-the-russians-now-dominating-as-the-west-destroys-itself/, Nov. 27, 2015

[28] "Blowback" or "law of unintended consequences" is one of the favorite   "limited hangouts" or ploys used by intelligence agencies to cover their tracks. Like other "accidental" or "spontaneous" explanations, it is a natural reflex – as when a child says, "the dish broke," rather than "I broke it."

John Negroponte & The Death-Squad Connection:
Bush Nominates Terrorist for National Intelligence Director.
by Frank Morales, Spring 2005 (excerpts)[29]

John Negroponte has a long and bloody criminal history, dating back to the early 1960s, of overseeing the training and arming of death squads, schooled in the techniques of torture, "forced interrogation," assassination and, as we shall see, even genocide. He has been described as an "old-fashioned imperialist," active for nearly four decades in Vietnam, Central America, the Philippines, Mexico and most recently Iraq. He got his start back in the days of the CIA's Phoenix program, which assassinated some 40,000 Vietnamese "subversives."

On Sept. 18, 2001, as the embers were still smoking at Lower Manhattan's Ground Zero, Negroponte was appointed U.S. Representative to the United Nations. His mission was to work the floor and backrooms in preparation for Colin Powell's infamous February 2003 presentation to the UN making the case for war on Iraq—which even Powell now admits was based on falsehoods. Then in April 2004, with a counter-insurgency war in Iraq rapidly spreading, Bush nominated Negroponte to be U.S. Ambassador to that occupied nation following the June 2004 hand-over of "sovereignty" to as-yet "undetermined Iraqi authorities."

As ambassador to Honduras from 1981 to 1985, Negroponte played a key role in establishing that country as a base of operations for the CIA's "Contra" guerrilla army then attempting to destabilize Nicaragua, with a 450-square-kilometer stretch along the border virtually turned over to the US-backed Nicaraguan rebels. He was also instrumental in the reign of terror then being overseen in Honduras by security chief Gen. Gustavo Alvarez Martinez, his good friend. Between 1980 and 1984, US military aid to Honduras jumped from $3.9 million to $77.4 million. Much of this went to facilitate the crushing of popular movements through a covert "low intensity" war.

Negroponte was in charge of the US Embassy when—according to a 1995 four-part series in the Baltimore Sun—hundreds of Hondurans deemed "subversives" were kidnapped, raped, tortured and killed by Battalion 316, a secret Honduran army intelligence unit (death squad) trained and supported by the Pentagon and the Central Intelligence Agency.[30]

---

[29] http://ww4report.com/node/379

[30] https://en.wikipedia.org/wiki/Battalion_3-16_(Honduras)

Intelligence Battalion 3–16 was the name of a Honduran army unit responsible for carrying out political assassinations and torture of suspected political opponents of the government during the 1980s.

Battalion members received training and support from the United States Central Intelligence Agency both in Honduras and at US military bases. At least 19 Battalion 3–16 members were graduates of the School of the Americas. Battalion 3–16 was also trained by Pinochet's Chile. [Its leader] General Gustavo Álvarez Martínez studied at the Argentine Military College, graduating in 1961.

By the end of 1981, i.e. during the Dirty War in Argentina during which up to 30,000 people were disappeared by Argentine security forces and death squads, more than 150 Argentine officers were in Honduras.

Battalion 316 also participated in the CIA's covert war against Nicaragua... Negroponte worked closely with Gen. Alvarez in overseeing the training of Honduran soldiers in psychological warfare, sabotage, torture and kidnapping. Honduras was the second largest recipient of U.S. military aid in the hemisphere at this time after neighboring El Salvador. Increasing numbers of both Honduran and Salvadoran soldiers were sent to the U.S. Army's School of the Americas to receive training. In El Salvador, the death squads were headed up by Major Roberto D'Aubuisson, a 1972 graduate of the School of the Americas.

Covert operations in Central America were paid for in part through the sale of cocaine... Ambassador Negroponte acquiesced in shutting down the Drug Enforcement Administration (DEA) office in Tegucigalpa, just as Honduras was emerging as an important base for CIA-facilitated cocaine trans-shipments to the United States, with profits going to the Contras. According to a 1989 Senate Foreign Relations Committee investigative report, "elements of the Honduran military were involved in the protection of the drug traffickers."

In 1982, the US negotiated access to airfields in Honduras and established a regional military training center there for Central American forces, principally directed at improving the lethal effectiveness of the Salvadoran military – at a time when the Salvadoran army was carrying out massacres...

Negroponte supervised the construction of El Aguacate Air Base where Nicaraguan Contras were trained by the US, said to be a secret detention and torture center.

Jack Binns, who served under president Jimmy Carter as the ambassador to Honduras prior to Negroponte, made numerous complaints about human rights abuses by the Honduran military. Recently, he stated regarding Negroponte, "I think he was complicit in abuses, I think he tried to put a lid on reporting abuses and I think he was untruthful to Congress about those activities." (NYT, March 29, 2005) In one early '80s cable, Binns reported that Gen. Alvarez was modeling his campaign against suspected subversives, on Argentina's "dirty war" of the 1970s.

When Bush announced Negroponte's nomination as ambassador to the UN shortly after coming to office, the move was met with widespread protest... the Bush administration did not back down – and even went so far as to silence potential witnesses who might have shed some light on Negroponte's criminal history... One of the deported Hondurans was none other than Gen. Luis Alonso Discua, the former commander of Battalion 3-16, then serving as Honduras' deputy ambassador to the UN!

Negroponte was sworn in as U.S. Representative to the United Nations on Sept. 18, 2001. By November 2002, he was strong-arming a resolution through the UN Security Council which called for the "disarming" of Iraq.

In March 2003, Negroponte walked out of the General Assembly after Iraq's UN envoy, Mohammed Al-Douri, accused the U.S. of preparing a war of

---

The CIA had a strong role in establishing, training, equipping and financing Battalion 3–16. The US Ambassador to Honduras at the time, John Negroponte, met frequently with General Gustavo Alvarez Martínez.

See also: Death squad, The Torture Manuals, Torture, Honduras, John Negroponte

aggression. "Britain and the United States are about to start a real war of extermination" he said, "that will kill everything and destroy everything."

On April 20, 2004, Bush nominated Negroponte as ambassador to Iraq.

Negroponte's US Embassy in Baghdad, housed in a palace that once belonged to Saddam Hussein, was and remains the largest embassy in the world, with a "diplomatic staff" of over 3,000. Opting for the kind of diplomacy he's most familiar with, he immediately "shifted more than $1 billion to build up the Iraqi Army," diverting the funds "from reconstruction projects" to military and intelligence projects.

By the first weeks of January 2005, Negroponte was said to be overseeing the formation of death squads in Iraq, prompting media reports about a "Salvador option." MSNBC reported on Jan. 8, 2005 that the Pentagon was

> intensively debating an option that dates back to a still-secret strategy in the Reagan administration's battle against the leftist guerrilla insurgency in El Salvador in the early 1980s. Then, faced with a losing war against Salvadoran rebels, the US government funded or supported 'nationalist' forces that allegedly included so-called death squads directed to hunt down and kill rebel leaders and sympathizers. Eventually, the insurgency was quelled, and many U.S. conservatives consider the policy to have been a success, despite the deaths of innocent civilians...

At least one pro-occupation death squad is already in operation. On Jan. 11, 2004, just days after the Pentagon plans regarding possible "new offensive operations" were revealed, a new militant group, "Saraya Iraqna," began offering big wads of American cash for insurgent scalps – up to $50,000.[31]

***

Question: what sort of man is Negroponte? Civil servant taking orders, patriot, mass murderer - or all of the above? There is yet another possibility – he suffers from the delusion that he is doing the right thing. At least, this may be the state of mind of the man who sent him to Iraq, GW Bush.

The eminent Malaysian Islamic scholar Imran Hosein has a fascinating anecdote in the description of his book *Gog and Magog*.[32]

> In 2003, G. Bush, on the eve of his invasion of Iraq, was trying to change the stance of France, which had refused to take part in this opening offensive of the Clash of Civilizations. He called [French President] Jacques Chirac, and told him about Gog and Magog, hoping this would make him realize the importance of joining this great battle of the End Times. Puzzled, the advisers at the Élysée Palace contacted a Protestant professor of theology. The answer: Bush is an

---

[31] Sheikh Imran Hosein tells anecdotes from his own circle of acquaintances, of a Syrian family whose son was given $1 million, and a Tunisian woman whose brother was given half a million, to join the "jihad" against Assad. "The Zionist Attack On Syria" https://www.youtube.com/watch?v=CISHTtNywyk, at 32-33 min. "They are not buying mujahideen, they are buying mercenaries... Saudi Arabia, Qatar and Turkey are all in the Zionist camp. These are the countries who are financing, who are supplying the weapons. Is this a legitimate jihad, or is this a Zionist attack on Syria?"

[32] *Gog et Magog*, http://www.amazon.fr/Gog-Magog-Hosein-Imran-N/dp/2367250596, Kontre Kulture, 2014

evangelical Christian, who believes that "God will be on the side of Israel in the final conflict of the End Times, and its enemies will belong to the camp of the Antichrist." If the French ministers would read this book, they would ... lead France on its own way, the way of peace.

So Bush meant well, he's off the hook, and the Iraq war was for Israel after all.

What else could Jesus say. "Forgive them, they have no idea what they're doing."

*****

John Negroponte is connected to Britain's royal family and British intelligence through his wife, Diana Villiers. Diana's father was Sir Charles Villiers, a merchant banker who would rise to become chairman of British Steel.[33] His father was a Greek shipping magnate. He graduated from Yale, then joined the Foreign Service. He has held five ambassadorial posts, and was Deputy Sec'y of State under Reagan and Bush 43. He was succeeded as Ambassador to Iraq by the Afghan-American, card-carrying neocon Zalmay Khalilzad.[34]

Khalilzad was Ambassador to Afghanistan, 2003-05, to Iraq 2005-07, and to the UN 2007-09. "His decisions, most especially his selection of puppet overseers to administer the conquered lands, were uniformly disastrous, contributing in large degree to the catastrophes of today." His role was to appoint underqualified prime ministers, Unocal consultant Karzai in Afghanistan, and small shopkeeper Maliki in Iraq, ensuring both nations a future as failed states and US colonies. The Afghans wanted to bring back their old king. Instead, Khalilzad parceled out fiefs to warlords and drug lords, to play them off against each other. Local tribes were so fed up they turned to the Taliban. In Iraq, Maliki and the US alienated Sunnis and plunged the country into abysmal corruption. Every office, including military commands, was for sale; no wonder the Iraq army melted away.[35]

Sheikh Hatem al-Suleiman[36] is the chief of the powerful Dulaim tribe in Ramadi, capital of Anbar province, Western Iraq. He was an early leader of the insurgency who changed sides and got "hundreds of millions" to join the US "Surge." But Sunni tribes are so bitter against Maliki that they have allied with ISIS to oppose him. Hatem blames the rise of ISIS on Maliki's sectarianism, but says "ISIS doesn't even represent 7 or 10 percent of the fighters."[37] In 2014, his tribal council hired a retired CIA officer to lobby Washington for Sunni autonomy: Jonathan Greenhill.[38] Current duties on *his* fascinating resumé include: "strategy for an Iraqi Sunni movement ... to halt Iranian influence in Iraq and to create ... an independent Sunni state" and "Promotion of foreign energy resources to U.S. Companies." Recent experience: "executed one of the Agency's most <u>successful counterterrorism covert action operations</u> while leading a CIA Base in a ... high stress war zone."[39] Sound familiar? Just like Iraq, but it says Afghanistan.

---

[33] http://www.apfn.org/apfn/negroponte.htm

[34] For a critical assessment, see "Zalmay Khalilzad—Bush's Theorist" in *Enemies by Design,* pp. 214-219, by Greg Felton, 2005.

[35] Andrew Cockburn, http://harpers.org/blog/2014/06/the-long-shadow-of-a-neocon/

[36] https://en.wikipedia.org/wiki/Ali_Hatem_al-Suleiman

[37] "Maliki Is 'More Dangerous' than ISIS" http://rudaw.net/english/interview/06072014

[38] http://www.newsmax.com/Newsfront/sunni-consultants-iraq-autonomy/2014/09/26/id/597110/

[39] http://www.zerohedge.com/news/2015-12-17/missing-link-islamic-state-iraq-and-now-documented-cia-connection; https://www.linkedin.com/in/jonathan-s-greenhill-6a500819

How the CIA Created ISIS –

The Libyan Connection[40]

The fact that the CIA was actively working to help the Libyan rebels topple Gaddafi was no secret,[41] nor were the airstrikes that Obama ordered against the Libyan government.[42]

However, little was said about the identity or the ideological leanings of these Libyan rebels. Not surprising, considering the fact that the leader of the Libyan rebels later admitted that his fighters included Al-Qaeda linked jihadists who fought against allied troops in Iraq.[43]

These jihadist militants from Iraq were part of what national security analysts commonly referred to as Al-Qaeda in Iraq. Remember Al-Qaeda in Iraq was ISIS before it was rebranded.

With the assistance of U.S. and NATO intelligence and air support, the Libyan rebels captured Gaddafi and summarily executed him in the street, all the while enthusiastically chanting "Allah Akbar". For many of those who had bought the official line about how these rebels were freedom fighters aiming to establish a liberal democracy in Libya, this was the beginning of the end of their illusions.

Prior to the U.S. and NATO backed intervention, Libya had the highest standard of living of any country in Africa. This according to the U.N.'s Human Development Index rankings for 2010.[44] In the years following the coup, the country descended into chaos, with extremism and violence running rampant. Libya is now widely regarded as a failed state (of course those who were naive enough to buy into the propaganda leading up to the war get defensive when this is said).

Now after Gaddafi was overthrown, the Libyan armories were looted, and massive quantities of weapons were sent by the Libyan rebels to Syria. The weapons, which included anti-tank and anti-aircraft missiles, were smuggled into Syria through Turkey, a NATO ally. The *Times of London* reported on the arrival of the shipment on September 14th, 2012.

This was just three days after Ambassador Chris Stevens was killed by the attack on the U.S. embassy in Benghazi. Chris Stevens had served as the U.S. government's liaison to the Libyan rebels since April of 2011. While a great deal media attention has focused on the fact that the State Department did not provide adequate security at the consulate, and was slow to send assistance when the attack started, Pulitzer Prize winning journalist Seymour Hersh released an

---

[40] Adapted from "Here is the Proof the CIA Created ISIS," May 18, 2015, http://www.conspiracyclub.co/2015/05/18/here-is-the-proof-cia-created-isis/

[41] https://sg.news.yahoo.com/cia-sends-teams-libya-us-considers-rebel-aid-20110331-065759-284.html

[42] http://articles.latimes.com/2011/mar/29/world/la-fg-obama-libya-20110329

[43] http://www.telegraph.co.uk/news/worldnews/africaandindianocean/libya/8407047/Libyan-rebel-commander-admits-his-fighters-have-al-Qaeda-links.html

[44] http://en.wikipedia.org/wiki/History_of_Libya_under_Muammar_Gaddafi#mediaviewer/File:UN_Human_Development_Report_2010_1.PNG

article in April of 2014[45] which exposed a classified agreement between the CIA, Turkey and the Syrian rebels to create what was referred to as a "rat line".

The "rat line" was a covert network used to channel weapons and ammunition from Libya, through southern Turkey and across the Syrian border. Funding was provided by Turkey, Saudi Arabia and Qatar.

With Stevens dead any direct U.S. involvement in that arms shipment was buried,[46] and Washington would continue to claim that they had not sent heavy weaponry into Syria. It was at this time that jihadist fighters from Libya began flooding into Syria as well.[47] And not just low level militants. Many were experienced commanders who had fought in multiple theaters.[48]

The U.S. and its allies were now fully focused on taking down Assad's government in Syria. As in Libya this regime change was to be framed in terms of human rights, and now overt support began to supplement the backdoor channels.[49] The growing jihadist presence was swept under the rug and covered up. As the rebels gained strength, however, the reports of war crimes and atrocities that they were committing began to create a bit of a public relations problem for Washington. It then became standard policy to insist that U.S. support was only being given to what they referred to as "moderate" rebel forces.[50]

This distinction obviously has zero relation to the reality of the situation. In an interview given in April of 2014, FSA commander Jamal Maarouf admitted that his fighters regularly conduct joint operations with Al-Nusra.[51] Al-Nusra is the official Al-Qa'ida branch in Syria. This statement is further validated by an interview in June of 2013 by Colonel Abdel Basset Al-Tawil, commander of the FSA's Northern Front. In this interview he openly discusses his ties with Al-Nusra, and expresses his desire to see Syria ruled by sharia law. (You can verify the identities of these two commanders here in this document from The Institute for the Study of War)[52]

Moderate rebels? Well it's complicated. Not that this should really come as any surprise. Reuters had reported in 2012 that the FSA's command was dominated by Islamic extremists,[53] and the *New York Times* had reported that same year[54]

[45] http://www.lrb.co.uk/v36/n08/seymour-m-hersh/the-red-line-and-the-rat-line

[46] http://www.businessinsider.com/us-syria-heavy-weapons-jihadists-2012-10

[47] http://www.telegraph.co.uk/news/worldnews/middleeast/syria/9606691/Syria-despatch-rebel-fighters-fear-the-growing-influence-of-their-Bin-Laden-faction.html

[48] http://www.longwarjournal.org/archives/2013/11/isis_praised_slain_c.php

[49] http://www.nytimes.com/2013/03/25/world/middleeast/arms-airlift-to-syrian-rebels-expands-with-cia-aid.html

[50] http://www.independent.co.uk/news/world/americas/syria-civil-war-us-will-arm-moderate-rebels-says-barack-obama-confirming-use-of-chemical-weapons-by-president-bashar-alassads-regime-8658368.html

[51] http://www.independent.co.uk/news/world/middle-east/i-am-not-fighting-againstalqaida-itsnot-our-problem-says-wests-last-hope-in-syria-9233424.html

[52] http://www.understandingwar.org/sites/default/files/Selected-Supreme-Military-Command-Members.pdf

[53] http://www.reuters.com/article/2012/12/07/us-syria-crisis-rebels-idUSBRE8B60QX20121207

[54] http://www.nytimes.com/2012/10/15/world/middleeast/jihadists-receiving-most-arms-sent-to-syrian-rebels.html

that the majority of the weapons that Washington was sending into Syria were ending up in the hands Jihadists. FOR TWO YEARS THE U.S. GOVERNMENT KNEW THIS WAS HAPPENING BUT DID NOTHING AND CONTINUED DOING IT.

And the FSA's ties to Al-Nusra are just the beginning. In June of 2014 Al-Nusra merged with ISIS at the border between Iraq and Syria.[55] In that context, the sarin gas attacks of 2013 turned out to have been committed by the Syrian rebels,[56] which makes a lot more sense doesn't it? If it wasn't enough that U.N. investigators,[57] Russian investigators,[58] and Pulitzer prize winning journalist Seymour Hersh[59] all pinned that crime on Washington's proxies, the rebels themselves threatened the West that they would expose what really happened if they were not given more advanced weaponry within one month. This threat was made on June 10th, 2013. In what can only be described as an amazing coincidence, just nine days later, the rebels received their first official shipment of heavy weapons in Aleppo.[60]

After the second sarin gas fiasco, which was also exposed and therefore failed to garner public support for airstrikes, the U.S. continued to increase its the training and support for the rebels.

In February of 2014, Haaretz[61] reported that the U.S. and its allies in the region, Saudi Arabia, Jordan and Israel, were in the process of helping the Syrian rebels plan and prepare for a massive attack in the south. According to Haaretz, Israel had also provided direct assistance in military operations against Assad four months prior. Then in May of 2014 PBS ran a report[62] in which they interviewed rebels who were trained by the U.S. in Qatar. According to those rebels they were being trained to finish off soldiers who survived attacks.

"They trained us to ambush regime or enemy vehicles and cut off the road," said the fighter, who is identified only as "Hussein." "They also trained us on how to attack a vehicle, raid it, retrieve information or weapons and munitions, and how to finish off soldiers still alive after an ambush."

This is a blatant violation of the Geneva conventions. It also runs contrary to conventional military strategy. In conventional doctrine soldiers are better off left wounded, because this ends up costing the enemy more resources. Executing captured enemy soldiers is the kind of tactic used when you want to strike terror in the hearts of the enemy. It also just happens to be standard operating

---

[55] http://www.telegraph.co.uk/news/worldnews/al-qaeda/10925602/Al-Qaeda-merges-with-Isis-at-Syria-Iraq-border-town.html

[56] http://scgnews.com/the-syrian-war-what-youre-not-being-told

[57] http://www.bbc.co.uk/news/world-middle-east-22424188

[58] http://www.reuters.com/article/2013/07/09/us-syria-crisis-chemical-russia-idUSBRE9680YZ20130709

[59] http://www.lrb.co.uk/v35/n24/seymour-m-hersh/whose-sarin

[60] http://www.telegraph.co.uk/news/worldnews/middleeast/syria/10131063/Syrian-rebels-get-first-heavy-weapons-on-the-front-line-of-Aleppo.html

[61] http://www.haaretz.com/news/middle-east/.premium-1.576083. Here's an archive: https://archive.today/qeRSZ

[62] http://www.pbs.org/wgbh/pages/frontline/foreign-affairs-defense/syria-arming-the-rebels/syrian-rebels-describe-u-s-backed-training-in-qatar/

procedure for ISIS. One month after this report, in June of 2014, ISIS made its dramatic entry, crossing over the Syrian border into Iraq, capturing Mosul, Baiji and almost reaching Baghdad. The internet was suddenly flooded with footage of drive-by shootings, large scale death marches, and mass graves. And of course any Iraqi soldier that was captured was executed.

Massive quantities of American military equipment were seized during that operation. ISIS took entire truckloads of humvees, they took helicopters, tanks, and artillery.[63] They photographed and video taped themselves and advertised what they were doing on social media, and yet for some reason Washington didn't even TRY to stop them. U.S. military doctrine clearly calls for the destruction of military equipment and supplies when friendly forces cannot prevent them from falling into enemy hands, but that didn't happen here. ISIS was allowed to carry this equipment out of Iraq and into Syria unimpeded. The U.S. military had the means to strike these convoys, but they didn't lift a finger, even though they had been launching drone strikes in Pakistan that same week.[64]

Those who know their history will remember that Zbigniew Brzezinski was directly involved in funding and arming the Islamic extremists in Pakistan and Afghanistan in order to weaken the Soviets. Officially the U.S. government's arming and funding of the Mujahideen was a response to the Soviet invasion in December of 1979. However, in his memoir entitled "From the Shadows," Robert Gates – director of the CIA under Ronald Reagan and George Bush Sr., and Secretary of Defense under both George W. Bush and Barack Obama – revealed that the U.S. actually began the covert operation six months prior, with the express intention of luring the Soviets into a quagmire.[65] The strategy worked. The Soviets invaded, and the ten years of war that followed are considered by many historians as being one of the primary causes of the fall of the USSR.

This example doesn't just establish precedent, what we're seeing happen in Iraq, Afghanistan and Syria right now is actually a continuation of an old story. Al-Nusra and ISIS are ideological and organizational descendants of these extremist elements that the U.S. government made use of thirty years ago. The U.S. then went on to create a breeding ground for them by invading Iraq in 2003. Had it not been for the vacuum of power left by the removal and execution of Saddam, Al-Qaeda in Iraq, aka ISIS, would not exist. And had it not been for Washington's attempt at toppling Assad by arming, funding and training shadowy militant groups in Syria, there is no way that ISIS would have been capable of storming into Iraq in June of 2014.

---

[63] http://www.news.com.au/world/iraqi-sunni-insurgents-seize-huge-cache-of-usmade-arms-and-equipment/story-fndir2ev-1226952811362

[64] http://www.nytimes.com/2014/06/13/world/asia/pakistan.html

[65]

http://books.google.com/books?id=M51ssIgLMl8C&pg=PA131&lpg=PA131&dq=arnold+horelic k+afghanistan

Syria's Fake Color Revolution[66]

By Joe Quinn

Hundreds of thousands of people have been repeatedly taking to the streets of Damascus to show their support for Syrian President Bashar al-Assad and demonstrate against the threat of a Libya-style foreign intervention.

Photo taken October 12, 2011.

This goes unreported by the mainstream media, who go to great lengths to mold world opinion to believe that events in Syria are yet another 'people's revolution,' while the facts point clearly to yet another US government-sponsored bloody 'regime change.'

This should be no surprise. History records that the CIA has orchestrated innumerable armed insurgencies in dozens of countries around the world, arming bands of mercenaries and death squads in an effort to overthrow national governments and expand American domination over every corner of the globe.

In 1988, former CIA station chief John Stockwell, who ran the CIA secret war in Angola, estimated the CIA had mounted approximately *3,000 major operations and 10,000 minor* operations of this nature, which killed over six million people. As quoted in the book *Addicted to War*,[67] he wrote,

> Now we have massive documentation of what they call the secret wars of the CIA. We don't have to guess or speculate. We had the Church committee investigate them in 1975, which gave us our first really in-depth powerful look inside this structure.
>
> Senator Church said in the 14 years before he did his investigation that he found that they had run 900 major operations and 3000 minor operations. And if you extrapolate that over the whole period of the 40 odd years that we've had a CIA,

---

[66] Introduction to the e-book edition of *Subverting Syria,* July 2012, adapted from "Syria's Bloody CIA Revolution - A Distraction?" by Joe Quinn, Feb. 2012, http://www.sott.net/article/241383-Syrias-Bloody-CIA-Revolution-A-Distraction . By distraction is meant a camouflage for a death squad operation.

[67] *Addicted to War,* Joel Andreas, AK Press, 2002, 2004, 2015. www.addictedtowar.com

you come up with 3000 major operations and over 10,000 minor operations. Every one of them illegal. Every one of them disruptive of the lives and societies of other peoples and many of them bloody and gory beyond comprehension, almost.

Each covert war is a violation of the US Constitution, which requires war to be declared by Congress, and not launched by an unelected, secret body.

To finance their business on such a scale they have control of the global drug trade, which is presumably the true reason for the American-Afghan war.

Stockwell's estimate did not include the NATO/Gladio operations in Europe, plus with 15 more years since with the CIA at work, probably at an increased tempo and with a widening global scope, it will by now have passed the mind-boggling figure of 20,000 such covert operations.

It should come as no great surprise to the reader, then, if evidence points to the current crisis in Syria as another CIA operation.

In an interview with Amy Goodman on March 2, 2007, U.S. General Wesley Clark (Ret.), explained that the Bush Administration planned to "take out" seven countries in five years: Iraq, Syria, Lebanon, Libya, Somalia, Sudan and Iran.

Syria has always been on the Israelis' 'to-do' list, especially as it is (now) the last independent, secular, multi-ethnic Arab country in the Middle East, a staunch supporter of Iran and, as such, an obstacle to Israeli hegemony over the entire Middle East.

But isn't Syria a dictatorship? This too is part of the grand game of NIGYSOB ('Now I've Got You you Son Of a Bitch'), whereby some Arab governments that refuse to submit to Western and Israeli dominance are continually harassed and destabilized to the point that they are forced, in order to survive, to develop a security infrastructure that is, to one extent or another, totalitarian. Western powers and the Israelis can then, when it suits them best, decry the lack of 'freedom' within the targeted nation and begin overthrowing the government. See Hugo Chavez's terms as Venezuelan president as an example of how this 'game' is played by Western powers.

So far, the Syrian 'revolution' has been a carbon copy of most other CIA-sponsored 'regime changes' over the past 60 years: mercenaries and death squads are imported into the country to 'stir things up' in advance of a bombing campaign when the time is right. In Libya, that's exactly what happened, with the British, Americans and Israelis pooling their resources and sharing the contents of their little black books of 'Al-Qaeda' fighters they have been recruiting over the years. Several leaders in the rebellion against Libya are now active in Syria, as witnessed by Spanish journalist Daniel Iriarte. These former Muslim terrorists turned NATO freedom fighters are nothing more than unscrupulous hired guns, who will fight for any cause as long as someone is willing to pay them hundreds of thousands of dollars.

In April 2011, Syrian state television aired the testimonies of three men arrested on suspicion of attacks on civilians and Syrian security forces. Anas al-Kanj, who presented himself as the head of an "armed terrorist group," is heard saying in a taped broadcast that he received "arms and money" from a member of Syria's banned Muslim Brotherhood.

Kanj said he was instructed "to incite people to protest, particularly outside the Ummayad Mosque in Damascus" and in the flashpoint protest towns of Daraa,

Latakia and Banias, to "incite protests to topple the regime and to carry out acts of sabotage". Agence France-Presse, citing Syria's Ath-Thawra newspaper, said that Kanj was instructed "to open fire on protesters in order to sow disarray and lead people to believe that the security forces were shooting on the demonstrators."

The idea is to get the people and the authorities up in arms against each other, while trumpeting in the world media that the regime is brutally repressing protests. This is a very interesting testimony because it captures several crucial steps in the Pentagon's Unconventional Warfare doctrine [See the chapter "Sociological Warfare"]. Here is an overview of the game plan as it applies to Syria:

- Fund NGO's to create a climate of protest in the target country

- Provocateurs organize demonstrations, then fire on protesters and security forces alike to stoke violence

- Staged and falsely attributed video footage creates the illusion of repression by the regime

- Mass media endlessly repeat the Big Lie that the nation's leader is a brutal dictator— "Give the dog a bad name and hang him."

- Invade border towns with special forces death squads, the CIA Foreign Legion of Al Qaeda psychopaths, fanatics and guns for hire

- Foment a civil war on ethnic divides, and fabricate pretexts for military intervention by the UN, or NATO

- Bomb the country into the stone age, to be conquered and ruled by NATO's Islamic terrorist puppets

- Eradicate Arab socialism and government for the people, replacing it with a corrupt clique beholden to Wall Street and London bankers

- US corporations write multi-billion-dollar contracts for "reconstruction" and "security," yielding an astronomical profit on the spoils of war

- Isolate Lebanon, Palestine, Iraq and Iran, giving free rein for Greater Israel to dominate the Middle East

In a December 2011 post on her web site, Turkish-American former FBI translator and whistleblower Sibel Edmonds stated that

> foreign military groups, estimated at hundreds of individuals, began to spread near the villages of the north-Jordan city of Al-Mafraq, which is adjacent to the Jordanian and Syrian border.

> According to one Jordanian military officer who asked to remain anonymous, hundreds of soldiers who speak languages other than Arabic were seen during the past two days in those areas moving back and forth in military vehicles between the King Hussein Air Base of al-Mafraq (10 km from the Syrian border), and the vicinity of Jordanian villages adjacent to the Syrian border.

In January 2012, the UK website 'Elite UK Forces' reported that "There has been growing chatter indicating that British Special Forces are in some way assisting forces aligned against the Syrian regime."

The US ambassador to Syria since 2010 until the closing of the US Embassy in Damascus has been Robert Stephen Ford ("Mr. Death Squad, Jr.") Before Syria, Ford was Political Counselor to the U.S. Embassy in Baghdad under John

Negroponte, who has been so infamously linked to death squads in Iraq. According to Wikipedia, "Former CIA intelligence officer Michael Scheuer has asserted that prior to Ford's removal he was traveling across the country [Syria] inciting groups to overthrow the government."

The Syrian 'revolution' proper began in March 2011 when fighting broke out in the relatively small town of Daraa on the Jordanian border, rather than in large cities like Damascus or Homs. Since then, the mainstream media has systematically misrepresented the size of the anti-government demonstrations and relied on biased reports for casualty counts.

For example, almost all of the first reports from fighting in Daraa in March made reference to police attacks on 'anti-government' protestors. Yet other reports point to more police being killed than demonstrators. So who, exactly, in this supposedly 'peaceful demonstration' was able to shoot and kill seven policemen? And what exactly did anyone expect the Syrian government to do in response? After seeing what US police do to actual peaceful protestors, like the OWS movement, we can only imagine what the US government would do if US cops came under fire from protestors.

In June 2011, Syrian state media reported that at least 120 members of the country's security forces were killed in a battle with what it called "armed organizations." According to NPR's Deborah Amos:

Syrian state television described a heated battle in the northern town of Jisr al-Shughour, near the Turkish border. Gangs armed with machine guns attacked security forces and set fire to government buildings, according to Syrian state TV. In the broadcast, a frantic resident called the evening news program to ask the government to save the town.

Notice that the reports of the most serious fighting come from border towns, which is indicative of incursions by armed groups from Turkey to the north, Jordan to the south and, of course, US-controlled Iraq to the east. Indeed, the main 'centers of unrest', as they're being called, are Daraa near Jordan, Talkalakh, Homs, Talbiseh and Al-Rastan near Lebanon, and Jisr ash-Shugur near Turkey, all located along Syria's borders. In November 2011, Albawaba reported that 600 fighters had already gone from Libya to Syria in order to support the newly established 'Free Syrian Army'.

Within a few weeks of the beginning of the CIA-sponsored uprising in Syria, the Syrian government expelled most foreign journalists from the country and tightly controlled the activities of those that remained. Given the nature of the Western media—the propaganda arm of the empire builders—this was an understandable reaction. Unfortunately, the Syrian government seems to have underestimated the extent to which the CIA had infiltrated Syria.

With little or no direct access to events in Syria, most Western media reports rely on the claims of unnamed 'opposition activists' who, frankly, could be anyone, and an organisation calling itself the 'Local Coordination Committees of Syria' (LCC), which claims to be a "collection of local committees in towns and cities across Syria that meet, plan and organize events on the ground." Strangely enough, however, the web sites associated with this LCC are based in Germany and owned by a person named Andreas Bertsch. It was the Local Coordination Committees of Syria that first broke the fake story that the hoax figure "Amina the Gay Girl from Damascus" had been arrested by Syrian police.

A video report from RT.com gave an example of the way in which reports of a Syrian government 'crack down' can be entirely fabricated:

Armed men came warning that the army and navy would attack Latakia - 2000 people fled, but came back in a couple days angry they had been lied to - no such attack came. The scare came the day after a big pro-Assad rally.

The attack never came, but the media omitted that. Over and over again, the media and Ms. "Heil" Hillary Clinton have jumped to vilify a "massacre by the Syrian government," before the dust settles and the facts emerge that the massacre was committed by the NATO-Salafist-mercenary death squads, or else it was a pitched battle between opposing armies.

In either case, it always turns out the Syrian Army was there doing its job protecting its people. But of course, the correction is never, ever heard in the media. Syria has realized the mistake of banning western journalists and has overturned the decision, but with the cards stacked for war fever, this still won't help them much in the media war.

What we are dealing with here is known in military circles as psychological warfare or 'psywar', which aims to influence a target audience's emotions, reasoning, behavior—usually by inventing lies and presenting them as truth.

High on the CIA's to-do list for 'regime change' in Syria—as was the case with the genocidal invasions of Afghanistan, Iraq and Libya—is the creation of an embryonic Syrian government-in-exile made up of right-wing hardliners and/or convicted conmen. Early last year, the Syrian National Council was created with its headquarters in Turkey. To get an idea of the political leaning of this clique, we need only look to the comments of its Chairman, Burhan Ghalioun, a French professor of political sociology and potential future President of Syria. On December 2, 2011 Ghalioun said that if his regime takes over Syria it would "end the military relationship to Iran and cut off arms supplies to Hezbollah and Hamas, and establish ties with Israel."

This fact alone points to strong Israeli backing and motivation in the effort to oust Assad. With a pro-US/Israel government in Syria, crucial Iranian support to Hizb'allah and the Palestinians would be cut off, leaving Israel free to enact its final solution for its 'Arab problem'.

George Galloway has pointed out that among the "opposition leaders" supported by the US and Saudi Arabia are personages responsible for crimes against humanity and the embezzlement of billions while they held high office in Syria under Hafez al-Assad: the expatriates Rifaat al-Assad and Abdul Halim Khaddam. Here again, note the parallel to "Iraqi Freedom" and that corrupt creature of the CIA, Ahmed Chalabi. Iraq and Libya are prime examples of the viciousness of this U.S. imperialism which mumbles on about "nation-building"—while smashing and plundering already highly-developed nations into ruins.

To quote cartoonist Walt Kelly from his famous Pogo comic strip, "We have met the enemy and he is us."

Unmasking ISIS

by George Washington's Blog

Introduction

Where did ISIS come from? How was it able to gain land, arms and money so quickly?

This book will answer those questions ... and unmask ISIS.

Part 1 shows that the U.S. – through bad policies and stupid choices – is largely responsible for the rise of ISIS.

Part 2 reveals the strange history of the leaders of ISIS ... Including one who never really existed, and another who – if you read mainstream media drivel – was killed ... then arrested ... and then killed *again*.

Part 3 delves into the little-known, secret history of Iraq and Syria ... and discusses the *real* motivations behind our current policies towards those countries.

And Part 4 reveals the shocking truth about who is really supporting ISIS.

So grab a cup of coffee, and prepare to learn the *real* story.

Part 1: Oops ... We Created a Monster

President Barack Obama noted[1] in an interview in March 2015:

ISIL [also known as ISIS] is a direct outgrowth of Al-Qaeda in Iraq that grew out of our invasion. Which is an example of unintended consequences. Which is why we should generally aim before we shoot.

He's correct. After all:

ISIS leaders *themselves* credit[2] the Iraq war for their success

- The New Yorker reports[3]: "ISIS is run by a council of former Iraqi generals .... Many are members of Saddam Hussein's secular Baath Party who converted to radical Islam in American prisons."

- Torture of Iraqis by Americans led to the rise of ISIS[4] ... and America's Guantanamo prison inspired ISIS atrocities5

- Al Qaeda *wasn't* even *in* Iraq[6] until the U.S. invaded that country, as admitted[7] by President George W. Bush to ABC News in 2008:

Bush: One of the major theaters against al Qaeda turns out to have been Iraq. This is where al Qaeda said they were going to take their stand. This is where al Qaeda was hoping to take ...

ABC News Interviewer: **But not until after the U.S. invaded.**

Bush: Yeah, **that's right**. So what?

- ISIS took over large swaths of Iraq using captured American weapons left over from the Iraq war[8]

In addition, the entire American policy of arming "moderate" Syrian rebels has backfired.

Lebanon's Daily Star reports9 that so-called "moderate" Syrian rebels support ISIS terrorists:

"**We are collaborating with the Islamic State** and the Nusra Front [another extremist and hard-line Islamic terrorist group][10] by attacking the Syrian Army's gatherings in ... Qalamoun," said Bassel Idriss, the **commander of an FSA-aligned rebel brigade**...

"**A very large number of FSA members have joined ISIS** and Nusra," Abu Fidaa [a retired Colonel in the Syrian army who is now the head of the Revolutionary Council in Qalamoun] said.

The so-called "moderate" Free Syrian Army has also signed a non-aggression pact[11] with ISIS[12].

The New York Times writes[13]:

President Obama's determination to train Syrian rebels to serve as ground troops against the Islamic State in Iraq and Syria leaves the United States dependent on a diverse group riven by infighting, with no shared leadership and with **hard-line Islamists as its most effective fighters**.

After more than three years of civil war, there are hundreds of militias fighting President Bashar al-Assad — and one another. Among them, **even the more secular forces have turned to Islamists for support and weapons** over the years, and **the remaining moderate rebels often fight alongside extremists** like the Nusra Front, Al Qaeda's affiliate in Syria...

Analysts who track the rebel movement say that **the concept of the Free Syrian Army as a unified force with an effective command structure is a myth**...

The Syrian rebels are a scattered archipelago of mostly local forces with ideologies that range from nationalist to jihadist. Their rank-and-file fighters are largely from the rural underclass, with **few having clear political visions beyond a general interest in** greater rights or **the dream of an Islamic state**...

Some European allies remain skeptical about the efficacy of arming the Syrian rebels. Germany, for instance, has been arming and training Kurdish pesh merga forces in Iraq, but has resisted doing the same for any groups in Syria — partly out of **fear that the weapons could end up in the hands of ISIS** or other radical groups.

"**We can't really control the final destination of these arms**," said Peter Wittig, the German ambassador to the United States...

The fluidity of battlefield alliances in Syria means that **even mainline rebels often end up fighting alongside the Nusra Front, whose suicide bombers are relied on by other groups** to soften up government targets.

"**Even the groups that the U.S. has trained tend to show up in the same trenches as the Nusra** Front eventually, because they need them and they are fighting the same battles," Mr. Lund said...

Current and former American officials acknowledge the government's lack of deep knowledge about the rebels. "**We need to do everything we can to figure out who the non-ISIS opposition is**," said Ryan C. Crocker, a former United States ambassador to Iraq and Syria. "Frankly, we don't have a clue."

And yet, as the Wall Street Journal[14], PBS[15], CNN[16], New York Times[17], Medium[18], Pulitzer prize-winning reporter Seymour Hersh[19] and others note, the U.S. and its allies have poured huge amounts of weapons and support to the Syrian Islamic "rebels". This is in *spite* of the CIA warning President Obama that arming rebels rarely works[20].

Washington wants regime change in Syria, so it's making up a myth of the "moderate Syrian rebel" who hates Assad and ISIS. But they "don't have a clue" as to whether such a mythical unicorn actually exists (spoiler alert: it doesn't).

The New York Times reported[21] in 2013 that *virtually all* of the rebel fighters in Syria are *hardline Islamic terrorists*. Things have gotten much worse since then … as the few remaining moderates have been lured away by ISIS' arms, cash and influence.

Michael Shank – Adjunct Faculty and Board Member at George Mason University's School for Conflict Analysis and Resolution, and director of foreign policy at the Friends Committee on National Legislation – warned[22] a year ago:

> The Senate and House Intelligence committees' about-face decision last week[23] to arm the rebels in Syria is dangerous and disconcerting. **The weapons will assuredly end up in the wrong hands** and will only escalate the slaughter in Syria. Regardless of the vetting procedures in place, the sheer factionalized nature of the opposition guarantees that the arms will end up in some unsavory hands. The same militant fighters who have committed gross atrocities are among the best-positioned of the rebel groups to seize the weapons that the United States sends to Syria…
>
> Arming one side of Syria's multi-sided and bloody civil war **will come back to haunt us**. Past decisions by the U.S. to arm insurgencies in Libya, Angola, Central America and Afghanistan helped sustain brutal conflicts in those regions for decades. In the case of Afghanistan, arming the mujahideen in the 1980s created the instability that emboldened extreme militant groups and gave rise to the Taliban, which ultimately created an environment for al Qaeda to thrive…
>
> Arming the enemies of our enemies hasn't made the U.S. more friends; it has made the U.S. more enemies…
>
> Some armed opposition factions, including powerful Islamist coalitions, reject negotiation altogether[24]. Yet these are the same groups that will **likely seize control of U.S.-supplied weapons, just as they've already seized control of the bulk of the rebels' weaponry**…
>
> When you lift the curtain on the armed groups with the most formidable military presence on the ground in Syria, you find the Al Nusra Front and Al Farough Brigades. Both groups are closely aligned with Al Qaeda and have directly perpetrated barbaric atrocities. The Al Nusra Front has been charged with **beheadings** of civilians, while a commander from the Al Farough Brigades reportedly ate the heart of a pro-Assad soldier.

Shank's warning was ignored, and his worst fears came to pass. And since the Obama administration is doubling-down on the same moronic policy, it will happen again …

And it's not as if we only started supporting the rebels after the Syrian civil war started. Rather, the U.S. started funding the Syrian opposition 5 years _before_ the civil war started … and started arming them 4 years beforehand[25].

And a leaked 2006 U.S. State Department Cable from the U.S. Ambassador to Syria discussed[26] plans to overthrow the Syrian government.

So it's not as if our intervention in Syria is for humanitarian reasons[27].

We summarized[28] the state of affairs in 2014:

The Syrian rebels are _mainly_ Al Qaeda, and the U.S. has been supporting these terrorists[29] for years. Indeed, as reported in the Wall Street Journal[30], the National[31] and other sources, Al Qaeda's power within the Syrian rebel forces is only growing _stronger_.

Rank-and-file Syrian rebels have:

- Burned[32] American flags33
- Threatened to attack America34
- Said: "When we finish with Assad, we will fight the U.S.!" 35
- Said: "We started our holy war here and won't finish until this [Al Qaeda] banner will be raised on top of the White House36. Keep funding them, you always do that, remember? Al Qaeda for instance."
- A former Syrian Jihadi says the rebels have a "9/11 ideology"37
- Indeed, they're _literally_ singing Bin Laden's praises[38] and celebrating the 9/11 attack[39]

In fact, one of the _heads_ of the Syrian rebels is also the _global boss_ of Al Qaeda ... and he is calling for fresh terrorist attacks on _America_. CBS News reports[40]:

> Al Qaeda chief Ayman al-Zawahiri called has called on Muslims to continue attacking Americans on their own soil in order to "bleed" the U.S. economy... "To keep up the hemorrhage in America's security and military spending, we need to keep the Unites States on a constant state of alert about where and when the next strike will blow," Zawahiri said.

Let's recap ... _Most_ of the Syrian "rebels" are Al Qaeda[41]. The U.S. government has designated these guys as terrorists[42].

Things are getting worse, not better: Al Qaeda is gaining _more and more power_[43] among the rebels....

Indeed, we've long known that _most_ of the weapons we're shipping to Syria are ending up in the hands of Al Qaeda[44]. And they apparently have chemical weapons[45].

Summary: We're arming the same guys who are threatening to blow us up.

Indeed, ISIS has tripled the size of its territory in Syria[46] and greatly expanded its territory in Iraq[47] even after the U.S. started its bombing campaign against ISIS. (Update: ISIS now has captured even more of Syria[48].)

Is something deeper going on behind the scene?

Part 2: ISIS' Strange Leadership

There is a question about whether the heads of ISIS are who we've been told.

For example, the New York Times reported[49] in 2007:

> For more than a year, the leader of one the most notorious insurgent groups in Iraq was said to be a mysterious Iraqi named Abdullah Rashid al-Baghdadi.
>
> As the **titular head of the Islamic State** in Iraq, an organization publicly backed by Al Qaeda, Baghdadi issued a steady stream of incendiary pronouncements. Despite claims by Iraqi officials that he had been killed in May, Baghdadi appeared to have persevered unscathed.

On Wednesday, a senior American military spokesman provided a new explanation for Baghdadi's ability to escape attack: He never existed.

Brigadier General Kevin Bergner, the chief American military spokesman, said the elusive Baghdadi was actually a fictional character whose audio-taped declarations were provided by an elderly actor named Abu Abdullah al-Naima.

The ruse, Bergner said, was devised by Abu Ayub al-Masri, the Egyptian-born leader of Al Qaeda in Mesopotamia, who was trying to mask the dominant role that foreigners play in that insurgent organization.

The ploy was to invent Baghdadi, a figure whose very name establishes his Iraqi pedigree, install him as the head of a front organization called the Islamic State of Iraq and then arrange for Masri to swear allegiance to him. Ayman al-Zawahiri, Osama bin Laden's deputy, sought to reinforce the deception by referring to Baghdadi in his video and Internet statements...

Bruce Riedel, a former CIA official and a Middle East expert, said that experts had long wondered whether Baghdadi actually existed. "There has been a question mark about this," he said...

American military spokesmen insist they have gotten to the truth on Baghdadi. Mashadani, they say, provided his account because he resented the role of foreign leaders in Al Qaeda in Mesopotamia.

The unmasking of the terror leader as being an actor's fictitious persona came after al-Baghdadi was – according to mainstream media reports – arrested in 2007[50], killed in 2007[51], arrested *again*[52] in 2009, and then killed *again*[53] in 2010.

The story of ISIS' previous leader – Abu Musab al-Zarqawi – was odd as well. He was declared dead[54] in 2004. Then he was said to be arrested[55] ... several different times[56]. Then he was supposedly killed again in 2006[57].

The Independent – in an article on "black propaganda" (i.e. intentional disinformation) by the U.S. government – cites[58] the forging by the U.S. government of a letter which it pretended was written by al Zarqawi, which was then unquestioningly parroted by the media as an authentic by Zarqawi letter. The Washington Post reported[59]:

One internal briefing, produced by the U.S. military headquarters in Iraq, said that Kimmitt [Brigadier General Mark Kimmitt, the U.S. military's chief spokesman in 2004, and subsequently the senior planner on the staff of the Central Command that directs operations in Iraq and the rest of the Middle East] had concluded that, "The Zarqawi PSYOP program is the most successful information campaign to date."

And CNN reported[60] that ISIS' *current* leader – Abu Bakr al-Baghdadi – was "respected" very much by the U.S. Army and allowed to communicate freely with other prisoners in the prison in which ISIS was hatched (see Part 1) and to travel without restriction at that prison.

Part 3: Deeper Background

To understand the deeper story behind ISIS, we have to go back more than half a century to look at U.S. history in the Middle East (and drill deep down for the black gold).

Target: Iraq

Between 1932 and 1948, the roots for the current wars in Iraq were planted. As Wikipedia explains[61]:

The Mosul–Haifa oil pipeline (also known as Mediterranean pipeline) was a crude oil pipeline from the oil fields in Kirkuk, located in north **Iraq**, through Jordan to Haifa (now on the territory of Israel). The pipeline was operational in 1935–1948. Its length was about 942 kilometres (585 mi), with a diameter of 12 inches (300 mm) (reducing to 10 and 8 inches (250 and 200 mm) in parts), and it took about 10 days for crude oil to travel the full length of the line. The oil arriving in Haifa was distilled in the Haifa refineries, stored in tanks, and then put in tankers for shipment to Europe.

The pipeline was built by the Iraq Petroleum Company between 1932 and 1935, during which period most of the area through which the pipeline passed was under a British mandate approved by the League of Nations. The pipeline was one of two pipelines carrying oil from the Kirkuk oilfield to the Mediterranean coast. The main pipeline split at Haditha with a second line carrying oil to Tripoli, Lebanon, which was then under a French mandate. This line was built primarily to satisfy the demands of the French partner in IPC, Compagnie Française des Pétroles, for a separate line to be built across French mandated territory.

The pipeline and the Haifa refineries were considered **strategically important by the British Government, and indeed provided much of the fuel needs of the British and American forces in the Mediterranean during the Second World War**.

The pipeline was a target of attacks by Arab gangs during the Great Arab Revolt, and as a result one of the main objectives of a joint British-Jewish Special Night Squad commanded by Captain Orde Wingate was to protect the pipeline against such attacks. Later on, the pipeline was the target of attacks by the Irgun. [Background[62].]

In 1948, with the outbreak of the 1948 Arab–Israeli War, the official operation of the pipeline ended when the Iraqi Government refused to pump any more oil through it.

Why is this relevant today? Haaretz reported[63] soon after the Iraq war started in 2003:

The United States has asked Israel to check the possibility of pumping oil from Iraq to the oil refineries in Haifa. The request came in a telegram last week from a senior Pentagon official to a top Foreign Ministry official in Jerusalem.

The Prime Minister's Office, which views the pipeline to Haifa as a "bonus" the U.S. could give to Israel in return for its unequivocal support for the American-led campaign in Iraq, had asked the Americans for the official telegram.

The new pipeline would take oil from the Kirkuk area, where some 40 percent of Iraqi oil is produced, and transport it via Mosul, and then across Jordan to Israel. **The U.S. telegram included a request for a cost estimate for repairing the Mosul-Haifa pipeline that was in use prior to 1948. During the War of Independence [what Jews call[64] the 1948 war to form the state of Israel], the Iraqis stopped the flow of oil to Haifa and the pipeline fell into disrepair over the years...**

National Infrastructure Minister Yosef Paritzky said yesterday that the port of Haifa is an attractive destination for Iraqi oil and that he plans to discuss this matter with the U.S. secretary of energy during his planned visit to Washington next month...

In response to rumors about the possible Kirkuk-Mosul-Haifa pipeline, Turkey has warned Israel that it would regard this development as a serious blow to Turkish-Israeli relations.

So the fighting over Iraq can be traced back to events occurring in 1948 and before.

But let's fast-forward to subsequent little-known events in Iraq.

The CIA plotted to poison the Iraqi leader[65] in 1960.

In 1963, the U.S. backed the coup which *succeeded*[66] in killing the head of Iraq.

And everyone knows that the U.S. also toppled Saddam Hussein during the Iraq war. But most don't know that neoconservatives planned regime change in Iraq once again in 1991[67].

4-Star General Wesley Clark – former Supreme Allied Commander of NATO – said:

> It came back to me … a **1991** meeting I had with Paul Wolfowitz...
>
> In 1991, he was the Undersecretary of Defense for Policy – the number 3 position at the Pentagon. And I had gone to see him when I was a 1-Star General commanding the National Training Center...
>
> And I said, "Mr. Secretary, you must be pretty happy with the performance of the troops in Desert Storm." And he said: "Yeah, but not really, because the truth is we should have gotten rid of Saddam Hussein, and we didn't … But one thing we did learn [from the Persian Gulf War] is that we can use our military in the region – in the Middle East – and the Soviets won't stop us. And we've got about 5 or 10 years to clean up those old Soviet client regimes – *Syria*, Iran, *IRAQ* – before the next great superpower comes on to challenge us."

And many people don't know that the architects of the Iraq War *themselves* admitted the war was about oil[68]. For example, former U.S. Secretary of Defense – and former 12-year Republican Senator – Chuck Hagel said[69] of the Iraq war in 2007:

> People say we're not fighting for oil. Of course we are. They talk about America's national interest. What the hell do you think they're talking about? We're not there for figs.

4 Star General John Abizaid – the former commander of CENTCOM with responsibility for Iraq – said[70]: "Of course it's about oil, it's very much about oil, and we can't really deny that."

Former Fed Chairman Alan Greenspan said[71] in 2007: "I am saddened that it is politically inconvenient to acknowledge what everyone knows: the Iraq war is largely about oil."

President George W. Bush said[72] in 2005 that keeping Iraqi oil away from the bad guys was a *key motive* for the Iraq war:

> If Zarqawi and [Osama] bin Laden gain control of Iraq, they would create a new training ground for future terrorist attacks. They'd seize oil fields to fund their ambitions.

John McCain said[73] in 2008:

> My friends, I will have an energy policy that we will be talking about, which will eliminate our dependence on oil from the Middle East that will — that will then prevent us — that will prevent us from having ever to send our young men and women into conflict again in the Middle East.

Sarah Palin said[74] in 2008:

> Better to start that drilling [for oil within the U.S.] today than wait and continue relying on foreign sources of energy. We are a nation at war and in many [ways] the reasons for war are fights over energy sources, which is nonsensical when you consider that domestically we have the supplies ready to go.

Former Bush speechwriter David Frum – author of the infamous "Axis of Evil" claim in Bush's 2002 State of the Union address – writes[75] in Newsweek:

> In 2002, Chalabi [the Iraqi politician and oil minister[76] who the Bush Administration favored to lead Iraq after the war] joined the annual summer retreat of the American Enterprise Institute near Vail, Colorado. He and Cheney spent

long hours together, contemplating the possibilities of a Western-oriented Iraq: **an additional source of oil**, an alternative to U.S. dependency on an unstable-looking Saudi Arabia.

Key war architect – and Under Secretary of State – John Bolton said[77]:

The critical oil and natural gas producing region that we fought so many wars to try and protect our economy from the adverse impact of losing that supply or having it available only at very high prices.

General Wesley Clark said[78] that the Iraq war – like all modern U.S. wars – were about oil.

A high-level National Security Council officer strongly implied that Cheney and the U.S. oil chiefs planned the Iraq war before 9/11 in order to get control of its oil[79].

The Sunday Herald reported[80]:

It is a document that fundamentally questions the motives behind the Bush administration's desire to take out Saddam Hussein and go to war with Iraq.

Strategic Energy Policy Challenges For The 21st Century describes how America is facing the biggest energy crisis in its history. It **targets Saddam as a threat to American interests because of his control of Iraqi oilfields and recommends the use of 'military intervention' as a means to fix the US energy crisis.**

The report is linked to a veritable who's who of US hawks, oilmen and corporate bigwigs. It was commissioned by James Baker, the former US Secretary of State under George Bush Sr, and **submitted to Vice-President Dick Cheney in April 2001** — a full five months before September 11. Yet it **advocates a policy of using military force against an enemy such as Iraq to secure US access to, and control of, Middle Eastern oil field**s.

One of the most telling passages in the document reads: '**Iraq remains a destabilising influence to … the flow of oil** to international markets from the Middle East. Saddam Hussein has also demonstrated a willingness to threaten to use the oil weapon and to use his own export programme to manipulate oil markets.

'This would display his personal power, enhance his image as a pan-Arab leader … and pressure others for a lifting of economic sanctions against his regime. The United States should conduct an immediate policy review toward Iraq including military, energy, economic and political/diplomatic assessments...

'Military intervention' is supported …..

The document also points out that 'the United States remains a prisoner of its energy dilemma', and that one of the 'consequences' of this is a 'need for military intervention'.

At the heart of the decision to target Iraq over oil lies dire mismanagement of the US energy policy over decades by consecutive administrations. The report refers to the huge power cuts that have affected California in recent years and warns of 'more Californias' ahead.

It says the 'central dilemma' for the US administration is that 'the American people continue to demand plentiful and cheap energy without sacrifice or inconvenience'. With the 'energy sector in critical condition, a crisis could erupt at any time [which] could have potentially enormous impact on the US ... and would affect US national security and foreign policy in dramatic ways.".

The response is to put oil at the heart of the administration — 'a reassessment of the role of energy in American foreign policy'...

Iraq is described as the world's 'key swing producer ... turning its taps on and off when it has felt such action was in its strategic interest". The report also says there is a 'possibility that Saddam may remove Iraqi oil from the market for an extended period of time', creating a volatile market...

Halliburton is one of the firms thought by analysts to be in line to make a killing in any clean-up operation after another US-led war on Iraq.

All five permanent members of the UN Security Council — the UK, France, China, Russia and the US — have international oil companies that would benefit from huge windfalls in the event of regime change in Baghdad. The best chance for US firms to make billions would come if Bush installed a pro-US Iraqi opposition member as the head of a new government.

Representatives of foreign oil firms have already met with leaders of the Iraqi opposition. Ahmed Chalabi, the London-based leader of the Iraqi National Congress, said: 'American companies will have a big shot at Iraqi oil.'

The Independent reported[81] in 2011:

Plans to exploit Iraq's oil reserves were discussed by government ministers and the world's largest oil companies the year before Britain took a leading role in invading Iraq, government documents show...

The minutes of a series of meetings between ministers and senior oil executives are at odds with the public denials of self-interest from oil companies and Western governments at the time...

Minutes of a meeting with BP, Shell and BG (formerly British Gas) on 31 October 2002 read: "Baroness Symons agreed that it would be difficult to justify British companies losing out in Iraq in that way if the UK had itself been a conspicuous supporter of the US government throughout the crisis."

The minister then promised to "report back to the companies before Christmas" on her lobbying efforts.

The Foreign Office invited BP in on 6 November 2002 to talk about opportunities in Iraq "post regime change". Its minutes state: "Iraq is the big oil prospect. BP is desperate to get in there and anxious that political deals should not deny them the opportunity."

After another meeting, this one in October 2002, the Foreign Office's Middle East director at the time, Edward Chaplin, noted: "Shell and BP could not afford not to have a stake in [Iraq] for the sake of their long-term future... We were determined to get a fair slice of the action for UK companies in a post-Saddam Iraq."

Whereas BP was insisting in public that it had "no strategic interest" in Iraq, in private it told the Foreign Office that Iraq was "more important than anything we've seen for a long time".

BP was concerned that if Washington allowed TotalFinaElf's existing contact with Saddam Hussein to stand after the invasion it would make the French conglomerate the world's leading oil company. BP told the Government it was willing to take "big risks" to get a share of the Iraqi reserves, the second largest in the world.

Over 1,000 documents were obtained under Freedom of Information over five years by the oil campaigner Greg Muttitt. They reveal that at least five meetings were held between civil servants, ministers and BP and Shell in late 2002.

The 20-year contracts signed in the wake of the invasion were the largest in the history of the oil industry. They covered half of Iraq's reserves – 60 billion barrels of oil ...

[Note: The 1990 Gulf war – while not a regime change – was also about oil. Specifically, Saddam Hussein's invasion of Kuwait caused oil prices to skyrocket. The U.S. invaded Iraq in order to calm oil markets[82]. In its August 20, 1990 issue, Time Magazine quoted[83] an anonymous U.S. Official as saying:

> Even a dolt understands the principle. We need the oil. It's nice to talk about standing up for freedom, but Kuwait and Saudi Arabia are not exactly democracies, and if their principal export were oranges, a mid-level State Department official would have issued a statement and we would have closed Washington down for August.]

Target: Syria

The history of western intervention in Syria is similar to our meddling in Iraq.

The CIA backed a right-wing coup in Syria in 1949[84]. Douglas Little, Professor, Department of Clark University History professor Douglas Little notes[85]:

> As early as 1949, this newly independent Arab republic was an important staging ground for the CIA's earliest experiments in covert action. The CIA secretly encouraged a right-wing military coup in 1949.

The reason the U.S. initiated the coup? Little explains:

> In late 1945, the Arabian American Oil Company (ARAMCO) announced plans to construct the Trans-Arabian Pipe Line (TAPLINE) from Saudi Arabia to the Mediterranean. With U.S. help, ARAMCO secured rights-of-way from Lebanon, Jordan and Saudi Arabia. The Syrian right-of-way was stalled in parliament.

In other words, Syria was the sole holdout for the lucrative oil pipeline.

The BBC reports[86] that – in 1957 – the British and American leaders seriously considered attacking the Syrian government using Muslim extremists in Syria as a form of "false flag" attack:

> In 1957 Harold Macmillan [then Prime Minister of the United Kingdom] and President Dwight Eisenhower approved a CIA-MI6 plan to stage fake border incidents as an excuse for an invasion by Syria's pro-western neighbours, and then to "eliminate" the most influential triumvirate in Damascus.... More importantly, Syria also had control of one of the main oil arteries of the Middle East, the pipeline which connected pro-western Iraq's oilfields to Turkey...

> The report said that once the necessary degree of fear had been created, frontier incidents and border clashes would be staged to provide a pretext for Iraqi and Jordanian military intervention. Syria had to be "made to appear as the sponsor of plots, sabotage and violence directed against neighbouring governments," the report says. "CIA and SIS should use their capabilities in both the psychological and action fields to augment tension." That meant operations in Jordan, Iraq, and Lebanon, taking the form of "sabotage, national conspiracies and various strong-arm activities" to be blamed on Damascus. The plan called for funding of a **"Free Syria Committee"** [hmmm ... sounds vaguely familiar[87]], and the **arming of**

"political factions with paramilitary or other actionist capabilities" within Syria. The CIA and MI6 would **instigate internal uprisings**, for instance by **the Druze** [a Shia Muslim sect[88]] in the south, help to free political prisoners held in the Mezze prison, **and stir up the Muslim Brotherhood in Damascus**.

Neoconservatives planned regime change in Syria once again in 1991[89] (as noted above in the quote from 4-Star General Wesley Clark).

And as the Guardian reported[90] in 2013:

According to former French foreign minister Roland Dumas[91], Britain had planned covert action in Syria as early as 2009:

"I was in England two years before the violence in Syria on other business," he told French television: "I met with top British officials, who confessed to me that they were preparing something in Syria. This was in Britain not in America. Britain was preparing gunmen to invade Syria.".

Leaked emails from the private intelligence firm Stratfor[92], including notes from a meeting with Pentagon officials[93], confirmed that as of 2011, US and UK special forces training of Syrian opposition forces was well underway. The goal was to elicit the "collapse" of Assad's regime "from within."..

In 2009 – the same year former French foreign minister Dumas alleges the British began planning operations in Syria – Assad refused to sign[94] a proposed agreement with Qatar that would run a pipeline from the latter's North field[95], contiguous with Iran's South Pars field, through Saudi Arabia, Jordan, Syria and on to Turkey, with a view to supply European markets – albeit crucially bypassing Russia. Assad's rationale was "to protect the interests of [his] Russian ally, which is Europe's top supplier of natural gas."

Instead, the following year, Assad pursued negotiations for an alternative $10 billion pipeline plan with Iran[96], across Iraq to Syria, that would also potentially allow Iran to supply gas to Europe from its South Pars field shared with Qatar. The Memorandum of Understanding (MoU) for the project was signed in July 2012 – just as Syria's civil war was spreading to Damascus and Aleppo – and earlier this year Iraq signed a framework agreement for construction of the gas pipelines[97].

The Iran-Iraq-Syria pipeline plan was a "direct slap in the face[98]" to Qatar's plans. No wonder Saudi Prince Bandar bin Sultan, in a failed attempt to bribe Russia to switch sides, told President Vladimir Putin that "whatever regime comes after" Assad, it will be "completely" in Saudi Arabia's hands[99] and will "not sign any agreement allowing any Gulf country to transport its gas across Syria to Europe and compete with Russian gas exports", according to diplomatic sources. When Putin refused, the Prince vowed military action.

It would seem that contradictory self-serving Saudi and Qatari oil interests are pulling the strings of an equally self-serving oil-focused US policy in Syria, if not the wider region. It is this – the problem of establishing a pliable opposition which the US and its oil allies feel confident will play ball[100], pipeline-style, in a post-Assad Syria – that will determine the nature of any prospective intervention: not concern for Syrian life.

[Footnote: The U.S. and its allies have toppled many other governments, as well[101].]

The war in Syria – like Iraq – is largely about oil and gas. International Business Times noted[102] in 2013:

[Syria] controls one of the largest conventional hydrocarbon resources in the eastern Mediterranean.

Syria possessed 2.5 billion barrels of crude oil as of January 2013, which makes it the largest proved reserve of crude oil in the eastern Mediterranean according to the Oil & Gas Journal estimate...

Syria also has oil shale resources with estimated reserves that range as high as 50 billion tons, according to a Syrian government source in 2010.

Moreover, Syria is a key chess piece[103] in the pipeline wars. Syria is an integral

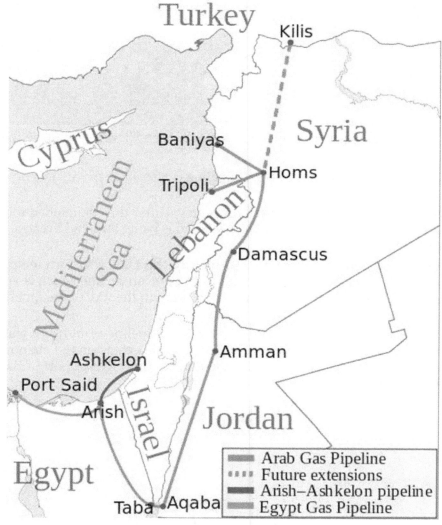

part[104] of the proposed 1,200km Arab Gas Pipeline:

Here are some additional graphics[105] courtesy of Adam Curry:
http://blog.curry.com/images/2012/02/07/arabGasPipeline.jpg
http://blog.curry.com/images/2012/02/07/syria-turkey.jpg and

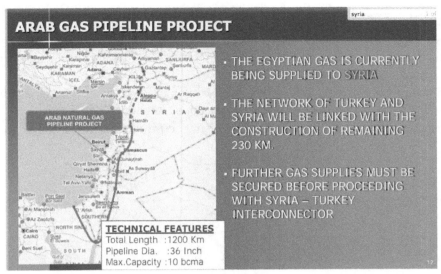

http://blog.curry.com/images/2012/02/07/levantprovince2.jpg,

Syria's central role in the Arab gas pipeline is also a key to why it is now being targeted.

Just as the Taliban was scheduled for removal after they demanded too much in return for the Unocal pipeline, Syria's Assad is being targeted because he is not a reliable "player".

Specifically, **Turkey, Israel and their ally the U.S. want an assured flow of gas through Syria**, and don't want a Syrian regime which is not unquestionably loyal to those 3 countries to stand in the way of the pipeline ... or which demands too big a cut of the profits.

A deal has also been inked to run a natural gas pipeline from Iran's giant South Pars field through Iraq and Syria[106] (with a possible extension to Lebanon). And a deal to run petroleum from Iraq's Kirkuk oil field to the Syrian port of Banias has also been approved:

KIRKUK-BANIAS PIPELINE

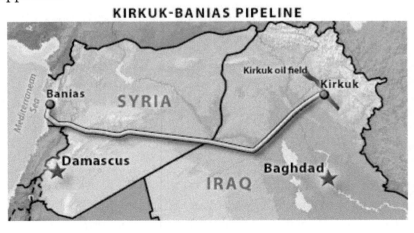

Turkey and Israel would be cut out of these competing pipelines.

Gail Tverberg- an expert on financial aspects of the oil industry – writes[107]:

One of the limits in ramping up Iraqi oil extraction is the limited amount of infrastructure available for exporting oil from Iraq. If pipelines through **Syria** could be added, this might alleviate part of the problem in getting oil to international markets.

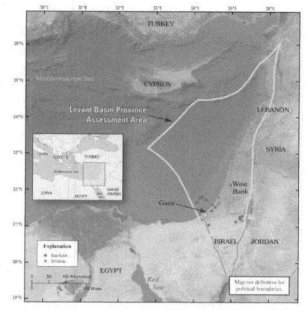

The Plan to Break Up Iraq and Syria?

In September 2015, Pentagon intelligence chief Lt. Gen. Vincent Stewart said[108] that he has "a tough time" seeing either Iraq or Syria really coming back together as sovereign nations. This may sound like a reaction to ISIS and the civil war raging in Syria. But – in reality – the hawks in the U.S. and Israel decided long ago[109] to break up Iraq and Syria into small fragments.

The Guardian noted[110] in 2003:

> President Hosni Mubarak of Egypt predicted devastating consequences for the Middle East if Iraq is attacked. "We fear a state of disorder and chaos may prevail in the region," he said...

> They are probably still splitting their sides with laughter in the Pentagon. But Mr Mubarak and the [Pentagon] hawks do agree on one thing: war with Iraq could spell disaster for several regimes in the Middle East. Mr Mubarak believes that would be bad. **The hawks, though, believe it would be good**.

> For the hawks, disorder and chaos sweeping through the region would not be an unfortunate side-effect of war with Iraq, but a sign that **everything is going according to plan**...

> The "skittles theory" of the Middle East – that one ball aimed at Iraq can knock down several regimes – has been around for some time on the wilder fringes of politics but has come to the fore in the United States on the back of the "war against terrorism".

> Its roots can be traced, at least in part, to a paper published in 1996 by an Israeli think tank, the Institute for Advanced Strategic and Political Studies. Entitled "A clean break: a new strategy for securing the realm", it was intended as a political **blueprint for the incoming government of Binyamin Netanyahu**. As the title indicates, it advised the right-wing Mr Netanyahu to make a complete break with the past by adopting a strategy "based on an entirely new intellectual foundation, one that restores strategic initiative and provides the nation the room to engage every possible energy on rebuilding Zionism ..."..

> The paper set out a plan by which Israel would "shape its strategic environment", beginning with the removal of Saddam Hussein and the installation of a Hashemite monarchy in Baghdad.

With Saddam out of the way and Iraq thus brought under Jordanian Hashemite influence, Jordan and Turkey would form an axis along with Israel to weaken and "roll back" Syria. Jordan, it suggested, could also sort out Lebanon by "weaning" the Shia Muslim population away from Syria and Iran, and re-establishing their former ties with the Shia in the new Hashemite kingdom of Iraq. "Israel will not only contain its foes; it will transcend them", the paper concluded...

The leader of the "prominent opinion makers" who wrote it was **Richard Perle – now chairman of the Defense Policy Board at the Pentagon**.

Also among the eight-person team was **Douglas Feith, a neo-conservative lawyer, who now holds one of the top four posts at the Pentagon as under-secretary of policy**...

Two other opinion-makers in the team were **David Wurmser and his wife, Meyrav** (see US thinktanks give lessons in foreign policy[111], August 19). Mrs Wurmser was co-founder of Memri, a Washington-based charity that distributes articles translated from Arabic newspapers portraying Arabs in a bad light. After working with Mr Perle at the American Enterprise Institute, David Wurmser is now at the State Department, as a special assistant to John Bolton, the under-secretary for arms control and international security.

A fifth member of the team was James Colbert, of the Washington-based Jewish Institute for National Security Affairs (Jinsa) – a bastion of neo-conservative hawkery whose advisory board was previously graced by Dick Cheney (now US vice-president), John Bolton and Douglas Feith...

With several of the "Clean Break" paper's authors now holding key positions in Washington, the plan for Israel to "transcend" its foes by reshaping the Middle East looks a good deal more achievable today than it did in 1996. Americans may even be persuaded to give up their lives to achieve it.

(Before assuming prominent roles in the Bush administration, many of the same people – including Richard Perle, Paul Wolfowitz, Dick Cheney, John Bolton and others[112] – advocated their imperial views during the Clinton administration via their American think tank, the "Project for a New American Century".)

Thomas Harrington – professor of Iberian Studies at Trinity College in Hartford, Connecticut – writes[113]:

[While there are some good articles on the chaos in Iraq, none of them] consider whether **the chaos now enveloping the region might, in fact, be the desired aim of policy planners in Washington and Tel Aviv**...

One of the prime goals of every empire is to foment ongoing internecine conflict in the territories whose resources and/or strategic outposts they covet...

The most efficient way of sparking such open-ended internecine conflict is to brutally smash the target country's social matrix and physical infrastructure...

Ongoing unrest has the additional perk of justifying the maintenance and expansion of the military machine that feeds the financial and political fortunes of the metropolitan elite.

In short ... divide and rule is about as close as it gets to a universal recourse the imperial game and that it is, therefore, as important to bear it in mind today as it was in the times of Alexander the Great, Julius Caesar, the Spanish Conquistadors and the British Raj.

To those—and I suspect there are still many out there—for whom all this seems too neat or too *conspiratorial*, I would suggest a careful side-by side reading of:

a) the "Clean Break" manifesto generated by the Jerusalem-based Institute for Advanced Strategic and Political Studies (IASPS) in 1996

and

b) the "Rebuilding America's Defenses" paper generated by The Project for a New American Century (PNAC) in 2000, a US group with deep personal and institutional links to the aforementioned Israeli think tank, and with the ascension of George Bush Junior to the White House, to the most exclusive sanctums of the US foreign policy apparatus.

To read the cold-blooded imperial reasoning in both of these documents—which speak, in the first case, quite openly of **the need to destabilize the region** so as to reshape Israel's "strategic environment" and, in the second of the need to dramatically increase the number of US "forward bases" in the region ....

To do so now, after the US's systematic destruction of Iraq and Libya—two notably oil-rich countries whose delicate ethnic and religious balances were well known to anyone in or out of government with more than passing interest in history—, and after them its carefully calibrated efforts to generate and maintain murderous and civilization-destroying stalemates in Syria and Egypt (something that is easily substantiated despite our media's deafening silence on the subject), is downright blood-curdling.

And yet, it seems that for even very well-informed analysts, it is beyond the pale to raise the possibility that foreign policy elites in the US and Israel, like all virtually all the ambitious hegemons before them on the world stage, might have quite coldly and consciously fomented open-ended chaos in order to achieve their overlapping strategic objectives in this part of the world.

Antiwar's Justin Raimondo notes[114]:

Iraq's fate was sealed from the moment we invaded: it has no future as a unitary state. As I pointed out again[115] and again[116] in the early days of the conflict, Iraq is fated to split apart into at least three separate states: the Shi'ite areas around Baghdad and to the south, the Sunni regions to the northwest, and the Kurdish enclave which was itching for independence since well before the US invasion. **This was the War Party's real[117] if unexpressed goal from the very beginning: the atomization of Iraq, and indeed the entire Middle East. Their goal, in short, was chaos** – and that is precisely what we are seeing today...

As I put it years ago[118]:

"[T]he actual purpose was to blow the country to smithereens: to atomize it, and crush it, so that it would never rise again.

"When we invaded and occupied Iraq, we didn't just militarily defeat Iraq's armed forces – we dismantled their army[119], and their police force, along with all the other institutions that held the country together. The educational system was destroyed, and not reconstituted. The infrastructure was pulverized[120], and never restored. Even the physical hallmarks of a civilized society – roads[121], bridges[122], electrical plants[123], water facilities[124], museums[125], schools[126] – were bombed out of existence or else left to fall into disrepair. Along with that, the spiritual and

psychological infrastructure that enables a society to function – the bonds of trust, allegiance, and custom – was dissolved[127]*, leaving Iraqis to fend for themselves in a war of all against all.*

"… What we are witnessing in post-Saddam Iraq is the erasure of an entire country. We can say, with confidence: We came, we saw, we atomized."

Why? This is the question that inevitably arises in the wake of such an analysis: why deliberately destroy an entire country whose people were civilized while our European ancestors were living in trees?

The people who planned, agitated for, and executed this war are the very same people who have advanced Israeli interests – at America's expense – at every opportunity. In "A Clean Break: A New Strategy for Securing the Realm[128]," a 1996 document prepared by a gaggle of neocons – Perle, Douglas Feith, James Colbert, Charles Fairbanks, Jr., Robert Loewenberg, David Wurmser, and Meyrav Wurmser – Israeli Prime Minister Benjamin Netanyahu was urged to "break out" - of Israel's alleged stagnation and undertake a campaign of "regime change" across the Middle East, targeting Lebanon, Libya, Syria, Iraq, and eventually Iran. With the exception of Iran – and that one's still cooking on the back burner – this is precisely what has occurred. In 2003, in the immediate wake of our Pyrrhic "victory" in Iraq, then Prime Minister Ariel Sharon declared[129] to a visiting delegation of American members of Congress that these "rogue states" – Iran, Libya, and Syria – would have to be next on the War Party's target list.

(Indeed[130].)

And Michel Chossudovsky points out[131]:

The division of Iraq along sectarian-ethnic lines has been on the drawing board of the Pentagon for more than 10 years.

What is envisaged by Washington is the outright suppression of the Baghdad regime and the institutions of the central government, leading to a process of political fracturing and **the elimination of Iraq as a country**.

This process of political fracturing in Iraq along sectarian lines will inevitably have an impact on Syria, where the US-NATO sponsored terrorists have in large part been defeated.

Destabilization and political fragmentation in Syria is also contemplated: Washington's intent is no longer to pursue the narrow objective of "regime change" in Damascus. What is contemplated is the break up of both Iraq and Syria along sectarian-ethnic lines.

The formation of the caliphate may be the first step towards a broader conflict in the Middle East, bearing in mind that Iran is supportive of the al-Maliki government and the US ploy may indeed be to encourage the intervention of Iran.

The proposed re-division of both Iraq and Syria is broadly modeled on that of the Federation of Yugoslavia (leader of the non-aligned bloc) which was split up by internecine warfare into seven "independent states" (Serbia, Croatia, Bosnia-Herzegovina, Macedonia (FYRM), Slovenia, Montenegro, Kosovo). According to Mahdi Darius Nazemroaya, the division of Iraq into three separate states is part of a broader process of redrawing the Map of the Middle East.

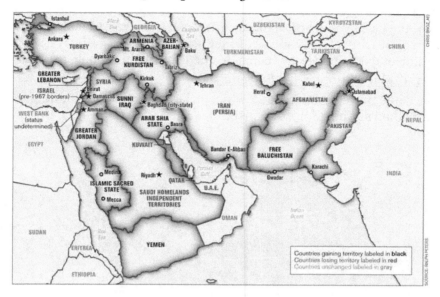

The above map was prepared by Lieutenant Colonel Ralph Peters. It was published in the Armed Forces Journal in June 2006, Peters is a retired colonel of the U.S. National War Academy. (Map Copyright Lt. Colonel Ralph Peters 2006).

Although the map does not officially reflect Pentagon doctrine, it has been used in a training program at NATO's Defense College for senior military officers". (See Plans for Redrawing the Middle East: The Project for a "New Middle East"[132] *By Mahdi Darius Nazemroaya[133], Global Research, November 2006)*

Similarly, Neooconservatives in the U.S. and Israel have long advocated for the balkanization of Syria into smaller regions based on ethnicity and religion. The goal was to *break up* the country, and to do away with the sovereignty of Syria as a separate nation.

In 1982, a prominent Israeli journalist formerly attached to the Israeli Foreign Ministry wrote[134] a book expressly calling for the break-up of Syria:

All the Arab states should be broken down, by Israel, into small units .... **Dissolution of Syria** and Iraq later on **into ethnically or religiously unique areas such** as in Lebanon, is Israel's primary target on the Eastern front in the long run.

In any event, it is well-documented that − in 1996 − U.S. and Israeli Neocons advocated[135] "Weakening, containing, and even **rolling back** Syria..."

As Michel Chossudovsky points out[136]:

Destabilization and political fragmentation in Syria is also contemplated: Washington's intent is no longer to pursue the narrow objective of "regime change" in Damascus. What is contemplated is the break up of both Iraq and Syria along sectarian-ethnic lines.

Indeed, in May 2015, one of the key architects[137] of the Iraq war − John Bolton − said:[138]

The Arabs divided between Sunnis and Shias − I think the Sunni Arabs are never going to agree to be in a state where the Shia outnumber them 3-1. That's what ISIS has been able to take advantage of.

I think **our objective should be a new Sunni state out of the western part of Iraq, the eastern part of Syria** run by moderates or at least authoritarians who are not radical Islamists. What's left of the state of Iraq, as of right now, is simply a satellite of the ayatollahs in Tehran. It's not anything we should try to aid.

U.S. and Allied Support for Extremists

There's one more historical fact which is key background to understanding ISIS: U.S. and allied support for extremists.

Front row, from left: Major Gen. Hamid Gul, director general of Pakistan's Inter-Services Intelligence Directorate (ISI), **Director of Central Intelligence Agency (CIA) William Webster**; **Deputy Director for Operations Clair George**; an ISI colonel; and senior CIA official, Milt Bearden at a Mujahideen training camp in North-West Frontier Province of Pakistan in 1987. (source RAWA)

Ronald Reagan meets Afghan Mujahideen Commanders at the White House in 1985 (Reagan Archives[139])

We Created Al Qaeda to Fight the Soviets in Afghanistan

Jimmy Carter's National Security Adviser Zbigniew Brzezinski admitted[140] on CNN that the U.S. organized and supported Bin Laden and the other originators of "Al Qaeda" in the 1970s[141] to fight the Soviets.

Brzezinski told[142] Al Qaeda's forefathers – the Mujahedin:

> We know of their deep belief in god – that they're confident that their struggle will succeed. That land over – there is yours – and you'll go back to it some day, because your fight will prevail, and you'll have your homes, your mosques, back again, because your cause is right, and god is on your side.

CIA director and Secretary of Defense Robert Gates confirmed[143] in his memoir that the U.S. backed the Mujahedin in the 1970s.

Former Secretary of State Hillary Clinton agrees[144].

MSNBC reported[145] in 1998:

> As his unclassified CIA biography states, bin Laden left Saudi Arabia to fight the Soviet army in Afghanistan after Moscow's invasion in 1979. By 1984, he was running a front organization known as Maktab al-Khidamar – the MAK – which funneled money, arms and fighters from the outside world into the Afghan war.

> What the CIA bio conveniently fails to specify (in its unclassified form, at least) is that the MAK was nurtured by Pakistan's state security services, the Inter-Services Intelligence agency, or ISI, the CIA's primary conduit for conducting the covert war against Moscow's occupation...

> The CIA, concerned about the factionalism of Afghanistan ... found that Arab zealots who flocked to aid the Afghans were easier to "read" than the rivalry-ridden natives. While the Arab volunteers might well prove troublesome later, the agency reasoned, they at least were one-dimensionally anti-Soviet for now. So bin Laden, along with a small group of Islamic militants from Egypt, Pakistan,

Lebanon, Syria and Palestinian refugee camps all over the Middle East, became the "reliable" partners of the CIA in its war against Moscow...

To this day, those involved in the decision to give the Afghan rebels access to a fortune in covert funding and top-level combat weaponry continue to defend that move in the context of the Cold War. Sen. Orrin Hatch, a senior Republican on the Senate Intelligence Committee making those decisions, told my colleague Robert Windrem that he would make the same call again today even knowing what bin Laden would do subsequently. "It was worth it," he said.

"Those were very important, pivotal matters that played an important role in the downfall of the Soviet Union," he said.

Indeed, the U.S. started backing Al Qaeda's forefathers *even before the Soviets invaded* Afghanistan. As Brzezinski told[146] *Le Nouvel Observateur* in a 1998 interview:

Question: The former director of the CIA, Robert Gates, stated in his memoirs ["From the Shadows"], that **American intelligence services began to aid the Mujahadeen in Afghanistan 6 months before the Soviet intervention**. In this period you were the national security adviser to President Carter. You therefore played a role in this affair. Is that correct?

Brzezinski: Yes. According to the official version of history, CIA aid to the Mujahadeen began during 1980, that is to say, after the Soviet army invaded Afghanistan, 24 Dec 1979. But **the reality, secretly guarded until now, is completely otherwise Indeed, it was July 3, 1979 that President Carter signed the first directive for secret aid to the opponents of the pro-Soviet regime in Kabul. And that very day, I wrote a note to the president in which I explained to him that in my opinion this aid was going to induce a Soviet military intervention...**

Q: And neither do you regret having supported the Islamic fundamentalism, having given arms and advice to future terrorists?

B: What is most important to the history of the world? The Taliban or the collapse of the Soviet empire? Some stirred-up Moslems or the liberation of Central Europe and the end of the Cold War?

The Washington Post reported[147] in 2002:

The United States spent millions of dollars to supply Afghan schoolchildren with textbooks filled with violent images and militant Islamic teachings ....

The primers, which were filled with talk of jihad and featured drawings of guns, bullets, soldiers and mines, have served since then as the Afghan school system's core curriculum. Even the Taliban used the American-produced books ....

The Council on Foreign Relations notes[148]:

The 9/11 Commission report (PDF)[149] released in 2004 said some of Pakistan's religious schools or madrassas served as "incubators for violent extremism." Since then, there has been much debate over madrassas and their connection to militancy...

New madrassas sprouted, funded and supported by Saudi Arabia and U.S. Central Intelligence Agency, where students were encouraged to join the Afghan resistance.

And see this[150]. Veteran journalist Robert Dreyfuss[151] writes:

For half a century the United States and many of its allies saw what I call the "Islamic right" as convenient partners in the Cold War...

In the decades before 9/11, hard-core activists and organizations among Muslim fundamentalists on the far right were often viewed as allies for two reasons, because they were seen a fierce anti-communists and because the opposed secular nationalists such as Egypt's Gamal Abdel Nasser, Iran's Mohammed Mossadegh...

By the end of the 1950s, rather than allying itself with the secular forces of progress in the Middle East and the Arab world, the United States found itself in league with Saudi Arabia's Islamist legions. Choosing Saudi Arabia over Nasser's Egypt was probably the single biggest mistake the United States has ever made in the Middle East.

A second big mistake ... occurred in the 1970s, when, at the height of the Cold War and the struggle for control of the Middle East, the United States either supported or acquiesced in the rapid growth of Islamic right in countries from Egypt to Afghanistan. In Egypt, Anwar Sadat brought the Muslim Brotherhood back to Egypt. In Syria, the United States, Israel, and Jordan supported the Muslim Brotherhood in a civil war against Syria. And ... Israel quietly backed Ahmed Yassin and the Muslim Brotherhood in the West Bank and Gaza, leading to the establishment of Hamas.

Still another major mistake was the fantasy that Islam would penetrate the USSR and unravel the Soviet Union in Asia. It led to America's support for the jihadists in Afghanistan. But ... America's alliance with the Afghan Islamists long predated the Soviet invasion of Afghanistan in 1979 and had its roots in CIA activity in Afghanistan in the 1960s and in the early and mid-1970s. The Afghan jihad spawned civil war in Afghanistan in the late 1980s, gave rise to the Taliban, and got Osama bin Laden started on building Al Qaeda.

Would the Islamic right have existed without U.S. support? Of course. This is not a book for the conspiracy-minded. But there is no question that the virulence of the movement that we now confront—and which confronts many of the countries in the region, too, from Algeria to India and beyond—would have been significantly less had the United States made other choices during the Cold War.

In other words, if the U.S. and our allies hadn't backed the radical violent Muslims instead of more stable, peaceful groups in the Middle East, radical Islam wouldn't have grown so large.

Pakistani nuclear scientist and peace activist[152] Pervez Hoodbhoy writes[153]:

Every religion, including Islam, has its crazed fanatics. Few in numbers and small in strength, they can properly be assigned to the "loony" section. This was true for Islam as well until 1979, the year of the Soviet invasion of Afghanistan. Indeed, there may well have been no 911 but for this game-changer...

Officials like Richard Perle, Assistant Secretary of Defense, immediately saw Afghanistan not as the locale of a harsh and dangerous conflict to be ended but as a place to teach the Russians a lesson. Such "bleeders" became the most influential people in Washington...

The task of creating such solidarity fell upon Saudi Arabia, together with other conservative Arab monarchies. This duty was accepted readily and they quickly made the Afghan Jihad their central cause.... But still more importantly, to go heart and soul for jihad was crucial at a time when Saudi legitimacy as the guardians of

Islam was under strong challenge by Iran, which pointed to the continued occupation of Palestine by America's partner, Israel. An increasing number of Saudis were becoming disaffected by the House of Saud – its corruption, self-indulgence, repression, and closeness to the US. Therefore, the Jihad in Afghanistan provided an excellent outlet for the growing number of militant Sunni activists in Saudi Arabia, and a way to deal with the daily taunts of the Iranian clergy...

The bleeders soon organized and armed the Great Global Jihad, funded by Saudi Arabia, and executed by Pakistan. **A powerful magnet for militant Sunni activists was created by the US. The most hardened and ideologically dedicated men were sought on the logic that they would be the best fighters. Advertisements, paid for from CIA funds, were placed in newspapers and newsletters around the world offering inducements and motivations to join the Jihad.**

American universities produced books for Afghan children that extolled the virtues of jihad and of killing communists. Readers browsing through book bazaars in Rawalpindi and Peshawar can, even today, sometimes find textbooks produced as part of the series underwritten by a USAID $50 million grant to the University of Nebraska in the 1980's . These textbooks sought to counterbalance Marxism through creating enthusiasm in Islamic militancy. They exhorted Afghan children to "pluck out the eyes of the Soviet enemy and cut off his legs". Years after the books were first printed they were approved by the Taliban for use in madrassas – a stamp of their ideological correctness and they are still widely available in both Afghanistan and Pakistan.

At the international level, Radical Islam went into overdrive as its superpower ally, the United States, funneled support to the mujahideen. Ronald Reagan feted jihadist leaders on the White House lawn, and the U.S. press lionized them.

And the chief of the visa section at the U.S. consulate in Jeddah, Saudi Arabia (J. Michael Springmann, who is now an attorney in private practice) says[154] that the CIA insisted that visas be issued to Afghanis so they could travel to the U.S. to be trained in terrorism in the United States, and then sent back to Afghanistan to fight the Soviets.

1993 World Trade Center Bombing

New York District Attorney Robert M. Morgenthau believed that the intelligence services could and should have stopped the 1993 bombing of the World Trade Center, but they were preoccupied with other issues cover.

As well-known[155] investigative journalist Robert I. Friedman wrote[156] in New York Magazine in 1995:

Sheikh Omar Abdel Rahman commands an almost deified adoration and respect in certain Islamic circles. It was his 1980 fatwa – religious decree – condemning Anwar Sadat for making peace with Israel that is widely believed to be responsible for Sadat's assassination a year later. (Rahman was subsequently tried but acquitted.)..

The CIA paid to send Abdel Rahman to Peshawar 'to preach to the Afghans about the necessity of unity to overthrow the Kabul regime,' according to Professor Rubin. By all accounts, Rahman was brilliant at inspiring the faithful.

As a reward for his services, the CIA gave the sheikh a one-year visa to the United States in May, 1990 – even though he was on a State Department terrorism watch list that should have barred him from the country.

After a public outcry in the wake of the World Trade Centre bombing, a State Department representative discovered that Rahman had, in fact, received four United States visas dating back to December 15, 1986. All were given to him by CIA agents acting as consular officers at American embassies in Khartoum and Cairo. The CIA officers claimed they didn't know the sheikh was one of the most notorious political figures in the Middle East and a militant on the State Department's list of undesirables. The agent in Khartoum said that when the sheikh walked in the computers were down and the Sudanese clerk didn't bother to check the microfiche file.

Says one top New York investigator: 'Left with the choice between pleading stupidity or else admitting deceit, the CIA went with stupidity.'..

The sheikh arrived in Brooklyn at a fortuitous time for the CIA. In the wake of the Soviet Union's retreat from Afghanistan, Congress had slashed the amount of covert aid going to the mujaheddin. The international network of Arab-financed support groups became even more vital to the CIA, including the string of jihad offices that had been set up across America with the help of Saudi and American intelligence. To drum up support, the agency paved the way for veterans of the Afghan conflict to visit the centres and tell their inspirational war stories; in return, the centres collected millions of dollars for the rebels at a time when they needed it most.

There were jihad offices in Jersey City, Atlanta and Dallas, but the most important was the one in Brooklyn, called Alkifah – Arabic for 'the struggle.' That storefront became the de facto headquarters of the sheikh...

On November 5, 1990, Rabbi Meir Kahane, an ultra-right-wing Zionist militant, was shot in the throat with a .357 magnum in a Manhattan hotel; El-Sayyid Nosair was gunned down by an off-duty postal inspector outside the hotel, and the murder weapon was found a few feet from his hand.

A subsequent search of Nosair's Cliffside Park, New Jersey home turned up forty boxes of evidence – evidence that, had the D.A.'s office and the FBI looked at it more carefully, would have revealed an active terrorist conspiracy about to boil over in New York...

In addition to discovering thousands of rounds of ammunition and hit lists with the names of New York judges and prosecutors, investigators found amongst the Nosair evidence classified U.S. military-training manuals...

Also found amongst Nosair's effects were several documents, letters and notebooks in Arabic, which when eventually translated would point to e terror conspiracy against the United States. The D.A.'s office shipped these, along with the other evidence, to the FBI's office at 26 Federal Plaza. 'We gave all this stuff to the bureau, thinking that they were well equipped,' says one source close to the D.A.'s office. 'After the World Trade Centre, we discovered they never translated the material.'

According to other sources familiar with the case, **the FBI told District Attorney Robert M. Morgenthau that Nosair was a lone gunman, not part of a broader conspiracy; the prosecution took this position at trial and lost, only convicting Nosair of gun charges. Morgenthau speculated the CIA may have encouraged**

the FBI not to pursue any other leads, these sources say. 'The FBI lied to me,' Morgenthau has told colleagues. 'They're supposed to untangle terrorist connections, but they can't be trusted to do the job.'

Three years later, on the day the FBI arrested four Arabs for the World Trade Centre bombing, saying it had all of the suspects, Morgenthau's ears pricked up. He didn't believe the four were 'self-starters,' and speculated that there was probably a larger network as well as a foreign sponsor. He also had a hunch that the suspects would lead back to Sheikh Abdel Rahman. But he worried that **the dots might not be connected because the U.S. government was protecting the sheikh for his help in Afghanistan**...

Nevertheless, **some in the D.A.'s office believe that until the Ryder van exploded underneath New York's tallest building, the sheikh and his men were being protected by the CIA. Morgenthau reportedly believes the CIA brought the sheikh to Brooklyn in the first place**....

As far as can be determined, no American agency is investigating leads suggesting foreign-government involvement in the New York terror conspiracy. For example, **Saudi intelligence has contributed to Sheikh Rahman's legal defense fund, according to Mohammed al-Khilewi**, the former first secretary to the Saudi mission at the U.N.

Friedman notes that intelligence agents had possession of notes which should have linked all of these terrorists, but failed to connect the dots prior to 1993.

CNN ran a special report in 1994 called "Terror Nation? U.S. Creation?"[157], which noted – as summarized by Congressman Peter Deutsch[158]:

Some Afghan groups that have had close affiliation with Pakistani Intelligence are believed to have been involved in the [1993] New York World Trade Center bombings...

Pro-Western afghan officials ... officially warned the U.S. government about Hekmatyar no fewer than four times. The last warning delivered just days before the [1993] Trade Center attack." Speaking to former CIA Director Robert Gates, about Gulbuddin Hekmatyar, Peter Arnett reports, "The Pakistanis showered Gulbuddin Hekmatyar with U.S. provided weapons and sang his praises to the CIA. They had close ties with Hekmatyar going back to the mid-1970's."

This is interesting because it is widely acknowledged that *Gulbuddin Hekmatyar* was enthusiastically backed by the U.S. For example, U.S. News and World Report says[159]:

[He was] once among America's most valued allies. In the 1980s, the CIA funneled hundreds of millions of dollars in weapons and ammunition to help them battle the Soviet Army during its occupation of Afghanistan. Hekmatyar, then widely considered by Washington to be a reliable anti-Soviet rebel, was even flown to the United States by the CIA in 1985.

As the New York Times[160], CBS News[161] and others reported, an FBI informant involved in the 1993 bombing of the World Trade Center begged the FBI to substitute fake bomb power for real explosives, but his FBI handler somehow let real explosives be used.

Bosnia

As professor of strategy at the Naval War College and former National Security Agency intelligence analyst and counterintelligence officer John R. Schindler documents, the U.S. supported Bin Laden and other Al Qaeda terrorists in Bosnia[162].

Libya

We reported[163] in 2012 that the U.S. supported Al Qaeda in Libya in its effort to topple Gaddafi:

> The U.S.-supported opposition which overthrew Libya's Gaddafi was largely comprised of Al Qaeda terrorists[164]. According to a 2007 report[165] by West Point's Combating Terrorism Center's center, the Libyan city of Benghazi was one of Al Qaeda's main headquarters – and bases for sending Al Qaeda fighters into Iraq – prior to the overthrow of Gaddafi:

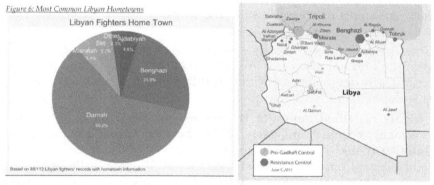

Figure 6: Most Common Libyan Hometowns

The Hindustan Times reported[166] last year:

> "There is no question that al Qaeda's Libyan franchise, Libyan Islamic Fighting Group, is a part of the opposition," Bruce Riedel, former CIA officer and a leading expert on terrorism, told Hindustan Times... It has always been Qaddafi's biggest enemy and its stronghold is Benghazi.

Al Qaeda is now largely in control of Libya. Indeed, Al Qaeda flags were flown over the Benghazi courthouse[167] once Gaddafi was toppled.

(Incidentally, Gaddafi was on the verge of invading Benghazi in 2011, 4 years after the West Point report cited Benghazi as a hotbed of Al Qaeda terrorists. Gaddafi claimed – rightly it turns out – that Benghazi was an Al Qaeda stronghold and a main source of the Libyan rebellion. But NATO planes stopped him[168], and protected Benghazi.)

Former top military and CIA officers said that the U.S intentionally armed Al Qaeda in Libya. The Daily Mail reported[169] in 2014:

> A self-selected group of former top military officers, CIA insiders and think-tankers, declared Tuesday in Washington that a seven-month review of the deadly 2012 terrorist attack has determined that it could have been prevented – if the **U.S.** hadn't been **helping to arm al-Qaeda militias throughout Libya** a year earlier.
>
> **'The United States switched sides in the war on terror with what we did in Libya, knowingly facilitating the provision of weapons to known al-Qaeda militias and figures,'** Clare Lopez, a member of the commission and a **former CIA officer**, told MailOnline.

She blamed the Obama administration for failing to stop half of a $1 billion United Arab Emirates arms shipment from reaching al-Qaeda-linked militants.

'Remember, these weapons that came into Benghazi were permitted to enter by our armed forces who were blockading the approaches from air and sea,' Lopez claimed. 'They were permitted to come in. ... [They] knew these weapons were coming in, and that was allowed..

'The intelligence community was part of that, the Department of State was part of that, and certainly that means that the top leadership of the United States, our national security leadership, and potentially Congress – if they were briefed on this – also knew about this.'..

'The White House and senior Congressional members,' the group wrote in an interim report released Tuesday, 'deliberately and knowingly pursued a policy that provided material support to terrorist organizations in order to topple a ruler [Muammar Gaddafi] who had been working closely with the West actively to **suppress al-Qaeda.'**

'Some look at it as treason,' said Wayne Simmons, a former CIA officer who participated in the commission's research.

Pulitzer-prize winning investigative reporter Seymour Hersh – who broke the stories of the Mai Lai massacre in Vietnam and the Iraq prison torture scandals, which rightfully disgraced the Nixon and Bush administrations' war-fighting tactics – also reported[170] in 2014:

A highly classified annex to the report, not made public, described a **secret agreement reached in early 2012 between the Obama and Erdoğan administrations**. It pertained to the rat line. By the terms of the agreement, funding came from Turkey, as well as Saudi Arabia and Qatar; **the CIA, with the support of MI6, was responsible for getting arms from Gaddafi's arsenals into Syria**. A number of front companies were set up in Libya, some under the cover of Australian entities. Retired American soldiers, who didn't always know who was really employing them, were hired to manage procurement and shipping. The operation was run by David Petraeus, the CIA director who would soon resign when it became known he was having an affair with his biographer. (A spokesperson for Petraeus denied the operation ever took place.)

The operation had not been disclosed at the time it was set up to the congressional intelligence committees and the congressional leadership, as required by law since the 1970s. The involvement of MI6 enabled the CIA to evade the law by classifying the mission as a liaison operation. The former intelligence official explained that for years there has been a recognised exception in the law that permits the CIA not to report liaison activity to Congress, which would otherwise be owed a finding. (All proposed CIA covert operations must be described in a written document, known as a 'finding', submitted to the senior leadership of Congress for approval.) Distribution of the annex was limited to the staff aides who wrote the report and to the eight ranking members of Congress – the Democratic and Republican leaders of the House and Senate, and the Democratic and Republicans leaders on the House and Senate intelligence committees. This hardly constituted a genuine attempt at oversight: the eight leaders are not known to gather together to raise questions or discuss the secret information they receive.

The annex didn't tell the whole story of what happened in Benghazi before the attack, nor did it explain why the American consulate was attacked. **'The consulate's only mission was to provide cover for the moving of arms,' the former intelligence official, who has read the annex, said. 'It had no real political role.'**

Secret intelligence reports from 2011, written before and during the illegal US-led attack on Libya and recently obtained by the Washington Times, state:[171] "There is a close link between al Qaeda, Jihadi organizations, and the opposition in Libya…"

Indeed, the Libyan rebel commander admitted[172] at the time that his fighters had links to Al Qaeda. And see this[173].

Iran

As noted by Seymour Hersh and others, the U.S. supports terrorists[174] within Iran. (See the next chapter "Born of the USA" by Wayne Madsen in this volume.)

Widespread Support for Terror

The director of the National Security Agency under Ronald Reagan – Lt. General William Odom said:[175] "**By any measure the US has long used terrorism**. In '78-79 the Senate was trying to pass a law against international terrorism – in every version they produced, the lawyers said the US would be in violation." (audio here[176]).

The Washington Post reported[177] in 2010: "The United States has long been an **exporter of terrorism**, according to a secret CIA analysis released Wednesday by the Web site WikiLeaks."[178]

Wikipedia notes[179]:

> Chomsky and Herman observed that terror was concentrated in the U.S. sphere of influence in the Third World, and documented terror carried out by U.S. client states in Latin America. They observed that of ten Latin American countries that had death squads, **all** were U.S. client states…
>
> They concluded that **the global rise in state terror was a result of U.S. foreign policy**…
>
> In 1991, a book edited by Alexander L. George [the Graham H. Stuart Professor of Political Science Emeritus at Stanford University] also argued that other Western powers sponsored terror in Third World countries. It concluded that **the U.S. and its allies were the main supporters of terrorism throughout the world**.

Indeed, the U.S. has created death squads in Latin America, Iraq and Syria[180].

Some in the American military have intentionally tried to "out-terrorize the terrorists"[181]. As Truthout notes[182]:

> Both [specialists Ethan McCord and Josh Stieber] say they saw their mission as a plan to "out-terrorize the terrorists," in order to make the general populace more afraid of the Americans than they were of insurgent groups. In the interview with [Scott] Horton, Horton pressed Stieber:
>
> "… a fellow veteran of yours from the same battalion has said that you guys had a standard operating procedure, SOP, that said – and I guess this is a reaction to some EFP attacks on y'all's Humvees and stuff that killed some guys – that from now on if a roadside bomb goes off, IED goes off, everyone who survives the

attack get out and fire in all directions at anybody who happens to be nearby ... that this was actually an order from above. Is that correct? Can you, you know, verify that?

Stieber answered:

"Yeah, it was an order that came from Kauzlarich himself, and it had the philosophy that, you know, as Finkel does describe in the book, that we were under pretty constant threat, and what he leaves out is the response to that threat. But the philosophy was that if each time one of these roadside bombs went off where you don't know who set it ... the way we were told to respond was to open fire on anyone in the area, with the philosophy that that would intimidate them, to be proactive in stopping people from making these bombs ..."

Terrorism is defined[183] as "The use of violence and threats to intimidate or coerce, especially for political purposes."

So McCord and Stieber are correct: this constitutes terrorism by American forces in Iraq.

False Flags

The U.S. and other "civilized" countries not only back terrorists, but sometimes carry out terrorist attacks themselves ... and falsely blame them on others.

Specifically, governments from around the world *admit* they've used the bully's trick ... attack first, and then blame the victim:

- Japanese troops set off a small explosion on a train track in 1931, and falsely blamed it on China in order to justify an invasion of Manchuria. This is known as[184] the "Mukden Incident" or the "Manchurian Incident". The Tokyo International Military Tribunal found[185]: "Several of the participators in the plan, including Hashimoto [a high-ranking Japanese army officer], *have on various occasions* admitted[186] their part in the plot and have stated that the object of the 'Incident' was to afford an excuse for the occupation of Manchuria by the Kwantung Army ...." And see this[187]

- A major with the Nazi SS admitted[188] at the Nuremberg trials that – under orders from the chief of the Gestapo – he and some other Nazi operatives faked attacks on their own people and resources which they blamed on the Poles, to justify the invasion of Poland. Nazi general Franz Halder also testified at the Nuremberg trials that Nazi leader Hermann Goering admitted[189] to setting fire to the German parliament building in 1933, and then falsely blaming the communists for the arson

- Soviet leader Nikita Khrushchev admitted[190] in writing that the Soviet Union's Red Army shelled the Russian village of Mainila in 1939 – while blaming the attack on Finland – as a basis for launching the "Winter War" against Finland. Russian president Boris Yeltsin agreed[191] that Russia had been the aggressor in the Winter War

- The Russian Parliament admits[192] that Soviet leader Joseph Stalin ordered his secret police to execute 22,000 Polish army officers and civilians in 1940, and then blamed it on the Nazis. Current Russian president Putin and former Soviet leader Gorbachev have also admitted[193] that the Soviets were responsible for the massacre

- Israel admits[194] that an Israeli terrorist cell operating in Egypt planted bombs in several buildings, including U.S. diplomatic facilities, then left behind "evidence" implicating the Arabs as the culprits (one of the bombs detonated prematurely, allowing the Egyptians to identify the bombers, and several of the Israelis later confessed) (and see this[195] and this[196])

- The CIA admits[197] that it hired Iranians in the 1950's to pose as Communists and stage bombings in Iran in order to turn the country against its democratically-elected prime minister

- The Turkish Prime Minister admitted[198] that the Turkish government carried out the 1955 bombing on a Turkish consulate in Greece – also damaging the nearby birthplace of the founder of modern Turkey – and blamed it on Greece, for the purpose of inciting and justifying anti-Greek violence

- The British Prime Minister admitted[199] to his defense secretary that he and American president Dwight Eisenhower approved a plan in 1957 to carry out attacks in Syria and blame it on the Syrian government as a way to effect regime change

- The former Italian Prime Minister, an Italian judge, and the former head of Italian counterintelligence[200] admit that NATO, with the help of the Pentagon and CIA, carried out terror bombings in Italy and other European countries in the 1950s and blamed the communists, in order to rally people's support for their governments in Europe in their fight against communism[201]. As one participant in this formerly-secret program stated: "You had to attack civilians, people, women, children, innocent people, unknown people far removed from any political game. The reason was quite simple. They were supposed to force these people, the Italian public, to turn to the state to ask for greater security"[202] (and see this[203])(Italy and other European countries subject to the terror campaign had joined NATO before the bombings occurred). And watch this BBC special[204]. They also allegedly carried out terror attacks in France, Belgium, Denmark, Germany, Greece, the Netherlands, Norway, Portugal, the UK[205], and other countries

- In 1960, American Senator George Smathers suggested[206] that the U.S. launch "a false attack made on Guantanamo Bay which would give us the excuse of actually fomenting a fight which would then give us the excuse to go in and [overthrow Castro]".

- Official State Department documents show that, in 1961, the head of the Joint Chiefs and other high-level officials discussed[207] blowing up a consulate in the Dominican Republic in order to justify an invasion of that country. The plans were not carried out, but they were all discussed as serious proposals

- As admitted by the U.S. government, recently declassified documents show that in 1962, the American Joint Chiefs of Staff signed off on a plan to **blow up AMERICAN airplanes** (using an elaborate plan involving the switching of airplanes), and also to **commit terrorist acts on American soil**, and then to blame it on the Cubans in order to justify an invasion of Cuba. See the following ABC news report[208]; the official documents[209]; and watch this interview [210]with the former Washington Investigative Producer for ABC's World News Tonight with Peter Jennings.

- In 1963, the U.S. Department of Defense wrote a paper promoting[211] attacks on nations within the Organization of American States – such as Trinidad-Tobago or Jamaica – and then falsely blaming them on Cuba.

- The U.S. Department of Defense even suggested[212] covertly paying a person in the Castro government to attack the United States: "The only area remaining for consideration then would be to bribe one of Castro's subordinate commanders to initiate an attack on Guantanamo."

- The NSA admits[213] that it lied[214] about what really happened in the Gulf of Tonkin incident[215] in 1964 … manipulating data to make it look like North Vietnamese boats fired on a U.S. ship so as to create a false justification for the Vietnam war

- A U.S. Congressional committee admitted[216] that – as part of its "Cointelpro" campaign – the FBI had used many provocateurs in the 1950s through 1970s to carry out violent acts and falsely blame them on political activists

- A top[217] Turkish general admitted[218] that Turkish forces burned down a mosque on Cyprus in the 1970s and blamed it on their enemy. He explained[219]: "In Special War, certain *acts of sabotage are staged and blamed on the enemy* to increase public resistance. We did this on Cyprus; we even burnt down a mosque." In response to the surprised correspondent's incredulous look the general said, "I am giving an example"

- The German government admitted[220] (and see this[221]) that, in 1978, the German secret service detonated a bomb in the outer wall of a prison and planted "escape tools" on a prisoner – a member of the Red Army Faction – which the secret service wished to frame the bombing on

- A Mossad agent says[222] that, in 1984, Mossad planted a radio transmitter in Gaddafi's compound in Tripoli, Libya which broadcast fake terrorist transmissions recorded by Mossad, in order to frame Gaddafi as a terrorist supporter. Ronald Reagan bombed Libya immediately thereafter.

- The South African Truth and Reconciliation Council found[223] that, in 1989, the Civil Cooperation Bureau (a covert branch of the South African Defense Force) approached an explosives expert and asked him "to participate in an operation aimed at discrediting the ANC [the African National Congress] by bombing the police vehicle of the investigating officer into the murder incident", thus framing the ANC for the bombing

- An Algerian diplomat and several officers in the Algerian army admit[224] that, in the 1990s, the Algerian army frequently massacred Algerian civilians and then blamed Islamic militants for the killings (and see this video[225]; and Agence France-Presse, 9/27/2002, French Court Dismisses Algerian Defamation Suit Against Author)

- An Indonesian fact-finding team investigated violent riots which occurred in 1998, and determined that "elements of the military had been involved in the riots, some of which were deliberately provoked[226]".

- Senior Russian Senior military and intelligence officers admit[227] that the KGB blew up Russian apartment buildings in 1999 and falsely blamed it on Chechens, in order to justify an invasion of Chechnya (and see this report[228] and this discussion[229])

- According to the Washington Post[230], Indonesian police admit that the Indonesian military killed American teachers in Papua in 2002 and blamed the murders on a Papuan separatist group in order to get that group listed as a terrorist organization.

- The well-respected former Indonesian president also admits[231] that the government probably had a role in the Bali bombings

- As reported by BBC[232], the New York Times[233], and Associated Press[234], Macedonian officials admit that the government murdered seven innocent immigrants in cold blood and pretended that they were Al Qaeda soldiers attempting to assassinate Macedonian police, in order to join the "war on terror"

- Senior police officials in Genoa, Italy admitted[235] that – in July 2001, at the G8 summit in Genoa – planted two Molotov cocktails and faked the stabbing of a police officer, in order to justify a violent crackdown[236] against protesters

- Although the FBI now admits that the 2001 anthrax attacks were carried out by one or more U.S. government scientists, a senior FBI official says that the FBI was actually *told* to blame the Anthrax attacks on Al Qaeda by White House officials[237] (remember what the anthrax letters looked like[238]). Government officials also confirm that the white House tried to link the anthrax to Iraq[239] as a justification for regime change in that country

- Similarly, the U.S. falsely blamed Iraq[240] for playing a role in the 9/11 attacks – as shown by a memo from the defense secretary[241] – as one of the main justifications[242] for launching the Iraq war. Even after the 9/11 Commission admitted[243] that there was no connection, Dick Cheney said[244] that the evidence is "overwhelming" that al Qaeda had a relationship with Saddam Hussein's regime, that Cheney "probably" had information unavailable to the Commission, and that the media was not 'doing their homework' in reporting such ties. Top U.S. government officials now admit[245] that the Iraq war was really launched for oil … not 9/11 or weapons of mass destruction (despite previous "lone wolf" claims, many U.S. government officials now say[246] that 9/11 was state-sponsored terror; but Iraq was *not* the state which backed the hijackers)

- Former Department of Justice lawyer John Yoo suggested[247] in 2005 that the US should go on the offensive against al-Qaeda, having "our intelligence agencies create a false terrorist organization. It could have its own websites, recruitment centers, training camps, and fundraising operations. It could launch fake terrorist operations and claim credit for real terrorist strikes, helping to sow confusion within al-Qaeda's ranks, causing operatives to doubt others' identities and to question the validity of communications."

- United Press International reported[248] in June 2005:

  U.S. intelligence officers are reporting that some of the insurgents in Iraq are using recent-model Beretta 92 pistols, but the pistols seem to have had their serial numbers erased. The numbers do not appear to have been physically removed; the pistols seem to have come off a production line without any serial numbers. Analysts suggest the lack of serial numbers indicates that the weapons were intended for intelligence operations or terrorist cells with substantial government backing. Analysts speculate that these guns are probably from either Mossad or the CIA. Analysts speculate that agent provocateurs may be using the untraceable weapons even as U.S. authorities use insurgent attacks against civilians as evidence of the illegitimacy of the resistance.

- Undercover Israeli soldiers admitted[249] in 2005 to throwing stones at other Israeli soldiers so they could blame it on Palestinians, as an excuse to crack down on peaceful protests by the Palestinians
- Quebec police admitted[250] that, in 2007, thugs carrying rocks to a peaceful protest were actually undercover Quebec police officers (and see this[251])
- At the G20 protests in London in 2009, a British member of parliament saw[252] plain clothes police officers attempting to incite the crowd to violence
- Egyptian politicians admitted[253] (and see this[254]) that government employees looted priceless museum artifacts in 2011 to try to discredit the protesters
- A Colombian army colonel has admitted[255] that his unit murdered 57 civilians, then dressed them in uniforms and claimed they were rebels killed in combat
- U.S. soldiers have admitted[256] that if they kill innocent Iraqis and Afghanis, they then "drop" automatic weapons near their body so they can pretend they were militants.
- The highly-respected writer for the Telegraph Ambrose Evans-Pritchard says that the head of Saudi intelligence – Prince Bandar – recently admitted[257] that the Saudi government controls "Chechen" terrorists
- High-level American sources admitted[258] that the Turkish government – a fellow NATO country – carried out the chemical weapons attacks blamed on the Syrian government; and high-ranking Turkish government officials admitted[259] on tape plans to carry out attacks and blame it on the Syrian government
- The former Ukrainian security chief admits[260] that the sniper attacks which started the Ukrainian coup were carried out in order to frame others
- Britain's spy agency has admitted[261] (and see this[262]) that it carries out "digital false flag" attacks on targets, framing people[263] by writing offensive or unlawful material … and blaming it on the target.

Part 4: What's the Real Story?

With the historical background in Parts 2 and 3, we can now look at the deeper story behind ISIS.

America's Closest Allies In the Mideast Support ISIS

America's top military official – the Chairman of the Joint Chiefs of Staff, General Martin E. Dempsey – and Senator Lindsey Graham admitted[264] last September in a Senate Armed Services Committee hearing that America's closest allies are supporting ISIS[265]:

SEN. LINDSEY GRAHAM (R), SOUTH CAROLINA, MEMBER OF ARMED SERVICES COMMITTEE: Do you know any major Arab ally that embraces ISIL?

GEN. MARTIN DEMPSEY, CHAIRMAN, JOINT CHIEFS OF STAFF: **I know major Arab allies who fund them**.

GRAHAM: Yeah, but do they embrace them? **They fund them because the Free Syrian Army couldn't fight Assad. They were trying to beat Assad**. I think they realized the folly of their ways.

Four-Star General Wesley Clark – who served as the Supreme Allied Commander of NATO – agrees[266].

So does Vice President Joe Biden[267].

A German minister says[268] that U.S. ally Qatar funds ISIS.

ABC News reports:[269] **"The Sunni rebels [inside Syria] are supported by the Islamist rulers of Saudi Arabia, Qatar and Turkey, as well as the U.S., France, Britain** and others."

The Independent headlines[270] "Iraq crisis: How **Saudi Arabia helped Isis** take over the north of the country":

> Some time before 9/11, Prince Bandar bin Sultan, once the powerful Saudi ambassador in Washington and head of Saudi intelligence until a few months ago, had a revealing and ominous conversation with the **head of the British Secret Intelligence Service, MI6, Sir Richard Dearlove**. Prince Bandar told him: "The time is not far off in the Middle East, Richard, when it will be literally 'God help the Shia'. More than a billion Sunnis have simply had enough of them."..

> There is no doubt about the accuracy of the quote by Prince Bandar, secretary-general of the Saudi National Security Council from 2005 and head of General Intelligence between 2012 and 2014, the crucial two years when al-Qa'ida-type jihadis took over the Sunni-armed opposition in Iraq and Syria. Speaking at the Royal United Services Institute last week, Dearlove, who headed MI6 from 1999 to 2004, emphasised the significance of Prince Bandar's words, saying that they constituted "a chilling comment that I remember very well indeed".

> He does not doubt that substantial and sustained funding from private donors in **Saudi Arabia and Qatar**, to which the authorities may have turned a blind eye, has played a central role in the Isis surge into Sunni areas of Iraq. He said: "**Such things simply do not happen spontaneously**." This sounds realistic since the tribal and communal leadership in Sunni majority provinces is much beholden to Saudi and Gulf paymasters, and would be **unlikely to cooperate with Isis without their consent**...

> Dearlove … sees Saudi strategic thinking as being shaped by two deep-seated beliefs or attitudes. First, **they are convinced that there "can be no legitimate or admissible challenge to the Islamic purity of their Wahhabi credentials as guardians of Islam's holiest shrines"**. But, perhaps more significantly given the deepening Sunni-Shia confrontation, the Saudi belief that they possess a monopoly of Islamic truth leads them to be "deeply attracted towards any militancy which can effectively challenge Shia-dom".

> **Western governments traditionally play down the connection between Saudi Arabia and its Wahhabist faith, on the one hand, and jihadism, whether of the variety espoused by Osama bin Laden and al-Qa'ida or by Abu Bakr al-Baghdadi's Isis. There is nothing conspiratorial or secret about these links: 15 out of 19 of the 9/11 hijackers were Saudis, as was Bin Laden and most of the private donors who funded the operation...**

> But there has always been a second theme to Saudi policy towards al-Qa'ida type jihadis, contradicting Prince Bandar's approach and seeing jihadis as a mortal threat to the Kingdom. Dearlove illustrates this attitude by relating how, soon after 9/11, he visited the Saudi capital Riyadh with Tony Blair.

He remembers the then **head of Saudi General Intelligence "literally shouting at me across his office: '9/11 is a mere pinprick on the West**. In the medium term, it is nothing more than a series of personal tragedies. What these terrorists want is to destroy the House of Saud and remake the Middle East.'" In the event, **Saudi Arabia** adopted both policies, **encouraging the jihadis** as a useful tool of Saudi anti-Shia influence abroad but suppressing them at home as a threat to the status quo. It is this dual policy that has fallen apart over the last year.

Saudi sympathy for anti-Shia "militancy" is identified in leaked US official documents. The then US Secretary of State **Hillary Clinton wrote in December 2009 in a cable released by Wikileaks that "<u>Saudi Arabia remains a critical financial support base for al-Qa'ida, the Taliban, LeT [Lashkar-e-Taiba in Pakistan] and other terrorist groups</u>.''**..

Saudi Arabia and its allies are in practice playing into the hands of Isis which is swiftly gaining full control of the Sunni opposition in Syria and Iraq...

For all his gargantuan mistakes, Maliki's failings are not the reason why the Iraqi state is disintegrating. What destabilised Iraq from 2011 on was the revolt of the Sunni in Syria and the takeover of that revolt by jihadis, who were often **sponsored by donors in Saudi Arabia, Qatar, Kuwait and United Arab Emirates**. Again and again Iraqi politicians warned that by not seeking to close down the civil war in Syria, Western leaders were making it inevitable that the conflict in Iraq would restart. "I guess they just didn't believe us and were fixated on getting rid of [President Bashar al-] Assad," said an Iraqi leader in Baghdad last week. Of course, US and British politicians and diplomats would argue that they were in no position to bring an end to the Syrian conflict. But this is misleading. By insisting that peace negotiations must be about the departure of Assad from power, something that was never going to happen since Assad held most of the cities in the country and his troops were advancing, the US and Britain made sure the war would continue...

Saudi Arabia has created a Frankenstein's monster over which it is rapidly losing control. **The same is true of its allies such as Turkey which has been a vital back-base for Isis** and Jabhat al-Nusra by keeping the 510-mile-long Turkish-Syrian border open.

The Daily Beast (a media company formerly owned by Newsweek[271]) notes[272], in a story entitled "America's Allies Are Funding ISIS":

The Islamic State of Iraq and Syria (ISIS), now threatening Baghdad, was funded for years by wealthy donors in Kuwait, Qatar, and Saudi Arabia, three U.S. allies that have dual agendas in the war on terror...

The extremist group that is threatening the existence of the Iraqi state was built and grown for years with the help of elite donors from **American supposed allies in the Persian Gulf region**...

A key component of ISIS's support came from wealthy individuals in the Arab Gulf States of Kuwait, Qatar and Saudi Arabia. Sometimes the support came with the **tacit nod of approval from those regimes** ....

Gulf donors support ISIS, the Syrian branch of al Qaeda called the al Nusrah Front, and other Islamic groups fighting on the ground in Syria ....

Donors in Kuwait, the Sunni majority Kingdom on Iraq's border, have taken advantage of Kuwait's weak financial rules to channel hundreds of millions of dollars to a host of Syrian rebel brigades, according to a December 2013 report by

The Brookings Institution, a Washington think tank that receives some funding from the Qatari government...

"The U.S. Treasury is aware of this activity and has expressed concern about this flow of private financing. But Western diplomats' and officials' general response has been a collective shrug," the report states.

When confronted with the problem, Gulf leaders often justify allowing their Salafi constituents to fund Syrian extremist groups ....

That's what Prince Bandar bin Sultan, head of Saudi intelligence since 2012 and former Saudi ambassador in Washington, reportedly told Secretary of State John Kerry[273] when Kerry pressed him on Saudi financing of extremist groups earlier this year. Saudi Arabia has retaken a leadership role in past months guiding help to the Syrian armed rebels, displacing Qatar, which was seen as supporting some of the worst of the worst organizations on the ground.

Business Insider notes[274]:

The Islamic State for Iraq and the Levant ... is also receiving private donations from wealthy Sunnis in **American-allied Gulf nations such as Kuwait, Qatar, and, possibly, Saudi Arabia**...

As far back as March[275], Iraqi Prime Minister Nouri al-Maliki has accused Saudi Arabia and Qatar of openly funding ISIS as his troops were fighting them.

"I accuse them of inciting and encouraging the terrorist movements. I accuse them of supporting them politically and in the media, of supporting them with money and by buying weapons for them," he told France 24 television.

In Kuwait, donors have taken advantage of weak terror financing control laws to funnel hundreds of millions of dollars to various Syrian rebel groups, including ISIS, according to a December 2013 report[276] by The Brookings Institution, which receives some funding from the government of Qatar.

"Over the last two and a half years, Kuwait has emerged as a financing and organizational hub for charities and individuals supporting Syria's myriad rebel groups," the report said, adding that money from donors in other gulf nations is collected in Kuwait before traveling through Turkey or Jordan to reach the insurgents...

Ironically, Kuwait is a staging area for individuals funneling money to an ISIS organization that is aligned with whatever is left of the Baathist regime once led by Saddam Hussein[277]. In 1990, the U.S. went to war with Iraq over Hussein's invasion and occupation of Kuwait.

Turkey Supports ISIS

NATO member Turkey has long been directly supporting ISIS[278].

The Jerusalem Post reports that an ISIS fighter says that Turkey funds the terrorist group[279].

A German news program – with English subtitles – shows that Turkey is sending terrorists into Syria: Opposition Turkish lawmakers say that the government is protecting and cooperating with ISIS and Al Qaeda terrorists[280], and providing free medical care to their leaders.

According to a leading Turkish newspaper (Today's Zaman), Turkish nurses are sick of providing free medical treatment to ISIS terrorists[281] in Turkish hospitals.

Now, Turkey is massively bombing the most effective on-the-ground fighters against ISIS. As Time Magazine pointed out[282] in June 2015:

> Ethnic Kurds—who on Tuesday scored their second and third significant victories over ISIS in the space of eight days—are **by far the most effective force fighting ISIS** in both Iraq and Syria.

And yet Turkey is trying to destroy the Kurds. Time writes[283]:

Since [Turkey announced that it was joining the war against ISIS] it has arrested more than 1,000 people in Turkey and carried out waves of air raids in neighboring Syria and Iraq. But **most of those arrests and air strikes**, say Kurdish leaders, **have hit Kurdish and left wing groups, not ISIS**.

Turkey is also supporting ISIS by buying its oil ... its main source of funding. The Guardian reported[284]:

> US special forces raided the compound of an Islamic State[285] leader in eastern Syria in May, they made sure not to tell the neighbours.

> The target of that raid, the first of its kind since US jets returned to the skies over Iraq last August, was an Isis official responsible for oil smuggling, named Abu Sayyaf[286]. He was almost unheard of outside the upper echelons of the terror group, but he was well known to Turkey. From mid-2013, the Tunisian fighter had been responsible for smuggling oil from Syria's eastern fields, which the group had by then commandeered. Black market oil quickly became the main driver of Isis revenues – and Turkish buyers were its **main clients**.

> As a result, the oil trade between the jihadis and the Turks was held up as evidence of an alliance between the two...

> In the wake of the raid that killed Abu Sayyaf, suspicions of an undeclared alliance have hardened. One **senior western official** familiar with the intelligence gathered at the slain leader's compound said that direct dealings between Turkish officials and ranking Isis members was now **"undeniable"**.

> "There are hundreds of flash drives and documents that were seized there," the official told the *Observer*. "They are being analysed at the moment, but the links are already so clear that they could end up having profound policy implications for the relationship between us and Ankara.".

> However, Turkey has openly supported other jihadi groups, such as Ahrar al-Sham[287], which espouses much of al-Qaida's ideology, and Jabhat al-Nusra, which is proscribed as a terror organisation by much of the US and Europe. "The distinctions they draw [with other opposition groups] are thin indeed," said the western official. "There is no doubt at all that they militarily cooperate with both.".

> One Isis member says the organisation remains a long way from establishing a self-sustaining economy across the area of Syria and Iraq it controls. "They need the Turks. I know of a lot of cooperation and it scares me," he said. "I don't see how Turkey can attack the organisation too hard. There are shared interests."

While the Guardian is one of Britain's leading newspapers, many in the alternative press have long[288] pointed[289] out[290] Turkey's support for ISIS.

And experts[291], Kurds[292], and Vice President Joe Biden[293] have accused Turkey of enabling ISIS.

Israel Supports ISIS

The Israeli air force has bombed[294] near the Syrian capital of Damascus, and attacked agricultural facilities and warehouses (the Syrian government is the other main opponent of ISIS in Syria besides the Kurds).

The Israeli military recently admitted[295] supporting Syrian jihadis. Specifically, the Times of Israel reported[296] in June 2015:

> **Defense Minister Moshe Ya'alon said Monday that Israel has been providing aid to Syrian rebels**, thus keeping the Druze in Syria out of immediate danger. Israeli officials have previously balked at confirming on the record that the country has been helping forces that are fighting to overthrow Syrian President Bashar Assad...
>
> "We've assisted them under two conditions," Ya'alon said of the Israeli medical aid to the Syrian rebels, **some of whom are presumably fighting with al-Qaeda affiliate al-Nusra Front** to topple Syrian President Bashar Assad. "That they don't get too close to the border, and that they don't touch the Druze."

(Al Nusra **is** Al Qaeda, and closely affiliated with ISIS[297].)

The Times of Israel reported[298] in 2014:

> A Free Syrian Army commander, arrested last month by the Islamist militia Al-Nusra Front, told his captors he collaborated with Israel in return for medical and military support, in a video released this week.
>
> In a video[299] uploaded to YouTube Monday ... Sharif As-Safouri, the commander of the Free Syrian Army's Al-Haramein Battalion, admitted to having entered Israel five times to meet with Israeli officers who later provided him with Soviet anti-tank weapons and light arms. Safouri was abducted by the al-Qaeda-affiliated Al-Nusra Front[300] in the Quneitra area, near the Israeli border, on July 22.
>
> "The [opposition] factions would receive support and send the injured in [to Israel] on condition that the Israeli fence area is secured. No person was allowed to come near the fence without prior coordination with Israel authorities," Safouri said in the video...
>
> In the edited confession video, in which Safouri seems physically unharmed, he says that at first he met with an Israeli officer named Ashraf at the border and was given an Israeli cellular phone. He later met with another officer named Younis and with the two men's commander, Abu Daoud. In total, Safouri said he entered Israel five times for meetings that took place in Tiberias.
>
> Following the meetings, Israel began providing Safouri and his men with "basic medical support and clothes" as well as weapons, which included 30 Russian [rifles], 10 RPG launchers with 47 rockets, and 48,000 5.56 millimeter bullets.

Haaretz reported[301] the same year:

> The Syrian opposition is willing to give up claims to the Golan Heights in return for cash and Israeli military aid against President Bashar Assad, a top opposition official told Al Arab newspaper, according to a report in Al Alam...
>
> The Western-backed militant groups want Israel to enforce a no-fly zone over parts of southern Syria to protect rebel bases from air strikes by Assad's forces, according to the report.

In a separate article, Haaretz also noted[302]:

According to reports, Israel has also been involved, and even provided active assistance in at least one attack by rebel troops four months ago, when its communications and intelligence base on Mount Hermon jammed the Syrian army's communications system and the information relayed between its fighting forces and their headquarters.

Jacky Hugi – an Arab affairs analyst for Israeli army radio – recently wrote[303]:

> The Israeli security establishment should gradually abandon its **emerging alliance**[304] **with the Syrian rebels** …..
>
> It is a dangerous, irresponsible gamble to choose Assad's enemies[305] and encourage his collapse — it would be playing with fire.

The U.S. Supports ISIS

Former CIA boss and 4-star general David Petraeus – who still (believe it or not) holds a lot of sway in Washington – suggests[306] we should arm Al Qaeda. Quite a few mainstream Americans are also saying[307] we should support Al Qaeda in Iraq and Syria.

Influential New York Times columnist Thomas Friedman asks[308] if we should arm *ISIS* itself, so as to counter Iranian influence. This isn't just empty rhetoric.

A former Al Qaeda commander says[309] that ISIS *already* works for the CIA.

Former FBI translator Sibel Edmonds – deemed credible by the Department of Justice's Inspector General, several senators[310] (free subscription required), and a coalition of prominent conservative and liberal groups[311] – says[312] that the CIA and NATO started recruiting and training people at a NATO base in Turkey – right near the Syrian border – to stage terrorist attacks in Syria to overthrow the Syrian government … and that this was the *birth* of ISIS:

> In 2011, months and months before Syria came in the headlines – anything about Syria was written on the New York Times, Washington Post and CNN – we broke a story [background here[313], here[314], here[315] and here[316]] based on my sources here in United States military but also in Turkey about the fact that special **CIA/NATO forces in a NATO base in Turkey**, which is in the southern portion of Turkey **very close to the Syrian border**, they were bringing in, in Turkey, **the CIA/NATO Gladio unit, they were recruiting and bringing in people from northern Syria into these camps, part of the US air force base in southern Turkey. They were training them – military training – they were arming them, and they were basically directing them towards create terror events inside Syria, not only against Assad, but also in various villages and regions against the people, against public**...
>
> **That was the training and beginning of the ISIS brand**. It started as ISIL and then turned to ISIS and now for short IS. This was completed by design, it was created and the people who are part of the so called ISIS they were carefully selected, brought into the U.S. NATO base in Turkey, they were trained they were funneled, and this is what they were told to do. They created a new brand and a new brand with purpose of replacing the old brand: Al Qaeda.

Sound like a conspiracy theory?

Unfortunately, an internal U.S. Defense Intelligence Agency (DIA) document produced recently shows that the U.S. knew that the actions of "the West, Gulf countries and Turkey" in Syria might create a terrorist group like ISIS and an Islamic caliphate[317].

By way of background, a non-profit organization called Judicial Watch has – for many years – obtained sensitive U.S. government documents through freedom of information requests and lawsuits. The government just produced documents[318] to Judicial Watch in response to a freedom of information suit which show that the West has long supported ISIS.

The documents were written by the U.S. Defense Intelligence Agency (DIA) on August 12, 2012 ... years *before*[319] ISIS burst onto the world stage. Here are excerpts from the documents (our emphasis on the relevant parts):

A. INTERNALLY, EVENTS ARE TAKING A CLEAR SECTARIAN DIRECTION.

B. THE SALAFIST, THE MUSLIM BROTHERHOOD, AND AQI ARE THE MAJOR FORCES DRIVING THE INSURGENCY IN SYRIA.

C. THE WEST, GULF COUNTRIES, AND TURKEY SUPPORT THE OPPOSITION; WHILE RUSSIA, CHINA. AND IRAN SUPPORT THE REGIME.

Why is this important? It shows that extreme Muslim terrorists – salafists[320], Muslim Brotherhood, and AQI (i.e. Al Qaeda in Iraq) – have *always* been the "major forces driving the insurgency in Syria."

This verifies what the alternative media has been saying for years: there *aren't any* moderate rebels[321] in Syria (and see this[322], this[323] and this[324]).

Moreover, the newly-declassified document continues:

TRAIN THEM ON THE IRAQI SIDE, IN ADDITION TO HARBORING REFUGEES (SYRIA).

C. IF THE SITUATION UNRAVELS THERE IS THE POSSIBILITY OF ESTABLISHING A DECLARED OR UNDECLARED SALAFIST PRINCIPALITY IN EASTERN SYRIA (HASAKA AND DER ZOR), AND THIS IS EXACTLY WHAT THE SUPPORTING POWERS TO THE OPPOSITION WANT, IN ORDER TO ISOLATE THE SYRIAN REGIME, WHICH IS CONSIDERED THE STRATEGIC DEPTH OF THE SHIA EXPANSION (IRAQ AND IRAN).

D. THE DETERIORATION OF THE SITUATION HAS DIRE CONSEQUENCES ON THE IRAQI SITUATION AND ARE AS FOLLOWS;

-1. THIS CREATES THE IDEAL ATMOSPHERE FOR AQI TO RETURN TO ITS OLD POCKETS IN MOSUL AND RAMADI AND WILL PROVIDE A RENEWED MOMENTUM UNDER THE PRESUMPTION OF UNIFYING THE JIHAD AMONG SUNNI IRAQ AND SYRIA, AND THE REST OF THE SUNNIS IN THE ARAB WORLD AGAINST WHAT IT CONSIDERS ONE ENEMY, THE DISSENTERS. ISI COULD ALSO DECLARE AN ISLAMIC STATE THROUGH ITS UNION WITH OTHER TERRORIST ORGANIZATIONS IN IRAQ AND SYRIA, WHICH WILL CREATE GRAVE DANGER IN REGARDS TO UNIFYING IRAQ AND THE PROTECTION OF ITS TERRITORY.

Yes, you read that correctly:

> ...**there is the possibility of establishing a declared or undeclared Salafist Principality in eastern Syria** (Hasaka and Der Zor), **and this is exactly what the supporting powers to the opposition want**, in order to isolate the Syrian regime ....

In other words, the powers supporting the Syrian opposition – the West, our Gulf allies, and Turkey **wanted** an Islamic caliphate in order to challenge Syrian president Assad.

This is a big deal. A former British Army and Metropolitan Police counter-terrorism intelligence officer and a former MI5 officer confirm[325] that the newly-released documents are a smoking gun.

And the former **head** of the DIA – Lieutenant General Michael Flynn – confirmed its importance as well. By any measure, Flynn was a top-level American military commander. Flynn served as[326]:

- The Director of the U.S. Intelligence Agency
- The Director of intelligence for Joint Special Operations Command (JSOC), the main military agency responsible for targeting Al-Qaeda and other Islamic terrorists
- The Commander of the Joint Functional Component Command for Intelligence, Surveillance and Reconnaissance
- The Chair of the Military Intelligence Board
- Assistant director of national intelligence

Flynn confirmed[327] the authenticity of the document in a subsequent interview, and said:

[Interviewer] So the administration turned a blind eye to your analysis?

*[Flynn] **I don't know that they turned a blind eye, I think it was a decision. I think it was a willful decision**.*

[Interviewer] A willful decision to support an insurgency that had Salafists, Al Qaeda and the Muslim Brotherhood?

*[Flynn] It was a **willful decision** to do what they're doing.*

NBC News[328], the Wall Street Journal[329], CNN[330] and others report that the U.S. has committed to provide air power to support Muslim jihadis in Syria.

World Net Daily reports that the U.S. trained Islamic jihadis – who would later join ISIS [331]– in Jordan.

Der Spiegel and the Guardian confirmed[332] that the U.S., France and England trained hundreds if not *thousands* of Islamic fighters in Jordan.

POSTSCRIPT:

ISIS does not represent mainstream Islam.

For example, the Intercept points out that ISIS has "more in common with Mao's Red Guards or the Khmer Rouge than it does with the Muslim empires of antiquity[333]".

Huffington Post reports[334]:

Can you guess which books the wannabe jihadists Yusuf Sarwar and Mohammed Ahmed ordered online from Amazon before they set out from Birmingham to fight in Syria last May? A copy of *Milestones* by the Egyptian Islamist Sayyid Qutb? No. How about *Messages to the World: the Statements of Osama Bin Laden*? Guess again. Wait, *The Anarchist Cookbook*, right? Wrong.

Sarwar and Ahmed, both of whom pleaded guilty to terrorism offences last month, purchased **Islam for Dummies and The Koran for Dummies**. You could not ask for better evidence to bolster the argument that the 1,400-year-old Islamic faith has little to do with the modern jihadist movement. The swivel-eyed young men who take sadistic pleasure in bombings and beheadings may try to justify their violence with recourse to religious rhetoric – think the killers of Lee Rigby screaming "Allahu Akbar" at their trial; think of Islamic State beheading the photojournalist James Foley as part of its "holy war" – but religious fervour isn't what motivates most of them.

In 2008, a classified briefing note on radicalisation, prepared by MI5's behavioural science unit, was leaked to the *Guardian*. It revealed that, "far from being religious zealots, a large number of those involved in terrorism do not practise their faith regularly. Many lack religious literacy and could . . . be regarded as religious novices." The analysts concluded that "a well-established religious identity **actually protects against violent radicalisation**", the newspaper said. [Here's the Guardian report[335].]

For more evidence, read the books of the forensic psychiatrist and former CIA officer Marc Sageman; the political scientist Robert Pape [Pape found that foreign occupation – and not religion[336] – made certain Arabs into terrorists; the CIA's top Bin Laden hunter agreed[337]]; the international relations scholar Rik Coolsaet; the Islamism expert Olivier Roy; the anthropologist Scott Atran. They have all studied the lives and backgrounds of hundreds of gun-toting, bomb-throwing jihadists and they all agree that Islam isn't to blame for the behaviour of such men (and, yes, they usually are men).

Instead they point to other drivers of radicalisation ....

When he lived in the Philippines in the 1990s, Khalid Sheikh Mohammed, described as "the principal architect" of the 11 September attacks by the 9/11 Commission, once flew a helicopter past a girlfriend's office building with a banner saying "I love you". His nephew Ramzi Yousef, sentenced to life in prison for his role in the 1993 World Trade Center bombing, also had a girlfriend and, like his uncle, was often spotted in Manila's red-light district. **The FBI agent who hunted Yousef said that he "hid behind a cloak of Islam"**. Eyewitness accounts suggest the 9/11 hijackers were visiting bars and strip clubs in Florida and Las Vegas in the run-up to the attacks. The Spanish neighbours of Hamid Ahmidan, convicted for his role in the Madrid train bombings of 2004, remember him "zooming by on a motorcycle with his long-haired girlfriend, a Spanish woman with a taste for revealing outfits", according to press reports.

No wonder Muslim leaders worldwide condemn ISIS[338].

Similarly, the 9/11 hijackers used cocaine and drank alcohol, slept with prostitutes and attended strip clubs ... but they *did not worship at any mosque.* See this[339], this[340], this[341], this[342], this[343], this[344], this[345] and this[346].

As such, Islamic terrorists do not represent Muslims as a whole.

Endnotes

1. noted: http://www.youtube.com/watch?v=2a01Rg2g2Z8?start=745&end=761
2. themselves credit: http://www.washingtonsblog.com/2014/08/isis-terrorists-credit-iraq-war-success.html
3. reports: http://www.newyorker.com/magazine/2014/09/29/fight-lives
4. led to the rise of ISIS: http://www.washingtonsblog.com/2014/12/u-s-torture-program-created-isis.html

5. Guantanamo prison inspired ISIS atrocities:
http://www.washingtonsblog.com/2015/02/guantanamo-inspires-isis-atrocities.html
6. wasn't even in Iraq: http://crooksandliars.com/cernig/bush-admits-al-qaeda-wasnt-iraq-invasion-so
7. admitted:
http://abcnews.go.com/Politics/BushLegacy/story?id=6460837&page=1&singlePage=true
8. captured American weapons leftover from the Iraq war:
http://www.washingtonsblog.com/2014/07/isis-taking-iraq-using-captured-american-weapons.html
9. reports: http://www.dailystar.com.lb/News/Lebanon-News/2014/Sep-08/269883-frustration-drives-arsals-fsa-into-isis-ranks.ashx#ixzz3CpSZVuEG
10. Nusra Front [another extremist and hard-line Islamic terrorist group] :
11. non-aggression pact: https://now.mmedia.me/lb/en/nowsyrialatestnews/563491-syria-rebels-is-in-non-aggression-pact-near-damascus
12. with ISIS: http://www.middleeasteye.net/news/syria-1651994714
13. writes: http://www.nytimes.com/2014/09/12/world/middleeast/us-pins-hope-on-syrian-rebels-with-loyalties-all-over-the-map.html
14. Wall Street Journal: http://www.wsj.com/news/articles/SB10001424
    0527023046263045795094018654 54762
15. PBS: http://www.pbs.org/wgbh/pages/frontline/foreign-affairs-defense/syria-arming-the-rebels/syrian-rebels-describe-u-s-backed-training-in-qatar/
16. CNN: http://www.cnn.com/2013/09/12/politics/syria-arming-rebels/
17. New York Times: http://www.nytimes.com/2012/06/21/world/middleeast/cia-said-to-aid-in-steering-arms-to-syrian-rebels.html?_r=0
18. Medium: https://medium.com/dan-sanchez/where-does-isis-get-those-wonderful-toys-77cea955731a
19. Pulitzer prize-winning reporter Seymour Hersh:
http://www.washingtonsblog.com/2014/04/real-benghazi-story.html
20. arming rebels rarely works: http://www.washingtonsblog.com/2014/10/cia-study-funding-rebels-rarely-works.html
21. reported: http://www.nytimes.com/2013/04/28/world/middleeast/islamist-rebels-gains-in-syria-create-dilemma-for-us.html?pagewanted=all&_r=0
22. warned: http://www.huffingtonpost.com/michael-shank/how-arming-syrian-rebels_b_3689592.html
23. committees' about-face decision last week: http://rt.com/usa/joint-chiefs-us-options-syria-445/
24. reject negotiation altogether: https://www.fas.org/sgp/crs/mideast/RL33487.pdf
25. 5 years before the civil war started … and started arming them 4 years beforehand:
http://www.washingtonsblog.com/2013/08/u-s-started-backing-syrian-opposition-years-before-the-uprising-started.html
26. discussed: http://www.youtube.com/watch?v=W3HWiydFlJc?start=340&end=485
27. humanitarian reasons: http://www.washingtonsblog.com/2015/03/original-sin-first-humanitarian-war.html
28. summarized: http://www.washingtonsblog.com/2014/05/america-switched-sides-now-backs-al-qaeda-nazis.html
29. mainly Al Qaeda, and the U.S. has been supporting these terrorists:
http://www.washingtonsblog.com/2013/09/syrian-rebels-slit-throat-of-christian-man-who-refused-to-convert-to-islam-taunt-fiance-jesus-didnt-come-to-save-him.html
30. Wall Street Journal:
http://online.wsj.com/news/articles/SB10001424052702304431104579547183675484314
31. the National: http://www.thenational.ae/world/middle-east/al-qaeda-expands-influence-in-syrias-southern-front
32. Burned: http://www.youtube.com/watch?feature=player_embedded&v=BZui1YVCVTY
33. flags: http://www.youtube.com/watch?feature=player_embedded&v=R5OtSNDz6lU

34. Threatened to attack America: http://www.washingtontimes.com/news/2013/sep/6/facebook-flap-syrian-rebels-post-image-selves-burn/

35. "When we finish with Assad, we will fight the U.S.!" : http://www.mcclatchydc.com/2012/12/02/176123/al-qaida-linked-group-syria-rebels.html#storylink=cpy

36. won't finish until this [Al Qaeda] banner will be raised on top of the White House: http://www.infowars.com/fsa-rebel-we-wont-stop-until-al-qaeda-flag-raised-over-white-house/

37. "9/11 ideology": http://www.israelnationalnews.com/News/News.aspx/175001#.U20gCaKaXYA

38. singing Bin Laden's praises: http://www.thestudentroom.co.uk/showthread.php?t=2665274

39. celebrating the 9/11 attack: http://www.youtube.com/watch?v=vsq5ZRir-0k

40. reports: http://www.cbsnews.com/8301-202_162-57602799/al-qaeda-boss-ayman-al-zawahri-marks-9-11-with-call-for-more-attacks-on-u.s-soil/

41. are Al Qaeda: http://www.washingtonsblog.com/2013/09/kerry-we-have-to-send-terrorists-into-syria-to-make-sure-that-chemical-weapons-dont-fall-into-the-hands-of-terrorists.html

42. designated these guys as terrorists: http://www.aljazeera.com/news/middleeast/2012/12/2012121117048117723.html

43. gaining more and more power: http://worldnews.nbcnews.com/_news/2013/09/11/20438772-jihadis-gain-ground-in-syrian-rebel-movement-as-moderates-grow-desperate?lite

44. ending up in the hands of Al Qaeda: http://www.nytimes.com/2012/10/15/world/middleeast/jihadists-receiving-most-arms-sent-to-syrian-rebels.html?pagewanted=all&_r=0

45. have chemical weapons: http://www.washingtonsblog.com/2013/09/classified-u-s-military-document-syrian-rebels-do-have-chemical-weapons.html

46. tripled the size of its territory in Syria: http://www.washingtonsblog.com/2015/01/islamic-state-tripled-territory-syria-u-s-started-airstrikes.html

47. greatly expanded its territory in Iraq: http://www.washingtonsblog.com/2015/05/in-iraq-isis-is-winning-and-the-united-states-is-losing.html

48. even more of Syria: http://static3.businessinsider.com/image/55eec098bd86ef15008b88be-1944-1716/2000px-syria15.png

49. reported: http://www.nytimes.com/2007/07/18/world/africa/18iht-iraq.4.6718200.html?_r=4&

50. arrested in 2007: http://web.archive.org/web/20070314153618/http://www.cnn.com/2007/WORLD/meast/03/09/iraq.main/index.html?eref=rss_latest

51. killed in 2007: http://edition.cnn.com/2007/WORLD/meast/05/03/iraq.main/

52. arrested again: http://www.huffingtonpost.com/2009/04/23/baghdad-suicide-bomber-ki_0_n_190455.html

53. killed again: http://www.reuters.com/article/2010/04/19/us-iraq-violence-alqaeda-idUSTRE63I3CL20100419

54. declared dead: http://www.nbcnews.com/id/4446084/ns/world_news-mideast_n_africa/t/iraq-militants-claim-al-zarqawi-dead/

55. said to be arrested: http://www.cbsnews.com/news/official-al-zarqawi-caught-freed/

56. several different times: http://www.chinadaily.com.cn/english/doc/2005-01/04/content_405831.htm

57. in 2006: http://www.cbsnews.com/news/whats-next-after-zarqawis-death/

58. cites: http://www.independent.co.uk/news/media/how-the-spooks-took-over-the-news-780672.html

59. reported: http://www.washingtonpost.com/wp-dyn/content/article/2006/04/09/AR2006040900890_pf.html

60. reported: http://www.youtube.com/watch?v=d-LbGW-8vig?start=625&end=751

61. explains: https://en.wikipedia.org/wiki/Mosul%E2%80%93Haifa_oil_pipeline

62. Background: http://en.wikipedia.org/wiki/Haifa#British_Mandate

63. reported: http://www.haaretz.com/print-edition/news/u-s-checking-possibility-of-pumping-oil-from-northern-iraq-to-haifa-via-jordan-1.98134

64. call: http://en.wikipedia.org/wiki/1948_Arab%E2%80%93Israeli_War
65. poison the Iraqi leader: http://en.wikipedia.org/wiki/CIA_activities_in_Iraq#Iraq_1960
66. backed the coup which succeeded:
http://en.wikipedia.org/wiki/CIA_activities_in_Iraq#Iraq_1963
67. in 1991: http://www.washingtonsblog.com/2011/11/neoconservatives-planned-regime-change-throughout-the-middle-east-and-northern-africa-20-years-ago.html
68. admitted the war was about oil: http://www.washingtonsblog.com/2013/03/top-republican-leaders-say-iraq-war-was-really-for-oil.html
69. said: http://discussion.guardian.co.uk/comment-permalink/22064968
70. said: http://www.youtube.com/watch?v=9sd2JseupXQ?start=1305
71. said:
http://web.archive.org/web/20110715222651/http://www.timesonline.co.uk/tol/news/world/article2461214.ece
72. said:
http://www.boston.com/news/nation/articles/2005/08/31/bush_gives_new_reason_for_iraq_war/
73. said: http://firstread.nbcnews.com/_news/2008/05/02/4431009-mccain-iraq-war-was-for-oil
74. said: http://www.businessweek.com/stories/2008-08-29/bartiromo-talks-with-sarah-palinbusinessweek-business-news-stock-market-and-financial-advice
75. writes: http://www.thedailybeast.com/newsweek/2013/03/18/the-speechwriter-inside-the-bush-administration-during-the-iraq-war.html
76. politician and oil minister: http://en.wikipedia.org/wiki/Ahmed_Chalabi
77. said: http://www.youtube.com/watch?v=uFbpKKOEnAE
78. said: http://www.youtube.com/watch?v=G1p_tFnKqMA
79. Cheney and the U.S. oil chiefs planned the Iraq war before 9/11 in order to get control of its oil:
http://www.washingtonsblog.com/2008/07/did-cheney-and-the-oil-bigs-plan-the-iraq-war-before-911.html
80. reported: http://web.archive.org/web/20030402124132/http://www.sundayherald.com/28224
81. reported: http://www.independent.co.uk/news/uk/politics/secret-memos-expose-link-between-oil-firms-and-invasion-of-iraq-2269610.html
82. in order to calm oil markets:
http://en.wikipedia.org/wiki/1990_oil_price_shock#Iraqi_invasion_of_Kuwait_and_ensuing_economic_effects
83. quoted: http://content.time.com/time/magazine/0,9263,7601900820,00.html
84. in 1949: http://en.wikipedia.org/wiki/March_1949_Syrian_coup_d%27%C3%A9tat
85. notes: http://coat.ncf.ca/our_magazine/links/issue51/articles/51_12-13.pdf
86. reports: http://m.guardian.co.uk/politics/2003/sep/27/uk.syria1?cat=politics&type=article
87. vaguely familiar: http://en.wikipedia.org/wiki/Free_Syrian_Army
88. Shia Muslim sect: http://en.wikipedia.org/wiki/Druze
89. in 1991: http://www.washingtonsblog.com/2011/11/neoconservatives-planned-regime-change-throughout-the-middle-east-and-northern-africa-20-years-ago.html
90. reported: http://www.theguardian.com/environment/earth-insight/2013/aug/30/syria-chemical-attack-war-intervention-oil-gas-energy-pipelines
91. Roland Dumas: http://www.youtube.com/watch?v=jeyRwFHR8WY
92. private intelligence firm Stratfor: http://blogs.channel4.com/alex-thomsons-view/syria-spooks-wikileaks-military/5502
93. a meeting with Pentagon officials: https://wikileaks.org/gifiles/docs/1671459_insight-military-intervention-in-syria-post-withdrawal.html
94. refused to sign:
http://www.google.com/hostednews/afp/article/ALeqM5jhPTvibpnk98IR09Amuc5QzWQsIQ?docId=CNG.c0b07c0fd43690568ae07ab83f87f608.6d1
95. run a pipeline from the latter's North field: http://www.thenational.ae/business/energy/qatar-seeks-gas-pipeline-to-turkey
96. an alternative $10 billion pipeline plan with Iran:
http://www.aljazeera.com/indepth/opinion/2012/08/201285133440424621.html

97. framework agreement for construction of the gas pipelines:
http://www.alarabiya.net/articles/2013/02/20/267257.html

98. direct slap in the face: http://oilprice.com/Geopolitics/Middle-East/IRAN-IRAQ-Pipeline-to-Syria-Ups-Ante-in-Proxy-War-with-Qatar.html

99. "completely" in Saudi Arabia's hands:
http://www.google.com/hostednews/afp/article/ALeqM5jhPTvibpnk98IR09Amuc5QzWQsIQ?docId=CNG.c0b07c0fd43690568ae07ab83f87f608.6d1

100. play ball: http://www.lawfareblog.com/2013/08/general-dempsey-on-syria-intervention/

101. many other governments, as well: http://www.washingtonsblog.com/2014/09/u-s-already-completed-regime-change-syria-iran-iraq-twice-oil-rich-countries.html

102. noted: http://www.ibtimes.com/syrian-oil-gas-little-known-facts-syrias-energy-resources-russias-help-1402405

103. key chess piece: http://www.washingtonsblog.com/2012/10/the-wars-in-the-middle-east-and-north-africa-are-not-just-about-oil-theyre-also-about-gas.html

104. integral part: http://www.hydrocarbons-technology.com/projects/arab-gas-pipeline-agp/

105. additional graphics: http://pipelines.curry.com/

106. from Iran's giant South Pars field through Iraq and Syria:
http://www.aljazeera.com/indepth/opinion/2012/08/201285133440424621.html

107. writes: http://oilprice.com/Energy/Energy-General/Depleted-Global-Oil-and-Gas-Reserves-have-Led-to-Greater-Interest-in-Syria.html

108. said: http://wlns.com/ap/intelligence-chief-iraq-and-syria-may-not-survive-as-states-2/

109. decided long ago: http://www.washingtonsblog.com/2014/06/mess-iraq-design.html

110. noted: http://www.theguardian.com/world/2002/sep/03/worlddispatch.iraq

111. US thinktanks give lessons in foreign policy:
http://www.guardian.co.uk/elsewhere/journalist/story/0,7792,777100,00.html

112. Richard Perle, Paul Wolfowitz, Dick Cheney, John Bolton and others:
http://en.wikipedia.org/wiki/Project_for_the_New_American_Century

113. writes: http://www.counterpunch.org/2014/06/17/is-open-ended-chaos-the-desired-us-israeli-aim-in-the-middle-east/

114. notes: http://original.antiwar.com/justin/2014/06/17/iraq-will-the-neocons-get-away-with-it-again/

115. again: http://original.antiwar.com/justin/2003/03/26/iraqi-pandora/

116. again: http://original.antiwar.com/justin/2005/01/31/iraq-election-sistanis-triumph/

117. real:
http://www.informationclearinghouse.info/pdf/The%20Zionist%20Plan%20for%20the%20Middle%20East.pdf

118. years ago: http://original.antiwar.com/justin/2012/01/31/iraq-in-retrospect/

119. dismantled their army:
http://www.slate.com/articles/news_and_politics/war_stories/2007/09/who_disbanded_the_iraqi_army.html

120. pulverized: http://www.google.com/search?hl=&q=airstrikes+iraq+2005&sourceid=navclient-ff&rlz=1B3GGLL_enUS412US413&ie=UTF-8&aq=0&oq=airstrikes+iraq+2005

121. roads: http://www.youtube.com/watch?v=uOrDHKwRXsg&feature=related

122. bridges: http://www.nytimes.com/2007/08/14/world/middleeast/14cnd-iraq.html

123. electrical plants: http://articles.latimes.com/2005/dec/25/world/fg-power25

124. water facilities: http://waterfortheages.org/2008/04/27/iraq-water-and-politics-in-a-war-torn-country/

125. museums: http://www.aam-us.org/pubs/mn/MN_JF07_lost-iraq.cfm

126. schools: http://iraqdailytimes.com/education-iraq-iraq-needs-to-5800-schools-to-meet-the-shortage/

127. dissolved: http://www.democracynow.org/2010/9/1/iraq_is_a_shattered_country_nir

128. A Clean Break: A New Strategy for Securing the Realm:
http://www.informationclearinghouse.info/article1438.htm

129.declared: http://www.haaretz.com/print-edition/news/sharon-says-u-s-should-also-disarm-iran-libya-and-syria-1.18707

130.Indeed: http://www.washingtonsblog.com/2011/11/neoconservatives-planned-regime-change-throughout-the-middle-east-and-northern-africa-20-years-ago.html

131.points out: http://www.globalresearch.ca/the-destruction-and-political-fragmentation-of-iraq-towards-the-creation-of-a-us-sponsored-islamist-caliphate/5386998

132.Plans for Redrawing the Middle East: The Project for a "New Middle East": http://www.globalresearch.ca/plans-for-redrawing-the-middle-east-the-project-for-a-new-middle-east/3882

133.Mahdi Darius Nazemroaya: http://www.globalresearch.ca/author/mahdi-darius-nazemroaya

134.wrote: http://www.amazon.com/Zionist-Plan-Middle-Special-Document/dp/0937694568

135.advocated: http://www.salon.com/2006/08/03/mideast_8/

136.points out: http://www.globalresearch.ca/the-destruction-and-political-fragmentation-of-iraq-towards-the-creation-of-a-us-sponsored-islamist-caliphate/5386998

137.key architects: http://www.msnbc.com/msnbc/10-years-later-the-architects-the-iraq-wa

138.said:: http://www.foxnews.com/transcript/2015/05/24/mike-huckabee-lays-out-path-to-2016-republican-nomination-amb-john-bolton-talks/

139.Reagan Archives: http://www.reagan.utexas.edu/archives/photographs/atwork.html

140.admitted: http://www.gwu.edu/%7Ensarchiv/coldwar/interviews/episode-17/brzezinski1.html

141.organized and supported Bin Laden and the other originators of "Al Qaeda" in the 1970s: http://www.thenation.com/article/blowback-prequel

142.told: http://www.youtube.com/watch?v=d4lf0RT72iw

143.confirmed: http://www.amazon.com/Shadows-Ultimate-Insiders-Story-Presidents/dp/0684834979/sr=8-1/qid=1163059092/ref=pd_bbs_1/102-8219747-6907339?ie=UTF8&s=books

144.agrees: http://www.youtube.com/watch?v=Dqn0bm4E9yw?rel=0&controls=0&showinfo=0

145.reported: http://www.msnbc.msn.com/id/3340101/#.UEaKb6BFbKc

146.told: http://www.globalresearch.ca/articles/BRZ110A.html

147.reported: http://pqasb.pqarchiver.com/washingtonpost/access/110956747.html?FMT=ABS&FMTS=ABS:FT&date=Mar+23%2C+2002&author=Joe+Stephens+and+David+B.+Ottaway&pub=The+Washington+Post&edition=&startpage=A.01&desc=From+U.S.%2C+the+ABC%27s+of+Jihad%3B+Violent+Soviet-Era+Textbooks+Complicate+Afghan+Education+Efforts

148.notes: http://www.cfr.org/publication/20364/pakistans_education_system_and_links_to_extremism.html

149.report (PDF): http://www.cfr.org/publication/10353/

150.this: http://www.guardian.co.uk/world/1999/jan/17/yemen.islam

151.Robert Dreyfuss: http://www.robertdreyfuss.com/bio.htm

152.nuclear scientist and peace activist: http://en.wikipedia.org/wiki/Pervez_Hoodbhoy

153.writes: http://www.physics.harvard.edu/%7Ewilson/pmpmta/2010_Hoodbhoy.doc

154.says: http://www.youtube.com/watch?v=iw6YHij-aCU

155.well-known: http://www.thenation.com/article/robert-i-friedman

156.wrote: http://books.google.com/books?id=l-MCAAAAMBAJ&pg=PA43&lpg=PA43&dq=%22According+to+other+sources+familiar+with+the+case,+the+FBI+told+District+Attorney+Robert+M.+Morgenthau+that+Nosair+was+a+lone+gunman,+not+part+of+a+broader+conspiracy;%22&source=bl&ots=Ri7bd4UFfI&sig=XSFrnaBeJ1cO5a402E6cQRthiPU&hl=en#v=onepage&q=%22According%20to%20other%20sources%20familiar%20with%20the%20case%2C%20the%20FBI%20told%20District%20Attorney%20Robert%20M.%20Morgenthau%20that%20Nosair%20was%20a%20lone%20gunman%2C%20not%20part%20of%20a%20broader%20conspiracy%3B%22&f=false

157.Terror Nation? U.S. Creation?: http://tv.msn.com/tv/episode/cnn-presents/terror-nation-us-creation/

158.summarized by Congressman Peter Deutsch: https://www.atsc.army.mil/crc/ISO6A10L/LessonPlan_TheCurrentThreatinAfghanistan.rtf

159. says: http://www.usnews.com/news/world/articles/2008/07/11/afghan-warlords-formerly-backed-by-the-cia-now-turn-their-guns-on-us-troops

160. the New York Times: http://web.archive.org/web/20071212122812/http://pqasb.pqarchiver.com/nytimes/access/116193080.html?did=116193080&FMT=ABS&FMTS=AI&date=Oct+28,+1993&author=By+RALPH+BLUMENTHAL&pub=New+York+Times++%281857_Current+file%29&desc=Tapes+Depict+Proposal+to+Thwart+Bomb+Used+in+Trade+Center+Blast

161. CBS News: http://www.youtube.com/watch?v=5F1Y6cGRXEs&eurl

162. supported Bin Laden and other Al Qaeda terrorists in Bosnia: http://www.amazon.com/Unholy-Terror-Bosnia-Al-Qaida-Global/dp/product-description/0760330034

163. reported: http://www.washingtonsblog.com/2012/11/why-did-cia-director-petraeus-suddenly-resign-and-why-was-the-u-s-ambassador-to-libya-murdered.html

164. largely comprised of Al Qaeda terrorists: http://www.telegraph.co.uk/news/worldnews/africaandindianocean/libya/8407047/Libyan-rebel-commander-admits-his-fighters-have-al-Qaeda-links.html

165. report: http://www.scribd.com/doc/111001074/West-Point-CTC-s-Al-Qa-ida-s-Foreign-Fighters-in-Iraq

166. reported: http://www.hindustantimes.com/world-news/Americas/Al-Qaeda-present-among-Libyan-rebels/Article1-679511.aspx

167. flown over the Benghazi courthouse: http://www.washingtonsblog.com/2011/11/did-we-overthrow-gaddafi-just-to-replace-him-with-al-qaeda.html

168. stopped him: http://www.telegraph.co.uk/news/worldnews/africaandindianocean/libya/8393843/Libya-Benghazi-about-to-fall...-then-came-the-planes.html

169. reported: http://www.dailymail.co.uk/news/article-2610598/Group-US-switched-sides-War-Terror-facilitating-500-MILLION-weapons-deliveries-Libyan-al-Qaeda-militias-leading-Benghazi-attack.html

170. reported: http://www.lrb.co.uk/v36/n08/seymour-m-hersh/the-red-line-and-the-rat-line

171. state: http://www.washingtontimes.com/news/2015/feb/1/hillary-clinton-libya-war-push-armed-benghazi-rebe/print/

172. admitted: http://www.telegraph.co.uk/news/worldnews/africaandindianocean/libya/8407047/Libyan-rebel-commander-admits-his-fighters-have-al-Qaeda-links.html

173. see this: http://www.washingtonsblog.com/2014/04/real-benghazi-story.html

174. supports terrorists: http://www.washingtonsblog.com/2011/01/biggest-terrorism-scaremongers-are-themselves-promoting-terrorism.html

175. said: http://hammernews.com/odomspeech.htm

176. here: http://hammernews.com/odom.ram

177. reported: http://www.washingtonpost.com/wp-dyn/content/article/2010/08/25/AR2010082506591.html

178. according to a secret CIA analysis released Wednesday by the Web site WikiLeaks: http://www.wikileaks.com/wiki/CIA_Red_Cell_Memorandum_on_United_States_%22exporting_terrorism%22,_2_Feb_2010

179. notes: http://en.wikipedia.org/wiki/United_States_and_state_terrorism

180. created death squads in Latin America, Iraq and Syria: http://www.globalresearch.ca/terrorism-with-a-human-face-the-history-of-americas-death-squads/5317564

181. "out-terrorize the terrorists": http://www.washingtonsblog.com/2010/09/the-warped-mission-of-the-american-military-out-terrorize-the-terrorists.html

182. notes: http://www.truth-out.org/second-soldier-alleges-former-tillman-commander-ordered-360-rotational-fire-iraq63153

183. defined: http://dictionary.reference.com/browse/terrorism

184. known as: http://en.wikipedia.org/wiki/Mukden_Incident

185.found:
https://books.google.com/books?id=rHainkH7pdEC&pg=PA321&dq=%22Several+of+the+partici
pators+in+the+plan,+including+Hashimoto,+have+on+various+occasions+admitted+their+part+in
+the+plot+and+have+stated+that+the+object%22&hl=en&sa=X&ei=NrOtVLiQGsm6ogT49oCQ
Ag&ved=0CB8Q6AEwAA#v=onepage&q=%22Several%20of%20the%20participators%20in%2
0the%20plan%2C%20including%20Hashimoto%2C%20have%20on%20various%20occasions%2
0admitted%20their%20part%20in%20the%20plot%20and%20have%20stated%20that%20the%20
object%22&f=false
186.admitted:
https://books.google.com/books?id=rHainkH7pdEC&pg=PA321&dq=%22Several+of+the+partici
pators+in+the+plan,+including+Hashimoto,+have+on+various+occasions+admitted+their+part+in
+the+plot+and+have+stated+that+the+object%22&hl=en&sa=X&ei=NrOtVLiQGsm6ogT49oCQ
Ag&ved=0CB8Q6AEwAA#v=onepage&q=%22Several%20of%20the%20participators%20in%2
0the%20plan%2C%20including%20Hashimoto%2C%20have%20on%20various%20occasions%2
0admitted%20their%20part%20in%20the%20plot%20and%20have%20stated%20that%20the%20
object%22&f=false
187.see this: http://lib.law.virginia.edu/imtfe/person/143
188.admitted: http://en.wikipedia.org/wiki/Gleiwitz_incident
189.admitted:
http://en.wikipedia.org/wiki/Hermann_G%C3%B6ring#Possible_responsibility_for_the_Reichsta
g_fire
190.admitted: https://en.wikipedia.org/wiki/Shelling_of_Mainila
191.agreed: https://en.wikipedia.org/wiki/Shelling_of_Mainila
192.admits: http://www.theguardian.com/world/2010/nov/26/russian-parliament-guilt-katyn-
massacre
193.admitted: http://www.theguardian.com/world/2010/nov/26/russian-parliament-guilt-katyn-
massacre
194.admits:
http://www.ynetnews.com/Ext/Comp/ArticleLayout/CdaArticlePrintPreview/1,2506,L-
3065838,00.html#n
195.this: http://www.stanford.edu/group/SHR/5-1/text/beinin.html
196.this: http://www.jewishvirtuallibrary.org/jsource/History/lavon.html
197.admits: http://www.nytimes.com/library/world/mideast/041600iran-cia-index.html
198.admitted:
http://books.google.com/books?id=SdubdhMwM1YC&pg=PA8&lpg=PA8&dq=the+riots+were+
purportedly+in+response+to+a+september+5+1955+greek+bombing+attack+on+the+turkish+con
sulate&source=bl&ots=O7OKEmcJrF&sig=y4vdM7vHk8Z8g1jH4gXDHTXw400&hl=en&sa=X
&ei=z2lKVIuEII3wgwTZ04HICA&ved=0CCQQ6AEwAQ#v=onepage&q=the%20riots%20were
%20purportedly%20in%20response%20to%20a%20september%205%201955%20greek%20bom
bing%20attack%20on%20the%20turkish%20consulate&f=false
199.admitted: http://www.washingtonsblog.com/2014/07/57-years-ago-u-s-britain-approved-use-
islamic-extremists-topple-syrian-government.html
200.former head of Italian counterintelligence:
http://www.guardian.co.uk/international/story/0,3604,462976,00.html
201.NATO, with the help of the Pentagon and CIA, carried out terror bombings in Italy and other
European countries in the 1950s and blamed the communists, in order to rally people's support for
their governments in Europe in their fight against communism:
http://en.wikipedia.org/wiki/Strategy_of_tension
202."You had to attack civilians, people, women, children, innocent people, unknown people far
removed from any political game. The reason was quite simple. They were supposed to force these
people, the Italian public, to turn to the state to ask for greater security":
http://web.archive.org/web/20051130003012/http://www.isn.ethz.ch/php/documents/collection_gl
adio/synopsis.htm
203.this: http://www.globalresearch.ca/articles/GAN412A.html

204. this BBC special:
https://video.search.yahoo.com/yhs/search;_ylt=AwrTca_5q89UIAwAVlsnnIlQ;_ylu=X3oDMTB
0MzkwOG5yBHNlYwNzYwRjb2xvA2dxMQR2dGlkA1lIUzAwNF8x?p=bbc+gladio&hspart=m
ozilla&hsimp=yhs-001
205. France, Belgium, Denmark, Germany, Greece, the Netherlands, Norway, Portugal, the UK:
http://en.wikipedia.org/wiki/Operation_Gladio
206. suggested: http://www.guardian.co.uk/theguardian/2012/aug/17/john-f-kennedy-fidel-castro
207. discussed: http://www.washingtonsblog.com/2010/02/nine-months-before-operation-
northwoods-government-leaders-suggested-false-flag-terror-in-the-dominican-republic.html
208. ABC news report: http://abcnews.go.com/US/story?id=92662&page=1
209. the official documents: http://www.gwu.edu/%7Ensarchiv/news/20010430/northwoods.pdf
210. this interview : http://www.youtube.com/watch?v=IygchZRJVXM
211. promoting:
http://en.wikipedia.org/wiki/Operation_Northwoods#Related_Operation_Mongoose_proposals
212. suggested:
http://en.wikipedia.org/wiki/Operation_Northwoods#Related_Operation_Mongoose_proposals
213. admits: http://www2.gwu.edu/%7Ensarchiv/NSAEBB/NSAEBB132/press20051201.htm
214. lied:
http://web.archive.org/web/20080203204207/http://rawstory.com/news/afp/Report_reveals_Vietna
m_War_hoaxes_f_01082008.html
215. Gulf of Tonkin incident: http://en.wikipedia.org/wiki/Gulf_of_Tonkin_incident
216. admitted: http://www.intelligence.senate.gov/churchcommittee.html
217. top: http://en.wikipedia.org/wiki/Sabri_Yirmibe%C5%9Fo%C4%9Flu
218. admitted: http://www.hurriyetdailynews.com/default.aspx?pageid=438&n=turkey-burned-
mosque-during-cyprus-war-gen-says-2010-09-24
219. explained: http://www.todayszaman.com/tz-web/news-222544-100-retired-general-confesses-
to-burning-mosque-to-fire-up-public.html
220. admitted: https://en.wikipedia.org/wiki/Celle_Hole
221. see this:
http://translate.google.com/translate?hl=en&sl=de&u=http://www.ndr.de/kultur/geschichte/chrono
logie/cellerloch102.html&prev=/search%3Fq%3Dhttp://www.ndr.de/kultur/geschichte/cellerloch1
02.html%26client%3Dfirefox-a%26hs%3DymV%26rls%3Dorg.mozilla:en-
US:official%26channel%3Dsb
222. says: http://www.amazon.com/Way-Deception-Victor-Ostrovsky-
ebook/dp/B002RL9NL2/ref=sr_1_1?s=books&ie=UTF8&qid=1422773938&sr=1-1
223. found: http://www.justice.gov.za/trc/decisions%5C2001/ac21233.htm
224. admit: http://www.encyclopedia.com/doc/1P1-68004301.html
225. this video: http://www.youtube.com/watch?v=HVJgsb5TuTw&feature=player_embedded
226. elements of the military had been involved in the riots, some of which were deliberately
provoked: http://www.fas.org/irp/world/indonesia/indonesia-1998.htm
227. admit:
http://web.archive.org/web/20060209100406/http://www.telegraph.co.uk/news/main.jhtml?xml=/
news/2004/01/13/wrus13.xml
228. this report: http://web.archive.org/web/20080413195430/http://www.sais-
jhu.edu/programs/res/papers/Satter_edited_final.pdf
229. this discussion: http://en.wikipedia.org/wiki/Russian_Apartment_Bombings
230. Washington Post: http://www.highbeam.com/doc/1P2-406202.html
231. admits: http://www.smh.com.au/news/National/Possible-police-role-in-2002-Bali-
attack/2005/10/12/1128796591857.html
232. BBC: http://news.bbc.co.uk/2/hi/europe/3674533.stm
233. New York Times:
http://www.nytimes.com/2004/05/17/international/europe/17mace.html?th=&pagewanted=all&po
sition=
234. Associated Press: http://www.highbeam.com/doc/1P1-94026683.html

235. admitted: https://web.archive.org/web/20030207160903/http://www.fair.org/activism/genoa-update.html

236. violent crackdown: http://www.theguardian.com/world/2010/may/19/g8-italian-police-sentenced

237. told to blame the Anthrax attacks on Al Qaeda by White House officials: http://www.nydailynews.com/news/us_world/2008/08/02/2008-08-02_fbi_was_told_to_blame_anthrax_scare_on_a.html

238. looked like: http://3.bp.blogspot.com/_MnYI3_FRbbQ/SJLfMP7mkrI/AAAAAAAAA94/irML20mNYDA/s400/anthrax.jpg

239. tried to link the anthrax to Iraq: http://www.nytimes.com/2001/12/22/national/22INQU.html?pagewanted=all

240. falsely blamed Iraq: http://www.washingtonsblog.com/2012/10/5-hours-after-the-911-attacks-donald-rumsfeld-said-my-interest-is-to-hit-saddam-he-also-said-go-massive-sweep-it-all-up-things-related-and-not-and-at-2.html

241. memo from the defense secretary: http://www.washingtonsblog.com/2013/02/newly-released-memos-of-donald-rumsfeld-prove-knowing-iraq-war.html

242. main justifications: http://www.washingtonsblog.com/2012/10/5-hours-after-the-911-attacks-donald-rumsfeld-said-my-interest-is-to-hit-saddam-he-also-said-go-massive-sweep-it-all-up-things-related-and-not-and-at-2.html

243. admitted: http://www.msnbc.msn.com/id/5223932/ns/us_news-security/t/panel-sees-no-link-between-iraq-al-qaida/#.UIde6fWUxqI

244. said: http://www.cnn.com/2004/ALLPOLITICS/06/18/cheney.iraq.al.qaeda/

245. admit: http://www.washingtonsblog.com/2013/03/top-republican-leaders-say-iraq-war-was-really-for-oil.html

246. say: http://www.washingtonsblog.com/2012/09/government-officials-say-911-was-state-sponsored-terrorism-but-disagree-about-which-nation-was-behind-attacks.html

247. suggested: http://www.aei.org/article/22833

248. reported: http://www.upi.com/Business_News/Security-Industry/2005/06/03/UPI-hears/UPI-64911117829623/

249. admitted: http://mondoweiss.net/2012/05/operation-glass-houses-idf-agent-provocateurs-admit-to-throwing-stones-at-the-idf-in-bilin.html

250. admitted: http://www.youtube.com/watch?v=gAfzUOx53Rg

251. see this: http://www.cbc.ca/news/canada/quebec-police-admit-they-went-undercover-at-montebello-protest-1.656171

252. saw: http://www.guardian.co.uk/politics/2009/may/10/g20-policing-agent-provacateurs

253. admitted: http://www.washingtonsblog.com/2011/01/prominent-former-egyptian-mp-and-presidential-candidate-the-looting-of-the-cairo-museum-was-carried-out-by-government-employees.html

254. see this: http://www.washingtonsblog.com/2011/02/washington-post-confirms-that-egyptian-looters-were-agents-provocateur.html

255. admitted: http://www.bbc.co.uk/news/world-latin-america-14149676

256. admitted: http://www.youtube.com/watch?v=SODTI_C1q_Q

257. admitted: http://www.telegraph.co.uk/finance/newsbysector/energy/oilandgas/10266957/Saudis-offer-Russia-secret-oil-deal-if-it-drops-Syria.html

258. admitted: http://www.washingtonsblog.com/2014/04/nato-member-conducts-false-flag-terror-try-whip-war.html

259. admitted: http://www.washingtonsblog.com/2014/04/nato-member-conducts-false-flag-terror-try-whip-war.html

260. admits: http://www.washingtonsblog.com/2014/03/former-ukranian-security-chief-alleges-new-government-behind-sniper-attacks.html

261. admitted: http://www.washingtonsblog.com/2014/02/nsa-engaged-internet-false-flag-attacks.html

262. see this: http://www.washingtonsblog.com/2014/02/false-flags-honey-traps.html

263. framing people: http://www.washingtonsblog.com/2014/07/spy-agencies-dirty-trick-powers-revealed-snowden.html

264. admitted: http://www.washingtonsblog.com/2014/09/top-u-s-military-official-arab-allies-support-isis.html

265. supporting ISIS: http://www.youtube.com/watch?v=nA39iVSo7XE?start=33

266. agrees: http://www.youtube.com/watch?v=QHLqaSZPe98

267. Vice President Joe Biden:
http://youtube%20http//www.youtube.com/watch?v=w04YE5zRmc8?start=67

268. says: http://www.rawstory.com/rs/2014/08/20/german-minister-accuses-qatar-of-funding-islamic-state-fighters/

269. reports: http://abcnews.go.com/International/hezbollah-al-qaeda-fighters-edging-closer-confrontation/story?id=19144119#.UagnQ5xGR8V

270. headlines: http://www.independent.co.uk/voices/comment/iraq-crisis-how-saudi-arabia-helped-isis-take-over-the-north-of-the-country-9602312.html

271. formerly owned by Newsweek: http://en.wikipedia.org/wiki/The_Daily_Beast

272. notes: http://www.thedailybeast.com/articles/2014/06/14/america-s-allies-are-funding-isis.html

273. told Secretary of State John Kerry: http://www.independent.co.uk/voices/comment/alqaida-the-second-act-is-saudi-arabia-regretting-its-support-for-terrorism-9198213.html

274. notes: http://www.businessinsider.com/isis-funding-us-allies-2014-6

275. far back as March: http://www.reuters.com/article/2014/03/09/us-iraq-saudi-qatar-idUSBREA2806S20140309

276. December 2013 report:
http://www.brookings.edu/%7E/media/research/files/papers/2013/12/06%20private%20gulf%20financing%20syria%20extremist%20rebels%20sectarian%20conflict%20dickinson/private%20gulf%20financing%20syria%20extremist%20rebels%20sectarian%20conflict%20dickinson.pdf

277. aligned with whatever is left of the Baathist regime once led by Saddam Hussein:
http://www.thedailybeast.com/articles/2014/06/14/america-s-allies-are-funding-isis.html

278. directly supporting ISIS: http://www.washingtonsblog.com/2014/09/turkey-israel-directly-supporting-isis-al-qaeda-syria.html

279. Turkey funds the terrorist group: http://www.breitbart.com/Big-Peace/2014/07/30/ISIS-Fighter-Claims-Turkey-Funds-the-Jihadist-Group

280. protecting and cooperating with ISIS and Al Qaeda terrorists:
http://www.hurriyetdailynews.com/chp-lawmakers-accuse-turkish-government-of-protecting-isil-and-al-nusra-militants.aspx?pageID=238&nID=67750&NewsCatID=338

281. medical treatment to ISIS terrorists: http://www.todayszaman.com/national_nurse-says-shes-tired-of-treating-isil-terrorists_358992.html

282. pointed out: http://time.com/3932515/the-kurds-are-building-a-country-with-every-victory-over-isis/

283. writes: http://time.com/3974399/turkey-kurds-isis/

284. reported: http://www.theguardian.com/world/2015/jul/26/isis-syria-turkey-us?CMP=share_btn_tw

285. Islamic State: http://www.theguardian.com/world/isis

286. Isis official responsible for oil smuggling, named Abu Sayyaf:
http://www.dailymail.co.uk/news/article-3084323/US-special-forces-kill-ISIS-commander.html

287. jihadi groups, such as Ahrar al-Sham: http://web.stanford.edu/group/mappingmilitants/cgi-bin/groups/view/523

288. long: http://www.washingtonsblog.com/2014/08/allegations-u-s-allies-back-isis-islamic-terrorists.html

289. pointed: http://www.washingtonsblog.com/2014/09/turkey-israel-directly-supporting-isis-al-qaeda-syria.html

290. out: http://www.washingtonsblog.com/2015/02/top-u-s-generals-american-allies-support-isis.html

291. experts: http://www.businessinsider.com/turkey-created-a-monster-and-doesnt-know-how-to-deal-with-it-2015-2

292. Kurds: http://www.newsweek.com/2014/10/31/kurds-accuse-turkish-government-supporting-isis-278776.html

293. Joe Biden: http://www.thegatewaypundit.com/2014/10/turkish-president-erdogan-demands-joe-biden-apologize-for-blaming-turkey-for-rise-of-isis/

294. Israeli air force has bombed: http://www.washingtonsblog.com/2014/12/israel-acts-isis-air-force-repeatedly-bombs-syria.html

295. recently admitted: http://www.washingtonsblog.com/2015/07/israeli-military-admits-to-supporting-syrian-jihadis.html

296. reported: http://www.timesofisrael.com/yaalon-syrian-rebels-keeping-druze-safe-in-exchange-for-israeli-aid/

297. is Al Qaeda, and closely affiliated with ISIS: http://www.washingtonsblog.com/2015/03/us-considering-openly-arming-syrian-al-qaeda-faction-al-nusra.html

298. reported: http://www.timesofisrael.com/syrian-rebel-commander-says-he-collaborated-with-israel/

299. a video: https://www.youtube.com/watch?v=6J1p6HR20_I

300. Safouri was abducted by the al-Qaeda-affiliated Al-Nusra Front: http://www.timesofisrael.com/syrian-al-qaeda-fighters-flee-southward-toward-israel-border/

301. reported: http://www.haaretz.com/news/diplomacy-defense/1.580169

302. noted: http://www.haaretz.com/news/middle-east/.premium-1.576083

303. wrote: http://www.al-monitor.com/pulse/originals/2015/07/israel-syria-war-bashar-al-assad-support-rebels-al-qaeda-is.html

304. emerging alliance: http://www.al-monitor.com/pulse/originals/2015/02/israel-syria-rebels-jihad-sunni-shiite-golan-heights.html

305. choose Assad's enemies: http://www.al-monitor.com/pulse/en/originals/2015/05/moderate-countries-saudi-arabia-israel-jihadists-dictators.html

306. suggests: http://www.thedailybeast.com/articles/2015/08/31/petraeus-use-al-qaeda-fighters-to-beat-isis.html

307. also saying: http://www.washingtonsblog.com/2015/03/mainstream-media-calls-supporting-al-qaeda-isis.html

308. asks: http://www.salon.com/2015/03/18/thomas_friedman_asks_if_us_should_arm_isis_to_fix_problems_created_by_policies_he_supported/

309. says: http://www.infowars.com/former-al-qaeda-commander-isis-works-for-the-cia/

310. the Department of Justice's Inspector General, several senators: http://www.nytimes.com/2005/01/15/national/15translate.html?ex=1153886400&en=13842175814b8e8c&ei=5070

311. coalition of prominent conservative and liberal groups: http://web.archive.org/web/20071031085021/http://www.libertycoalition.net/state-secrets-privelage/coalition-letter-to-the-house-committee-on-oversight-and-government-reform-on-criminal-activities-by-the

312. says: http://www.globalresearch.ca/silencing-a-whistle-blower-gladio-b-and-the-origins-of-isis-sibel-edmonds/5475126

313. here: http://www.boilingfrogspost.com/2011/11/21/bfp-exclusive-syria-secret-us-nato-training-support-camp-to-oust-current-syrian-president/

314. here: http://www.boilingfrogspost.com/2011/12/03/us-media-distorters-of-reality-gravediggers-of-truth/

315. here: http://www.boilingfrogspost.com/2011/12/11/bfp-exclusive-developing-story-hundreds-of-us-nato-soldiers-arrive-begin-operations-on-the-jordan-syria-border/

316. here: https://www.youtube.com/watch?v=-v1h1bUfCVc

317. might create a terrorist group like ISIS and an Islamic caliphate: http://www.washingtonsblog.com/2015/05/newly-declassified-u-s-government-documents-the-west-supported-the-creation-of-isis.html

318. documents: http://www.judicialwatch.org/wp-content/uploads/2015/05/Pg.-291-Pgs.-287-293-JW-v-DOD-and-State-14-812-DOD-Release-2015-04-10-final-version11.pdf

319. years before: http://www.cnn.com/2014/08/08/world/isis-fast-facts/

320. salafists: http://www.washingtonsblog.com/2014/08/closest-u-s-allies-middle-east-hotbeds-islamic-fundamentalism.html

321. aren't any moderate rebels: http://www.washingtonsblog.com/2014/09/war-3.html

322. this: https://www.google.com/search?q=no+moderate+rebels+syria&ie=utf-8&oe=utf-8&aq=t&rls=org.mozilla:en-US:official&client=firefox-a&channel=sb

323. this: http://www.washingtonpost.com/blogs/worldviews/wp/2014/10/06/behind-bidens-gaffe-some-legitimate-concerns-about-americas-middle-east-allies/

324. this: http://news.firedoglake.com/2014/08/11/obama-admits-arming-moderate-syrian-rebels-has-always-been-a-fantasy/

325. confirm: https://medium.com/insurge-intelligence/secret-pentagon-report-reveals-west-saw-isis-as-strategic-asset-b99ad7a29092

326. served as: https://en.wikipedia.org/wiki/Michael_T._Flynn

327. confirmed: http://www.youtube.com/watch?v=SG3j8OYKgn4?start=675&end=769

328. NBC News: http://www.nbcnews.com/storyline/middle-east-unrest/u-s-launches-airstrikes-aid-american-trained-syrian-rebels-n401906

329. Wall Street Journal: http://www.wsj.com/articles/u-s-to-give-some-syria-rebels-ability-to-call-airstrikes-1424208053?mod=djemalertNEWS

330. CNN: http://www.cnn.com/2015/08/02/middleeast/syrian-rebels-u-s-air-cover/

331. U.S. trained Islamic jihadis – who would later join ISIS :
http://www.wnd.com/2014/06/officials-u-s-trained-isis-at-secret-base-in-jordan/

332. confirmed: http://www.reuters.com/article/2013/03/10/us-syria-crisis-rebels-usa-idUSBRE9290FI20130310

333. more in common with Mao's Red Guards or the Khmer Rouge than it does with the Muslim empires of antiquity: https://firstlook.org/theintercept/2014/09/26/isis-islamic/

334. reports: http://www.huffingtonpost.co.uk/mehdi-hasan/jihadist-radicalisation-islam-for-dummies_b_5697160.html?utm_hp_ref=tw

335. Here's the Guardian report:
http://www.theguardian.com/uk/2008/aug/20/uksecurity.terrorism1

336. foreign occupation – and not religion: http://www.washingtonsblog.com/2013/10/u-s-war-on-terror-has-increased-terrorism.html

337. top Bin Laden hunter agreed: http://www.washingtonsblog.com/2014/07/head-cia-unit-tasked-killing-bin-laden.html

338. Muslim leaders worldwide condemn ISIS:
http://www.washingtonsblog.com/2014/08/muslims-condemn-isis.html

339. this:
http://web.archive.org/web/20011010224657/http://www.bostonherald.com/attack/investigation/ausprob10102001.htm

340. this: http://web.archive.org/web/20010916150533/http://www.sun-sentinel.com/news/local/southflorida/sfl-warriors916.story

341. this: http://www.newsweek.com/2001/10/14/cracking-the-terror-code.html

342. this:
http://web.archive.org/web/20011023132702/http://interactive.wsj.com/articles/SB1003180286455952120.htm

343. this:
http://web.archive.org/web/20090213114442/http://articles.latimes.com/2002/sep/01/nation/na-plot

344. this:
http://www.historycommons.org/context.jsp?item=a091101beforepinkpony#a091101beforepinkpony

345. this: http://www.firstcoastnews.com/news/local/story.aspx?storyid=23296

346. this: http://www.youtube.com/embed/_qC0rEG_f3Y

Born of the USA:

The Real Origins of ISIL

By Wayne Madsen

The comments of two U.S. generals, one active duty and the other retired, exposed for the entire world the covert U.S. backing enjoyed by the Islamic State of Iraq and the Levant (ISIL) in its rise to power in Syria and Iraq. The retired director of the Defense Intelligence Agency, Lieutenant General Michael Flynn, revealed that U.S. support for the most radical Islamist guerrillas in Syria led to the creation of the Islamic State in that country. Provided with arms via a Central Intelligence Agency (CIA)-initiated covert supply chain from post-Muammar Qaddafi Libya, itself decimated by a U.S. - and NATO-created civil war, ISIL was successful in seizing territory from the Syrian government of President Bashar al-Assad. ISIL then turned its attention to Iraq and seized a large swath of territory in Iraq's western and northern regions. The net result of this U.S. backing for the Islamic State was the creation of a brutal Islamic Caliphate stretching from the outskirts of Baghdad and Damascus to eastern Libya, northern Nigeria, and pockets in Egypt's Sinai Peninsula.

The ISIL insurgents, many of them foreign mercenaries who are considered more dangerous than Al Qaeda by many Pentagon and U.S. intelligence specialists, have disturbing links to intelligence services of the United States, Israel, France, and Britain.

The deeper one digs into the operations surrounding the ISIL, or, as it is variably called, "Islamic State of Iraq and al-Sham" (ISIS), "Al Dawlah" (the State), or "Da'ish" (an acronym of *"al-Dawla al-Islamiya fi Iraq wa al-Sham")*, the more the Islamist insurgent group's links to Western and Israeli intelligence are revealed. ISIL is an outgrowth of the Organization of Jihad's Base in the Country of the Two Rivers or Al Qaeda in Iraq (AQI), which was once led by Abu Musab al-Zarqawi. As with the current leader of ISIL, Abu Bakr al-Baghdadi, questions also surrounded the background of Zarqawi.

Zarqawi's real name was Ahmed Fadeel Nazal al-Khalayleh. He was born in the Jordanian town of Zarqa. Abu Musab al-Zarqawi was an alias as much as Abu Bakr al-Baghdadi was an alias for the alleged leader of ISIL. Al Baghdadi, a native of Samarra, Iraq, was actually Ibrahim ibn Awwad ibn Ibrahim ibn Ali ibn Muhammad al-Badri al-Samarrai. Before he joined the mujaheddin war against the Soviets in Afghanistan, Zarqawi was a video store clerk who was known as a drunk and drug abuser, hardly material for the fundamentalist Islamists bankrolled by Saudi Arabia and the Gulf emirates.

After the American invasion of Iraq, Zarqawi proclaimed himself the "Emir of Al Qaeda in the Country of the Two Rivers" and he quickly became public enemy number one for U.S. occupation forces. Zarqawi was recruited in Jordan by "The Base" or "Al Qaeda" to serve in the ranks of Arab legions fighting the Soviets in Afghanistan. As the late British Foreign Secretary pointed out, "The Base" or "Al Qaeda" was a CIA database containing the names of various CIA recruiters, financiers, exporters, and other personnel required to maintain the flow of mercenaries, weapons, and money to Afghanistan and Pakistan to sustain the campaign against the Soviets in Afghanistan.[68]

Al Qaeda leader Osama bin Laden was also allegedly known to the CIA by his agency cover name "Tim Osman" and by his Arab Afghani volunteers as the "Hero of Jaji." Jaji was the location of an Afghan battlefield where Bin Laden was victorious against the Soviets. Reports of Bin Laden's past connections to the CIA, including an alleged arms procurement meeting he held with CIA agents in Sherman Oaks, California in 1986, have been relegated to relatively obscure publications and websites in an obvious campaign by the CIA to downplay its one-time association with the jihadist insurgent leader.[69] In fact, it is known that Bin Laden ran the *Maktab al-Khidamar* - the MAK - for the CIA and Saudis. MAK ensured the flow of fighters, money, and weapons to the Afghan insurgency on behalf of the CIA's Al Qaeda operation.

After the Soviets withdrew from Afghanistan, Zarqawi, who befriended Bin Laden, returned to Jordan but was jailed by the authorities for setting up *Jund al-Sham*, a "caliphate" liberation movement with the goal of establishing an Islamist state in Syria, Lebanon, Jordan, Palestine, Cyprus, and southern Turkey. It is no coincidence that *Jund al-Sham* had similar goals to those of the later-proclaimed Islamic State. It also turned out that *Jund al-Sham* was thoroughly infiltrated by Jordanian intelligence,[70] which informed the CIA about all the group's members.

Zarqawi was released by Jordan in 2001. He traveled to Afghanistan to battle against the U.S. occupation forces there and he eventually found his way into Iraq where he organized jihadists for the forthcoming U.S. invasion. CIA "evidence" that Zarqawi was in Iraq was used to justify the 2003 U.S. invasion of the country. Jordanian intelligence and the CIA also had evidence that Zarqawi was involved in the 2005 bombings in Amman of the Radisson SAS Hotel, the Grand Hyatt, and the Days Inn. The attacks were used by Jordan and the U.S. to beef up America's military presence in the Hashemite Kingdom.

One time CIA deputy director Michael Morell wrote that Zarqawi's and AQI's rise to power in Iraq were a direct result of two schemes by the Bush administration neocons in the wake of the U.S. occupation of Iraq. One was the edict by the U.S. Coalition Provisional Authority to "remove anyone who had been a member of Saddam's Baath Party from a position inside the Iraqi government." The second was "to disband any organization with close ties to the Baath Party," which "resulted in the collapse of the Iraqi military and security services." Morell wrote that the resulting vacuum was filled by, among others, AQI.[71] It cannot be stressed enough that the neocons in charge of Iraq knew that

---

[68] Robin Cook, "The struggle against terrorism cannot be won by military means," The Guardian, July 8, 2005.

[69] Mike Blair, "Public Enemy No. 1 was guest of the Central Intelligence Agency," *American Free Press*, January 7/14, 2002.

[70] Harmony Project, Combating Terrorism Center at West Point, *Al Qaeda's (Mis)Adventures in the Horn of Africa*, Darby, PA: Diane Publishing, 2009. p. 122.

[71] Michael Morell, *The Great War of Our Time*, New York: Twelve, 2015, pp. 305-6.

the country would fall into the hands of jihadists financed by the Saudis and armed and trained by Al Qaeda.

Beginning in 2003, Zarqawi was accused of carrying out a number of terrorist attacks against Western interests inside Iraq, as well as in Casablanca, Madrid, and Istanbul. Zarqawi's base of operations in Iraq was in the northern Kurdistan region, in the area later claimed by ISIL and Baghdadi. In May 2004, AQI released a video in which American Nick Berg was claimed by the CIA to have been beheaded by a masked Zarqawi. The video allegedly posted by AQI was "found" on the Internet by the Washington, DC-based Search for International Terrorist Entities Institute or "SITE," run by Rita Katz, an individual with close ties to Israel's Mossad. The Berg beheading was the only video said to have been made by Zarqawi. Zarqawi's other media releases in which he issued threats against the West were audio recordings. Although the CIA stated that it confirmed Zarqawi's voice on the Berg beheading video, there were no independent verifications of Zarqawi's voice being on either the beheading videotape or the various audio recordings.

Zarqawi's exploits in Iraq were hyped further after he was said to have personally beheaded in September 2004 American contractor Owen Eugene Armstrong, an employee of Gulf Supplies Commercial Services of the United Arab Emirates, and supposedly ordered the beheading of British engineer Ken Bigley in October 2004. Zarqawi was also said to have ordered the 2002 assassination of U.S. diplomat Lawrence Foley in Jordan and the bombing in August 2003 of the Canal Hotel in Baghdad, the headquarters of the United Nations, an attack that killed United Nations Secretary General's special envoy Sergio Vieira de Mello and 21 other people. Zarqawi became the name the U.S. associated with almost every Sunni terrorist attack in Iraq, including the 2006 bombing of the Shi'a al-Askari Mosque in Samarra, Shi'a shrines in Karbala and Najaf, and thousands of killings of Iraqi civilians. A document later found in one of Zarqawi's Iraq safe houses revealed plans for him to goad the U.S. into attacking Iran. Such a plan would have fit in nicely with U.S. Vice President Dick Cheney's and Israel's long range goals for the region.

In his February 5, 2003, address to the UN Security Council, Secretary of State Colin Powell, who lied about Iraq possessing biological weapons of mass destruction and mobile bio-warfare laboratories, also stated that Saddam Hussein was linked to Zarqawi. Iraq's intelligence service later stated that it could not even locate Zarqawi in Iraq. Unquestionably, Zarqawi was as much a threat to Saddam as he was to the U.S. or Jordan. Had Saddam captured the jihadist leader, he would have likely been tortured for information and then executed on the spot and on Saddam's personal orders.

In the 2006 Senate Report on Prewar Intelligence, the Senate Intelligence Committee concluded: "Postwar information indicates that Saddam Hussein attempted, unsuccessfully, to locate and capture al-Zarqawi and that the regime did not have a relationship with, harbor, or turn a blind eye toward Zarqawi."[72] It turned out that the "intelligence" linking Zarqawi to Saddam had emanated from the Pentagon's notorious Mossad mole, Undersecretary of Defense for Policy and

---

[72] Mark Mazzetti, "C.I.A. Said to Find No Hussein Link to Terror Chief," *The New York Times*, September 9, 2006.

Plans Douglas Feith, who leaked the information in a classified memorandum to Stephen Hayes, the columnist for the neo-conservative *Weekly Standard*.

Zarqawi: The man and the myth

Some U.S. intelligence sources claimed that Zarqawi was a "myth" invented by the neocons to justify continued U.S. military operations in Iraq. Iraqi Sunni and Shi'a leaders rarely agree, however. A Sunni insurgent leader told *The Daily Telegraph* that he believed that Zarqawi was an American or Israeli agent[73] and Iraqi Shi'a leader Muqtada al Sadr claimed that Zarqawi was a fake *takfir* (a Muslim who declares that other Muslims, such as the Shia's, are heretics) and was in the employment of the United States. Shi'a imam Sheikh Jawad Al-Khalessi repeated the accusation that Zarqawi was a myth in 2005. According to *The Washington Post*, General Mark Kimmitt, the U.S. Central Command's chief public affairs officer in Iraq stated in a 2004 internal CENTCOM briefing that "The Zarqawi PSYOP program is the most successful information campaign to date."[74]

The Afghan Northern Alliance claimed that Zarqawi was killed in a 2002 missile attack in Afghanistan. There were a number of reports of Zarqawi having been killed by either U.S. missiles or bombs in 2003. Some reports claimed that Zarqawi had lost a leg in Afghan combat operations. Other reports said he had both of his legs. The "Zarqawi" in the Berg beheading video had both legs, and an autopsy X-ray of the person said to have been Zarqawi and who was reportedly killed in a 2006 U.S. air strike showed a fracture to the lower right leg, said to have been lost in Afghanistan.

Zarqawi was captured in Iraq by coalition forces in 2004 but released. The explanation given at the time was that the Iraqis and Americans failed to recognize America's public enemy number one in Iraq. Zarqawi's eventual successor as the head of AQI, al-Baghdadi, was also captured by U.S. forces in Iraq in 2004 and held at Camp Bucca from February to December 2004 before being released. Al-Baghdadi took over the AQI operation in May 2010 after his predecessor Abu Omar al-Qurashi al-Baghdadi, actual name Hamid Dawud Mohamed Khalil al Zawi, was killed in a U.S.-Iraqi rocket attack. In 2007, Bin Laden intermediary Khaled al-Mashhadani, also known as Abu Shahid, claimed Abu Omar al-Baghdadi, the predecessor to the current ISIL chief, was a fictional character designed by Al Qaeda in Iraq to give an Iraqi face to a foreign-led insurgency. Mashhadani said audio statements attributed to Abu Omar were being read by an Iraqi actor.[75] Suspiciously, the Abu Omar recordings were all released by the SITE Institute.

U.S. forces claimed they killed Zarqawi near Baqubah, Iraq in a June 7, 2006 targeted killing by two precision-guided bombs.

---

[73] Obituary, Abu Musab al-Zarqawi, *The Daily Telegraph*, June 9, 2006.

[74] Thomas Ricks, "Military Plays Up Role of Zarqawi," *The Washington Post*, April 9, 2006.

[75] Dean Yates, Reuters, "Senior Qaeda figure in Iraq a myth: U.S. military," July 18, 2007.

Enter Al-Baghdadi II

While Zarqawi was hyped as one of America's most dangerous enemies, the man who eventually succeeded him as the head of ISIL in Syria, Abu Bakr al-Baghdadi, became one of America's trusted allies. Al-Baghdadi, along with the leaders of the Al Nusra Front, initially placed their forces under the umbrella of the Free Syrian Army. In May 2013, U.S. Senator John McCain, a chief water carrier for the neocon interventionists and Israeli interests, covertly met with Syrian rebel leaders after crossing into rebel-held Syrian territory from Turkey. McCain was accompanied by General Salem Idris, the head of the Free Syrian Army's Supreme Military Council, as he met with the commanders of a number of Syrian rebel units.

One of these rebel commanders was none other than Abu Bakr al-Baghdadi, the current head of ISIL. McCain's office has denied that Al-Baghdadi was present at the meetings, but photographic evidence of the ISIL chief's meeting with McCain and the U.S.-supported Free Syrian Army officials is overwhelming.

The Commander of the U.S. Special Operations Command, General Lloyd Austin, testified before the Senate Armed Services Committee in September 2015 that, to date, the United States had trained a grand total of "four or five" moderate Syrian fighters in the alleged U.S. war against ISIL.[76] Hundreds of millions of dollars had been spent on the Pentagon's "train and equip" program

for the alleged Syrian "moderates," however, the money seemed to have gone elsewhere. Austin's testimony revealed, perhaps unwittingly, that American weapons and training had found their way into the hands of ISIL and allied groups like Al Nusra Front and Khorasan Group.

---

[76] Luis Martinez, "General Austin: Only '4 or 5' US-Trained Syrian Rebels Fighting ISIS," ABC News, September 16, 2015.

America's response to ISIL's threat to turn Iraq, Syria, Lebanon, Jordan, and other countries into an Islamic Caliphate were as perplexing as American indifference over proclaimed caliphates by initially U.S.-supported Islamist radicals in Libya and by Boko Haram in Nigeria and Ansar Dine in Mali. The lackadaisical attitude by the CIA and the White House over these groups, which kidnapped, raped, tortured, burned, bombed, and beheaded their way into international headlines, was exactly what would be expected from a scenario in which radical Islamist groups were created by the CIA, Mossad, and MI-6 to create permanent conflict situations between the West and Islam, and between Muslims themselves.

"Al-Baghdadi II" – a contrivance of Mossad and Western intelligence agencies

There is a wealth of material to strongly suggest that America's "public enemy number one" during its occupation of Iraq, Abu Musab al-Zarqawi and the "two al-Baghdadis" – Omar and Abu Bakr – who followed him, were psychological warfare creations of the CIA, Mossad, and the British MI-6 Secret Intelligence Service.

Abu Bakr al-Baghdadi, or "Al Baghdadi II," released audio statements claiming that he is the new caliph of the Islamic State, that he would march on Rome to conquer the Mediterranean region, including all of Spain and Italy for his caliphate, and that he will kill Russian President Vladimir Putin and Pope Francis I. There are elements in Wall Street and in the power centers of Washington, London, and Jerusalem that would not have minded at all if Putin and the Pope were "eliminated," and if it were done by ISIL, so much the better for Western globalization plans.

But was "al-Baghdadi II" real or as much a fake as Zarqawi?

Nabil Na'eem, a former top Al Qaeda commander and founder of the Islamic Democratic Jihad Party in Lebanon, told Beirut's Al-Maydeen television network that ISIL is a creation of the CIA and Mossad. Na'eem also stated that the intent of ISIL is to implement Israeli Prime Minister Binyamin Netanyahu's "Clean Break" policy that dates from the 1990s.[77] Al-Baghdadi II is reported to have undergone Mossad military and Islamist theology training in Israel for a year. Na'eem also said that the commander of the Al-Nusra Front, Mohammed al-Jawlani, who swore allegiance to ISIL, is a CIA operative.[78]

A videotaped speech by Al Baghdadi at the Great Mosque of al-Nuri in Mosul, in which he claimed to be the caliph of all Muslims, was deemed a fake by an Iraqi government official.

There is every indication that ISIL had significant links to Israel. Although there are claims to the contrary, ISIL absorbed most of the ranks of the Al Qaeda-affiliated Jabhat al-Nusra (Al Nusra Front) Islamist insurgent group in Syria. Al Nusra Front coordinated its seizure of Syrian army positions along the Golan

---

[77] The Clean Break was complementary to the 1982 "Yinon Plan," crafted by Likud Party loyalist and journalist Oded Yinon, which called for the destruction of the modern Arab nation-states and their replacement with warring caliphates and warlords.

[78] Wayne Madsen, "The Looming American Quagmire in Iraq and Syria," Strategic Culture Foundation, September 19, 2014.

Heights border with the Israeli Defense Force (IDF). Rather than hit back at Al Nusra positions on the Syrian side of the Golan frontier, the Israelis attacked Syrian army positions, giving a boost to the Syrian campaigns of Al Nusra in particular and ISIL in general. There were reports that the Israeli military was given the coordinates of Syrian army and Hezbollah forces, as well as "Committees for the Defense of the Homeland" militia forces of Alawites, Shi'as, Christians, and Druze, by Al-Nusra/ISIL to launch missile and drone attacks from the Israeli side of the border.

Israel was so sanguine about ISIL, the Israeli daily *Ha'aretz* reported, that Israeli authorities routinely permitted Israeli tourists, armed only with cameras and binoculars, to visit the Golan Heights and peer out over the valley of Quneitra to witness Al-Nusra/ISIL jihadists fighting the Syrian army. Israel even supplied large telescopic viewers for Israelis to spy on the fighting in the valley.[79] Israelis, some who brought their lunch, coffee, and lawn chairs, spent the entire day watching Arabs killing other Arabs. The Israeli complacency about the jihadists suggested a deal had been worked out between the Israeli government and the Syrian jihadists not to bring the conflict across the Golan frontier into Israel. Or, the Syrian jihadists were under some type of operational control by Mossad and the IDF, and were under strict orders to not attack Israeli targets under any circumstance.

After Al-Nusra/ISIL rebels seized control of United Nations peacekeeping facilities in the Golan, Philippines Army chief General Gregorio Catapang stated that the UN's French Under-Secretary-General for Peacekeeping Operations, Herve Ladsous, ordered 81 Philippines troops to hand their weapons over the jihadists. Although the Philippines troops refused Ladsous's order and were subsequently permitted to "escape" into Israel, there was no information on the fate of 45 Fijian peacekeepers captured by Al-Nusra/ISIL. Nor was Ladsous forthcoming on what happened to the Fijians' weapons.

Catapang also stated that the UNDOF (United Nations Disengagement and Observation Force) Commander, General Iqbal Singh Singha of India, wanted the Philippines peacekeepers to hand over their weapons to the jihadists because of a demand by the rebels that they would harm their Fijian captives if they did not surrender their weapons. Catapanga's Fijian counterpart, Fiji Army Chief Brigadier General Mosese Tikoitoga, stated that it was Singha who ordered the 45 Fijian peacekeepers, most if not all of them being Christians, to surrender to Al Nusra/ISIL, along with handing over of their weapons to the terrorists. Al-Nusra/ISIL intended to try the Fijians under Islamic sharia law for "war crimes."[80] Without the UNDOF force present in the Golan, Israel was able to violate the UN cease fire agreement at will and move weapons and personnel across the Syrian frontier in support of Al-Nusra/ISIL.

It was later reported that Singha and Ladsous also ordered Irish peacekeeping troops who served at the Breiqa UN encampment with the Philippines troops to also surrender to Al-Nusra/ISIL, enriching the Islamist terrorists with even more

---

[79] Judy Maltz, "On Golan, Israelis Grab a Front-row Seat to the War in Syria, *Ha'aretz*, September 7, 2014.
[80] ABS-CBN News, "UN backs Golan commander, denies PH's claims," September 4, 2014.

captured weapons. The Irish troops were permitted to "escape" into Israel with the assistance of the IDF.

Ultimately, the decision to order the Philippines and Fijian troops to surrender to Al-Nusra/ISIL rested on Under-Secretary-General for Political Affairs Jeffrey Feltman, a former U.S. ambassador to Lebanon and Undersecretary of State for Near Eastern Affairs who was a rock solid member of the neocon and Israel agent-of-influence infrastructure and who wormed his way from the State Department into the UN. Feltman was champion of arming Syrian rebels, including the Islamists, against the Assad government and Hezbollah volunteers from Lebanon. Feltman also served in the U.S. embassy in Tel Aviv in the 1990s during the time when U.S. ambassador Martin Indyk, a key agent-of-influence for Israel, lost his security clearance after a compromise of classified U.S. information to the Israeli government. Secretary of State Madeleine Albright, yet another water carrier for Israel, quickly restored Indyk's security clearance after a watered-down official "investigation." A U.S. embassy Tel Aviv source revealed that among the information compromised were the codes used for secure telephone units to discuss classified information between the embassy and the U.S. government in Washington.

The American grand master for Israel's expansionist policies, former U.S. Secretary of State Henry Kissinger, stated that Iran was a bigger threat than ISIL.[81] Prospective Democratic presidential candidate Hillary Clinton had earlier lavished praise on Kissinger in a review of his new book, *World Order*. Kissinger's comments came after reports that the U.S. military was coordinating its attacks on ISIL in northern Iraq with Iranian Revolutionary Guard forces that were aiding Kurdish Peshmerga forces in Iraqi Kurdistan, and a day after Iran's Supreme Ayatollah, Ali Hosseini *Khamenei*, ordered Iran's forces to cooperate with the United States in attacking ISIL. Kissinger, in his usual role as an agent-of-influence for Israel, sloughed off ISIL as a "group of adventurers" who would have to conquer more territory to become as threatening as Iran. Kissinger's giving a pass to ISIL appeared coordinated with Israel's tacit support for the group. Ever since Netanyahu commissioned the "Clean Break" policy in the early 1990s, it was the wish of the Zionist parties in Israel to not only kill off the Palestinian peace process and absorb the West Bank, Gaza, and the Golan Heights into Israel, but also to create ethnic and religious divisions in various Arab countries, with a goal of creating Israeli-managed statelets. That policy came to full fruition in Syria, Iraq, Libya, and Yemen.

The beheading videos

Just as Zarqawi was said to have beheaded British engineer Bigley in 2004, Al-Baghdadi II ordered the beheading of British contractor David Cawthorne Haines. Bigley's videotaped beheading by AQI came after the videotaped beheadings of Americans Berg and Armstrong. Ten years later, ISIL beheaded the Briton Haines after the videotaped beheadings of U.S. journalist James Foley and dual-nationality U.S.-Israeli journalist Steven Sotloff.

It was a London-accented ISIL jihadist who allegedly beheaded Foley and Sotloff. Known as "Jihad John" and said to be London rapper Abdel-Majed Abdel

---

[81] "Kissinger: Iran Is a Bigger Threat Than Islamic State," *Ha'aretz*, September 7, 2014.

Bary, a British-Egyptian, the alleged beheader reportedly received his inspiration from British Muslim cleric Anjem Choudary, who was permitted to use London to issue pro-ISIL statements. The beheading of the Briton and Americans came as British Prime Minister David Cameron issued an elevated alert for ISIL-led terrorism in the United Kingdom. It appeared that Cameron's gambit was to scare Scottish independence referendum voters into opting for continued "protection" from Merry Old England.

President Obama was always reluctant to order a massive U.S. military attack on ISIL. Was that because he knew that his Saudiphile CIA chief, John O. Brennan, authorized the training of ISIL guerrillas at a secret base near the town of Safawi in Jordan's northern desert region and at another installation near the American airbase at Incirlik in Turkey? Was the initial reluctance of Britain and France to engage ISIL the result of their military instructors helping the CIA train ISIL insurgents at Safawi and Incirlik?

There were also questions about the "journalistic" roles of Foley and Sotloff in covering the wars in Syria, Libya, and Iraq. The two both had a very questionable relationship with a combination freelance videographer and mercenary from Baltimore named Matthew VanDyke.

VanDyke fought with Islamist guerrillas against Muammar Qaddafi's forces during the Libyan civil war and was detained by the Qaddafi government, along with Foley, for entering Libya illegally and being found embedded with rebel forces. Sotloff also covered Libya from the vantage point of the Islamist insurgent forces, some of whom later took control of Tripoli. VanDyke, Foley, and Sotloff also entered Syria illegally and reported only from the ranks of the Islamist guerrilla side. E-mail was released between journalists for *The New York Times, The Wall Street Journal, The Washington Post,* and other publications on one hand and the CIA on the other showing collusion between the reporters and the CIA in writing stories. Questions were also raised about Foley's relationship with the seemingly under-capitalized but worldwide-present *GlobalPost.com* of Boston and why Sotloff, who wrote for a publication owned by the neo-conservative *Jerusalem Post*, was embedded with Islamist *takfiris*,[82] and even had his Twitter photograph taken manning a jihadist truck-mounted machine gun in Syria. The *Journalist Creed* deters such practices, whether they were alleged journalist VanDyke fighting with guerrillas in Libya, or Sotloff manning an insurgent machine gun in Syria, or Foley only embedding with Islamist guerrillas in Syria or Libya.

After writing an article about the CIA's possible use of journalists in covert operations abroad, an overturning of a longtime ban on such practices, this writer was immediately attacked by the Israeli-friendly on-line media. Evidently, a very sensitive nerve was hit.

---

[82] The term derives from the root "Kaffir" or infidel, unbeliever. A *takfiri* is one who calls everyone else an apostate. Like the old story of the two bums in the slums. One said, "The whole world is crazy, except us." The other replied, "Yep – and I'm not too sure about you."
Seriously, *takfiri* is a more accurate term than "jihadist," because *Jihad* does not mean a holy war or a crusade, it is a general term for any kind of struggle.

McCain's consorting with terrorists exposed

Senator McCain's links to ISIL pointed to the close links between the group and a network in Washington that not only includes McCain, the chairman of the Senate Armed Services Committee, but also to Brennan's CIA.

McCain's Middle East adviser Elizabeth O'Bagy, who falsely claimed to have had a PhD from Georgetown University, accompanied McCain on an unofficial trip to Syria in 2013 where the two met and were photographed with Abu Bakr al-Baghdadi and Mohammed Nour of the Northern Storm Brigade of the ISIL-linked Al Nusra Front. Standing next to Salim Idriss, the former head of the Supreme Military Council of the "Free Syrian Army" who lived in exile in Doha, Qatar, was O'Bagy.

While McCain was meeting with Nour, the Northern Storm Brigade had already kidnapped Shi'a pilgrims in Syria, as well as a Lebanese journalist. Had any other Americans met with documented terrorists such as Nour and al-Baghdadi, unlike McCain and O'Bagy, they would have been arrested and charged with aiding and abetting a terrorist group. Several Americans were serving long prison terms for doing much less than McCain and O'Bagy had done in Syria and were entrapped in FBI sting operations merely because they were Muslims.

At the time O'Bagy accompanied McCain to Syria to meet in Bab Salama with the chief of ISIL and other terrorist leaders, including 20 Syrian rebel brigade commanders representing Al Nusra and the nascent ISIL, O'Bagy worked for Kimberly Kagan, the wife of arch-neocon Zionist Frederick Kagan of the right-wing American Enterprise Institute, and sister-in-law of Robert Kagan, a resident neocon scholar at the Brookings Institution, and his wife, Victoria Nuland, the neo-conservative Assistant Secretary for European and Eurasian Affairs at the State Department. Nuland was primarily responsible for funding and coordinating the coup in Ukraine that resulted in a bloody civil war between Russian-speaking eastern Ukraine and the Nazi- and Zionist-dominated central government in Kiev.

Working under Kimberly Kagan, O'Bagy was the Syria analyst in the Institute for the Study of War (ISW), another neocon operation in Washington that wielded undue influence over U.S. foreign policy in the Middle East and elsewhere. After it was disclosed that she committed resumé fraud by falsely claiming to have a PhD from Georgetown, O'Bagy was officially "fired" by ISW but continued on as the Political Director of the Syrian Emergency Task Force (SETF) NGO, a nonprofit that sought donations from other NGOs, including the neoconservative Freedom House and the Foundation for the Defense of Democracies. SETF admitted to having "sub-contracts with the U.S. and British governments to provide aid to the Syrian opposition." O'Bagy also served officially as a legislative assistant to McCain. The SETF was an extreme anti-Bashar al-Assad organization that used Pentagon-grade psychological warfare tactics to demonize the Assad government and falsely blame him for atrocities carried out by Syrian rebels, including sarin and chlorine gas attacks in Syria.

O'Bagy's operations security (OPSEC) left something to be desired as she voraciously sent out Twitter messages during her clandestine visit to Syria with McCain in 2013. After the visit was publicized, O'Bagy deleted her Twitter messages.

O'Bagy was most infamous for writing an August 30, 2013 Op-Ed in *The Wall Street Journal* that was cited by both McCain and Secretary of State John Kerry. The article, titled "On the Front Lines of Syria's Civil War," was cited by McCain during a Senate hearing as "an important op-ed by ***Dr.*** Elizabeth O'Bagy." Kerry also cited the article in testimony before the House Foreign Affairs Committee, calling it a "very interesting article." [83]

In the article, O'Bagy, who claimed to have made a number of trips to Syria to liaise with Syrian rebels, falsely stated that Syrian "moderates" were leading the fight against the Syrian government in Damascus. The Op-Ed called for the United States to provide "sophisticated weaponry" to the rebels and enter the civil war militarily. Obama refused to follow this advice, a decision that earned him the scorn of McCain and other neocons. McCain continued to suggest that the Syrian "moderate" rebels had a chance to seize control of Syria.

In her "tweets," O'Bagy took responsibility for everything from McCain's attire in Syria to the individuals with whom he met. It was later learned that these individuals not only included al-Baghdadi and Nour, but other terrorist commanders. O'Bagy was also at pains to distance her Syrian rebel friends from Abu Sakkar, aka Khalid bin Hamad, the rebel commander who was filmed eating the heart of a Syrian soldier. O'Bagy denied that Abu Sakkar was a member of the Free Syrian Army's Homs-based Farooq Brigades, but independent news reports stated that he was indeed a commander of the brigades. O'Bagy also misidentified bin Hamad as a non-threatening Farouq Mustaqila, a familiar tactic of the neocons and no surprise from an individual who lied about having a PhD.

ISIL and the Saudis, Qataris, and Israelis

ISIL/Al Nusra was also enriching itself from ransom payments for hostages, money mostly received from Qatar. Qatar paid ransom payments to Al Nusra-ISIL units for some Syrian nuns and captured Lebanese Army soldiers. Meanwhile, Saudi Arabia was training so-called Free Syrian Army "moderates" the Assad government. In the past, the Saudis conducted such training in order to radicalize Sunni Muslim volunteers for the Syrian civil war and funnel them to ISIL units in Syria and Iraq.

Israel was also reported to be transporting Al Nusra/ISIL terrorists across the Golan frontier into Israel, ostensibly for medical treatment, but also for intelligence and other military training. Netanyahu's Twitter statement that "Hamas is ISIS" was a crude attempt to confuse those in the West who did not understand what was at the root of the ISIL insurrection.

The Wall Street Journal, which provided the government of Israeli Prime Minister Netanyahu with unending editorial support, reported that Israel provided logistical support in Syria to Al Qaeda and its affiliate, *Jabhat al-Nusra*. The paper reported that Al-Nusra "hasn't bothered Israel since seizing the border area last summer" along the Golan Heights. In fact, the core Al Qaeda and its

---

[83] Elizabeth O'Bagy, "On the Front Lines of Syria's Civil War," *The Wall Street Journal*, August 30, 2013.

official branches never "bothered" Israel.[84] Israel provided medical assistance to some 2000 Syrians, a number of them members of the Nusra Front and Al Qaeda.

France was also not an idle bystander to the creation and nurturing of ISIL. Terrorist Boubaker El-Hakim, a French national of Tunisian descent, had close ties to French intelligence. There was yet another ISIL affiliate operative who worked for the French external intelligence service, *Direction générale de la sécurité extérieure* – DGSE. That ex-French agent, David Drugeon, actually became a leader of the Khorasan Group in Syria.

On October 5, 2014, McClatchy news service reported that Drugeon "defected" from DGSE to Al Qaeda. Although Western intelligence finds it useful to separate ISIL or the Islamic State, the Khorasan Group, Al Qaeda, and the Al Nusra Front, on the Syrian and Iraqi battlefields these groups fight under the same command and same black and white jihadist banner. [85]

Drugeon was raised Catholic in Vannes, Brittany. He allegedly converted to Salafist Islam and took the name of Daoud. He was known by the nickname "Français d'Al Qaïda." Afterwards, Drugeon is said to have received military-like training from a civilian French government organization.[86] The quarters that immediately questioned the veracity of the McClatchy report were all neo-conservative in nature, with the loudest shouting coming from a very noisy neo-con cell at the U.S. Naval War College whose job appeared to be to attack journalists who reported information that ran counter to the memes issued by the neocon-controlled press. The McClatchy report was also attacked by the Foundation for the Defense of Democracies, a virtual Mossad front in Washington; the pro-business *L'Opinion* of France; and the Rothschild banking family-linked *L'Express* of Paris.

Intelligence observers in Europe believed that Drugeon was placed by DGSE within the ranks of Khorasan to give it as much gravitas as that already possessed by ISIL, in order to justify greater Western military involvement in Syria. In fact, the U.S. Director of National Intelligence James Clapper said Khorasan was as "great a threat to the homeland" as ISIL. The U.S. Central Command stated that Khorasan included seasoned core fighters who took part in operations for Al Qaeda and the Al Nusra Front. Drugeon reportedly provided Khorasan with advanced bomb-making capabilities.

Israel's military and intelligence services also provided assistance to Al Nusra in Syria and ISIL in Iraq. Hakem al-Zameli, the chairman of the Iraqi Parliament's National Security and Defense Committee, stated that Iraq's armed forces shot down two British planes that were carrying weapons to ISIL in Anbar province, the same province where Israeli commandos have been witnessed transferring weapons to ISIL forces. Al-Zameli also said that his committee is receiving daily reports from Anbar province about successive U.S. coalition

---

[84] Yaroslav Trofimov, "Al Qaeda a Lesser Evil? Syria War Pulls U.S., Israel Apart," *The Wall Street Journal*, March 12, 2015.
[85] McClatchy News, "Sources: U.S. air strikes in Syria targeted French agent who defected to al Qaida," October 5, 2014.
[86] Ibid.

planes airdropping weapons and other materials for ISIL in areas held by the jihadist group.[87]

Khalaf Tarmouz, the head of the Anbar Provincial Council said local officials have discovered U.S., European, and Israeli weapons from the areas liberated from ISIL in the Al-Bagdadi region. The Iraqi government also revealed that U.S. coalition forces airdropped weapons to support ISIL in Salahuddin, Al-Anbar and Diyala provinces. Member of Parliament Majid al-Gharawi said he was aware of U.S. airdrops of weapons for ISIL in Salahuddin and other Iraqi provinces.

Al-Zameli said, "The US drops weapons for the ISIL on the excuse of not knowing about the whereabouts of the ISIL positions, and it is trying to distort the reality with its allegations." He said evidence was provided by Iraqi army officers and other Iraqi forces.

Iranian Brigadier General Massoud Jazayeri confirmed the Iraqi government reports. He said, "The U.S. and the so-called anti-ISIL coalition claim that they have launched a campaign against this terrorist and criminal group – while supplying them with weapons, food and medicine in Jalawla region [in Diyala Governorate].[88]

Western intelligence links to ISIL began to be systematically exposed around the world. Chechen President Ramzan Kadyrov declared that ISIL's leader, Ibrahim Samarrai, aka "Abu Bakr al-Baghdadi," was a Central Intelligence Agency operative who received financial backing from Western intelligence services. From reports coming from Iraq and Syria, the links between the violent jihadists and their CIA, MI-6, DGSE, and Mossad overseers were becoming abundantly clear.

It was revealed in May 2015 that the U.S.-trained commander of Tajikistan's OMON Special Forces, Colonel Gulmurod Khalimov, had defected to ISIL to serve as one of the group's top field commanders in Syria. After his defection, Khalimov said in a video, "Listen, you American pigs, I've been three times to America, and I saw how you train fighters to kill Muslims . . . God willing, I will come with this weapon to your cities, your homes, and we will kill you."[89] . Khalimov was reportedly trained by U.S. Special Operations forces, Blackwater, and the CIA during a number of official visits to the United States

The leader of Lebanon's Druze Progressive Socialist Party, Walid Jumblatt, who was always an erratic on-and-off supporter of Israel, concluded an agreement with the Al Nusra Front and its Al Qaeda affiliate in Syria. Jumblatt concluded the agreement even though his fellow Druze in Idlib, Syria were given an ultimatum by ISIL to convert to Wahhabi Islam and destroy their shrines, mausoleums, and religious icons or face execution. Jumblatt is reported by the Lebanese press to have arranged for the forced conversions of the Idlib Druze in exchange for their lives using the offices of the United Arab Emirates.[90]

---

[87] Fars News Agency, "Iraqi Army Downs 2 UK Planes Carrying Weapons for ISIL," February 23, 2015.

[88] *Ibid.*

[89] Ishan Tharoor, "The U.S.-trained commander of Tajikistan's special forces has joined the Islamic State," The Washington Post, May 28, 2015.

[90] *Daily Star*, "Jumblatt, Nusra reach agreement on Idlib's Druze: report," March 2, 2015.

It was also reported in the Lebanese press that Israel helped arrange for contacts, using Jordanian intelligence interlocutors, between Al Nusra/Al Qaeda and the Syrian Druze. Israel offered military and intelligence support to the Syrian Druze if they attacked Syrian government forces and their Lebanese Hezbollah allies in Syria.

Other Israeli fingerprints on ISIL:

The Israeli press reported that gardeners in the northern Israeli city of Nazareth Illit discovered a bag containing about 25 new black-and-white ISIL flags. The discovery of the flags further implicated the Israeli government in providing not only military and logistical support to ISIL, but propaganda support, as well.

Turkish foreign minister Mevlut Cavusoglu revealed that Turkish authorities arrested a foreign intelligence agent, believed to be an asset of the Canadian Security and Intelligence Service (CSIS), who was charged with helping three British schoolgirls travel from Britain through Turkey and then into Syria to join ISIL. Under the Stephen Harper government, Canadian intelligence was ordered to assist Mossad in all matters requested by the Israelis. The arrested agent was Mohammed Mehmet Rashid, aka "Doctor Mehmet Rashid," Mohammed al Rashid, and Mohammad Al Rashed, who reported to Bruno Saccomani, the Canadian ambassador to Jordan and Iraq. Saccomani is a former Royal Canadian Mounted Police (RCMP) officer who was the head of Harper's personal security detail until he was appointed ambassador to Amman. Saccomani was criticized by other RCMP officers for his "bullying" tactics. The appointment was roundly criticized by the Canadian opposition because Saccomani had no diplomatic experience. Al Rashid met the three British school girls at Gaziantep near the Syrian border and personally delivered them into ISIL hands in Syria. Saccomani served as the RCMP liaison officer at the Canadian embassy in Rome in 1997 where he developed a close working relationship with Israeli intelligence and law enforcement officials.

Russian President Vladimir Putin's aide Alexander Prokhanov charged in December 2014 that Mossad was training ISIL's leadership.

News reports from around the Middle East revealed that Abu Bakr Al Baghdad, the self-proclaimed ISIL "caliph," received a year of intensive language and Islamic theology training from his Mossad handlers.

Adrian Kaba, a member of Sweden's ruling Social Democratic Party who served on the Malmo City Council and the regional government, wrote in 2014 that Mossad provided training to ISIL. Kaba wrote on his Facebook page that "ISIS is being trained by the Israeli Mossad. Muslims are not waging war, they are being used as pawns by other peoples' game."

Israeli foreign minister Avigdor Lieberman suggested ISIL-style beheadings for Israeli Arabs suspected of supporting terrorism.

Prince Bandar bin Sultan, the godfather behind the creation of ISIL, returned to an influential position advising the late King Abdullah after having earlier been sacked as Saudi intelligence chief in April 2014. Bandar's new title was "adviser to the King and his special envoy." Bandar had never actually left the Saudi inner circle. Even after being sacked as intelligence chief, Bandar retained his position as secretary general of the Saudi National Security Council, a position similar to that held by Susan Rice as the White House National Security Adviser and director of the National Security Council.

The House of Saud was a major bank-roller of ISIL since the beginning of the insurgent group's role in Syria's civil war. The Al Nusra Front (Jabhat al-Nusra), on the other hand, was mainly funded by Qatar. The Al Nusra Front, far from being a rival to ISIL, pledged its support for the group as its forces spread across northern and western Iraq.

The actual aim of Saudi Arabia was to destabilize Iraq and Syria, hoping that the Iraqi Shi'a-dominated government and Bashar al Assad's government in Damascus would be overthrown and replaced with radical Sunni regimes beholden to the Saudis.

Bandar had longstanding ties to Jihadist terrorism. On a pre-Sochi Olympics trip to Moscow, he offered a lucrative weapons deal if Russia would cease its support for Assad. Bandar also told Putin that if Russia rejected Saudi Arabia's offer, Saudi-backed Islamist terrorists in the Caucasus region would be free to launch terrorist attacks on the Winter Olympics in Sochi. Putin reportedly ordered Bandar out of his office in the Kremlin. There are also reports that Saudi-financed Islamist terrorists from Chechnya and Dagestan were active fighting against Russian-speaking separatists in eastern Ukraine. In some cases, Islamist terrorists have joined Israeli paramilitary units in Ukraine in support of the Kiev government's military actions against eastern Ukraine. In Syria, there have been reports of Mossad coordination with ISIL units in attacks against Syrian government forces, including in the region north of the Golan Heights.

Bandar's name was reportedly contained in the classified 28 pages from the Joint Congressional 9/11 Inquiry report on Saudi Arabia's role in the 9/11 attack. Attempts to have the 28 pages declassified met with strong opposition from Brennan and the CIA, as well as the Obama White House and Saudi and Israeli lobbies in Washington. Former Senator Bob Graham (D-FL), who chaired the Senate Intelligence Committee at the time the report was written, called for the 28 pages to be made public. A reliable source reported that Graham was cold-shouldered when he visited the White House in 2014 to press for full disclosure. Graham was shuffled off to meet with a low-level White House staffer instead of any influential White House policy makers.

DIA exposes Western backing for ISIL

A formerly SECRET NOFORN (No Foreign Dissemination) message, dated August 5, 2012, to the Defense Intelligence Agency (DIA) from a redacted U.S. government agency, provided more evidence that ISIL was a construct of U.S. intelligence.

The message, declassified as the result of a Freedom of Information Act request submitted by Judicial Watch, a conservative organization, indicates that the intelligence on ISIL was "not finally evaluated," which means it was not sanitized and editorialized by the political operatives within the U.S. intelligence community.

The message released was unusual in that some of the action and information "addees" were redacted, which was not normally the case with declassified message traffic, whether they originated with the Defense Department, State Department, or U.S. intelligence agencies.

The message led off with the following: "The Salafist, the Muslim Brotherhood, and AQI [Al Qaeda in Iraq] are the major forces driving the insurgency in Iraq." The message goes on to state: "The West, Gulf countries, and Turkey support the [Syrian] opposition; while Russia, China, and Iran support the regime." The "regime" was the government of Syrian President Bashar al-Assad.

The message also stated: "AQI supported the Syrian opposition from the beginning, both ideologically and through the media . . . and conducted a number of operations in several under the name of Jaish al Nusra (Victorious Army), one of its affiliates."

There was also a direct reference to the similarity of Western support for the Syrian and Iraqi jihadists and those who emerged in Libya following the overthrow of Muammar el-Qaddafi. This support was directed to internationally-supported "safe havens" harboring the jihadist and Salafist forces: "Opposition forces are trying to control the eastern areas (Hasaka and Der Zor), adjacent to the western Iraqi provinces (Mosul and Anbar), in addition to neighboring Turkish borders. *Western countries, the Gulf countries and Turkey are supporting these efforts* [emphasis added]. This hypothesis is most likely in accordance with the data from recent events, which will help prepare safe havens under international sheltering, similar to what transpired in Libya when Benghazi was chosen as the command center of the temporary government." What the message does not state is that the "safe havens" in Syria, Iraq, and Benghazi were the locations where the Islamic State and its allies declared a caliphate (the Islamic caliphate in Syria and Iraq) and an emirate (the Emirate of Derna in eastern Libya).

The operative paragraph stated that the "supporting powers to the opposition" wanted to establish a "declared or undeclared Salafist principality in eastern Syria (Hasaka and Der Zor), and this is <u>exactly</u> what the supporting powers [Western countries, the Gulf countries and Turkey] want, in order to isolate the Syrian regime, which is considered the strategic depth of the Shia expansion (Iraq and Iran)."

C. IF THE SITUATION UNRAVELS THERE IS THE POSSIBILITY OF ESTABLISHING A DECLARED OR UNDECLARED SALAFIST PRINCIPALITY IN EASTERN SYRIA (HASAKA AND DER ZOR), AND THIS IS EXACTLY WHAT THE SUPPORTING POWERS TO THE OPPOSITION WANT, IN ORDER TO ISOLATE THE SYRIAN REGIME, WHICH IS CONSIDERED THE STRATEGIC DEPTH OF THE SHIA EXPANSION (IRAQ AND IRAN).

The Western powers – the United States, Britain, France, and, more importantly, Israel – working in concert with the Gulf countries [Saudi Arabia, Qatar, United Arab Emirates, Kuwait, and Bahrain], as well as Turkey, according to U.S. intelligence, created ISIL to destroy the Shia-dominated nations of Syria and Iraq. The fall of Palmyra in Syria and Ramadi in Iraq were a result of this conspiracy of "supporting powers." The civil war in Yemen that saw the very same "supporting powers," including Egypt, provide military forces to fight the Shi'a-aligned Houthi rebels was, like the civil wars in Syria and Iraq, of U.S. Saudi, Israeli, and Turkish design. Ultimately, Iran was the ultimate target for the "supporting powers" of ISIL and its allies.

While ISIL forces ransacked and destroyed Shi'a shrines and mosques in Iraq and Syria, Saudi war planes leveled Shi'a mosques and revered buildings in Yemen. In another example of how the Saudis and ISIL are on the same page, it was a Saudi military checkpoint that allowed an ISIL terrorist unit to enter the town of Qadih in eastern Saudi Arabia to bomb a Shi'a mosque in May 2015. There was not one criticism of the Saudi regime in the official statement issued by ISIL taking credit for the deadly blast at the mosque. And of course, the ISIL statement, as usual, was discovered by the SITE Institute, Mossad's intelligence operation that spins alleged jihadist communiqués to the international media.

There were also suspicious links between ISIL and the Iranian exiled terrorist group Mojahedin-e-Khalq (MEK) through CIA and Israeli Mossad interlocutors. These links included personal contacts between the husband-and-wife leadership of the MEK, Massoud and Maryam Rajavi, and the senior leadership of ISIL. These contacts were reportedly authorized by ISIL's self-proclaimed "caliph" Abu Bakr al-Baghdadi. ISIL and the MEK also jointly approached the Baluchi terrorist group *Jundallah*, which operated in western Pakistan, on conducting joint terrorist operations against Iran. These contacts were facilitated by Saudi Arabia, the CIA, and Mossad.

MEK paramilitary units continued to be based at Camp Liberty, also known as Camp Hurriya, to the west of Baghdad, where they were protected by CIA contractor personnel. Iranian intelligence was well aware of contacts between the MEK and ISIL units fighting in the western environs of Baghdad and in some cases witnessed MEK and ISIL guerrillas and CIA contractors involved in joint operations against Iraqi army personnel.

The CIA-supported MEK had been described as a "cult" by members who managed to escape its control. There were credible reports from witnesses concerning torture by the MEK of 3000 internees at Camp Liberty. MEK members were moved to Camp Liberty by the United States from the group's former Iraqi base at Camp Ashraf. Named after Massoud Rajavi's first wife, Camp Ashraf was once supported by Iraqi President Saddam Hussein.

ISIL was also deemed a non-Islamic "cult" by a number of Middle Eastern intelligence services who cited the large number of French Jews who have joined the organization. On October 14, *Ha'aretz* reported the following: "There are a number of Jews among the more than 1,000 French citizens who have joined the Islamic State, a French government official told Israel's Channel 2 news."[91] ISIL also attracted Buddhists from Japan, Hindus from India, Catholics from Italy, and Protestants from Canada and Australia as recruits. Some of them were so-called recent "converts" to Islam while others had not converted.

Both the MEK and ISIL hold dissident members hostage against their will. The MEK, like ISIL, received training, weapons, and funding from the Mossad. The Israel Lobby in the U.S. arranged for its many political supporters, including former New York Mayor Rudolph Giuliani, former Vermont Governor Howard Dean, former Pennsylvania Governor Ed Rendell, former Obama national security adviser General James Jones, former New Jersey senator Robert Torricelli, former CIA directors James Woolsey and Porter Goss, former U.S.

---

[91] *Ha'aretz*, "More Jews Have Joined Islamic State, French Official Says," October 14, 2014.

ambassador to the UN John Bolton, and Harvard professor Alan Dershowitz, to publicly support the goals of the MEK. In 2012, Secretary of State Hillary Clinton de-listed the MEK as a foreign terrorist organization and permitted the group to re-open its office in Washington, DC. The MEK office in the National Press Building was originally closed by the Bush administration in 2003.

The current MEK-ISIL alliance made all the aforementioned political notables witting or unwitting enablers of ISIL operations in Iraq, Syria, and, reportedly, operations inside Iran with the assistance of MEK units.

The CIA's and Pentagon's support for a terrorist grouping like ISIL and its allies is not new in American history. The Pentagon's crazed scheme to launch terrorist attacks on U.S. and allied targets in the early 1960s and blame them on Fidel Castro's Cuba – Operation Northwoods – is legendary in the annals of U.S. state-supported terrorism. Other examples include the CIA's Operation Gladio that saw right-wing groups carry out deadly terrorist attacks in Europe during the 1970s and 80s that were blamed on leftist groups and the CIA's Operation Phoenix that saw the U.S. randomly assassinate South Vietnamese village leaders and Buddhist clerics.

Former U.S. commander in Iraq and director of the CIA General David Petraeus called for the U.S. to ally with Al Qaeda against ISIL. Many CIA veterans understand that there is no real difference between the rank and file members of Al Qaeda and ISIL, and they know that Al Qaeda in Iraq morphed into ISIL in both Iraq and Syria. The Ivy League denizen Petraeus was personally involved in training Iraqi Sunni insurgents during his time in Iraq. Ironically, the two training programs that saw U.S. weapons and training provided to the nascent Al Qaeda and ISIL forces were code named IVY SERPENT and IVY CYCLONE. These covert operations, in addition to COPPER GREEN, which identified potential Sunni agents of influence for the United States inside the Abu Ghraib prison and other Iraqi detention centers, created the two al-Baghdadis.

To quote cartoonist Walt Kelly from his famous Pogo comic strip, "We have met the enemy and he is us."

Sociological Warfare

Going Rogue: America's Unconventional Warfare in the Mideast

By Sharmine Narwani - May 25, 2012

"The intent of U.S. Unconventional Warfare (UW) efforts is to exploit a hostile power's political, military, economic, and psychological vulnerabilities by developing and sustaining resistance forces to accomplish U.S. strategic objectives... <u>For the foreseeable future, U.S. forces will predominantly engage in irregular warfare (IW) operations.</u>"

So begins the 2010 Unconventional Warfare Manual of the US Military's Special Forces.[92]...

But most of us have not had the pleasure of leafing through this truly revelatory blueprint that shows how America wages its dirty wars. These are the secret wars that have neither been approved by Congress, nor by the inhabitants of nations whose lives – if not bodies – are mauled by the directives on these pages.

A quote from President John F. Kennedy in 1962 opens the document. These few lines illustrate a core Washington belief that US forces have the right to destabilize, infiltrate, assassinate, subvert – all in service of questionable foreign policy objectives, with no evident consideration of a sovereign state's preparedness or desire for change:

> *There is another type of warfare—new in its intensity, ancient in its origin—war by guerrillas, subversives, insurgents, assassins; war by ambush instead of by combat, by infiltration instead of aggression, seeking victory by eroding and exhausting the enemy instead of engaging him. It preys on unrest.*

Target: Middle East

The Bush Doctrine paved the way for the mainstreaming of unconventional warfare... The prime targets of UW have traditionally been nations and groups that oppose US primacy in the region – mainly the Resistance Axis consisting of Iran, Syria, Hezbollah and Hamas.

The most nefarious aspect of UW - aside from the obvious violations of international law pertaining to sovereignty, territorial integrity and loss of human life/property, etc – is the proactive and aggressive effort to psychologically sway a population against its government. It is at this entry point where UW fails every American test of "values..."

Prime examples are Iran, Syria and Libya – all of which have been UW targets in the past year, at different levels of infiltration and with markedly different results.

Here is a chart from the Special Forces UW manual that demonstrates the scope of activity at the early stages...

---

[92] http://www.al-akhbar.com/sites/default/files/pdfs/Special_Forces_Report.pdf

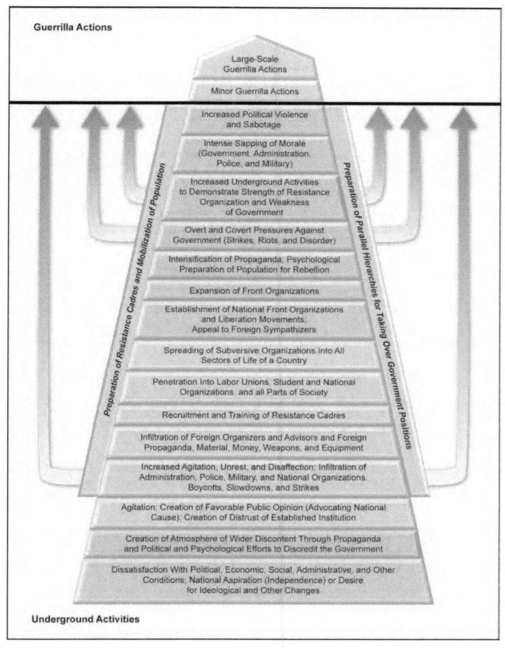

Figure 2-2. Structure of an insurgency or resistance movement

[Note that in Libya and Syria, the warfare began at the top of the pyramid, with sabotage and guerrilla attacks.]

The use of social media to coordinate protests and widely disseminate anti-regime narratives in Iran's post-election period marked a new era in the internet revolution globally. The Pentagon lost no time in claiming cyberspace as an "operational domain" and in the past year has substantially increased its budgetary allocation to subversion activities on the web.

Last July (as I wrote in Salon.com[93]) the technology arm of the Department of Defense, DARPA, announced a $42 million program to enable the U.S. military to "detect, classify, measure and track the formation, development and spread of ideas and concepts (memes)" within social media.

Wired magazine calls the project the Pentagon's "social media propaganda machine" because of its plans for "counter messaging of detected adversary influence operations."

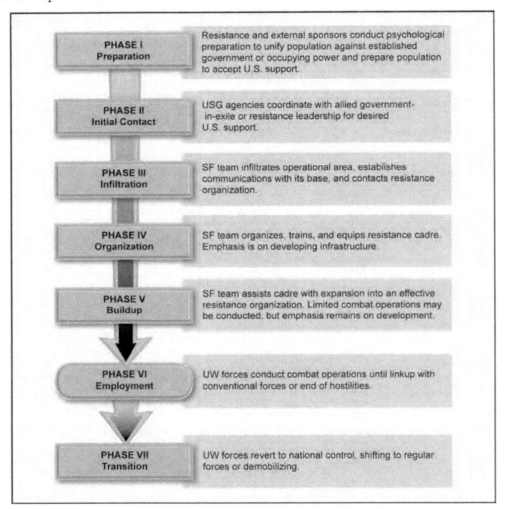

PHASE I Preparation — Resistance and external sponsors conduct psychological preparation to unify population against established government or occupying power and prepare population to accept U.S. support.

PHASE II Initial Contact — USG agencies coordinate with allied government-in-exile or resistance leadership for desired U.S. support.

PHASE III Infiltration — SF team infiltrates operational area, establishes communications with its base, and contacts resistance organization.

PHASE IV Organization — SF team organizes, trains, and equips resistance cadre. Emphasis is on developing infrastructure.

PHASE V Buildup — SF team assists cadre with expansion into an effective resistance organization. Limited combat operations may be conducted, but emphasis remains on development.

PHASE VI Employment — UW forces conduct combat operations until linkup with conventional forces or end of hostilities.

PHASE VII Transition — UW forces revert to national control, shifting to regular forces or demobilizing.

Figure 1-3. Phases of unconventional warfare

The UW campaign in Iran appears to more or less have faltered at technology sabotage, social media infiltration and assassinations. Libya is at the other extreme – and the following chart gives a bird's eye view of the UW manual's playbook for operations of that magnitude:

---

[93] http://www.salon.com/2011/10/26/pentagon_game_to_divide_iranians_and_arabs/

(Plain text versions of these two charts are given in Appendix 2 at the end of the book.)

The Libyan scenario of course was slightly different in that it was conducted under NATO cover, with the US military "leading from behind." In addition, the large-scale UW operation's success relied less on ground combat than on air cover and intelligence-sharing for attacks conducted largely by Libyan rebels.

Target: Regime Change in Syria

In Syria, the UW task would have been a mix of the two. Because of the domestic popularity and strength of Syrian President Bashar al-Assad revealed here in a 2006 Wikileaks Cable, UW activities would necessarily need to start with some subversion of the population...

"For the resistance to succeed, it must convince the uncommitted middle population...to accept it as a legitimate entity. A passive population is sometimes all a well-supported insurgency needs to seize political power."

To turn the "uncommitted middle population" into supporting insurgency, UW recommends the "creation of atmosphere of wider discontent through propaganda and political and psychological efforts to discredit the government..."

Then, the "infiltration of foreign organizers and advisors and foreign propaganda, material, money, weapons and equipment."

The next level of operations would be to establish "national front organizations [i.e. the Syrian National Council] and liberation movements [i.e. the Free Syrian Army]" that would move larger segments of the population toward accepting "increased political violence and sabotage" – and encourage the mentoring of "individuals or groups that conduct acts of sabotage in urban centers."

Now, how and why would an uncommitted – and ostensibly peaceful - majority of the population respond to the introduction of violence by opposition groups? The UW manual tells us there is an easy way to spin this one:

> If retaliation [by the target government] occurs, the resistance can exploit the negative consequences to garner more sympathy and support from the population by emphasizing the sacrifices and hardship the resistance is enduring on behalf of "the people." If retaliation is ineffective or does not occur, the resistance can use this as proof of its ability to wage effect combat against the enemy. In addition, the resistance can portray the inability or reluctance of the enemy to retaliate as a weakness, which will demoralize enemy forces and instill a belief in their eventual defeat...

The Ugly American just got uglier.

***

Sharmine Narwani is a commentator and political analyst covering the Middle East. You can follow Sharmine on twitter@snarwani. (Note: This article has been censored by AOL-Huffington Post)

Unconventional and Hybrid War

by John-Paul Leonard

The color revolution technology seen in Eastern Europe and the Arab Spring is only one variant of sociological warfare. In the Syrian crisis, the tactics of manipulating youthful idealists with democratic slogans were used mainly to deceive the public outside of Syria. As Paul Antopolous has noted, there never was an "Arab Spring" within Syria; it was a cover story for a foreign-supported resurgence of islamist extremist violence, a repeat of the uprising by the Muslim Brotherhood in Hama in 1982.

Thirty years later, the Syrian Arab Army again fight back against terrorism to protect its people, gaining strong support for itself and for Assad's government. Syria's long history of distrust of foreign manipulation frustrated the divide and conquer efforts of the French Mandate in the 1930's. So it was clear that regime change via the hypothetical Unconventional Warfare pyramid was not an option. The base of the pyramid, distrust of the government, was weak, while fear and hatred of the insurgent terrorists and foreign invaders was intense. It was not a war for Syrian hearts and minds, but a war on Syria, to degrade, destroy and break up the country – a premeditated crime against humanity.

The pyramid is not only a model of developments over time, it is also a scale from soft to hard. If political warfare doesn't work, then UW escalates to the deadlier options at the top, as in Libya and Syria. While it seems abhorrent to weaponize sociology, the warmakers might consider themselves benign and innovative for developing the "soft warfare" alternative for soft targets!

Building the pyramid over time from the bottom might seem like it would take generations, but remember that the Anglo-American empire has been on the scene for many generations already. There is already a legacy of influence, and of groups like the Moslem Brotherhood to build on.

The lower levels of the pyramid also look like something the Soviet Union could have undertaken to draw nations into the communist fold. Thus, the UW study might also be used by the Pentagon to identify and counter competing programmes – "counter-messaging," as Narwani notes.

So instead of being a nation with an army to defend our political freedoms, we are now attacking other nations by subverting their political freedoms?

The Deception Within the Deception

It is scandalous and offensive to our ideals, to see them abused and turned upside down in this way. Yet not everyone will be outraged. Those with a *Realpolitik* mentality will agree with Brzezinski that it's cheaper and more humane – at least in appearance – than full-scale invasion.

The rot goes deeper than that. The "leaked" Wikileaks cable and UW manual were themselves a cover story for the real operation. The story about a color revolution, NGO's, social media and protesters was for consumption by the world media, to mobilize support for military intervention. On the ground, the reality was that death squads set up by the US and its allies were randomly killing people, while the embedded globalist media were twisting that to blame the murders on Assad, as grist for the war propaganda mill.

I know there was a "Twitter war" for Syria, between anonymous "FSA supporters" (or "revtards," retards believing in revolution) and "pro-Syrian" activists, because I took part in it, although only in English, and it was a battle for cyberspace. I can remember only one pro-FSA tweeter who was clearly a real Syrian in Syria. He went by the name "Edward Dark," and lived in Aleppo, and was sought out by the Western media for interviews. No "shabiha" or secret police came after him. But when the terror brigades got to Aleppo, and he saw them senselessly destroying his home city, he changed sides. His Twitter followers were in shock. They thought he had been killed, bought out or lost his mind. It wasn't that. Edward Dark had seen the light. Too many millions of people world-wide have learnt the difference between democracy and demagoguery this way – the hard way.

To sum up,

1. Color revolutions in the Arab World, the Arab Spring, were never meant to bring in democracy, but to install Muslim Brotherhood regimes, as in Tunisia and Egypt, or even worse in Syria and Libya. This is part of a long-standing divide-and-conquer strategy to isolate Muslims from the world and each other.

2. The planners knew this would never work against the strong and popular regimes in Iraq, Syria and Libya, so the Arab Spring was mainly a mask to fool world opinion into supporting an armed intervention. On the ground there were death squads dressed up as jihadist terrorists, to carry out coups by armed force.

3. In the case of Iraq, there was no color revolution at all. ISIS came after an armed invasion and occupation by the US to smash the old regime and fragment Iraqi society. In Libya, Islamist terror brigades launched a civil war, with the support of NATO air power.

In the primary debates in the year 2000, John McCain said that if elected, he would tackle Iraq using UW techniques:

Q: What area of international policy would you change immediately?

A: Our policies concerning rogue states: Iraq, Libya, North Korea-those countries that continue to try to acquire weapons of mass destruction and the means to deliver them. I'd institute a policy that I call 'rogue state rollback.' I would arm, train, equip, both from without and from within, forces that would eventually overthrow the governments and install free and democratically-elected governments. As long as Saddam Hussein is in power, I am convinced that he will pose a threat to our security.

Yet he now admits that evidence of Saddam's WMD, "with the benefit of hindsight, was very flimsy."[94]

Hybrid War
More observations on Sociological Warfare.

Has the US advanced to the stage of a post-industrial power, or regressed to a pre-industrial stage of plunder? Certainly, military know-how is one of the few product lines where she still excels, and the return on investment can be huge. The US was recently able to take over and exploit the energy resources of Iraq and Libya, much as Britain long ago installed her puppets in the Arabian Peninsula and the Gulf. The UK earmarked $500 million for NATO's intervention in Libya, to gain reconstruction contracts valued at over $300 *billion*.[95]

[94] http://dailycaller.com/2014/07/18/mccain-if-id-won-in-2000-we-wouldnt-have-gone-to-war-in-iraq/
[95] "Make money, make war," RT, Nov. 11, 2011, cited in *Subverting Syria*, p. 25.

Target nations are actively working on defenses. Multiple attempts at a color revolution in Venezuela failed, even with the support of the elitist-owned media, because over 80% of the people benefit from the policies of Chavez. He died suddenly and suspiciously of cancer, a known CIA murder technique, and his successor Maduro has accused Obama of plotting to kill him, too.

> Sixty-Two Years after a CIA Coup Ousted Iranian Prime Minister Mossadegh for Nationalizing His Nation's Oil Reserves: US Foreign Policy Still Relies on Color Revolutions, which Must be Outlawed like Poison Gas.[96]

Civilization demands a halt to radical new developments in offensive weapons. The neutron bomb was a scandal because it would target people while sparing buildings. Color revolutions are even more selective, targeting the democratic due process and national self-determination. The arsenal of sociological warfare should be banned by international treaty.

The CIA has now admitted to the 1953 coup in which Kermit Roosevelt worked to install the Shah. With G W Bush calling Iran "The Axis of Evil" and the Ayatollah Khomeini calling the US "The Great Satan," few observers noticed that the CIA also installed Khomeini to subvert a popular, secular revolt.

> Brzezinski did everything to overthrow the Shah, and then to make sure that no secular politician like Shapour Baktiar took power in his stead: US Air Force Gen. Robert Huyser from Al Haig's NATO staff was sent to Iran with the message that only Khomeini would be acceptable to the United States... Khomeini's Iran did become a center of propagation of Islamic fundamentalist ideology, just as Brzezinski had intended.[97]

Since Khomeini, Iran has been able to pursue a more progressive course, and is firm friends with secular and largely Sunni Syria. Yet the US strategy did succeed in marking the region with a deep Sunni-Shi'a divide that would be exploited by the neocons. It halted a spontaneous surge of grassroots committees and workplace democracy, the *shora* movement. Khomeini's "Revolutionary Guards" broke strikes, liquidated local committees and shut down the revolution.[98]

It so happens that corruption is one of the key ways the empire can enmesh nations into its corporate and political network, and that the best cure for corruption is local accountability in small, democratically-run entities. So a grassroots popular revolution, like Iran had at the start, is a threat to corrupt cliques everywhere. Iran-Contra showed Khomeini was corrupt to the core.

At the "outlaw like poison gas" page there is a link to the book *Hybrid Wars: The Indirect Adaptive Approach to Regime Change*[99] by a perceptive Russian scholar, Andrew Korybko. The term "hybrid war" has been bandied about by Western media as a label for Putin's adept handling of the Ukraine crisis, especially in Crimea and the Donbass. Korybko says that on the contrary, it was the recent wars by the USA on Ukraine, Libya, and Syria that were a hybrid – of

---

[96] http://theinternationalreporter.org/2015/08/20/webster-tarpley-color-revolutions-must-be-outlawed-like-poison-gas-video/ Tells how Iranians have distrusted the US ever since the 1953 coup against Iran's elected government. The CIA finally admitted it was behind the coup.
[97] Webster Tarpley, *9/11 Synthetic Terror*, 5th ed., p. 256.
[98] https://libcom.org/history/1978-1979-the-iranian-revolution
[99] http://orientalreview.org/wp-content/uploads/2015/08/AK-Hybrid-Wars-updated.pdf

color revolution and unconventional warfare tactics: "the US is far ahead of any other country in practicing this new method of warfare, as no other state has attempted a Color Revolution thus far, let alone transitioned it into an Unconventional War."

The Color Revolution brand was created with a pronounced "non-violent" label to capture the "moral high ground," in the campaign to overthrow Milosevic in Serbia. The Unconventional Warfare (UW) manual is itself a hybrid, with a basis of building pro-democracy networks, capped by direct warfare methods. In Libya and Syria, the UW script was started from the end. There was no need to patiently build radical revolutionary movements. These already exist – the *takfiri* sectarian extremists, fostered and fed for two centuries by Britain's grand assets, the Saudi princes.

What they don't tell you about is the real mutant horror which is actually implemented: Where the Color Revolution is just a screen given to the mass media to cover for the work of death squads, blame the killing on the regime and agitate world wide for the green light to attack the country under the "R2P" doctrine (responsibility to protect civilians). Where there is only a show of an opposition working towards reform and democracy, while the sole aim is to sow chaos and destruction – to knock the country back to the stone age, not only in terms of infrastructure, but of society, in setting up a regime of feudal fanatics.

In Iraq, Saddam Hussein was already the product of an earlier CIA palace coup. Why take the long difficult road to build the UW pyramid to overthrow him, and have his replacement government eventually become independent again. Instead, use death squads to create two separate and opposed political structures, a double pyramid, a grotesque parody of UW. Create a state of permanent war, where US power will always be the arbiter between the factions, as in Afghanistan.

The Green Revolution failed in Iran. This was the Axis of Resistance, like Syria, where a color revolution had no chance of success, except as a screen for the Salvador and Somalia options. In Ukraine, the Orange Revolution of 2004 was gradually neutralized by Russia. The 2013 "Euromaidan" protests involved a nonviolent color revolution screen with protesters on stipends. In the background, neo-fascist elements were mobilized, the notorious Pravy Sektor, with their own death squad legacy. Sniper provocateurs from their ranks, and not the protests themselves, brought down the government. An old recipe: Revolution as a way of conduiting a palace coup.

In 2007, in a *New Yorker* article entitled "The Redirection," Seymour Hersh revealed "how the United States, Israel, and Saudi Arabia, along with Abdel Nour's Hariri faction in Lebanon, were preparing a regional army of sectarian extremists to destabilize" Iran and Syria – playing the Shia vs. Sunni card.[100]

---

[100] http://www.newyorker.com/magazine/2007/03/05/the-redirection, cited by Tony Cartalucci in *Subverting Syria*, 2012.

The New Gladio in Action?

'Swarming Adolescents' and 'Rebellious Hysteria'[101]

By Jonathan Mowat

"Gene Sharp started out the seminar by saying 'Strategic nonviolent struggle is all about political power.' And I thought, 'Boy is this guy speaking my language,' that is what armed struggle is about — Col. Robert Helvey

Washington, DC, March 19, 2005 — The U.S. government and allied forces' year-end installation of Victor Yushchenko as president of Ukraine has completed the field-testing of the "Postmodern Coup." Employing and fine-tuning the same sophisticated techniques used in Serbia in 2000 and Georgia in 2003 (and tried unsuccessfully in Belarus in 2001), it is widely expected that the United States will attempt to apply the same methods throughout the former Soviet Union...

The same networks are also increasingly active in South America, Africa, and Asia. Top targets include Venezuela, Mozambique, and Iran, among others.

The method employed is usefully described by *The Guardian*'s Ian Traynor in a Nov. 26, 2004, article entitled "US campaign behind the turmoil in Kiev," during the first phase of the coup.

> With their websites and stickers, their pranks and slogans aimed at banishing widespread fear of a corrupt regime, the democracy guerrillas of the Ukrainian Pora youth movement have already notched up a famous victory...
>
> [T]he campaign is an American creation, a sophisticated and brilliantly conceived exercise in western branding and mass marketing that, in four countries in four years, has been used to try to salvage rigged elections and topple unsavoury regimes.
>
> Funded and organised by the U.S. government, deploying U.S. consultancies, pollsters, diplomats, the two big American parties and US non-government organisations, the campaign was first used in Europe in Belgrade in 2000 to beat Slobodan Milosevic at the ballot box.
>
> Richard Miles, the U.S. ambassador in Belgrade, played a key role. And by last year, as U.S. ambassador in Tbilisi, he repeated the trick in Georgia, coaching Mikhail Saakashvili in how to bring down Eduard Shevardnadze. Ten months after the success in Belgrade, the U.S. ambassador in Minsk, Michael Kozak, a veteran of similar operations in central America, notably in Nicaragua, organised a near identical campaign to try to defeat the Belarus hard man, Alexander Lukashenko.
>
> The operation — engineering democracy through the ballot box and civil disobedience — is now so slick that the methods have matured into a template for winning other people's elections.

Much of the coup apparatus is the same that was used in the overthrow of President Fernando Marcos of the Philippines in 1986, the Tiananmen Square destabilization in 1989, and Vaclav Havel's "Velvet revolution" in Czechoslovakia in 1989. As in these early operations, the National Endowment for Democracy (NED), and its primary arms,

---

[101] Excerpted from *Obama, the Postmodern Coup: The Making of a Manchurian Candidate*, Webster G. Tarpley, 2008, p, 243 ff.

the National Democratic Institute for International Affairs (NDI) and International Republican Institute (IRI), played a central role. The NED was established by the Reagan Administration in 1983, to do overtly what the CIA had done covertly, in the words of one of its legislative drafters, Allen Weinstein. The Cold War propaganda and operations center, Freedom House, now chaired by former CIA director James Woolsey, has also been involved, as were billionaire George Soros's foundations, whose donations always dovetail those of the NED.

What is new about the template bears on the use of the Internet (in particular chat rooms, instant messaging, and blogs) and cell phones (including text-messaging), to rapidly steer angry and suggestible "Generation X" youth into and out of mass demonstrations and the like — a capability that only emerged in the mid-1990s...

A CIVILIAN REVOLUTION IN MILITARY AFFAIRS

The emphasis on the use of new communication technologies to rapidly deploy small groups suggests that we are seeing the civilian application of Defense Secretary Donald Rumsfeld's "Revolution in Military Affairs" doctrine, which depends on highly mobile small group deployments "enabled" by "real-time" intelligence and communications. Squads of soldiers taking over city blocks with the aid of "intelligence helmet" video screens that give them an instantaneous overview of their environment, constitute the military side. Bands of youth converging on targeted intersections in constant dialogue on cell phones constitute the doctrine's civilian application...

The "revolution" in warfare that such new instruments permit has been pushed to the extreme by several specialists in psychological warfare...

The new techniques of warfare include the use of *both* lethal (violent) and nonlethal (nonviolent) tactics... It is what is known as *cyberwar*. For example, the tactic of swarming is a fundamental element in both violent and nonviolent forms of warfare...

Dr. Peter Ackerman, the author of *Strategic Nonviolent Conflict*, proposed that youth movements, such as those used to bring down Serbia, could bring down Iran and North Korea, and could have been used to bring down Iraq — thereby accomplishing all of Bush's objectives without relying on military means. And he reported that he has been working with the top U.S. weapons designer, Lawrence Livermore Laboratories, on developing new communications technologies that could be used in other youth movement insurgencies. "There is no question that these technologies are democratizing," he stressed, in reference to their potential use in bringing down China, "they enable decentralized activity. They create, if you will, a digital concept of the right of assembly."

Dr. Ackerman is the founding chairman of International Center on Nonviolent Conflicts of Washington, DC, of which former U.S. Air Force officer Jack DuVall is president. Together with former CIA director James Woolsey, DuVall also directs the Arlington Institute of Washington, DC. It was created by former Chief of Naval Operations advisor John L. Petersen in 1989 "to help redefine the concept of national security in much larger, comprehensive terms" through introducing "social value shifts into the traditional national defense equation."

"SWARMING ADOLESCENTS" AND "REBELLIOUS HYSTERIA"

As in the case of the new communication technologies, the potential effectiveness of angry youth in postmodern coups has long been under study. As far back as 1967, Dr. Fred Emery, then director of the Tavistock Institute, and an expert on the "hypnotic effects" of television, specified that the then-new phenomenon of "swarming adolescents" found at rock concerts could be effectively used to bring down the nation-state by the end of the 1990s... because the phenomenon was associated with "rebellious hysteria." The British military created the Tavistock Institute as its psychological warfare arm following World War I; it has been the forerunner of such strategic planning ever since. Dr. Emery's concept saw immediate application in NATO's use of "swarming adolescents" in toppling French President Charles de Gaulle in 1967...

Dr. Howard Perlmutter, a professor of "Social Architecture" at the Wharton School, and a follower of Dr. Emery, stressed that "rock video in Katmandu," was an appropriate image of how states with traditional cultures could be destabilized, thereby creating the possibility of a "global civilization." There are two requirements for such a transformation, he added, "building internationally committed networks of international and locally committed organizations," and "creating global events" through "the transformation of a local event into one having virtually instantaneous international implications through mass-media."

This brings us to the final ingredient of these new coups — the deployment of polling agencies' "exit polls" broadcast on international television to give the false (or sometimes accurate) impression of massive vote-fraud by the ruling party, and put targeted states on the defensive. Polling operations in the recent coups have been overseen by such outfits as Penn, Schoen & Berland Associates, top advisors to Microsoft and Bill Clinton. Praising their role in subverting Serbia, then-Secretary of State (and later Chairman of NDI) Madeleine Albright, in an October 2000 letter to the firm quoted on its website, stated: "Your work with the National Democratic Institute and the Yugoslav opposition contributed directly and decisively to the recent breakthrough for democracy in that country..." Penn, Schoen, together with the Organization for Security and Cooperation in Europe (OSCE), also ran the widely televised "exit poll" operations in the Ukrainian elections.

In the aftermath of such youth deployments and media operations, **more traditional elements come to the fore. That is, the forceful, if covert, intervention** by international institutions and governments threatening the targeted regime, and using well-placed operatives within the target regime's military and intelligence services to ensure no countermeasures can be effectively deployed. Without these traditional elements, of course, no postmodern coup could ever work.

GLADIO AND JAMES BOND GET A YOUTH GROUP

The creation and deployment of coups of any kind requires agents on the ground. The main handler of these coups on the "street side" has been the Albert Einstein Institution, which was formed in 1983 as an offshoot of Harvard University under the impetus of Dr. Gene Sharp, and which specializes in "nonviolence as a form of warfare." Dr. Sharp had been the executive secretary to A. J. Muste, the famous U.S. Trotskyite labor organizer and peacenik. The group is funded by Soros and the NED. Albert Einstein's president is Col. Robert Helvey, a former U.S. Army officer with 30 years of experience in Southeast Asia. He has served as the case officer for youth groups active in the Balkans and Eastern Europe since at least 1999.

Col. Helvey reports, in a January 29, 2001, interview with film producer Steve York in Belgrade, that he first got involved in "strategic nonviolence" upon seeing the failure of military approaches to toppling dictators — especially in Myanmar, where he had been stationed as military attaché... Helvey

> was an officer of the Defense Intelligence Agency of the Pentagon, who had served in Vietnam and, subsequently, as the US Defense Attaché in Yangon, Myanmar

(1983 to 85), during which he clandestinely organised the Myanmarese students to work behind Aung San Suu Kyi and in collaboration with Bo Mya's Karen insurgent group... He also trained in Hong Kong the student leaders from Beijing in mass demonstration techniques which they were to subsequently use in the Tiananmen Square incident of June 1989 ... and is now believed to be acting as an adviser to the Falun Gong, the religious sect of China, in similar civil disobedience techniques.

Reflecting Albert Einstein's patronage, one of its first books was Dr. Sharp's *Making Europe Unconquerable: The Potential of Civilian-Based Deterrence and Defense,* published in 1985 with a foreword by the famous "Mr. X," George Kennan, the 1940's architect of the Cold War and founder of the CIA's Operations division. There, Sharp reports that "civilian-based defense" could counter the Soviet threat through its ability "to deter and defeat attacks by making a society ungovernable by would be oppressors..." The book was promptly translated into German, Norwegian, Italian, Danish, and other NATO-country languages...

Such formulations suggest that Albert Einstein Institution activities were, ironically, coherent with (or, possibly updating) the infamous NATO's "Gladio" stay-behind network, whose purpose was to combat possible Soviet occupation through a panoply of military and nonmilitary means. The investigations into Gladio, and those following the 1978 assassination of former Prime Minister Aldo Moro, also shed some light (immediately switched off) on a professional apparatus of destabilization that had been invisible to the public for several decades.

It is noteworthy that the former deputy chief of intelligence for the U.S. Army in Europe, Maj. Gen. Edward Atkeson...

As we shall see below, with such backing, Col. Helvey and his colleagues have created a series of youth movements including Otpor in Serbia, Kmara in Georgia, Pora in Ukraine, and the like...

THE SERBIAN VIRUS

The networks and methods used in the Serbian through Ukraine sequence were first publicly revealed in a *Washington Post* article on Dec. 11, 2000, by Michael Dobbs, entitled "U.S. Advice Guided Milosevic Opposition: Political Consultants Helped Yugoslav Opposition Topple Authoritarian Leader." Dobbs reports that:

> U.S.-funded consultants played a crucial role behind the scenes in virtually every facet of the anti-Milosevic drive, running tracking polls, training thousands of opposition activists and helping to organize a vitally important parallel vote count. U.S. taxpayers paid for 5,000 cans of spray paint used by student activists to scrawl anti-Milosevic graffiti on walls across Serbia, and 2.5 million stickers with the slogan "He's Finished," which became the revolution's catchphrase...

> During the seminar, the Serbian students received training in such matters as how to organize a strike, how to communicate with symbols, how to overcome fear and how to undermine the authority of a dictatorial regime. The principal lecturer was retired U.S. Army Col. Robert Helvey, who has made a study of nonviolent resistance methods around the world, including those used in modern-day Burma and the civil rights struggle in the American South...

Otpor's leaders knew that they "couldn't use force on someone who ... had three times more force and weapons than we did," in the words of Lazendic. "We knew what had happened in Tiananmen, where the army plowed over students with tanks..."

This relatively sophisticated knowledge of how to develop nonviolent power was not intuitive. Miljenko Dereta, the director of a private group in Belgrade called Civic Initiatives, got funding from Freedom House in the U.S. to print and distribute 5,000 copies of Gene Sharp's book, *From Dictatorship to Democracy: A Conceptual Framework for Liberation*... activists also received direct training from Sharp's colleague, Col. Robert Helvey, at the Budapest Hilton in March 2000.

Helvey emphasized how to break the people's habits of subservience to authority, and also how to subvert the regime's "pillars of support," including the police and armed forces. Crucially, he warned them against "contaminants to a nonviolent struggle," especially violent action, which would deter ordinary people from joining the movement and alienate the international community, from which material and financial assistance could be drawn. As Popovic put it: "Stay nonviolent and you will get the support of the third party."

That support, largely denied to the Serbian opposition before, now began to flow. Otpor and other dissident groups received funding from the National Endowment for Democracy, affiliated with the U.S. government... The U.S. Agency for International Development, the wellspring for most of this financing, was also the source of money that went for materials like T-shirts and stickers.

NO LACK OF OPPORTUNITIES FOR EMPLOYMENT

In the aftermath of the Serbian revolution, the National Endowment for Democracy, Albert Einstein Institution, and related outfits helped establish several Otpor-modelled youth groups in Eastern Europe, notably Zubr in Belarus in January 2001; Kmara in Georgia, in April 2003; and Pora in Ukraine in June 2004. Efforts to overthrow Belarus President Alexsander Luschenko failed in 2001, while the U.S. overthrow of Georgian President Eduard Schevardnadze was successfully accomplished in 2003, using Kmara as part of its operation...

Saakashvili with McCain

[In 2003], before becoming president in Georgia, the U.S.-educated Mr. Saakashvili travelled from Tbilisi to Belgrade to be coached in the techniques of mass defiance. [He has since been posted to Ukraine as governor of the restive Odessa province.]

An Associated Press article by Dusan Stojanovic, on Nov. 2, 2004, entitled "Serbia's Export: Peaceful Revolution," elaborates:

In Ukraine and Belarus, tens of thousands of people have been staging daily protests — carbon copies of the anti-Milosevic rallies — with "training" provided by the Serbian group... Otpor's clenched fist was flying high on white flags again — this time in Georgia, when protesters stormed the parliament in an action that led to the toppling of Shevardnadze.

Last month, Ukrainian border authorities denied entry to Alexandar Maric, a member of Otpor and an adviser with the U.S.-based democracy watchdog

Freedom House. A Ukrainian student group called Pora was following the strategies of Otpor.

Timeline:

• Otpor founded in Belgrade, Serbia in October 1998. Postmodern Coup overthrows Slobodan Milosevic on Oct. 5, 2000. Subsequently forms Center for Nonviolent Resistance to spread revolutions.

• Clinton Administration's Community of Democracies launched in Warsaw, Poland, in June 2000.

• Zubr founded in Minsk, Belarus, on Jan. 14, 2001. Election-Coup efforts fail in Sept. 9, 2001.

• Mjaft founded in Tirana, Albania, on March 15, 2003.

• Kmara founded in Tblisi, Georgia in April 2003. "Rose revolution" overthrows President Eduard Shevardnadze on Nov. 23, 2003.

• Pora founded in Kiev, Ukraine in June 2004. "Orange revolution" installs Victor Yushchenko into power on December 26, 2004.

• Kmara overthrows Abashidze of Ajaria (western Georgian secessionist province) May 5, 2004.

THE COUP PLOTTERS

The Albert Einstein Institution

The Albert Einstein Institution (AEI) has played the key role in recent years in training and deploying youth movements to help prepare the conditions for coups through fostering the impression that the targeted regimes are deeply unpopular, and through destabilizing those regimes through their demonstrations and the like. The group, which is funded by the Soros foundations and the U.S. government, is led by former DIA officer Col. Robert Helvey, and Harvard University's Dr. Gene Sharp...

According to Sharp, "If the issue is to bring down a dictatorship, then it is not good enough to say, 'we want freedom.' It's necessary to develop a strategy, or a super-plan, to weaken a dictatorship and that can only be done by identifying its sources of power. These [sources of power] include: authority, human resources skills, knowledge, tangible factors, economic and material resources and sanctions like police and troops."

For this reason, Sharp reports, he has written numerous books on nonviolent struggle to help oppressed peoples develop a "superplan." These works, of which the major one is *The Politics of Nonviolent Action*, have been translated into 27 languages...

***

Editor's note. The manual includes a list of 198 methods rebels can use to destabilize a government. The AEI has also produced a film starring the aging Gene Sharp, *How to Start a Revolution*. Available in many languages, it makes a strong emotional appeal to values like idealism, hope and heroism. Watching it one may have conflicting emotions, like Ulysses tied to the mast, listening to the siren song, yet reminding oneself what a dangerous deception it is.

For a good read on the tentacles of the Soros Octopus, see this story on the color revolution in Macedonia. It details many of the organizations and color revolutions he has funded. His activist networks are very powerful in small countries that don't have other civic groups to counter them. http://balkanblog.org/2015/07/24/george-soros-cia-freedom-house-ned-nato-and-the-western-color-revolution-in-macedonia/ .
Balkanization slices up countries small enough so each fat cat can run one of his own.

Eyewitness Reports: Analyst in Damascus

Adapted from Thierry Meyssan at VoltaireNet

Thierry Meyssan is a very astute observer of the world political scene, and the founder and main writer of the prodigious geopolitical website VoltaireNet (Réseau Voltaire). He moved from Paris to Beirut some years ago, which has augmented his rare insight into Near Eastern politics. In 2011, Meyssan was reporting from Tripoli, Libya at great personal risk, and denied the false reports of the fall of the city, revealing it as a psychological warfare ploy by NATO.

The United States say they want to destroy the Islamic Emirate ISIS which they created to carry out the ethnic cleansing for their remodeling of the "New Middle East". Stranger still, they say they want to fight in Syria alongside the "moderate opposition," which are interchangeable with ISIS. And very odd indeed, they destroyed buildings in Raqqa two days after ISIS evacuated them.[102]

Erdogan's Errors – Turkey's Tragedy – Syria's Sorrow

Turkey has long been a nation with a split identity. It straddles Europe and Asia; there are more ancient Greek ruins to be found in Turkey than in Greece. The Byzantine Empire was Orthodox Christian, a faith not quite of the West nor of the East. Constantinople became Istanbul, and the Ottoman Empire inherited the mantle of the Caliphate, the protector of Islam.

There is a precedent to Erdogan's baiting Russia at NATO's urging. In the Crimean War of 1853, France and Britain put Turkey up to declaring war on Russia. Absurdly, the *casus belli* was supposedly, "Who was to be named protector of the Christians in the Middle East" - Russia (Orthodox) or France (Catholic) - even though the churches themselves came to an agreement.

Today, the post of Protector of the Christians in the Middle East has gone unfilled for perhaps a century – certainly by France, Britain and the US. So that mantle is there for Russia to pick up.

Turkey's Ottoman Empire was on Britain's hit list to be humbled and carved up in the Great War. In the aftermath, Kamal Ataturk did hold Turkey together, but at the price of adopting Western secularism, the Latin alphabet, and nationalism, which meant "ethnic cleansing" of minorities, brutal suppression of Sufi religious orders, and abstaining from dreams of empire.

This was formally a 20th-century democracy, which the generals could suspend when needed. For decades, Turkey aspired to membership in the European Union; there was always an excuse to keep her out. Meanwhile she became a regional industrial power.

Beneath the superficial glitter, the deeply rooted Islamic faith remained strong.

When the Islamist AKP party came to power in Turkey in 2003, they aimed for a new foreign policy strategy as the foundation for a new Ottoman empire. They started by trying to cultivate good relations with all their Muslim neighbors plus

---

[102] "Behind the anti-terror alibi, the gas war in the Levant," Oct. 3, 2014, http://www.voltairenet.org/article185495.html

Israel (the "zero problem policy). This worked well enough until the Israeli massacres against Gaza in 2009, which put Turkey on a pro-Palestinian pivot. There was the Turkish flotilla to bring aid to Gaza, and the founding of a common market with Iran, Iraq and Syria.[103]

This happy state of things was soon overturned in 2011, by the war waged by the US, UK and France on Libya and Syria. These two Arab nations were important economic partners for Turkey, but Erdogan's cooperation with the cruel wars against them was procured by promising him a new Caliphate that would reign over Islamist regimes rising from the Arab Spring across the Muslim world. At the behest of the US, the Muslim Brotherhood would replace the secular, nationalist, egalitarian Arab governments, thorns that had long been festering in the side of the Western globalist world order. Their economies would become tributaries of the Empire of the West... as "foreshadowed by the genocidal 5-year plan to destroy 7 nations, which Gen. Wesley Clark made public in 2007: 'We're going to take out seven countries in five years, starting with Iraq, and then Syria, Lebanon, Libya, Somalia, Sudan and, finishing off, Iran.'"

– JPL

The role played by Erdoğan in the coordination of international terrorism after the attack on Saudi prince Bandar bin Sultan.[104]

Erdogan played a key role in NATO's destruction of Libya by mobilizing the Misrata tribes against Gaddafi.[105]

> Turkey was aware that by attacking Libya, it would lose a very important market, but it hoped to take control of the governments held by the Muslim Brotherhood, already present in Tunisia, then probably in Libya, Egypt and Syria. This in fact came to pass in the two former states in 2012, but did not last.

Erdogan apparently is thinking that the "Caliphate" of ISIS is the entering wedge for his "New Ottoman Empire." But the real existing US empire will play Turkey off against its neighbors in a classic divide and conquer ploy, Erdogan is dreaming if he thinks they will let the Turks set up shop as a regional empire under the aegis of the US.[106]

> So Turkey joined in the war against Syria, and became the forward base for NATO operations. During the first phase of the war, from February 2011 to the Geneva Conference of June 2012, NATO infiltrated its al-Qaïda brigades from Libya into Syria via Turkey to create the so-called "Free Syrian Army". Mr. Erdoğan supplied

---

[103] Clinton, Juppé, Erdoğan, Daesh and the PKK, Aug. 3, 2015,
http://www.voltairenet.org/article188337.html
[104] Nearing the end of the Erdoğan system, June 15, 2015.
http://www.voltairenet.org/article187879.html
[105] Misrata tribes: "Turkish Jews who had converted to Islam and settled in Libya in the 18th and 19th centuries... in extremis, Recep Tayyip Erdoğan supported NATO's project... Immediately, Ankara mobilised the citizens of Misrata in Libya. These are mostly the descendants of the Jewish soldiers of the Ottoman Empire, the Adghams, and the nomadic merchants descended from black slaves, the Muntasirs, who had supported the Young Turks. They formed the only significant Libyan group capable of attacking Tripoli."
[106] See for example http://southfront.org/foreign-policy-diary-turkey-seeks-to-become-new-ottoman-empire/. Dec. 26, 2015

rear bases disguised as "refugee camps", while the blind Western press saw nothing other than a "democratic revolution" along the lines of the so-called "Arab Spring."

In the space of two years, more than 200,000 mercenaries arrived from all over the world and transited by Turkey in order to wage jihad in Syria. The MIT, or Turkish secret services, set up a vast system to supply weapons arms and funds, mainly paid for by Qatar and supervised by the CIA.

In May 2014, Turkey's MIT sent a special train to "Daesh," the Syrian terrorists, loaded with heavy weapons and new Toyota pick-ups courtesy of Saudi Arabia. The Islamic Emirate, or ISIS, which at the time numbered only a few hundred fighters, grew within a month into an army of tens of thousands, and invaded Iraq.

On Jan. 19th, 2015, on a warrant from the public prosecutor's department, the police intercepted a convoy transporting weapons for Daesh. However, the search was halted because the convoy was being led by MIT agents. The prosecutors and the police colonel were then arrested for "treason" [against the Erdogan system of "justice"]. During the preliminary investigation, a magistrate made it known that the MIT had chartered a total of 2,000 truckloads of weapons for Daesh. [107]

Mr. Erdoğan installed three al-Qaïda training camps on his soil, including one next to the NATO base at Incirlik. He organised them as terrorist academies on the lines of the School of the Americas.

The Turkish police and Justice system have shown that Mr. Erdoğan – like ex-US Vice President Dick Cheney - was a personal friend of Yasin al-Qadi, known as the "al-Qaïda banker" by the FBI and the UN – until he was taken off the international terrorist list in 2012. While he was still a wanted man, "al-Qadi took a secret trip to Ankara in a private plane. Mr. Erdoğan's bodyguards came to pick him up at the airport, having first de-activated the surveillance cameras.

Turkey made a huge profit from the war against Syria. Firstly by organising the pillage of its archeological treasures. A public market was set up in Antioch so that collectors from all over the world could come and buy the stolen objects and place orders for works to be stolen. Secondly, by organising the industrial pillage of Aleppo, the economic capital of Syria. The Chamber of Commerce and Industry of Aleppo revealed how their factories had been systematically dismantled, and the machines-tools transferred to Turkey under the vigilant eye of the MIT.

ISIS steals oil, which is taken to Turkey in tank trucks, then it goes by pipeline to Ceyhan, and shipped to Israel. Israeli authorities provide false certificates of origin from Eilat, then it is exported to the European Union, which pretends to believe it's Israeli oil.

On May 27, 2015, Massoud Barzani, long-term Israeli client and president of the Kurdish regional government in Iraq, went to Amman to coordinate the invasion of Iraq by Iraqi Kurds together with ISIS. In early June, ISIS and the Kurdish forces went on the attack. ISIS was tasked with spreading terror in order to complete the ethnic cleansing that the US army had begun in 2003.[108]

---

[107] "Nearing the end of the Erdoğan system," Ibid.

[108] "Behind the anti-terror alibi, the gas war in the Levant," Oct. 3, 2014, http://www.voltairenet.org/article185495.html

Erdogan expected the US and NATO to attack Syria as they had Libya, but they were blocked by Russia and China in the Security Council, and all efforts at toppling Assad seemed only to increase his popular support. Meyssan contends that the US and UK stopped believing in the war on Syria already in 2012 (a fact which had escaped me, whilst living in the US and being regularly regaled with the belligerent rhetoric of our hawkish politicians), leaving Turkey and France in the game.

Both Meyssan and Iran's *Press TV*[109] implicate Turkey and France in the assassination attempt on Syrian President Assad and his foreign affairs minister Walid al Muallem pn July 18, 2012. The bombing in Damascus killed a number of high Syrian officials and generals. During the next week, without the discretion of delay, the Saudi Kingdom named Prince Bandar Chief of Intelligence. Two days afterwards he was seriously wounded in a bombing attack, which pro-Assad websites ascribe to Syria.

> The Saudi services, with logistical support from the CIA, had managed to blow up the headquarters of the Syrian National Security during a Crisis Cell meeting... This operation, called "Damascus Volcano" was the signal for the attack on the capital by a swarm of mercenaries, mainly coming from Jordan.[110]

Bandar had been the chief organizer of the "insurgency" against Syria, and as his post was now open, Erdogan eagerly stepped in to take over the job.

Erdogan also arranged the Ghouta false flag chemical attacks to try and bring NATO in. The war hysteria was well orchestrated, the necessary evidence was faked, but Putin made his famous diplomatic intervention, and the British parliament balked. Obama suddenly remembered he is supposed to be a Constitutional scholar, said something about passing the buck to Congress, and the mania passed.

Erdogan's son Bilal is believed to run the smuggling of massive quantities of ISIS-looted Syrian and Iraqi oil to Turkey - the number of trucks in service approached the capacity of a pipeline. The Erdogans buy it at one third of the world price; the total proceeds for ISIS have been reckoned at nearly a billion dollars, so the Turks have made astronomical sums.

Bilal Erdogan is also involved in a scandal in Italy, where he is accused of laundering money gotten by illegally taking possession of the plaintiff's business. For good measure, his sister Sümeyye Erdogan runs a hospital for wounded ISIS fighters. And journalists who reported on the smuggling of weapons to ISIS were jailed – Erdogan wants life sentences.[111]

One reason Erdogan eagerly signed agreements with Russia in December 2014, says Meyssan, was his concern over the US peace talks with Iran, which might leave Turkey out in the cold. The accord was signed in July 2015, and shortly thereafter,

---

[109] http://www.presstv.com/detail/2013/03/03/291672/france-turkey-plot-to-kill-assad/
[110] "Syria reportedly eliminated Bandar bin Sultan in retaliation for Damascus bombing," July 29, 2012 http://www.voltairenet.org/Syria-reportedly-eliminated-Bandar
[111] Martin Berger, Dec. 28, 2015, "Erdogan's Family Caught in New Scandal," http://journal-neo.org/2015/12/28/erdogans-family-got-caught-in-a-new-scandal/

Erdoğan received, on the 24th July, an ultimatum from President Obama, requiring him to immediately renounce the Russian gas pipe-line project, cease his support of Daesh – of which he had become the executive chief behind the screen of caliph Abu Bakr al-Baghdadi – and go to war with them.

Erdogan made amends by agreeing to let the US use the Turkish airbase at Incirlik, then made an end-run by teaming up with Gen. John Allen, who was supposed to be running the war on ISIS, but is really much more interested in a war on Syria. Together, they turned the US anti-ISIS effort into a war on the Kurds. Webster Tarpley has written extensively in his TWSP newsletters on the tensions and intrigues between Obama and the hawks like Allen and Defense Secretary Ashton Carter.

Three months later, Russian intervention upset Erdogan's apple cart, and the Russian gas pipe-line was put on hold anyway. Erdogan's bungling has let one more fault line open wide: doing America's bidding, he has lost the friendship of his most powerful neighbor Russia, and it will cost Turkey dearly.

Meyssan sums him up: "He is a petty criminal who joined the Muslim Brotherhood, was propelled to power with the help of the CIA, and he now behaves like a true mafia boss."

Turkish "Islamists" like Erdogan and "Pan-Turkish nationalist" Gladio outfits like Turan and the Grey Wolves are even playing the Al-Qaida terrorist card against China, by training Muslim Uighur militants in Xinjiang.[112]

A History of the Muslim Brotherhood[113]

The war in Syria

is not a war opposing different communities, but a war between two projects for society.

On one side, a modern, secular Syria, in other words, a society which is respectful of ethnic, religious, and political diversity; on the other, the ideology of the Muslim Brotherhood, who, since their creation in 1928, have been seeking to re-establish the Ottoman caliphate by means of jihad...

From 1954, although the Muslim Brotherhood had assassinated two Egyptian Prime Ministers, the CIA decided to use them to destabilize the Soviet Union as well as to combat the Arab nationalist movements.

Note the close parallel with NATO's use of Gladio, ostensibly on guard against the Soviet Union, but actually implemented against progressive nationalist governments in Europe.

From 1978 to 1982 the Brotherhood carried out terrorist attacks against the Syrian regime of Hafez Assad, who finally crushed their force in their stronghold at Hama.

In 1979, the West used the Brotherhood to fight the Russians in Afghanistan; thus was born Al Qaeda, which was later used against Serbia, and against Russia in Chechnya.

---

[112] Tony Cartalucci, Sept. 23, 2015, "Turkish-Uyghur Terror Inc. – America's Other Al Qaeda," http://journal-neo.org/2015/09/23/turkish-uyghur-terror-inc-americas-other-al-qaeda/,
[113] Thierry Meyssan, "Let's unite against the project by Al-Qaïda and Daesh," Sept. 30, 2015 http://www.voltairenet.org/article188854.html

Then came the Arab Spring in 2011, the Petraeus plan for the Brotherhood to supplant all the Arab secular regimes. The US forced Mubarak to resign from power in Egypt, and he was replaced by the creepy dictator Morsi from the Brotherhood, but Egyptian society violently rejected them. In 2012, the FSA - Daesh - ISIS branch declared an Islamic Caliphate in Homs, which was eventually decimated in a bitter siege by the Syrian Army.

Why does France want to overthrow the Syrian Arab Republic[114]

Fairly well-known, are

the personal links that ex-President Nicolas Sarkozy[115] entertained with Qatar, sponsor of the Muslim Brotherhood, and those of President François Hollande, not only with Qatar, but now also with Saudi Arabia. Both Presidents obtained illegal financing for their electoral campaigns from these states.

Not so well known is how this relates to the history of French colonialism in Syria, going back to the secret agreement between France and Britain to carve up the colonies of the Central Powers after the Great War, in particular, the Sykes-Picot agreement that made Syria a French colony or "mandate."

In 2009, two staunch Zionists, Secretary of State Hillary Clinton and Nicolas Sarkozy, a CIA asset and stepson of Frank Wisner, Jr., decided "to re-launch the Franco-British colonial project under the guidance of the United States – this is known as the theory of 'leading from behind'." The formal signing came in November 2010 with the

Lancaster House Agreements... the secret part of the Agreements anticipates the attacks on Libya and Syria, on the 21st March 2011... The attack on Syria never took place, however, because its commander, the United States, changed its mind...

On the 29th of July 2011, France created the Free Syrian Army (the "moderates")... the first elements engaged were not Syrians, but Libyan members of al-Qaïda. The Free Syrian Army (FSA) is supervised by French legionnaires... The FSA now fights under the French colonial flag...[116] It was also the FSA who broadcast a video of one of their cannibal leaders eating the heart and liver of a Syrian soldier. The only difference between the moderates and the extremists is their flag – either the French colonial flag or that of the jihad.

At the beginning of 2012, French legionnaires escorted the 3,000 combatants of the FSA to Homs, the ancient capital of French colonialism, in order to make it the "revolutionary capital". They moved into the new area of Baba Amr, where they proclaimed an Islamic Emirate [Islamic State]. A revolutionary tribunal condemned to death more than 150 inhabitants who had stayed in the area, and had their throats cut in public. The FSA held out for a month against a siege, protected by fire stations of Milan anti-tank missiles offered to them by France...

---

[114] "Why does France want to overthrow the Syrian Arab Republic?" Oct. 12, 2015
http://www.voltairenet.org/article189006.html
[115] "Operation Sarkozy: how the CIA placed one of its agents at the presidency of the French Republic," Oct. 12, 2015, http://www.voltairenet.org/article157821.html
[116] The so-called "opposition flag," with green and black bars and three red stars, which Wikipedia has been showing in first place in its article on the Syrian flag, claiming there are two governments due to the "civil war." One of a myriad examples of a complete matrix of fake reality created about Syria from 2011 onwards. The official flag has red and black bars with two green stars.

On Sept. 27th, 2015,

> ex-President Valéry Giscard d'Estaing said – "I am wondering about the possibility of creating a UN mandate for Syria, for a duration of five years". The UN has never once given a "mandate" since it was created. The very word itself harks back to the worst of colonisation...

> It is pertinent here to recall that Geneviève, the sister of François Georges-Picot (of the Sykes-Picot Agreements), married senator Jacques Bardoux – a member of the "Colonial Party". As for their daughter, May Bardoux, she married the President of the Société Financière Française et Coloniale, Edmond Giscard d'Estaing, the father of the ex-President of France.

> So the solution to the Syrian problem, according to the grand-nephew of the man who negotiated the French mandate for Syria with the British, is to recolonise the country.

France and Israël launch a new war in Iraq and Syria[117]

A third phase of the Syrian war has been opened.

The first war was the Arab Spring, from Feb. 2011 to Jan. 2013. It was instigated by the US, and its aim was to replace secular regimes with Moslem Brotherhood dictatorships.

The second was a war of attrition against Syria and its army, lasting from July 2012 to October 2015. It was promoted by US hawks Hillary Clinton and David Petraeus, financed by Saudi Arabia, Qatar and Turkey, and some multinationals. This war was ended by Russia's massive intervention against ISIS and on behalf of the Syrian army.

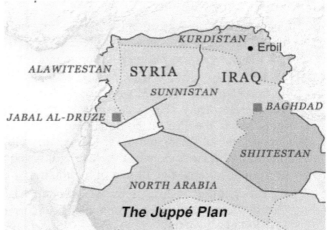

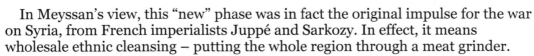

The Juppé Plan

The third phase reverts to the Juppé plan to create a new Kurdish statelet in the northern sector of Syria and Iraq, to balkanize and weaken those countries, as well as the bordering states of Turkey and Iran.

***

In Meyssan's view, this "new" phase was in fact the original impulse for the war on Syria, from French imperialists Juppé and Sarkozy. In effect, it means wholesale ethnic cleansing – putting the whole region through a meat grinder.

The reason that France and the UK are suddenly eager to join the war now is not the Paris attacks, but to dictate the outcome in Syria. Left to Russia, it will be the restoration of Syrian sovereignty. In Iraq, the US recently used its airpower to support the liberation of Sinjar and its Yazidi population from ISIS – and turn it

---

[117] "France and Israël launch a new war in Iraq and Syria," Nov. 23, 2015, http://www.voltairenet.org/article189385.html

over to the Kurds, who are long-time clients of Israel. Amnesty International reports that the Kurds are burning and bulldozing the homes and businesses of Arabs who were driven out by ISIS, and not letting them return.[118] Gordon Duff went so far as to write, "Face It, Iraqi Kurds are ISIS": while fighting ISIS in Kobane, the Kurds are the lifeline of the ISIS oil smuggling. They supply ISIS with oil, transport and contacts with the Erdogan clan and the Turkish mafia.[119]

The Russian intervention turned ISIS into a PR problem for the US, so the US will shift more chips on the Kurdish card. This will make a war so confused and chaotic that we can't keep track of what's going on, giving them cover in plausible deniability again. The FSA has been resurrected under the wing of the Kurds as "Syrian Democratic Forces," to fight – you guessed it, ISIS and Assad. ISIS mercenaries may be expected to come over to the SDF for better pay and safety from Russian airstrikes. – JPL

The unavowable project for a pseudo-Kurdistan

In 2011, Alain Juppé (France) and Ahmet Davutoğlu (Turkey) came to a secret agreement to employ a terrorist organisation (Daesh) to force the creation of a Sunni state and a Kurdistan, both straddling Iraq and Syria. This Juppé plan was to "resolve the Kurdish question" without "damaging the integrity of Turkish territory», in other words, the creation of a pseudo-Kurdistan in Syria.

Only 1% of Syria's population was Kurdish before it took in two million refugees from the Turkish civil war of 1980-90. Turkey now wants to expel the rest of them into a Kurdish enclave carved out of Syria: by colonising the country which has generously sheltered them.[120]

September 2016: The current Kurdistan project, supported by France and the United States, has no connection with the legitimate project which was recognised by the same countries during the Sèvres Conference of 1920. It is not even situated anywhere near the same territory! This pseudo-Kurdistan is no more than a Western bribe intended to turn the Syrian Kurds against Damascus.[121]

Meyssan's analysis proved to be very accurate, as shown by the maneuverings of the US in Syria since the Russian intervention in fall 2015 greatly weakened ISIS. The US is supporting any forces that rival the sovereign government, including ISIS under other names, like Al Nusra.

Tarpley Sees Death Squads, not Freedom Fighters in Syria

Geopolitical scientist Webster Tarpley spent a week in Syria in Nov. 2011 to investigate events on the ground, and he gave a number of interviews on his findings.[122]

---

[118] https://www.rt.com/news/329520-kurds-bulldoze-arabs-iraq/
[119] http://journal-neo.org/2016/01/02/face-it-iraqi-kurds-are-isis/
[120] http://www.voltairenet.org/article189562.html Dec. 7, 2015
[121] http://www.voltairenet.org/article193142.html Sept. 26, 2016
[122] For a full length account see World Crisis Radio, Nov. 26, 2011 "More Truth on Syria" https://vimeo.com/32769466. KPFA's *Guns and Butter* has hour-long interviews from both his Syria and Libya visits: "NATO's Assault On Syria" https://kpfa.org/episode/76242/

Stirring Syria: Mossad vs Assad? 'CIA death squads behind Syria bloodbath'. Russia Today, Nov. 21, 2011.

https://www.rt.com/news/syria-terrorism-cia-destabilization-863/
(highlights of an 8 minute video interview)

The West is doing its best to destabilize the situation in Syria, author and journalist Webster Tarpley told RT. According to him, civilians have to deal with death squads and blind terrorism, which is typical of the CIA.

"What average Syrians of all ethnic groups say about this is that they are being shot at by snipers. People complained that there are terrorist snipers who are shooting at civilians, blind terrorism simply for the purpose of destabilizing the country. I would not call this civil war – it is a very misleading term. What you are dealing with here are death squads, you are dealing with terror commandos; this is a typical CIA method. In this case it's a joint production of CIA, MI6, Mossad, it's got money coming from Saudi Arabia, The United Arab Emirates and Qatar," he explained.

He added that Syrian society is the most tolerant society in the Middle East, the one place where all kinds of people live together in remarkable harmony, Muslims and Christians of all kinds.

"This is a model of a peaceful coexistence of various ethnic groups. The US policy right now is to smash the Middle East according to ethnic lines...

"After Libya becoming a bloodbath with 150,000 dead and now with Egypt showing what it was all along – there was no revolution there, it was a complete failure and now people are beginning to understand ... this bankrupt model of the colour revolution, backed up by terrorist troops – people from Al-Qaeda and the Muslim Brotherhood..."

"What we have here in Syria is a cynical media campaign, because I've been in Homs. When you go to Homs and you go to this Zahra neighborhood which is supposed to be the hottest point in the whole country, you find people who are pro-Assad... They'll say, 'We want the Syrian army to come in here. We want the Syrian army posted on the roofs of the houses with helicopters, and tanks, stop these snipers from killing us.' Don't let these black hooded figures, which is what they are, pretending to be deserters when they're really maybe from Chechnya, they're from Libya, they're from Afghanistan or Pakistan. Foreign fighters have been brought in here by the CIA and the other western services...

Of course when Al Jazeera arrives, they say those deaths are the responsibility of the Syrian army. That is absolute baloney. This is a Goebbels Big Lie campaign, there is no civil war here, there is no insurrection, there is no mass political movement against Assad.

The Embedded Mainstream Media Version

http://www.cnn.com/2011/12/28/world/meast/syria-homs-scene/

"Homs has been the focus of opposition to the regime of President Bashar al-Assad, with almost daily protests since the summer... government snipers prowl the city picking off their victims apparently indiscriminately and at will."

---

and "Report From Tripoli" https://kpfa.org/episode/71085/

Mother Agnes:[123] Witnesses from Homs

In May 2011, Mother Agnes published two witness accounts on the alleged protests in Homs. [124]

Testimony of a Teacher

"The protestors we saw on Palm Sunday were not from Homs. They didn't know their way around in the city, some of them even asked us for directions. A lot of them were children walking around in scruffy sandals which they ended up losing in the streets. These adolescents explained they "were making money". Some of them were given 500 Syrian Pounds (10 USD), others 1000 Syrian Pounds (20 USD) to participate in the protests...

The protestors continued their way, breaking down shops, they knifed passersby and putting tires on fire... people were shot from short range and they were cut up in pieces to cause the greatest fear among the people... Homs was in panic and thousands of people came together to acclaim the name of the President. But the foreign media didn't give any importance to this incident. They attribute all positive protests to "organized schemes" of the regime...

All night we heard them proclaiming frightening slogans: "The front of Homs proclaims the Jihad, people of Homs, to Jihad!" But no inhabitant of Homs joined them.

Testimony of M.S. Student of Qâra, residing in Homs

"On Wednesday, 19th of April I was in Homs... Apart from the protesters I saw well equipped jeeps having large machine guns fixed on the back. The man operating the machine gun was holding down the trigger, spraying bullets with live ammunition at all the shops... some policemen opened fire on the car which skidded off the road. We ran after the car and captured them. They were three. We were astonished to see their inexplicable behavior, they were like drugged. The one operating the machine gun had been struck by a bullet which penetrated deeply in his arm. But he was laughing really hard, insensitive to the pain..."

When gathering testimonies from our friends in various neighborhoods of Damascus... the Palestinian refugee camps which operate a large arms trafficking business... or Daraa, Suwaida, Lattakia and Jezzirah, we hear more or less the same scenarios. The people, adults and younger people, gather when leaving the mosques or on other occasions. They march out in a peaceful demonstration. Within the group there are a few select people who start to arouse the tension. The slogans become more violent and fanatic. At a certain moment these infiltrators begin to commit violent acts: break stores, burn cars, hassle passersby or the police force. The whole of the protestors are not fully aware of the aggressions which take place at the protest. At a certain moment hidden snipers

---

[123] "Mother Superior Agnes Mariam de la Croix ... of the monastery of St James the Mutilated in Syria, a Melkite Greek Catholic monastery in the town of Qara in the Homs diocese. She is outspoken regarding the Syrian Civil War." – Wikipedia

[124] "In the Flood of Disinformation, the Situation in Syria" http://silviacattori.net/article1754.html . The Homs "protestors" were poor folk who had been hired and bussed in from desert villages.

on the roof or people within the crowd start firing on the protestors and the police. Chaos erupts. **The video sequences are shot at that very moment supposedly as evidence that the police force has shot on a peaceful crowd...**

The Homs mosques publically proclaimed: "Jihad! He who wants money, let him come and claim it, we're giving it away". The places where these protests occur are not by chance. They occur in strategic places...

It's evident for impartial observers that this must be a well-thought-out scenario mounted by secret services and orchestrated by global media that have mastery of the use of key, psychologically charged concepts...

Why interfere in Libya in favor of the protestors while in Bahrain they interfered against the protestors? ...

We are far from acknowledging these protests... as the "springtime" of a new political order. On the contrary... we only see a miserable attempt to enroll us in a new fabrication which pleases the masters of the world. And the proof is substantial; we read in the Figaro of the 18th of April that the USA has financed the opposition in Syria.

Gearóid Ó Colmáin

Gearóid Ó Colmáin visited Syria in April 2011. In November of that year he wrote an article, "Unknown Snipers and Western backed 'Regime Change:' A Historical Review and Analysis."[125] It was reprinted in 2014, after the Maidan sniper attacks blamed on Yanukovich toppled the government in Ukraine:

> Unknown snipers played a pivotal role throughout the so-called "Arab Spring Revolutions" yet, in spite of reports of their presence in the mainstream media, surprisingly little attention has been paid to their purpose and role.

> The Russian investigative journalist Nikolay Starikov has written a book which discusses the role of unknown snipers in the destabilization of countries targeted for regime change by the United States and its allies.

Colmáin then lists a series of major historical events when a government was destabilized or overthrown by blaming it for sniper attacks on civilians:

Romania 1989, Russia 1983 (Yeltsin's counter-coup), Venezuela 2002, Thailand and Kyrgyztan 2010, Tunisia, Egypt, Libya and Syria 2011.

Here is what he wrote on Libya and Syria:

Snipers and Western backed 'Regime Change'

During the destabilization of Libya, a video was aired by Al Jazeera purporting to show peaceful "pro-democracy" demonstrators being fired upon by "Gaddafi's forces". The video was edited to convince the viewer that anti-Gaddafi demonstrators were being murdered by the security forces. However, the unedited version of the video is available on youtube. It clearly shows pro-Gaddafi demonstrators with Green flags being fired upon by unknown snipers. The attribution of NATO-linked crimes to the security forces

[125] http://www.globalresearch.ca/unknown-snipers-and-western-backed-regime-change/27904

of the Libyan Jamahirya was a constant feature of the brutal media war waged against the Libyan people.

The people of Syria have been beset by death squads and snipers since the outbreak of violence there in March. Hundreds of Syrian soldiers and security personnel have been murdered, tortured and mutilated by Salafist and Muslim Brotherhood militants. Yet the international media corporations continue to spread the pathetic lie that the deaths are the result Bachar Al Assad's dictatorship.

The people of Syria have been beset by death squads and snipers since the outbreak of violence there in March. Hundreds of Syrian soldiers and security personnel have been murdered, tortured and mutilated by Salafist and Muslim Brotherhood militants. Yet the international media corporations continue to spread the pathetic lie that the deaths are the result Bachar Al Assad's dictatorship.

When I visited Syria in April of this year, I personally encountered merchants and citizens in Hama who told me they had seen armed terrorists roaming the streets of that once peaceful city, terrorizing the neighbourhood. I recall speaking to a fruit seller in the city of Hama who spoke about the horror he had witnessed that day. As he described the scenes of violence to me, my attention was arrested by a newspaper headline in English from the Washington Post shown on Syrian television: "CIA backs Syrian opposition". The Central Intelligence Agency provides training and funding for groups who do the bidding of US imperialist interests. The history of the CIA shows that backing opposition forces means providing them with arms and finance, actions illegal under international law...

Many of the crimes attributed to the Syrian army have been committed by the armed gangs, such as the dumping of mutilated bodies into the river in Hama, presented to the world as more proof of the crimes of the Assad regime...

There is a minority of innocent opponents of the Assad regime who believe everything they see and hear on Al Jazeera and the other pro-Western satellite stations. These people simply do not understand the intricacies of international politics.

But the facts on the ground show that most people in Syria support the government. Syrians have access to all internet websites and international TV channels. They can watch BBC, CNN, Al Jazeera, read the New York Times online or Le Monde before tuning into their own state media. In this respect, many Syrians are more informed about international politics than the average European or American. Most Europeans and American believe their own media. Few are capable of reading the Syrian press in original Arabic or watching Syrian television. The Western powers are the masters of discourse, who own the means of communication. The Arab Spring has been the most horrifying example of the wanton abuse of this power.

Disinformation is effective in sowing the seeds of doubt among those who are seduced by Western propaganda. Syrian state media has disproved hundreds of Al Jazeera lies since the beginning of this conflict. Yet the western media has refused to even report the Syrian government's position, lest fair coverage of the other side of this story encourage a modicum of critical thought in the public mind.

Conclusion.

The use of mercenaries, death squads and snipers by Western intelligence agencies is well documented. No rational government attempting to stay in power would resort to unknown snipers to intimidate its opponents. Shooting at innocent protestors would be counterproductive in the face of unmitigated pressure from Western governments determined to install a client regime in Damascus. Shooting of unarmed protestors is only acceptable in dictatorships that enjoy the unconditional support of Western governments such as Bahrain, Honduras or Colombia.

A government which is so massively supported by the population of Syria would not sabotage its own survival by setting snipers against the protests of a small minority.

The opposition to the Syrian regime is, in fact, miniscule. Tear gas, mass arrests and other non lethal methods would be perfectly sufficient for a government wishing to control unarmed demonstrators.

Snipers are used to create terror, fear and anti-regime propaganda. They are an integral feature of Western sponsored regime change.

If one were to make a serious criticism of the Syrian government over the past few months, it is that they have failed to implement effective anti-terrorism measures in the country. The Syrian people want troops on the streets and the roofs of public buildings.

***

Youtube terminated the account that posted the video Colmáin mentioned, "Censored - Libya - Unidentified Snipers". Videos of Syrian snipers have also disappeared down the Google-Youtube memory hole:

> CIA / Mossad Snipers in Syria
>
> Many members of these death squads have been captured by the Syrian Government and many have confessed in detail their operations, where they received their support, weapons etc. Many have been caught with US produced M40A3 snipers and US openly admits they have supported terrorists in and outside Syria with 50 million (USD).
>
> This video finally shows visual evidence of these US death squads.

(Link at http://counterpsyops.com/2011/12/08/cia-mossad-snipers-in-syria/)

The following video was uploaded to YouTube in July 2011. It is a collection of video footage showing snipers firing from the rooftops of tall buildings in Syrian cities. Towards the end, there is also footage of what appear to be Western agents trying to escape the scene with very high-powered rifles

(link at https://www.sott.net/article/242143-CIA-or-Mossad-Snipers-Caught-in-Syria)

Washington's Blog also commented on the use of snipers: "Brutal ... but effective and cheap. Because it doesn't cost much to hire one or a handful of snipers to access rooftops or bridge overpasses, create chaos, and then quietly disappear."[126]

In the Flood of Disinformation, the Situation in Syria

by Mother Agnès-Mariam de la Croix[127]

May 1, 2011

I work in Syria for the renovation of a monastery from the sixth century that had fallen into ruin...

---

[126] http://www.globalresearch.ca/the-momentum-for-regime-change-snipers-are-commonly-used-as-false-flag-terrorists/5372178
[127] http://silviacattori.net/article1754.html

We receive about 20,000 visitors a year. This rush of people, along with our local network and the regional friendships of the community, permits us to have a quite objective idea of the situation...

The reality that we see here in Syria lies in stark, not subtle but stark contrast to what the news channels choose to highlight...

It is as if there was a new brand of totalitarianism, one that manipulates public opinion on an international scale. It is easy to see that the information reported by the media is thin on fact and heavy on psychology—playing on emotions, preconceptions and images rather than on substance... crafted so as to present a particular image...

Lured by the bait of money or 15 minutes of fame, a lot of images and videos are being transmitted whose content is unexplained and totally open to any and every interpretation. One of our foremen at our monastery showed me a video clip accompanying a popular Arabic song which had been filmed by local Syrian youth. Here we see a group of youth dressed in black and riding in convertible cars, they have guns to make themselves look like security guards. To our great shock this same video was later shown on Al-Jazeera as proof of the "arrogance of the Syrian secret police!"

We would take up a lot of time if we had to go back to all the fictions and psychologically charged 'montages'... the channels succeed in reporting the contrary of what the interviewed persons say...

The *Guardian* refers to a video on YouTube. In this video the interviewer is harassing a wounded soldier to get a forced confession from him stating that he refused to shoot the people. "Question: when you didn't shoot, what happened?" He replies: "Nothing, bullets were coming at us from all directions". But in reality the soldier didn't understand the question because he had just said that he didn't receive orders to shoot the crowd. The interviewer repeats his question in a different way asking: "Why do you shoot at us Muslims?" The soldier responds: "I too am a Muslim". So the interviewer continues: "Why then were you planning to shoot us?" to which the soldier replies: "We didn't shoot the people, we were being shot at out of nowhere." ...

Since all the major channels are saying basically the same things at the same time, everything passes under the false flag of objectivity. Somehow it has been decided that the Arab people must revolt and blindly change their regime whatever the cost...

Not later than yesterday a truck was intercepted which contained weapons, it passed by our monastery which is between the border and the village of Qâra. Since the sixties the Sunni fundamentalists have been trying to grow within the womb of Arab regimes. Held back by these regimes the Muslim Brotherhood and the Salafist jihadists have formed **secret networks which these last years have been filled by unemployed youth. Some of them in our village are being enrolled to fight on the side of al-Qaeda in Iraq and have been killed.** We've known that what were thought to be simple Egyptian workers, Jordanian residents, Lebanese or refugee Iraqis are in fact members of "sleeper cells" which are gradually equipping themselves for a scenario where the regime is brutally toppled. These networks are widely spread over several bases, and they are funded or trained by the secret services of certain great powers and some Arab countries.

Daraa, the Spark of the Firestorm

Robert Fisk: "Despite the narrative now peddled in the West, armed men were present on the streets of Syrian cities and villages since the very early days of the Syrian awakening [i.e., nightmare] 18 months ago."[128]

To get a clear understanding of what set off the Syria crisis, it is best to focus on the earliest acts that incited it. Later, in the cycle of reprisals and the fog of full-scale war, it is hard to see who shot first.

The earliest outbreaks of protests and killings occurred in the town of Daraa on the border with Jordan, in March, 2011. A close look at these events shows that *from the start, this was a war of violent aggression by islamist extremist fanatics against a stable secular government*.

There never ever was an early uprising of democratic dreamers, yearning yuppies or any such photogenic forces which was then hijacked by ISIS and other bushy-bearded RPG-toting rag-heads, screaming "Allah al-akbar, God is Great," on camera for each atrocity they commit. The Syria War (2011-20??) was a straight update of the same old Moslem Brotherhood insurgency against Ba'athist Syrian nationalism; Assad the Elder had crushed their rebellion in 1982.

Accounts by several authors of the Ides of March, 2011, follow here.

The day before Deraa: How the war broke out in Syria

By Steven Sahounie to the *American Herald Tribune*, Aug. 10, 2016[129]

Deraa was teeming with activity and foreign visitors to Syria well before the staged uprising began its opening act.

The Omari Mosque was the scene of backstage preparations, costume changes and rehearsals. The Libyan terrorists, fresh from the battlefield of the US-NATO regime change attack on Libya, were in Deraa well ahead of the March 2011 uprising of violence. The cleric of the Omari Mosque was Sheikh Ahmad al Sayasneh ...

The participation of local Muslim Brotherhood followers, who would assist the foreign Libyan mercenaries/terrorists, was an essential part of the CIA plan, which was well scripted and directed from Jordan... The local men were the 'front' for the operation...

In reality, the uprising in Deraa in March 2011 was not fueled by graffiti written by teenagers, and there were no disgruntled parents demanding their children to be freed. That was part of the Hollywood-style script written by skilled CIA agents, who had been given a mission: to destroy Syria for the purpose of regime change. Deraa was only Act 1: Scene 1...

The staged uprising in Deraa had some locals in the street who were unaware of their participation in a CIA-Hollywood production. They were the unpaid extras in the scene about to be shot...

---

[128] http://www.independent.co.uk/voices/commentators/fisk/robert-fisk-the-bloody-truth-about-syrias-uncivil-war-8081386.html
[129] http://ahtribune.com/world/north-africa-south-west-asia/syria-crisis/1135-day-before-deraa.html

The Libyans stockpiled weapons at the Omari Mosque well before any rumor spread about teenagers arrested for graffiti. The cleric, visually impaired and elderly, was unaware of the situation inside his Mosque, or of the foreign infiltrators in his midst.

The weapons came into Deraa from the CIA office in Jordan. The US government has close ties to the King of Jordan...

Deraa's location directly on the Jordanian border is the sole reason it was picked for the location-shoot of the opening act of the Syrian uprising... The access to the weapons from Jordan made Deraa the perfect place to stage the uprising which has turned into an international war. Any person with common sense would assume an uprising or revolution in Syria would begin in Damascus or Aleppo, the two biggest cities. Even after 2 ½ years of violence around the country, Aleppo's population never participated in the uprising, or called for regime change. Aleppo: the large industrial powerhouse of Syria wanted nothing to do with the CIA mission...

The weapons were all supplied by the United States of America, from their warehouse at the dock of Benghazi, Libya. The US-NATO regime change mission had ended in success in Libya, with America having taken possession of all the weapons and stockpiles formerly the property of the Libyan government, including tons of gold bullion taken by the US government from the Central Bank of Libya.

Shortly before the Deraa staged uprising began, Brad Pitt and Angelina Jolie were in Damascus and being driven around by the President and First Lady. Pitt and Jolie had come to visit and support the Iraqi war refugees in Damascus. Brad Pitt was amazed that the Syrian President would drive him around personally, and without any body guards or security detail. Pitt and Jolie were used to their own heavy security team in USA. Pres. Assad explained that he and his wife were comfortable in Damascus, knowing that it was a safe place. Indeed, the association of French travel agents had deemed Syria as the safest tourist destination in the entire Mediterranean region, meaning even safer than France itself.

However, the US strategy was to create a "New Middle East", which would do away with safety in Syria; through the ensuing tornado, aka 'winds of change'.

Tunisia, Libya, Egypt and then Syria were the stepping stones in the garden of the "Arab Spring"...

We can't under-estimate the role that mainstream media had to play in the destruction of Syria. For example, Al Jazeera's Rula Amin was in Deraa and personally interviewed the cleric Sayasneh at the Omari Mosque. Al Jazeera is the state-owned and operated media for the Prince of Qatar. The Prince of Qatar was one of the key funders of the terrorists attacking Syria. The USA was sending the weapons, supplies and providing military satellite imagery, however the cash to make payroll, to pay out bribes in Turkey, and all other expenses which needed cold cash in hand was being paid out by the Prince of Qatar and the King of Saudi Arabia, who were playing their roles as closest Middle East allies of the United States of America. This was a production team between USA, EU, NATO, Turkey, Jordan, Israel and the Persian Gulf Arab monarchies of Saudi Arabia and Qatar primarily. The CIA has no problem with covert operations in foreign countries, and even full scale attacks, but the matter of funding needs to come from a foreign country, because the American voters don't care about killing people in Syria, but they would never agree to pay for it...

Rula Amin and others of the Al Jazeera staff, and including the American CNN, the British BBC and the French France24 all began a deliberate political propaganda campaign against the Syrian government and the Syrian people, who were suffering from the death and destruction brought on by the terrorists who were pretending to be players in a local uprising...

The actual Syrians living inside Syria, who read in English online, were baffled. Syrians were wondering how Western writers could take the side of the terrorists who were foreigners, following Radical Islam and attacking any unarmed civilian who tried to defend their home and family. The media was portraying the terrorists as freedom fighters and heroes of democracy, while they were raping, looting, maiming, kidnapping for ransom and murdering unarmed civilians who had not read the script before the shooting began in Deraa. There was one global movie trailer, and it was a low budget cell phone video which went viral around the world, and it sold the viewers on the idea of Syria being in the beginning of a dramatic fight for freedom, justice and the American way. From the very beginning, Al Jazeera and all the rest of the media were paying $100.00 for any amateur video shot in Syria. A whole new cottage industry sprang up in Syria, with directors and actors all hungry for the spotlight and fame. Authenticity was not questioned; the media just wanted content which supported their propaganda campaign in Syria.

The Sheikh who Shook the World

The Blind Leading the Blind

"Since the very first moment when I ascended the rostrum of Al-Omari mosque in Deraa, I called for a revolution against the unjust regime... Jihad against the Assad regime and its gang is an obligation on everyone— Muslim or non-Muslim, the Syrians, and all people all over the world." [130] *– The Blind Sheikh Ahmad al Sayasneh, imam of the Omari Mosque in Daraa.*

Until the protests of March 18, 2011, Sayasneh was banned from preaching his message of Jihad hate against the state.

Through a mutual acquaintance I struck up a correspondence with a Syrian writer who had lived in Daraa until shortly before the outbreak of hostilities there. The following is his report on the "spark of Daraa," based partly on information from people he knew there, and partly his own conversations with visitors to Daraa, who related some aspects of the operation during its preparation.

This report differs from the preceding one by Steven Sahounie in one respect: that the blind sheikh was not so blind to the operation being launched under his nose in the Omari mosque. On the contrary, the Imam Sayasneh had personally adopted about 200 poor youths and trained them as fanatics and fighters, perhaps on the lines of Hasan al-Sabah and his legendary crew of Assassins.

130

http://www.syrianobserver.com/EN/Features/26086/Jihad+Against+Assad+is+a+Must+for+Muslims+and+NonMuslims+a+Deraa+sheikh+says

According to this account, the anti-government graffiti action by teenagers in late February 2011 was a planned provocation. The youngsters were members of the two major Muslim Brotherhood (MB) families of Daraa. After they were arrested, the Imams of the MB and Al Nusra gave sermons at Friday prayers calling for mass protests. Extremists took this as a call to start an uprising, and torched a number of government buildings. Then, with Al Jazeera cameras in place, snipers fired on the protest marchers, making it appear like an unprovoked and bloody repression.

The snipers who killed the police and the protesters during the uproar, according to this report, were fanatical followers of Imam Sayasneh, and this fact was widely known in Daraa. After the incendiary sermon, they put on masks and police or army uniforms, took their guns which were stored in the mosques, and went up on the roofs. From there they fired on and killed four members of the two powerful MB families of the town.

These killings and the constant calls to jihad from the pulpit were the fuel that set Daraa and the whole country on fire. MB sleeper cells throughout the country awoke now, after the long wait for the call to avenge their defeat in the 1982 uprising in Hama. Al Jazeera broadcast its inverted version of events, inciting a violent reaction among many more Syrian Muslims who believed the lies. However, the protests were never broad-based, even in Daraa, where even the largest demonstration never gathered more than 5,000 protestors.

President Assad sent a delegation to Daraa to make generous concessions and efforts at reconciliation, and the teenagers who had sprayed graffiti were released. The army was ordered to withdraw and not to shoot, but the peacemakers themselves came under attack; many police and soldiers were killed. The gangs committed various crimes which were blamed on "regime forces." They killed soldiers and hung their heads at the entrances to the city.

Syria had a large military presence in Daraa, around 12,000 troops, because it is the front line in any potential conflict with Israel. The Syrian Army stopped the Israeli tank offensive here in the 1973 war, and people still talk about those tank battles. So Assad could easily have crushed the militants, but he chose to seek reconciliation. He met all the demands of the protestors, including the release of prisoners. The extremists and the freed prisoners took advantage of the withdrawal of the army to seize the city center, and proclaim an Islamic Emirate of Daraa. They stormed the army barracks, killed hundreds of soldiers, took tons of weapons and many hostages to exchange for prisoners of the Muslim Brotherhood , the Fatah al-Islam and Jund al-Sham terrorist groups.

Sheikh Sayasneh recruited 4,000 young men, offering them a salary and military training in Jordan, at the camp run by Blackwater and Jordanian intelligence. The "opposition" then claimed these young men had been kidnapped and disappeared by the "Assad regime." Blackwater had its operations base just a couple miles from the border. Sheik Sayasneh had close ties to Jordan and Qatar, and was generously funded by them. In January 2012 the Arab League inspectors helped him escape to Jordan, where he stayed a year before moving to Qatar.

Sayasneh issued a fatwa that the Assad regime are Zionists and infidels and that it is the duty of Muslims to oppose them, when of course the great collaborators with Zionism are the rulers of Jordan and Qatar.

Sayasneh's active role is corroborated by Syrian government reports on confessions of arrested terrorists in Daraa.

Televised Confessions of Captured Terrorists[131]

27 April 2011. DAMASCUS. The Syrian Television on Wednesday broadcast confessions of two members of two terrorist organizations... Ahmad Mohammad Hussein, a member of an extremist terrorist cell that was arrested in Daraa, admitted to assaulting the army and security forces and opening fire on passing cars on Daraa highway on Monday... he said that on Monday he heard a voice from a mosque calling the people of al-Gharia to jihad, saying "your brothers are being killed in Daraa and you are sitting..."

He said that the sheikh instructed them to climb atop buildings and hide as not to be seen, and when the army arrives they would throw the gasoline bottles at them... "some of the groups on the barrier had machineguns, automatic rifles, pump-action shotguns, pistols..."

He went on to say that sheikh Walid brought the weapons from sheikh Ahmad al-Sayasneh who affirmed to them that those who kill the army and security forces and work to change the system are martyrs...

"Sheikh Walid Majed al-Munawer has been calling people to jihad for a month, saying that when they call for jihad they must be stationed here and must be martyred in dying for the sake of God," Hussein concluded...

In Lattakia, Ghassan Selwaya, a member of an extremist terrorist organization that committed murder and vandalism against the army, security and forces and innocent citizens in the government, confessed...

"A man came to us and said that there are protests on Friday at Khaled bin al-Walid mosque... we said that we're ready but we want weapons... he provided us with the weapons we used against the army, security forces and the citizens," Selwaya said.

He said that the protests they participated in were called "peaceful" in order for nothing to touch them, but in fact they were armed, concluded by saying "we used weapons... we opened fire on the security and the army to kill them."

The Syrian Television broadcast pictures of youths carrying weapons during a protest. The pictures were on Selwaya's mobile phone who said that these pictures were of him and his accomplices when they were killing and assaulting during the protests.

Earlier on Tuesday, Syrian Television broadcast confessions of Mustafa bin Yousef Khalifa Aiyash, who was arrested in Daraa being a member of the extremist terrorist cell... Khalifa Aiyash said he lives in Manshiyat Al Balad in Daraa and was seeing people go to Al Omari Mosque in the city and participate and meet a group of sheikhs (religious men), among them he mentioned skeikh Ahmad Al Sayasneh...

---

[131] "Members of Extremist Terrorist Cell were arrested in Syria," DayPress, http://www.dp-news.com/en/detail.aspx?articleid=81969

Khalifa Aiyash added that some of those sheikhs were calling for calming the situation. "Others, however, were calling for 'Jihad' saying that those who are facing us are 'Zionists' and everybody who dies while confronting them will be considered 'a martyr'."

"Among those was someone called Ibrahim Al Nayef Masalmeh who gave me SYP 50,000 [$100] and asked me to answer the call to 'Jihad'," Khalifa Aiyash said.

"Ibrahim Masalmeh promised me SYP 1 million [$2000] which I will get after the end of the demonstration..." said Khalifa Aiyash, pointing out that large amounts of weapons were available and there were more than 500 people involved.

Syria: how the violence began, in Daraa

An excellent overview by Tim Anderson[132]

"The claim that armed opposition to the government has begun only recently is a complete lie. The killings of soldiers, police and civilians, often in the most brutal circumstances, have been going on virtually since the beginning." – Professor Jeremy Salt, October 2011 (Ankara)

There is no doubt that there was popular agitation in Syria in early 2011, after the events in Egypt and Tunisia. There were anti-government and pro-government demonstrations, and a genuine political reform debate. However the serious violence that erupted in March 2011 has been systematically misreported, in line with yet another US-NATO "regime change" agenda.

For many months the big powers and the corporate media pretended that armed opposition in Syria did not exist at all. All violence was government forces against "peaceful protestors". In the words of the US-based Human Rights Watch (strongly linked to the US Council on Foreign Relations), "protestors only used violence against the security forces" in response to killings by the security forces or "as a last resort". This was a dreadful deceit. Washington and its allies (Saudi Arabia, Qatar, Turkey and some elements in Lebanon) were sponsoring armed attacks within Syria from the very beginning.

With the revelations of foreign Islamist fighters in Syria, engaged in kidnappings, torture and executions, we can see a "revised imperial line". These "jihadis" or "Al Qaeda" groups are said to be "on the fringes" of the rebel "Free Syrian Army" (FSA), which is said to be led by defectors from the Syrian Arab Army. An alternative line is that the genuine "revolution" is in danger of being "hijacked" by the fundamentalists.

Daraa: the killings begin

In February 2011 some anti-government demonstrations began. They were met in March with even larger pro-government demonstrations. In early March some teenagers in Daraa were arrested for graffiti that had been copied from North

---

[132] http://www.opednews.com/articles/Syria-how-the-violence-be-by-Tim-Anderson-130513-875.html

Africa "the people want to overthrow the regime". It was reported that they were abused by local police. Time magazine reported that President Assad intervened, the local governor was sacked and the teenagers were released.

What followed is highly contested. The western media version is that protestors burned and trashed government offices and that "provincial security forces opened fire on marchers, killing several" (Time, 22 March). After that, "protestors" staged demonstrations in front of the al-Omari mosque, but were in turn attacked. The western media exaggerated the demonstrations, claiming crowds of up to 300,000, with 15 anti-government "protesters" killed (AP 23 March). Daraa is a border town with 150,000 inhabitants.[133]

The Syrian government, on the other hand, stated that armed attacks had begun on security forces, killing several police, along with the burning of government offices. There was corroboration of this account. While its headline blamed security forces for killing "protesters", the British Daily Mail showed pictures of guns, AK47 rifles and hand grenades that security forces had recovered after storming the al-Omari mosque. The paper noted reports that "an armed gang" had opened fire on an ambulance, killing "a doctor, a paramedic and a policeman".

Israeli and Lebanese media gave versions of the events of 17-18 March closer to that of the Syrian government. An Israel National News report (21 March) said "Seven police officers and at least four demonstrators in Syria have been killed "and the Baath party headquarters and courthouse were torched". The police had been targeted by rooftop snipers.

Al Jazeera (29 April), owned by Qatar's royal family, implied the rooftop snipers in Daraa were government forces. "President Bashar al Assad has sent thousands of Syrian soldiers and their heavy weaponry into Deraa for an operation the regime wants nobody in the world to see". However the Al Jazeera claim that secret police snipers were killing "soldiers and protestors alike" was both illogical and out of sequence.

The armed forces came to Daraa precisely because police had been killed by snipers. Once in Daraa they engaged in more gun-fire and stormed the local mosque to seize the guns and grenades stored by "protesters". Michel Chossudovsky wrote: "The deployment of armed forces including tanks in Daraa [was] directed against an organised armed insurrection, which has been active in the border city since March 17-18."

Saudi Arabia, a key US regional ally, had armed and funded extremist Sunni sects (Salafists and Wahabis) to move against the secular government. From exile in Saudi Arabia, Sheikh Adnan Arour called for a holy war against the liberal Allawi muslims, who dominated the government: "by Allah we shall mince them in meat grinders and feed their flesh to the dogs". The Salafist aim was a theocratic sate or "caliphate". Sheikh Muhammed al Zughbey said the Alawites were "more infidel than the Jews and the Christians". The original North African slogan was rapidly replaced by a Salafist slogan "Christians to Beirut, Alawites to the grave". They would soon act on these threats.

---

[133] According to the 2004 census, Daraa City had a population of 98,000; while the metropolitan area had 146,000.

Saudi official Anwar Al-Eshki later confirmed to BBC television that arms had indeed been provided to groups within Syria, and they had stored them in the al-Omari mosque.

While the Syrian Baathist system has been authoritarian, it has also been secular and inclusive. The Saudi-Qatari and US-NATO backed armed insurgency aims to derail the reform program led by President Bashar al-Assad. If a more compliant government cannot be formed in Damascus, the big powers will probably settle for a country mired in sectarian chaos. That is, after all, what we see across the border in Iraq.

Tim Anderson on parallels with the 1982 Hama insurrection[134]

In early 2011 Syrians were well aware of a piece of history few western observers would remember: a strikingly similar Islamist insurrection took place in the town of Hama, back in 1982...

US intelligence (DIA 1982) and the late British author Patrick Seale (1988) give independent accounts of what happened at Hama. After years of violent, sectarian attacks by Syria's Muslim Brotherhood, by mid-1980 President Hafez al Assad had 'broken the back' of their sectarian rebellion, which aimed to impose a Salafi-Islamic state. One final coup plot was exposed and the Brotherhood 'felt pressured into initiating' an uprising in their stronghold of Hama. Seale describes the start of that violence in this way:

> 'At 2am on the night of 2-3 February 1982 an army unit combing the old city fell into an ambush. Roof top snipers killed perhaps a score of soldiers ... [Brotherhood leader] Abu Bakr [Umar Jawwad] gave the order for a general uprising ... hundreds of Islamist fighters rose ... by the morning some seventy leading Ba'athists had been slaughtered and the triumphant guerrillas declared the city 'liberated' (Seale 1988: 332).

However the Army responded with a huge force of about 12,000 and the battle raged for three weeks...

Two months later a US intelligence report said: 'The total casualties for the Hama incident probably number about 2,000. This includes an estimated 300 to 400 members of the Muslim Brotherhood's elite 'Secret Apparatus' (DIA 1982: 7). Seale recognises that the Army also suffered heavy losses...

[But if you google on Hama 1982, what comes up is the Hama Massacre, not the Hama Insurrection, naturally.]

> 'The guerrillas were formidable opponents. They had a fortune in foreign money ... [and] no fewer than 15,000 machine guns' (Seale 1988: 335). Subsequent Muslim Brotherhood accounts have inflated the casualties, reaching up to '40,000 civilians', and attempting to hide the vicious insurrection by claiming that Hafez al Assad had simply carried out a 'civilian massacre' (e.g. Nassar 2014). The then Syrian President blamed a large scale foreign conspiracy for the Hama insurrection. Seale observes that Hafez was 'not paranoical', as many US weapons were captured and foreign backing had come from several US collaborators: King Hussayn of Jordan, Lebanese Christian militias (the Israeli-aligned 'Guardians of the Cedar') and Saddam Hussein in Iraq (Seale 1988: 336-337).

---

[134] http://www.globalresearch.ca/daraa-2011-syrias-islamist-insurrection-in-disguise/5460547

[Nothing new under the sun!]

The Dirty War on Syria[135]

Who pulled the trigger first? Who had the motive and the plan?

A favorite opposition argument is that peaceful protesters restrained themselves for a long time, until the "brutal crack-down by the Assad regime" stoked their rage and they started to fight back. However, the facts show that violence began almost from the start, so quickly that it is very hard to figure out who fired first. Michel Chossudovsky of Global Research analysed the evidence in a May 2011 article, "Syria: Who is Behind The Protest Movement? Fabricating a Pretext for a US-NATO 'Humanitarian Intervention." He writes,

> The Western media has presented the events in Syria as part of the broader Arab pro-democracy protest movement, spreading spontaneously from Tunisia, to Egypt, and from Libya to Syria.
>
> Media coverage has focused on the Syrian police and armed forces, which are accused of indiscriminately shooting and killing unarmed "pro-democracy" demonstrators... what the media failed to mention is that among the demonstrators there were armed gunmen as well as snipers who were shooting at both the security forces and the protesters.[136]

Chossudovsky notes that the protests started not in Damascus, where the authentic internal opposition is based, but in Daraa (or Deraa), a small town of 75,000 souls on the border with Jordan. The pattern has held throughout – the FSA always concentrates on targets near borders, as they must be supplied from foreign countries.

The first fatalities in Daraa were seven policemen and four armed protesters, in March 2011. Some or all of the dead may have been shot by mysterious snipers on rooftops, who were shooting at BOTH police and protesters. In Syrian state TV footage *used by the BBC*, it says on the screen, "You are seeing gunmen shooting at unarmed civilians and security forces." When Tarpley visited Homs in November 2011, he found that all the victims were shot by snipers, while the army had orders not to shoot.

Why shoot at both sides? To stoke enmity and violence between the two sides. What would be the motive? For violent elements to take over the protest movement and overthrow the state. The last thing any government wants, be it a dictator or a democracy, would be civil war.

In other words, as the BBC themselves put it in their emotion-charged video "Inside the Secret Revolution," the snipers were "agents provocateur." But the Beeb claims these provocateurs were plainclothes government thugs – the "Shabiha." The word means "spooks," and refers to a gang of Latakia port smugglers, among them a nephew of Hafez Assad, during the 70's and '80s. He suppressed them in the 90s, and they were disbanded in 2000. Some of them might have then been recruited by the CIA. Syria participated in the CIA

---

[135] From the blog, by John-Paul Leonard, Aug. 26, 2012 http://progressivepress.com/blog/dirty-war-syria

[136] http://www.globalresearch.ca/syria-who-is-behind-the-protest-movement-fabricating-a-pretext-for-a-us-nato-humanitarian-intervention/24591

rendition (torture outsourcing) program, and the Turkish Gladio unit, Ergenekon, was also involved in smuggling.

Drumbeaters for war on Syria have blamed terrorist killings on the Shabiha. Yet there is very little evidence for their "ghostly" existence (other than the usual "unconfirmed activist reports" and dubious videos).

The last thing any government wants, be it a dictator or a democracy, is a civil war. The Syrian regime was doing what any state does, to try and maintain law and order, not to pour oil on flames and engulf themselves. Rather than "cracking down," the authorities immediately tried to calm the situation by offering to release the students who had been arrested, but the mobs went ahead and set fire to government buildings. Were they paid or incited to do this?

The Biased Broadcasting Corporation, or BBC

The BBC don't try to explain why the government would want to provoke violence. We know, however, from the US Unconventional Warfare manual TC 18-01, that the US does use this kind of violent destabilization tactic. The BBC then present a "witness" (with face dramatically hidden from the camera), allegedly a Syrian army defector. His wild tale would have fetched a good price on the Lebanese border (where foreign journalists pay for stories to feed the MSM war propaganda mill). Officers allegedly ordered their men at gunpoint to shoot, saying, "Don't shoot the 'armed groups,' they are with us. There are no rebels, no conspirators, just the people. Shoot the people." According to this Hollywood-cartoon-villain self-indictment, the officers shot dead seven men because they had refused to shoot the protesters! A shocking but inherently absurd script with a slick presentation that still makes a strong impression.

A month later, as the army occupies Daraa to try to restore order, Al-Jazeera reports this hellish scenario: people don't dare to go in the streets because "plain clothes thugs and secret police" snipers on rooftops are shooting both civilians and soldiers. Based on "unconfirmed activist reports" – but how would they know who these snipers are working for? No government would choose to destabilize its own regime.

Anyway, why did the Assad regime start randomly shooting citizens the day death-squad honcho Robert Ford arrived? Were they "in cahoots?" In the section "Eyewitness Reports" we see that the Syrian people blamed outside terrorists and wanted the army to protect them.

Deraa, April 2011. Unidentified gunmen.

This Associated Press footage shows the snipers were still at it in April, looking just like tramps on a grassy knoll.

Freelance journalist Alaa Ebrahim:

> I've been to Daraa for the better part of April and May 2011... The four people who were killed in the first protests in Daraa: I've interviewed protesters who were along with them, and I've interviewed security officers and policemen who were at the scene... Something that all the people that I have interviewed have agreed upon is they don't know who shot at the protesters who were killed the first day. Protesters have told me that the shooting took place from a high place over a water tank in the city, and they couldn't identify the people who were shooting.[137]

Syrian media showed demonstrations of millions of people against US intervention – practically the whole able-bodied population was out on the streets waving the real Syrian flag. Western media ignored that, and made a big show over tiny anti-Assad protests, numbering a few knots of people, at most a couple hundred, many of them likely hired, hungry beggars.

The media with their fakery are absolutely guilty of enabling these war crimes, which could never occur without their "coverage" (or rather, coverups.)

Review of *Syria: The Flood* - 57 minute documentary

Oct 3, 2013 http://www.youtube.com/watch?v=cMCWVQ3avWg

The first few minutes of The Flood are an absolute must-watch. The film opens with interviews from participants in the early stages of protest, telling how the poor and desperate were paid to go to demonstrations, how the numbers were greatly exaggerated, how snipers shot people and police to provoke an explosion. To create the impression of a general strike, they forced shopkeepers to close their shops at gunpoint.

Later testimony covers the funding by Saudis, Qataris and others, and some of the criminal acts of the brigands such as kidnapping, rape, car bombs, smuggling weapons, killing prisoners, stealing cars at gunpoint to sell them. They advance to destroying infrastructure, hospitals, plundering storehouses, homes and shops, until the inhabitants

---

[137] Lizzie Phelan and Mostafa Afzalzadeh, "Manufacturing Dissent: The Truth About Syria," GlobalResearchTV, Oct. 15, 2013, https://www.youtube.com/watch?v=RtYvDCEKKTY . Image: Screen shot of AP footage of snipers at 4:38 .

fled as refugees. Dismantling factories and selling the machines to Turkey to buy arms, which they smuggled into Syria over back roads. Some of the weapons received were from Saudi Arabia or Israel. Gangsters taking Islamic names to get funds from Saudis, who come and lecture them on Jihad, the houris, and pay them princely wages.

Mossad instructors trained brigades on how to take out Syrian air defenses. Now the goal was to destroy the Syrian Arab Army, to allow Israel and the USA to invade Syria without resistance. Saudi emirs gave them orders to attack military bases, airports and missile sites and plunder the weapons and missiles. They were given complete details of the targets and instructions how to attack. The missiles were taken to a hiding place where Turkish and Libyan experts were there to advise. While dismantling one missile to get the explosive, it and 2 other missiles exploded, causing great damage, which the rebels blamed on a Syrian Army helicopter barrel bomb. Their work helped Israel target the research center near Damascus, an unprovoked act of aggression.

But the rebels couldn't succeed on their own, so the Zionist axis had to intervene directly to destroy Syria, the last citadel of Arab resistance. In the final minutes the witnesses express immense regret, "We received money from abroad to destroy our homeland with our own hands." "We thought we were doing the best for our homeland, but it turns out we were destroying it." "They deceived us in the name of religion."

The Not so Independent *Independent*?

Posted by John-Paul Leonard in the Dirty War on Syria blog,[138] August 25, 2012

Dear Mr Fisk,

I'd like to ask if in repeating that "the revolt began after secret police officers tortured to death a 13-year-old boy," have you checked into this or are you trusting the media – the corrupt warmongering mainstream media? There are two sides to every story and every time I dig out the Syrian side, I find that the tale put out everywhere by the CIA-trained FSA is a Big Lie.

In the case of Hamza al Khateeb, he was 17, not 13, and he was not arrested and tortured for writing graffiti. He joined an armed mob that was firing at a police station, and was killed by three bullets – whether fired by the police or perhaps even by provocateurs, commandos tasked with stoking violence. The cause of death – gunshot wounds, and not torture – was established by the coroner before it was known who Hamza was. His body was taken from the scene of the shootings directly to the hospital.

The Syrian government narrative "True Story of Hamza al-Khateeb's Death Belies Media Fabrications" can be found online as well as a youtube video "Medical Examiner Interview about Hamza Al-Khateeb."

I think you too, the more you dig into the Syria story, the more you will find it is a dirty war based on a Big Lie against a small, proud, nation that dares to be INDEPENDENT.

---

[138] https://rickrozoff.wordpress.com/2012/08/26/the-dirty-war-on-syria/

Statements by Statesmen

Excerpts from Vladimir Putin's speeches.

At the 12th annual meeting, themed "Societies Between War and Peace: Overcoming the Logic of Conflict in Tomorrow's World," Valdai Club, Sochi, Russia, Oct. 22, 2015

Success in fighting terrorists cannot be reached if using some of them as a battering ram to overthrow disliked regimes...

Why play with words dividing terrorists into moderate and not moderate. What's the difference? in the opinion of some experts... so-called moderate bandits behead people moderately

We are being criticized for allegedly hitting wrong targets. Tell us which targets are correct, if you know. But they keep silence. Tell us which targets we must not hit — they also refuse to.

Speech to Western journalists at the Valdai Club, Oct. 15, 2015[139]

Another threat that President Obama mentioned was ISIS. Well who on earth armed them? Who armed the Syrians that were fighting with Assad? Who created the necessary political-informational climate that facilitated this situation? Who pushed for the delivery of arms to the area? Do you really not understand who is fighting in Syria? They are mercenaries, mostly. Do you understand they are paid money? Mercenaries fight for whichever side pays most. So they arm them and pay them a certain amount. I even know what these amounts are. So they fight, they have the arms, you can't get them to return the weapons of course, at the end...

Then they discover elsewhere pays a little more... so they go fight there. Then they occupy the oil fields – wherever; in Iraq, in Syria. They start extracting the oil – this oil is purchased by somebody. Where are the sanctions on the parties purchasing this oil? Do you believe the US does not know who is buying it? Is it not their allies that are buying oil from ISIS? Do you not think the US has the power to influence their allies? Or is the point that they indeed do not wish to influence them? Then why bomb ISIS?

In areas where they started extracting oil and paying mercenaries more – in those areas, the rebels from the "civilized" Syrian opposition forces immediately joined ISIS because they are paid more...

When it comes to the consideration of our national interests I would really like it if people like you who posed the questions, would one day head your government. Maybe then we can somehow reverse the situation. If that doesn't happen, I will at least ask you to deliver my messages to your government... Tell them that we do not want, or look for, any confrontation whatsoever. When you start to consider our national interests in your actions any other disagreements we may have – they will self-regulate. This needs to be done, not just talked about.

---

[139] "Banned in USA: Putin explains who supports ISIS," transcript in comment by Beth Ashe, https://www.youtube.com/all_comments?v=W_uBmoPZOwc

You must consider the interests of others and you must respect other people. You cannot "squeeze" others, having considered only the benefits that you require from whatever... in economics; in your military activities, in everything. Look at Iraq, the situation is terrible... Look at Libya and what you did there, that got your Ambassador murdered. Was it us that did this? You even had a Security Council decision for this – to establish a no fly zone. What for? It was so Gaddafi's airforce couldn't fly over and bomb the rebels. This wasn't the smartest decision. But okay... What did you proceed to do yourselves?

You started bombing the territory. This is in clear contravention of the Security Council resolution. It is even outright aggression over a state. Was it us that did this? You did this with your bare hands and it ended with the murder of your Ambassador... do not look around for somebody to blame when it is you making these mistakes. You must do the opposite; rise above the endless desire to dominate. You must stop acting out of imperialistic ambitions. Do not poison the consciousness of millions of people; like there can be no other way but imperialistic politics.

We will never forget our relationship when we supported the US in the War of Independence. We will never forget that we collaborated in both World Wars, as allies. I personally believe that the geostrategic interests of Russia and the US are essentially the same. We must focus on this interrelationship.

[Editor's comment. The Tsar supported the US in the War of Independence and in the Civil War both for ideological reasons – sympathy for democracy – and strategic reasons – the enmity of Britain, which always was busy to crush rival powers. Russia's historical support is never mentioned in the US school curriculum. Fifty years ago, we were still taught that the British "redcoats" were the enemy, but now that has been scrubbed too. The problem is that US "leaders" are not working in our interests, but for foreign taskmasters.]

Speech to the United Nations, Sept. 28, 2015

We also remember certain episodes from the history of the Soviet Union. Social experiments for export, attempts to push for changes within other countries based on ideological preferences, often led to tragic consequences and to degradation rather than progress.

It seemed, however, that far from learning from others' mistakes, everyone just keeps repeating them, and so the export of revolutions, this time of so-called democratic ones, continues. It would suffice to look at the situation in the Middle East and North Africa...

Rather than bringing about reforms, an aggressive foreign interference has resulted in a brazen destruction of national institutions and the lifestyle itself. Instead of the triumph of democracy and progress, we got violence, poverty and social disaster. Nobody cares a bit about human rights, including the right to life.

I cannot help asking those who have caused the situation, do you realize now what you've done? But I am afraid no one is going to answer that. Indeed, policies based on self-conceit and belief in one's exceptionality and impunity have never been abandoned.

It is now obvious that the power vacuum created in some countries of the Middle East and North Africa through the emergence of areas of anarchy, which immediately started to be filled with extremists and terrorists.

Tens of thousands of militants are fighting under the banners of the so-called Islamic State. Its ranks include former Iraqi servicemen who were thrown out into the street after the invasion of Iraq in 2003. Many recruits also come from Libya, a country whose statehood was destroyed as a result of a gross violation of the U.N. Security Council Resolution 1973. And now, the ranks of radicals are being joined by the members of the so-called moderate Syrian opposition supported by the Western countries.

First, they are armed and trained and then they defect to the so-called Islamic State. Besides, the Islamic State itself did not just come from nowhere. It was also initially forged as a tool against undesirable secular regimes.

Having established a foothold in Iraq and Syria, the Islamic State has begun actively expanding to other regions. It is seeking dominance in the Islamic world.

Speech to the Valdai International Discussion Club, Oct. 24, 2014

Instead of sovereign and stable states we see the growing spread of chaos, and instead of democracy there is support for a very dubious grouping ranging from open neo-fascists to Islamic radicals.

Why do they support such people? They do this because they decide to use them as instruments along the way in achieving their goals but then burn their fingers and recoil. I never cease to be amazed by the way that our partners just keep stepping on the same rake, as we say here in Russia, that is to say, make the same mistake over and over.

Only the current Egyptian leadership's determination and wisdom saved this key Arab country from chaos and having extremists run rampant. In Syria, as in the past, the United States and its allies started directly financing and arming rebels and allowing them to fill their ranks with mercenaries from various countries. Let me ask where do these rebels get their money, arms and military specialists? Where does all this come from? How did the notorious ISIL manage to become such a powerful group, essentially a real armed force?

As for financing sources, today, the money is coming not just from drugs, production of which has increased not just by a few percentage points but many-fold, since the international coalition forces have been present in Afghanistan. You are aware of this. The terrorists are getting money from selling oil too.

Where do they get new recruits? In Iraq, after Saddam Hussein was toppled, the state's institutions, including the army, were left in ruins. We said back then, be very, very careful. You are driving people out into the street, and what will they do there? Don't forget (rightfully or not) that they were in the leadership of a large regional power, and what are you now turning them into?

What was the result? Tens of thousands of soldiers, officers and former Baath Party activists were turned out into the streets and today have joined the rebels' ranks. Perhaps this is what explains why the Islamic State group has turned out so effective? In military terms, it is acting very effectively and has some very professional people. Russia warned repeatedly about the dangers of unilateral military actions, intervening in sovereign states' affairs, and flirting with extremists and radicals. We insisted on having the groups fighting the central Syrian government, above all the Islamic State, included on the lists of terrorist organisations. But did we see any results? We appealed in vain.

We sometimes get the impression that our colleagues and friends are constantly fighting the consequences of their own policies, throw all their effort into addressing the risks they themselves have created, and pay an ever-greater price.

From Putin's Op-Ed in the *New York Times*[140]

Sept. 11, 2013

Syria is not witnessing a battle for democracy...

There are few champions of democracy in Syria. But there are more than enough Qaeda fighters and extremists of all stripes battling the government. The United States State Department has designated Al Nusra Front and the Islamic State of Iraq and the Levant, fighting with the opposition, as terrorist organizations. This internal conflict, fueled by foreign weapons supplied to the opposition, is one of the bloodiest in the world...

No one doubts that poison gas was used in Syria. But there is every reason to believe it was used not by the Syrian Army, but by opposition forces, to provoke intervention by their powerful foreign patrons, who would be siding with the fundamentalists...

It is alarming that military intervention in internal conflicts in foreign countries has become commonplace for the United States. Is it in America's long-term interest? I doubt it. Millions around the world increasingly see America not as a model of democracy but as relying solely on brute force, cobbling coalitions together under the slogan "you're either with us or against us."

But force has proved ineffective and pointless. Afghanistan is reeling, and no one can say what will happen after international forces withdraw. Libya is divided into tribes and clans. In Iraq the civil war continues, with dozens killed each day...

The world reacts by asking: if you cannot count on international law, then you must find other ways to ensure your security. Thus a growing number of countries seek to acquire weapons of mass destruction. This is logical: if you have the bomb, no one will touch you...

We must stop using the language of force and return to the path of civilized diplomatic and political settlement...

I would rather disagree with a case he [Obama] made on American exceptionalism, stating that the United States' policy is "what makes America different. It's what makes us exceptional." It is extremely dangerous to encourage people to see themselves as exceptional, whatever the motivation. There are big countries and small countries, rich and poor, those with long democratic traditions and those still finding their way to democracy. Their policies differ, too. We are all different, but when we ask for the Lord's blessings, we must not forget that God created us equal.

---

[140] http://www.nytimes.com/2013/09/12/opinion/putin-plea-for-caution-from-russia-on-syria.html

Interview with Syrian President Assad

October 7, 2013 (Excerpts) [141]

DAMASCUS, (ST) – In an interview with the German *Der Spiegel* News Magazine, President Bashar Al-Assad said that through Western support, now there are thousands of al-Qaeda fighters from 80 countries in Syria.

Der Spiegel: Mr. President, do you love your country?

President Al-Assad: Of course, and in this I am no different from most people. This is not merely about emotions, but rather about what one can do for his country if he has the power and especially in times of crisis; and at this particular time, I realize more than ever how much I love my country and so I must protect it.

Der Spiegel: Wouldn't you be more patriotic if you stepped down and allowed for ?

President Al-Assad: The Syrian people determine my fate; no other party can determine this issue. As for the armed opposition or factions, who do they represent - the Syrian people? If so, this can be proven only through the ballot box.

Der Spiegel: Are you prepared to run in the next elections?

President Al-Assad: My term ends in August next year. The presidential elections should take place before that time...

Der Spiegel: Will you seriously consider giving up power?

President Al-Assad: This is not about me or what I want. It's about what people want. The country is not mine alone, it's the country for all Syrians.

Der Spiegel: But some people say that you are the cause of the rebellion, because people want to get rid of corruption and tyranny...

President Al-Assad: Do these people speak for themselves, or do they speak on behalf of the Syrian people or on behalf of the countries that are backing them? ... These people live in five-star hotels, they are dictated to by their financial backers and have no grass roots in Syria.

Der Spiegel: Do you deny that there is a strong opposition against you in your country?

President Al-Assad: ... What country doesn't have opposition? ...

Der Spiegel: It's not only us who deny the legitimacy of your presidency. U. S. President Barack Obama said at the U. N. General Assembly meeting in New York that a leader who kills his people and gases children to death has forfeited any right to rule his country.

President Al-Assad: ... what he says in reality has no foundation whatsoever...

Der Spiegel: For us, it seems that you are ignoring reality. By stepping down, you save the people a great deal of suffering.

President Al-Assad: ... Killing innocent people and terrorizing them by explosions and car bombs, brought to our country by al-Qaeda, is what causes pain to the Syrian people...

Der Spiegel: It is relevant because your forces and security services have committed some of these atrocities and you are responsible for that.

---

[141] http://www.presidentassad.net/index.php?option=com_content&view=article&id=1171

President Al-Assad: Despite the fact that the protests were not peaceful at all, it was our policy from the beginning to respond to the demands of the demonstrators. In the first weeks, we lost soldiers and policemen who were killed in those protests...

Der Spiegel: Was the Houla massacre also the result of mere individual failure?

President Al-Assad: ... it was the armed gangs and the extremists who attacked the families who supported the government... We can give you the names of the victims who were killed because they stood against terrorism.

Der Spiegel: We have evidence. Our reporters were in Houla[142]... President Al-Assad: With respect to your reporters, we Syrians, know our country better, know the truth better and can fully document that.

Der Spiegel: The culprits were 'shabiha', members of the militias with links to your regime.

President Al- Assad: Do you have any evidence to prove that?

Der Spiegel: We heard this from people we consider credible.

President Al- Assad: I'll be candid and even blunt with you: your question is based on wrong information. What you are asserting has no ground in reality. A lie is a lie, no matter how you phrase it or present it.

Der Spiegel: That's right. So, you don't acknowledge that your 'shabiha' took part in the massacre.

President Al-Assad: What do you mean by 'shabiha?

Der Spiegel: The militias close to your regime.

President Al-Assad: ...when armed groups attack remote areas, and the army and police cannot provide sufficient protection to citizens, villagers arm themselves and create patrols in self-defense... they are defending against al-Qaeda terrorists that have been attacking them for months.

Der Spiegel: So, it was only the other side who committed massacres and terrorism, and your soldiers, militias, security forces and intelligence services have nothing to do with that?

President Al-Assad: ... The truth is not always black and white; but, in principle this is true. We are defending ourselves...

Der Spiegel: ... As a result of the gas attack against your people, you forfeited every right to be in your position.

President Al-Assad: We did not use chemical weapons; this is not true. And the picture you are drawing of me is not true. The United States, the entire western world, the richest countries in the Arab world and neighbouring Turkey are against me, and terrorists are crossing the borders from Iraq. On top of all of this, I kill my people, who support me nevertheless! Am I superhuman? No. So, why am I still in power two and half years on? The answer is simple: because a large segment of the Syrian people support me...

Der Spiegel: After the U. N. investigation of this crime, U. S. President Obama had no doubt that your regime used chemical weapons on August 21 in an attack that claimed the lives of over a thousand people, including hundreds of children.

---

[142] See my blog, http://www.progressivepress.com/blog/dirty-war-syria, and YouTube video, "The Big Lie & Dirty War on Syria: the Foreign Subversive Army Massacres its Human Shields in Daraya," for the false flag attack on families in Houla
https://www.youtube.com/watch?v=_6YAOJ35yMk

President Al-Assad: Once again, Obama never provided one shred of evidence. The only things he provided were lies.

Der Spiegel: But the conclusions reached by the U. N. investigators ...

President Al-Assad: What conclusions? When the investigators came to Syria, we asked them to continue their work and we hope that they will provide an explanation of who is responsible for this act.

Der Spiegel: The trajectory of the gas shells could be traced back from their point of impact to their point of launching. And it shows that they were launched from 4th division installations.

President Al-Assad: This doesn't prove anything. These terrorists can be anywhere; they are even in Damascus itself. They could fire a missile next to my home.

Der Spiegel: But launching rockets containing Sarin gas cannot be done by your enemies. They don't have the capabilities to do that because it requires military equipment, training and accuracy.

President Al-Assad: Who says so? Terrorists used Sarin gas in a Tokyo attack in the 1990s. Sarin is called the "kitchen gas" because anyone can make it anywhere, in any room... They are in possession of Sarin and they already used it in Aleppo.

Der Spiegel: ... Have you conducted any investigations of your own?

President Al-Assad: Every investigation should start with identifying the number of the real victims. The armed groups speak about 350. The United States speaks about 1,400. Médecins Sans Frontières mention about 280. This cannot be right. Even the photos taken of the victims contain discrepancies. For instance, a dead child appears in two different locations.

Der Spiegel: You mean that the photos of the victims have been manipulated?

President Al-Assad: I want to say this case should be verified thoroughly; and no one has done that so far. We cannot do it, because it is an area where terrorists operate...

Der Spiegel: Do you think you can regain control of the areas you lost?

President Al-Assad: It is not about winning or losing in territorial terms. We are not two states, one controlling an area belonging to the other, as in the case with Israel, which occupies our Golan Heights. This is about terrorism, which should be eliminated. When we liberate a certain area, as we have done in many areas of Syria, it doesn't mean that we are winning, because the terrorists withdraw to another area and destroy it. That's why we are also concerned about our citizens' security. It is also important for us to win the support of our population: we win with their support and vice versa.

Der Spiegel: Do you still control the chemical weapons stockpiles?

President Al-Assad: Yes, certainly. Furthermore, to assure you, I would like to add that the stored materials haven't been activated; and no one can use them before they are prepared for that purpose.

Der Spiegel: This doesn't rule out that the army was responsible for the attack. Western intelligence services intercepted phone calls in which your commanders urge the general command to use poisonous gas.

President Al-Assad: This is complete fabrication and forgery and I will not waste my time with such allegations.

Der Spiegel: Isn't it puzzling that we, in the West, have a completely different assessment of the situation?

President Al-Assad: In fact, your region is always late in recognizing reality and is extremely slow in understanding this reality. In the beginning, we talked about violent protests, while you talked about peaceful demonstrations. When we started talking about extremists, you were still talking about "some militants." When we talked about al-Qaeda, you were still talking about a few terrorists, although they are actually the majority... Secretary of State Kerry still sticks to the past and talks about 20%. This is exactly what I meant with the reality deficit you have.

Der Spiegel: Is the reluctance the West to trust your assessments due to the lack of confidence in you...

President Al-Assad: I think the West prefers to trust al-Qaeda rather than to trust me.

Der Spiegel: This is absurd!!

President Al-Assad: I mean it... all the decisions you have taken in the West for the past ten years have been in support of al-Qaeda... through Western support, now we have thousands of al-Qaeda fighters from 80 countries... Even when we get rid of thousands of them, their ranks are replenished by other jihadists.

Der Spiegel: Yet, you believe you will win in this conflict?

President Al-Assad: Even if there was no chance of winning the fight, we have no other choice but to defend our country.

Der Spiegel: On the subject of trust, we want to remind you that you have always denied that you possessed chemical weapons, while now you acknowledge that you have them.

President Al-Assad: We never stated that we had no chemical weapons...

Der Spiegel: And the international community should simply accept that you haven't hidden secret stockpiles somewhere?

President Al-Assad: In international relations, things are not about trust and believing, they are about setting up the mechanisms on which the approach can be based... What is important for me is to win the trust of the Syrian people and not the West. What is important for me is Syria not the West.

Der Spiegel: Don't you need the West?

President Al- Assad: Of course, but not to replace the Syrians, or the Russians who are real friends. They understand better than the West the truth about what is happening here in reality... You rely too much on the United States in your policies...

Der Spiegel: The fact of the matter is that the Russians have strategic interests in Syria.

President Al-Assad: You can discuss that with President Putin. But I will say that some Europeans have come and signaled that they are convinced with our political position and that they share our analyses and explanations of the situation. But they cannot say this in public because it's difficult for them at this moment in time.

Der Spiegel: And this applies to the poisonous gas attack?

President Al-Assad: Of course... 51% of the American people reject a military strike against Syria. The British Parliament was against the strike too... Because most people didn't believe Obama's story.

Der Spiegel: Is Germany part of the contacts you are making?...

President Al-Assad: I would be happy if German envoys visited Damascus to engage with us directly... If they think that by not engaging with us, they are isolating us, I tell them: you are isolating yourselves from reality; so, it's about their interests. What do they gain when al-Qaeda is in their backyard wreaking havoc on the world?

Der Spiegel: As a result of the violence of the conflict, a quarter of the Syrian population, i. e. five million people have become refugees.

President Al-Assad: We don't have accurate figures; but even four million is an exaggerated figure. Many of those who are displaced within Syria go to live with relatives and don't appear in any statistics.

Der Spiegel: You talk about this issue as if it were an issue of paying taxes and not a humanitarian disaster.

President Al-Assad: The exact opposite is true. You in the West use these figures as if you were reading a spreadsheet: four, five, six, seven million. These figures are of your making: seventy thousand victims, eighty thousand, ninety thousand, one hundred thousand, as if it were an auction.

Der Spiegel: The reason for this exodus is that people are fleeing you and your regime.

President Al-Assad: Is this a question or a statement? If it's a statement, then it's completely wrong. If people flee, they do so for a number of reasons, first of which is fear of the terrorists...

President Putin knows from his experience in fighting terrorism in Chechnya what we are going through here.

Der Spiegel: That's why you are confident Moscow will provide you with the S300 air defense system, which you have been waiting months for?

President Al-Assad: He has said more than once that he will support Syria in different fields and that he is committed to the contracts signed between us...

Der Spiegel: The international community will do everything to prevent arming you.

President Al-Assad: What right do they have? We are a sovereign state, and we have the right to defend ourselves. We don't occupy anybody's land. Why isn't the international community bothered when Israel gets all kinds of weapons? Why should Israel receive three submarines from Germany, despite the fact that it is an occupying power and still occupies our land? We have the right to arm ourselves in accordance with the U. N. charter. This is why the West isn't objective in this position; it's because of these double standards that we don't trust the West.

Der Spiegel: When will you win against al-Qaeda?

President Al-Assad: When we restore stability; that's why we must get rid of the terrorists. Then, we need to get rid of their ideology that has infiltrated certain areas of Syria, because it is more dangerous than terrorism itself. This ideology, which encourages an eight-year old boy to slaughter a man while adults and children watch and cheer as if they were watching a football match. This actually happened in northern Syria. Getting rid of this mentality and liberating ourselves from it is going to be more difficult than getting rid of the chemical weapons.

Der Spiegel: Such scenes might not be strange in states like Somalia, Liberia and Sierra Leone, but in Syria?

President Al-Assad: The brutality we are witnessing in Syria is incredible...

Der Spiegel: Somalia, Liberia and Sierra Leone have been "failed" states for decades. Yet, you believe you can restore Syria back to pre-rebellion times?

President Al-Assad: Concerning stability, yes, when an end is put to billions of dollars flowing from Saudi Arabia and Qatar, when Turkey stops its logistical assistance to the terrorists. Then we can solve the problem in a few months...

Der Spiegel: For the international community, you are responsible for escalating this conflict, which has no end in sight. How can you cope with such guilt?

President Al-Assad: It's not about me, but about Syria. The situation in Syria worries and saddens me; that's where my concern is, I am not concerned for myself.

Der Spiegel: Has it crossed your mind that your end will be similar to President Ceausescu of Romania, when he was killed by a group of his soldiers?

President Al-Assad: I am not worried about myself. Had I been worried and fearful, I would have left Syria a long time ago.

***

Blessed are ye, when men shall revile you, and persecute you, and shall say all manner of evil against you falsely, for my sake.

– Jesus

***

Donald Trump Slams US Middle East Policy[143]

Trump on CBS, October 4, 2015

Todd: They [Russia] are hitting the people we trained!

Trump: Excuse me, they are hitting people, we are talking about people that we don't even know ... the rebel group ... we have NO IDEA! I was talking to a general two days ago, and he said, we have no idea who these people are. We are training people we don't who they are, we are giving them billions of dollars to fight Assad. And you know what, it's very possible...

And I am not saying Assad is a good guy, he is probably a bad guy, but I watched him interviewed many times, and you can make a case...

If you look at Libya, look what we did there - it's a mess, if you look at Saddam Hussein with Iraq, look what we did there - it's a mess! It's going to be the same thing!

Todd: Do you think the Middle East would be better today if Saddam and Qaddafi were still there, and Assad was stronger?

Trump: It's not even a contest, Chuck! It's not even a contest! Iraq is a disaster!...

We've spent now 2 trillion in Iraq, probably a trillion in Afghanistan. We are destroying our country

Todd: You would pull out of what we are doing in Syria now?

Trump: I would sit back and this is not usually me talking, because I am very proactive, as you probably know, but I would sit back and see what's going on...

Here is the problem: we are fighting Assad, and we are fighting for people and helping people that we don't even know who they are, and they may be worse than Assad, they may be worse, ok? They may be worse!...

---

[143] fortruss.blogspot.com/2015/10/donald-trump-middle-east-would-be-safer.html

If you didn't have a problem in Syria, You wouldn't have the migration... And now they are talking about taking 200 thousand people, that we don't even know who they are and bringing them into the United States? The whole thing is ridiculous!

Donald Trump Slams Hillary Clinton on Fox News[144]

Dec. 14, 2015

[Hillary Clinton said about me,] "I think he's dangerous." I'm dangerous. She is the one that caused all this problem with her stupid policies. You look at what she did with Libya, what she did with Syria. Looks at what happened with Egypt - a total mess. We don't back any of our allies. You look, she was truly, if not the, one of the worst secretary of States in the history of the country.

She talks about me being dangerous; she's killed hundreds of thousands of people with her stupidity... Look at what happened. The Middle East is a total disaster under her. She traveled back and forth, but look at all the problems. Look at, as an example, Iraq. Total disaster. They didn't get us in but they got us out badly. Total, we spent two trillion dollars, thousands of lives, wounded warriors all over. Look at Libya, look at Benghazi, our ambassador, he wired her five or six hundred times, asking for help."

Teleprompter Glitch Gives Obama the Wrong Script?

President Obama: "The fall of Ramadi has galvanized the Iraqi government, so with the additional steps I ordered last month, we're speeding up training of ISIL forces, including volunteers from Sunni tribes in Anbar province."[145]

---

[144] https://www.youtube.com/watch?v=KVuZs2Mk9Oc "This video is no longer available because the YouTube account associated with this video has been terminated. Sorry about that."
[145] "Obama Slips Up: 'We're Training ISIL'" https://www.youtube.com/watch?v=p2NkjNvwuaU

Syrian Girl Superstar

"Syrian Girl Partisan" is the screen name of Mimi al-Laham, who became an activist on Twitter, Facebook and YouTube to protest and expose the dirty war on her country, Syria. Born in Damascus, Syrian Girl was raised in Australia. Her intelligence, political acumen and rare beauty would make her a Superstar – if she were peddling the mainstream line. (As it was, the best the MSM could muster was a blogger they fell for named "Gay Girl in Damascus," see "Just Tell Us What We Want to Hear Our real Syrian Girl has been fairly named "The World's Hottest Political Blogger."

Syrian Girl's family belonged to the political elite but left because of the Baathist regime, and she is not a long-term Assad supporter, rather a patriot striving to defend her country. As a graduate student in chemistry, she played an important role in exposing the lies about the chemical weapon rocket attacks in Ghouta in 2013. The embedded, weaponized Western media machine blamed the Syrian government for the attacks, coming very close to triggering US airstrikes on Syria. In fact, the rockets were probably supplied by Turkey to rebel forces to stage a false flag, precisely to bring on a NATO intervention. Syrian Girl had warned of the risk of a false-flag chemical weapons attack for at least a year before the incident. She opposed Syria's giving up its chemical weapons, as its only strategic defense against foreign nuclear attack. Syrian Girl also goes by the name Maram Susli. She is now a regular columnist at Near Eastern Outlook.

***

Videos:

Eight Reasons Why the NWO Hates Syria

No Rothschild central bank, NO IMF debt, No Genetically modified food, Oil and pipelines, Anti-secret societies, Anti-Zionism, Secularism, Nationalism

SyrianGirlPartisan Channel on YouTube, published Dec 17, 2012. 418,483 views. https://www.youtube.com/watch?v=TP3mXVRd89Y

Syrian Girl: This is Syrian Girl. I want to talk to you about why the New World Order hates Syria and why they are attacking the country now. The New World Order is the plan to bring all nations under the control of one power.

People might argue about who the real power is behind the agenda, but those who are observant will notice that this New World Order is the end game.

1. Syria's Central Bank is State-Owned

Syria has always resisted and in the front line against the New World Order. One of the ways that Syria resists is Syria does not have a Rothschild Central Bank. A Rothschild Central Bank is a bank that has been bought by the Rothschild family, one of the richest and most powerful families in the world. It is a bank which is under the control of the "Bank of International Settlements" which decides how much money is worth in a nation and how much debt a nation has. In Libya one of the first things that happened after NATO took over the country is their Central Bank was turned into a Rothschild Central Bank.

2. Syria has no debt to the IMF

Another way in which Syria resists the New World Order is it has no loans from the International Monetary Fund or IMF. Syria before the crisis began was a totally debt free country. If it has ever taken out loans it was not with the IMF but with a trusted ally like Russia. The first thing that Egypt's new President Morsi did when he came to power was saddle Egypt with $4.8 billion worth of IMF debt. Even though he claims to be a Muslim and Islam is against debt and interest.

Because Syria owes no money to world powers and their bank is free from foreign control she's able to choose her own foreign policy. This is why Syria can oppose imperialism like in Palestine, Libya and Iraq and ban genetically modified food.

3. Syria has no GMO

Syria has never had genetically modified food and has recently formalized this into law. Companies like Monsanto are among the war profiteers or "dogs of war". When Iraq was invaded one of the first things the US government changed in the Iraqi constitution was to make it illegal for farmers to store their own seeds and force them to buy genetically modified seed from Monsanto.[146] Genetically modified seeds are very expensive and carry a promise of being better than natural seeds. Many Indian farmers who bought the seeds and had their crops fail that year committed suicide because they had no money to buy new seeds from Monsanto and couldn't have saved their own seeds because they had entered a contractual agreement to purchase seeds from Monsanto. Famine reigned as a result.[147]

Controlling food supplies is yet another constraint the New World Order uses to keep countries in check and bring them under the control of the one-world government. Syria resists these steps to control her.

4. Syrians are aware of the global conspiracy

Syrian state media doesn't shy away from discussion of secret societies. In Syria talk of secret societies is not seen as a fringe conspiracy, but mainstream.

---

[146] "US Declares Iraqis Must Destroy Their Own Seeds", Iman Khaduri, Feb. 1, 2005, http://www.globalresearch.ca/articles/KHA501A.html

[147] Headlines: "'Bitter Seeds' Film Tells of Suicide and GMO Effects on India's Farmers;" "Monsanto's GMO Seeds Contributing to Farmer Suicides Every 30 Minutes"

Don't they tell you it is not significant that the two US presidential candidates, Bush and Kerry, were both members of the same tiny secret society, Skull and Bones? They are willingly blind.

5. Syria has gas and plans to build pipeline

Oil and energy flow is another way in which world powers bring nations to their knees and yet another reason why Syria is a target. Syria recently discovered gas off its coast and she was working on a new pipeline going through Iran, Iraq, and Syria to Europe that would drive out the BTC pipeline currently going through Israel. Forcing oil to pass through Israel through the BTC pipeline is the way in which the New World Order uses Israel as their hub of control of the oil flow between Europe, Asia and Africa. They can turn off the tap whenever they want and that brings nations under their umbrella. Syria's attempts to give the world an alternative route for oil and gas could have been a way to free the world and put a wrench in the plans of the global dominators.[148]

6. Syria opposes Zionism and "Israel"

And I've spoken about this at length because Syria is one of the last countries left that does not recognize the apartheid state of Israel and resists the Zionist agenda which is a large part of the New World Order. This is one of the main reasons the New World Order sees Syria as an obstacle to its plans and this point requires an individual video.

7. Syria the last secular country in the Middle East

Another reason why then New World Order hates Syria is that it is a secular country in the Middle East. Afghanistan, Libya, Iraq and much of North Africa were secular nations, but after the Iraq war Iraq was given a more theocratic, Shiite government. After the Arab Spring and NATO bombardment of Libya it was given a Wahhabi extremist government, and recently Egypt became a Muslim Brotherhood nation, another theocracy. And with Israel being an extremist Jewish theocracy in the region, Syria is really the last secular country left in the Middle East. In Syria, asking someone what their religion is, is insulting, and if an outsider asks you what it is, you can't help but feel a little bit defensive, and the common answer is "I am Syrian." All the primary religions have lived there in peace for hundreds of years and with freedom to practice. Divide and conquer is a strategy which the world powers use to control nations, and Syria's unity has been a way to resist that.

8. A strong national identity

Syria has a very strong national and cultural identity. If you have ever travelled the world you will notice you can find the same shops and same culture being spread everywhere. You can find the same clothing lines in a shop in Dubai that you can find in a shop in France. This is not the case for Syria. Syria holds onto its uniqueness and its own production. Coca Cola and other foreign companies used to be banned in Syria, but years ago the current president unbanned them, which

---

[148] In other videos, Syrian Girl has commented that the idea is to keep the area destabilized, break it into three parts, which will block the Iran-Iraq-Syria pipeline to Europe. Balkanization will also end the alliance between Iran and Syria. -

I believe was a huge mistake. Syria had its own cola production companies that were even more delicious that had to close down as a result of Coca Cola being unbanned. But these reforms really only went so far to open up Syria's economy, and Syrians still resisted entry of foreign companies, and I think this is one of the other reasons that Syria is hated by the New World Order.

Syria is one for the last countries that remain distinct from everywhere else, and I believe there is a clear new world order agenda to make everywhere look pretty much the same and thereby create no more nations and one world government. What a boring world that would be. The New World Order hates Syria because Syria is free, so Orwellian it is that they shout "free Syria" when they really try to enslave her. If Syria falls, it could be a tipping point that ends up in victory for the New World Order, like Stalingrad was a tipping point between Germany and Russia in World War II. Syria resists in spite of all the massive power of the nations against her. She resists not just for herself but for every free person.

As I said earlier, Syria is the front line against the New World Order, so fight alongside us until the end.

"Every person has two homelands... His own and Syria." – Historian André Parrot

***

Editor's Observations: One of the important functions of ISIS is of course to shock ordinary citizens of Western countries and turn them against the Muslim world, and this obviously helps the Zionist cause enormously. But there is another side as well. What the power elite are most concerned about is keeping their privileges and their lion's share of everything. Any country that isn't plugged into their debt bondage threatens to upset the apple cart. People in the West might learn that in places like Syria the government isn't in debt to the banks, and you don't have to fork out a big part of your income for that, or for health care, while Wall Street demands cuts in Social Security. People in the US realize that the system is not fair, but they don't realize there are alternatives out there. The headlines about chaos and terror and bloodshed overseas reinforce the notion that, after all, we're lucky to have this old system we have, because this is as good as it gets. If examples like Syria or Qaddafi's Libya are followed by more countries, the empire could lose its grip. People were not supposed to find out that Libya was an egalitarian system sharing the wealth with the little people. Instead they had to link Libya with Lockerbie (which I have read was a false flag op by the Mossad and CIA). They had to be terrified by terrorism.

The Truth about ISIS

"Syrian Women Speak Out on the Syrian Conflict" on Australian TV "SBS Insight" programme, Oct. 30, 2012. SyrianGirlPartisan YouTube channel "SyrianGirl debates FSA" 243,661 views https://www.youtube.com/watch?v=GrEPadG0pQk

Hanadi Assoud, Hands Off Syria: I have family there, they're telling us what going on.

Insight: What are they telling you?

Hanadi: They are telling us that they've been targeted being the minority. If you are not with them...

Insight: Targeted by whom?

Hanadi: By the rebels. They come in... You see I come from Homs, from the same city that the Doctor comes from. The areas that I've noticed... I mean Mother Agnes was here, she said that 80,000 Christians were forced out of Homs so were other....

Male: Not true.

Hanadi: It is true and Mother...

Male: It's not true I'm from Homs.

Hanadi: I'm sorry can I finish what I'm saying?

Insight: Yeah. Don't try to finish what she's saying. I'll come to you in a minute let her finish what she's saying.

Hanadi: When she came, she was in Australia, and she was interviewed. She said, "And I know a lot of people." We have Christians here they can tell you their story as well. They have families that have been killed, we have people that have been beheaded and this is their slogan "If you're not with us you are to be beheaded." But why? If they want to fight a government why don't they go and fight them in a place where there's no civilians? If they care about the people of Syria, they care about civilians why use them as human shields? Why force the people outside their houses and use their houses? Is that how you fight?

Mimi: I think this whole debate is ignoring the main point here. Which is that the "rebel uprising" or the "democratic uprising" is not that – it's a Muslim Brotherhood uprising. The Muslim Brotherhood was the main opposition group in Syria for the last 40 years and they're the one that want to remove the secular government. And I'm not a government supporter. I am for the reform process just like the majority of Syrian people, but the fact is... don't interrupt me sir.

The fact is it is American and NATO governments and Israel that are funding these Al Qaeda terrorists and Muslim Brotherhood extremists. That is the point everybody here is missing and the fact is that... Excuse me sir but you do have a stake in Syria because we have Russia emerging as a super power and you have China emerging as a super power and America and NATO want to control the Mediterranean Sea. They want to cut off this new pipeline deal that is happening between Syria, Iraq and Iran. They want to cut off ties between Syria and Iran. Which is why these people hate Iran so much and it is why these sectarians are against any unity between Syria and Iran. Because they want to see Syria get destroyed and that is what this is about, destroying Syria.

Insight: Mimi, what sort of government do you want?

Mimi: Of course I would like to see a government that has less corruption, but also maintains our foreign policy which is of the utmost importance. Because we have an imperialist Zionist entity right next door to us, Israel. Which is funded by NATO, and the whole crisis is being created by our enemies: Israel, NATO, America, European countries.

Insight: Can I just ask you though; do you want Assad to survive?

Mimi: Right now Assad has to survive because his replacement is going to be Islamic extremists, the Muslim Brotherhood...

Insight: But do you want him to survive?

Mimi: I want him to survive for now...

Insight: Okay final comment from you Hanadi.

Hanadi: I just want to say we're not Assad regime supporters. We are Syrians, therefore we've seen the uprisings in the Middle East, we've seen that so called Islamic Brotherhood uprising and the proof is in Egypt. The leader now is a Brotherhood extremist, in Tunisia the leader is a Brotherhood extremist, in Libya, Tunisia and Egypt, this is what concerns us. We want Syria to stay secular, we've lived there. I've lived there for 8 years myself. Everybody practiced his religion freely, we've all had free education, we've had it all. What is it they want? I want a reform, we all want reforms. We do know every country has corruption, we want that to go. However, we don't want extremists to come and run our country. That's all we're saying.

Next up on YouTube was the full programme. The "Male" who tried to interrupt Mimi, draped with the French Mandate "FSA" flag scarf, starts parroting the Big Lie that the MSM are awash with: "The government is deliberately targeting civilians."

This is the operative lie which is instrumental to taking the crisis from the death squads launched by the US, to the objective of a "responsibility to protect" invasion by NATO and installation of a Moslem Brotherhood puppet regime.

During the programme, arguments erupt between Syrians in the studio audience who have had relatives killed in Syria, some say by rebels and others say by unknown killers, or relatives jailed by the regime.
https://www.youtube.com/watch?v=B4dEeoL6QP8

***

Who is backing ISIS? What is the agenda behind the group's takeover of Iraq and the Middle East?

The Truth about ISIS with Syrian Girl.
YouTube video by Paul Joseph Watson on Jul 9, 2014. 1,316,798 views,
https://www.youtube.com/watch?v=IQ2KzjNtDTc

Paul Joseph Watson: In the last month we've seen ISIS jihadists completely overrunning the Iraqi military in many areas of the country. They've stolen a huge arsenal of military vehicles, weapons including Stinger missiles, they got chemical weapons. They've seized towns, committed atrocities and now they're destroying mosques. So where did this group come from, who's responsible for its expansion, how did it become so powerful?

Mimi: So, actually ISIS was formed in Iraq in 2007. One of its captured leaders in fact admitted that for the first year of its life it existed solely on the internet. But that didn't stop most of the foreign media, especially Qatar's Al-Jazeera TV station, from promoting their existence. The group was basically designed to crush any unity between Sunnis and Shias in Iraq, so that the resistance would be divided and conquered.

Even in 2003 we were told that Al Qaeda was already operating in Iraq, but as we know that was a lie, there wasn't any Al Qaeda in Iraq until the US brought it with the invasion. We were told in 2004 that Abu Musab Zarqawi was in Fallujah, even though no one had actually ever seen him there, and any politician who was interviewed at the time said, he's never made an appearance. So he's very much like a WMD. Abu Musab Zarqawi was the then leader of Al Qaeda which at the time didn't have the name ISIS or ISIL. So he's referred to as another WMD, basically something that is an invention just to create a pretext for war.

It was only by 2006 that this IS or ISIS group emerged, and pre-existing factions in Iraq which were resistance movements that used to be unified but were more nationalist, they took ISIS to be a threat, and they at the beginning clashed with it. But ISIS was too strong. And that leads us to the question, Why ISIS emerged as the most powerful of all the groups? And you have to ask first of all, is it possible that this could happen without a state backer. In my opinion it is not. I think that there is definitely an organization that is backing this ISIS group.

And if we look at who benefits the most, the introduction of the Maliki government after the fall of Iraq, basically handed Iraq to Iran's influence. So it was largely influenced by a sort of unholy alliance between the US in Iraq and Iran at the time. And now that this influence has overtaken the US in the region, the obvious beneficiaries for the Maliki government being destabilized and weakened and Iranian influence to be weakened also, are the usual suspects, Saudi Arabia and Qatar, [News Headline: "America's Allies Are Funding ISIS. ISIS was funded for years by wealthy donors in Kuwait, Qatar, and Saudi Arabia, three US allies that have dual agendas in the war on terror"] and the United States and Israel. Hillary Clinton in fact even called for Maliki to step down, now at the worst possible time, so this would be the US basically fighting alongside ISIS.

However, in spite of all of this, I don't actually believe that ISIS is as powerful as the media is making them out to be. That perception of invincibility is creating more members and more people being recruited. Because the lack of clarity who's behind it is driving easily manipulated youth into actually believing that ISIS is backed by God, like that must be the secret to its strength. And finally, ISIS has a sort of "You're either with us or against us" policy, there's no middle ground with these people. They rule with fear and barbarism, and so even if the sheikhs may secretly give them money, unless they publicly support ISIS, ISIS considers them enemies. Out of fear actually they get many defections.

PJW: So basically you're saying this whole PR campaign about ISIS being very powerful, very militant, very influential in the region of course is making many even in the West go and travel to join ISIS, we've seen many stories about that. The result of that now is that people flying through airports in Britain and other countries on the way to America, they're being harassed more and more because of what as you said seems to be a PR campaign on the behalf of the Western media which in fact is bolstering ISIS to a level which it otherwise wouldn't achieve, is that correct?

Mimi: They told us only a few weeks ago that ISIS was going to be in Baghdad in a week, and Baghdad is about to fall I read in some media. Yeah, ISIS is strong, but it's certainly not as strong as they make it out to be. It's certainly not invincible. The groups that get the most attention are the groups that grow the largest.

PJW: Given what we know about ISIS, is their takeover of Iraq really a failure of US foreign policy, as it's been characterized, or did it take Washington by surprise, or is there another wider agenda behind it?

Mimi: I don't believe it is against the US agenda, I don't believe it was unplanned, unpredicted, I know that on the surface a lot of people are thinking that the ISIS victory in Iraq appears to humiliate US foreign policy in the short term. Like Oh, they failed to create a stable Iraq, now militias are taking it over. But in reality, this was all by design. Anyone who was observant during the US occupation of Iraq, even though the media was claiming the US was trying to build a viable state and wanted to end any kind of sectarianism, everything that they did was to push "divide and conquer" and to pit Sunnis and Shias against each other. They of course helped the Dawa party of the Iraqi Shias, which is more of a religious party rather than a secular party to get into power, and of course with their unholy alliance with Iran.

Al-Baghdadi, the current leader of Isis, was actually released from Iraqi prison in 2009. In Basra, some British troops were caught dressed up as Arabs, these are special forces troops, shooting at Iraqi police. James Steele, Gen. Petraeus, Robert Ford, they all openly conducted the El Salvador option in Iraq. They created these death squads like the Badr Brigade and they trained them in torture. And then those militias actually joined the Interior Ministry of the Iraq government. The torture that they committed was actually exposed to the people.

These groups are sectarian Shiite groups that went around cutting off heads of Sunnis who just so happened to not like the Iraqi government or the occupation. So they created all this hatred and this tension. And in the meantime, the flip side of that coin was they created ISIS and helped it grow alongside Saudi Arabia. So any sort of nationhood that existed in Iraq in 2004, where Sunnis and Shias were protesting against the occupation – and I remember at the time Fox News, and excuse my language, said "The Shiites have hit the fan" – Any sort of unity was crushed by 2004, and it was turned into a solely Sunni-Shia war.

The objective is to turn Iraq into three states, a Kurdish north, a Sunni center and a Shiite south. And the exact same Balkanization strategy is playing out in Syria. A Kurdish north, an Alawite coast and a Sunni center. The idea is to create a perpetual war between states divided along religious lines, without any nationalist, cultural or historical connection.

PJW: On this subject of Balkanization, given the relative success, security and prosperity of the Kurdish area of Iraq post 2003, some would see Balkanization as a good option for the Iraqi people. Why is that not the case in your view?

Mimi: Balkanization, as we saw with Pakistan when it was cut off from India, basically resulted in a perpetual war. It resulted in an arms race, it resulted in Hindus burning Muslims alive, and Muslims attacking Hindus, and the hatred just built up from there, because of external forces. India was one before the occupation and the divide. Balkanizing these countries is not an end to war, it's a beginning of war. Apart from the Kurds, the only thing that would divide people are these religious affiliations, which have no basis in culture, or history or real nationality. The Kurds do have an opinion of their own nationality. But the circumstances by which a Kurdistan might occur cannot be at the expense of weak nations, and it cannot be unreasonable either. There are lands that the Kurds lay claim to that do not historically belong to them. They just happen to be oil-rich. I think that Israel wants an ally in the region and that's why they cultivate a Kurdistan as well. But Turkey, if you noticed, is not the one that's being destabilized, even though it has the largest population of Kurds. Balkanization, if you're a nationalist, it is not a solution.

PJW: Turning to Syria itself, which of course is where ISIS really got their power in the first place, you of course were very accurate last year when you predicted the false flag chemical weapon attack which would be used to justify the attack on Syria. That was derailed at the last minute, then we have the MIT report and others coming out confirming that the narrative that Assad was behind the attack was basically a complete nonsense, there was no evidence for it. In terms of the ISIS crisis, do you think this is going to be hijacked by NATO, by the US, as a pretext for a second bite on the cherry when it comes to an assault on Syria?

Mimi: If you recall what I did say specifically to Infowars at the time, was that after the chemical weapons attack, the US military government was not going to use it to attack Syria, they were going to use it to disarm Syria of chemical weapons. The reason I thought that a possibility of an attack could happen was I didn't expect Syria to actually agree to disarm. So I was thinking it might result in a regional war. But I did not believe that the US ever really intended to attack Syria, as I repeated many times - at the time it was too strong, just because of the WMDs, and it's anti-air missiles, and its allies of course. But that's exactly what happened, and now I guess I have to repeat a little bit.

The US may intervene a little bit, in terms of ISIS, potentially they'll have drones flying over Iraq skies, and they hope to have some drones flying over Syrian skies as well. But like with Pakistan, they don't actually ever want to defeat these extremist groups, they just want to keep things going, just enough to maintain instability, and have their foot in the door. So I don't think we're going to see the US have a full-blown invasion again, but that is not going to stop the US government from killing people with drones.

PJW: So again it goes back to this idea of needing instability, needing tension in the region, which is why the Global War on Terror needs a steady supply of terrorists to justify it, to justify the military-industrial complex, the sales of all those weapons, and that's precisely what ISIS is providing at the moment. "Obomber" recently announced that the US will be sending $500 million to so-called "moderate rebels" in Syria. We've heard that one before. Given that the US actually trained ISIS members in Jordan in 2012, can we really trust the White House's judgment on who it considers to be "moderate?"

Mimi: It's really interesting because Obama himself recently told the media that the idea of a "ready-made moderate force that we can arm, that can have any chance at defeating the Syrian government, is a fantasy." So why is he dropping $500 million on a fantasy? [Did YouTube captions offer a hint? Fantasy rendered as "fun to see."]

So we can safely say that they're not ignorant of the fact that there is no moderate force that has any sort of influence. Ignorance isn't driving US policy. They know where the money's going to end up. They know that the moderate rebels will either defect to ISIS and take the money with them, or that they're going to be killed, and the money's going to be pocketed by ISIS anyway, or, it's going to go into the hands of corrupt individuals, which happens a lot.

The interesting thing though, that even if the money and training does not end up in the hands of ISIS due to defection, these moderate rebel groups that they're talking about, the only existing ones are led by a man called Jamal Maarouf, who recently told the Independent, that Al-Qaeda is not his problem, it's America's problem, and he has no problem with Al-Qaeda because he's fighting alongside it – the Jabhat al Nusra faction, which the media seems to very conveniently now forget. So these "moderate rebels" might have some kind of territorial dispute with ISIS, but that's not stopping them from fighting alongside the other factions of Al-Qaeda, although ISIS is supposedly fighting with Al-Qaeda now, but that doesn't stop them from fighting alongside Jabhat al-Nusra, AKA Al-Qaeda. That's who the $500 million is going to. In reality, on the ground, the most powerful groups in Syria are ISIS, Jabhat al Nusra and Ahrar al-Sham. All of them are Al-Qaeda factions. The leftovers are only taking sides with either one of these groups.

P. Of course many of these so-called moderate rebels, as far back as 18 months ago, had stories that they were all defecting and pledging allegiance to Jabhat al-Nusra. So even if the money and the arms go to the moderate rebels in the first place, they can defect as they have done, and then you know you have Stinger missiles in the hands of these radical jihadists. Moving on to Abu Bakr al-Baghdadi, the salt of the earth militant jihadist who likes to wear flashy Rolex watches, he recently announced the birth of a global Islamic caliphate in the aftermath of this ISIS takeover of Iraq. What's the real story of this Caliphate, is it a genuine threat and how does it play into this idea of a clash of civilizations that we've heard so much about from the neo-cons?

M. Basically what ISIS really wants, what they stand for, is they have a strange belief that God is a real estate agent. And they join other extremist factions of other religions, for example, during the Crusades, Christianity went through something like that, and in more recent years, Judaism went through something like that, with Zionism, where they think they have a right to other people's land, because it's what their religion tells them. So a Pakistani living in London, believes himself to have more claim over Syrian land than a Christian or a Muslim Syrian who was born of that land and whose ancestors go back to that land for tens of thousands of years. Basically if that Pakistani in London has this belief that ISIS has, that all of this land is "Islamic land" and it belongs to the "true Muslims" and not just anybody else, so the rest can just get sunk into the sea or get shot, it doesn't matter. But anybody that isn't Syrian, they have a right to live in Syria? So currently the Caliphate that they're declaring is contained in countries that already have a majority of Muslims living there, and also some that were part of the Umayyad dynasty of hundreds and hundreds of years ago, but eventually they intend to take the whole world. And that might lead to problems for the UK, and Europe, more so than just terrorism. You might have people saying, Well, now, South London is part of the Islamic State.

PJW: Are they powerful enough to pull that off or is it all just fear-mongering.

Mimi: No, I don't think they're that powerful enough to pull it off, but they're stupid enough to believe they are, and even now they think they're taking over the world. They think, this is it, this is the rise of the Islamic empire – that isn't Islamic in any way. In fact it's Wahhabi to the core, which is a relatively new cult. It's a throwback to thousands and thousands of years ago, this used to be a standard practice around the world, that thieves get their hands cut off, they're taking us back to thousands of years ago.

[Wahhabi-Saudi justice: Steal an egg, and lose your hand, steal a kingdom – and found a dynasty. – *Ed.*]

I did want to say that the "moderate rebels" may not want to create an Islamic state around the entire globe, but they do want to create an Islamic state – or let's be more truthful, a Wahhabi state – inside Syria and Iraq. These "moderate rebels", you notice that the media uses the word "moderate" because they cannot use the word "secular," because these groups are in no way secular, and that's clear as anybody can see. So they use the word "moderate." You know, moderate relative to Al-Qaeda and Wahhabi deranged lunatics. But these moderates are the same ones that eat hearts [on screen: "Face-to-face with Abu Sakkar, Syria's 'heart-eating cannibal', by BBC News"] and chop off heads anyway, but that doesn't matter.

If the US genuinely wants to defeat ISIS, they wouldn't be trying to destabilize and weaken the Syrian and Iraqi state and military. These destabilizations, and the border being porous, and Turkey allowing ISIS and Jabhat al-Nusra in, and Turkey recently took Jabhat al-Nusra off the anti-terror list, and Turkey is a NATO member, so it does take orders from the United States. If the US was serious about defeating ISIS, they wouldn't be destabilizing Syria and Iraq, they would be strengthening them, and they wouldn't allow Turkey and the neighboring states to boost these groups.

PJW: Just something that sprang to mind when you mention chopping people's hands off, of course, we posted many stories on Infowars about all the atrocities committed not only by ISIS but by these other rebel groups, Jabhat al-Nusra etc. and a lot of the comments, usually along the lines of you know, Kill all Muslims. As a Muslim how do you feel when people react to seeing these atrocities committed by extremist groups and then making them somehow representative of all Muslims.

Mimi: Well, I think it's basically the most ignorant reaction anyone can make because the people who are suffering from these groups are Muslims. They're Muslims like me, Muslims like my friend's parents who are very religious and very conservative, and very very good, and these are the people who have been suffering the most, it's not the West. So for them to just turn around and say, Kill all Muslims, what have we done to you, we are already being killed by these groups that the US government is supporting. This cult never existed in the Middle East before. It's a growing thing, and it's Muslims that have been dying the most and suffering the most from all of these events.

PJW: Okay, just drop in a note with ISIS, I mean in a couple sentences, what is the truth about ISIS that we're not hearing in the mainstream narrative.

Mimi: In a couple of sentences, ISIS is backed by the United States and allies Qatar and Saudi Arabia. We're talking about governments not people, and if the people knew, they would not accept it. It's just a cause to destabilize, divide and conquer these lands that unfortunately seem to have a lot of resources, but not enough power to just defend their own borders.

PJW: OK, we're going to wrap it up with that. Tell people where they can reach you on Twitter.

Mimi: You can reach me on Twitter on Partisan Girl and on YouTube on Syrian Girl Partisan.

The Truth Behind Isis and the Middle East

Alex Jones Channel on YouTube, July 21, 2014. 38,309 views.
https://www.youtube.com/watch?v=GWr8iK_rw94

Alex Jones: Syrian Girl has been one of the most accurate reporters out there and pundits exposing what's happening in Syria. Now ISIS has gone into Iraq, killing tens of thousands there, they estimate 300,000 dead in the last three or four years of globalist-backed destabilization in Syria...

Mimi: Just recently ISIS has actually pushed out all of the Christians from Mosul in Iraq, where they've been for 2,000 years. And it appears they've actually been marking their homes, just like the Nazis would mark the homes in Germany just before and during WWII. So of course they've been destroying Iraq's historical artifacts, following on the trend of the destruction of Iraq's history since the start of the war in 2003. They've been stoning women, and basically their goal is to turn back time to 1400 years ago... they believe that land automatically belongs to them and they're allowed to just go in there and steal people's homes, steal people's oil, slaughter people, not give anything to society but just create war and destruction. It's basically like a zombie horde...

In 2004 if you recall, many people were protesting against the occupation, that were both Sunni and Shia, and the country was sort of united against the occupation. And of course, in order to divide and conquer them, the thinkers of the time, such as James Steele, Robert Ford, who created the El Salvador option, they decided to back death squads from both the Shia side and the Sunni side. So on the Shia side of the coin, they supported the Badr brigades... And on the other side of that coin, they created ISIS which of course sees all Shias as basically lambs for the slaughter.

Alex: Just like Israel created Hamas to counter Hezbollah in 1974 or 75, this is Full Spectrum Dominance, where you create the two groups to wreck the country. The target is the women and children. The target is civilization. The target is movie theaters, the target is running water... These are absolutely war crimes by the Rand Corporation, Pentagon... If you're wearing a suit and tie and don't have a big beard, you're dead. You haven't attacked anybody and want to work with people, you're dead. You want to run about like psychos and kill people all day and go from country to country, you're going to be put in charge.

How are things going with your family back in Syria with the war?...

Mimi: The situation in Damascus is getting much better, checkpoints are no longer very close to the city... on the other hand in Aleppo, I have a friend in Aleppo, and he tells me that in that city of two million people, they've been without running water for two months, because the Al Qaeda rebels actually blew up the water supply. And this isn't ISIS, this is Jabhat al Nusra, the other al-Qaeda rebels – the "moderate" rebels that they keep telling us about... People have been taking water from rivers and dragging it back to their homes. You never hear about that from the humanitarians. But I just wanted to go back to Hamas just for a little bit because of what's going on in Gaza and what you mentioned about its creation, I just wanted to say, Yes, they were created to weaken other groups which were based on nationalism and secularism rather than religion, but maybe Hamas just wasn't sectarian enough, because in 2001 the Mossad actually was caught trying to start an al-Qaeda cell in Gaza, so that's really interesting. It's also interesting that it's ISIS that claimed to have captured the three illegal Israeli settlers, not Hamas. Hamas actually said they have nothing to do with it. And that was the event that was the precursor to Israel's starting to bomb Gaza. So it's interesting how Isis HAS been tying in to that plan, and one of the other plans that ISIS has really been tying in to, is the Balkanization of Iraq and Syria, to each country being split into three separate states, which has been one of the main goals of a lot of these think tanks, such as the Brookings Institute, that suggested this would be really beneficial towards the US and Israel. Of course that means the creation of Kurdistan, supporting the Peshmerga there.

Alex: Let's be clear. All these big think tanks are bragging about how great this is going. I wonder how everybody in Israel deals with Netanyahu openly endorsing Isis a month ago and saying, what's going on in Iraq is good for us? How is joining with evil, killing innocent people, causing civil war, how is that good for Israel?

Mimi: Well, they just want more land, it's like they just want to continue their ethnic cleansing of all the Palestinians that live amongst them. So that's the state agenda. I don't think it's good for the Jewish people. I think it's good only for the state that wants to grow. The state has a mind of its own it doesn't care.

Alex: Exactly, that's why all these governments act the same.

***

Why Al Qaeda is Al CIAda

By 108morris108, Feb 17, 2012 188,136 views
https://www.youtube.com/watch?v=qCqmI1SQB5o

Morris: Syrian girl today you're going to tell us about Al Qaeda I believe. Is that correct?

Syrian Girl: Yes, or as otherwise known as, Al-CIAduh.

So wherever Al Qaeda is there's some Shin Bet, Mossad or CIA agents controlling it and it's not a new tactic. I mean in Ireland MI5 and MI6 they too used it against the Irish resistance.

Morris: Same method.

Syrian Girl: Exactly, and they tried to use it to destroy the Iraq resistance in fact, but the Sunni Resistance, they wouldn't bite. They actually clashed with Al Qaeda for many many years. There was an organization called the ISI, if anybody remembers that and actually the leaders of this "ISI" movement were basically Al Qaeda in Iraq...

The biggest news agency that promotes Al Qaeda as a real organization, that takes their videos and plays them to people is Al Jazeera [in Qatar]. Now you're seeing Al Jazeera taking basically all the revolutions, almost all the revolutions have been in the Middle East right now and using them to gain influence over the countries. So basically in conclusion Al Qaeda, the CIA and Qatar are one entity.

Morris: Sounds right. You've got some Al Qaeda cells working in Syria, coming from Lebanon and Turkey is that correct?

Syrian Girl: I think we're starting to see that a little bit now because the movement in Syria, I'm not going to say all of the Syrian opposition is this way, but the most powerful element currently amongst the Syrian opposition, the most heavily funded and the one that's probably going to be set up to take power is an Islamic Salafist Movement which coincides with Al Qaeda's beliefs. So yeah I would say that "they are Al Qaeda", you know. If Al Qaeda is not really a legitimate organization, it's just a name or some puppets that are being controlled by America.

Morris: So do you think all the Arab world could become Al Qaeda or Muslim Brotherhood? I don't know if it's fair to combine the two in the same sentence.

Syrian Girl: It's not exactly fair because the Muslim Brotherhood is more like ...Christian democrats but I think that even they are being pushed more and more to the extremist Salafist side. It seems that only the secular countries are being targeted and they're being turned into this Islamic Emirate and the powers that be for some reason they wish to see the whole Middle East being turned into theocracies whether being run by Wahhabi Salafist as in Saudi Arabia or otherwise.

Morris: I've heard it said that Israel would like to see religiously run countries all around it. I mean also it might just be a reaction to Israel given that Israel is waving a religious flag, just food for thought.

Syrian Girl: Maybe or you might say that this is just the Sunni Islamic states like Qatar and Saudi Arabia trying to gain influence over everything in opposition to Iran which is a Shia government. But maybe somebody is puppeting everybody from the outside trying to create a huge clash between religions. In order to do that you can't have any secular states left.

If you think about it the only secular states in the Middle East is the Levant region which is Syria, Lebanon, and Palestine ... and you know even Palestine not so much anymore because of Hamas's strong religious ticket. So the only country left with the secular stuff at the moment in the whole Middle East is Syria.

Morris: It's not very fashionable right now, secularism.

Syrian Girl: No it isn't. It seems to have been I think from the 70s or 60s... I wanted to make one comparison. If anybody has read the book George Orwell's *1984* there's a character in that, his name is Goldstein. By the end of the book, I'm sorry it's a spoiler, you learn that this Goldstein character was supposed to be against the government and leading this insurgent terrorist organization against the government. He turns out to be a puppet of the government all along and he wasn't even real, he's just an actor and the whole organization he was supposed to be a part of was used to get dissidents to expose themselves by attempting to join it. And one of the other interesting things about the book was the hate minute. This was when this Goldstein character would appear on television and talk about why you should oppose the government. That always reminded me of the hate minute we received watching Osama Bin Laden on either CNN or Al Jazeera, you know, just clips of his speeches and we're supposed to just sit there and rage at this creature.

Morris: It's the signature of our ruling powers now to demonize certain characters. It's terrible and you're absolutely right it's about everybody get angry and hate somebody for a minute.

The Truth About U.S. Air Strikes on Syria

YouTube video by Paul Joseph Watson on Sep 24, 2014. 228,347 views, https://www.youtube.com/watch?v=8nyUnWW5Hh0

Mimi: The wolf changed into sheep's clothing and now many people believe the US is attacking Syria on the basis of fighting ISIS, the new Al Qaeda, but that is not the truth. In this video I'm going to tell you exactly why and how these air strikes will not defeat ISIS.

The US government and military industrial machine have basically three excuses they cycle through to sell their wars to the American people. Number one democracy and regime change, number two WMD's and chemical weapons, and number three fighting Al Qaeda and terrorism. A decade ago in the lead off to the Iraq war all three of these excuses were used, and these exact same excuses are now being used to start a war with Syria – from WMD's, to regime change and now finally fighting Al Qaeda, which seems to be the easiest one to sell. So please don't buy it because even whilst the US was backing Al Qaeda in Libya and Syria, some of us already knew they would eventually use them as an excuse to start a war...

Let Hillary Clinton tell you herself.

Hillary: I mean let's remember here the people we're fighting today we funded. Let's deal with the ISI and the Pakistani military and let's go recruit these Mujahideen and that's great, let some to come from Saudi Arabia and other places importing their Wahhabi brand of Islam.

Mimi: You see the US government needed groups like ISIS in order to weaken Syria before they could attack. Syria has a powerful air defense system and the Pentagon admitted that would make Syria difficult to attack. So again I predicted that the US could attack Syrian soil once ISIS takes out Syrian Air Defenses near Raqqa. I said this in a video last month. Tabqa Airbase near Raqqa may contain S300 Anti War Missile Defense Systems. This is why ISIS, the US government proxy army, are now throwing everything they have at the airbase and have been for last few days. Without this airbase the US airplanes could potentially fly over that region without being harassed by Syria's air defenses and that is exactly what happened with the fall of Tabqa Air Base...

It's a big joke that the US coalition against ISIS includes Saudi Arabia, the country who has conducted more beheadings than ISIS this month. Saudi Arabia is an example of the kind of state that ISIS wants to create, minus the McDonald's of course. Both coalition members, Saudi Arabia and Qatar are the main bankrollers of Al Qaeda...

[Interestingly, two of the most notorious beheading videos featured foreign executioners: "Jihadi John" the Brit, and the one who decapitated Egyptian Copts, who spoke with an American accent.]

If the US really wanted to fight Al Qaeda they would not let their ally Israel provide Al Qaeda-Jabhat al-Nusra faction with air defenses, and medical aid on the Golan Heights border. Just today Israel shot down a Syrian MiG that was targeting Jabhat al-Nusra in order to defend them. It's ironic that for the last three years those liberal humanitarian war mongers were calling for US humanitarian intervention against Syria to save Syrian children, but when the US bombs ISIS, levels Homs and kills babies in Idlib, these so called humanitarians including Amnesty International are oddly silent. Killing babies in order to save babies? I think not. These wars are not about humanitarianism or protecting minorities or fighting ISIS, there are other objectives here...

The US government's real objectives in attacking Syria are to destroy it: the Syrian state, military and the country, breaking it up into three pieces, creating a scenario for perpetual war. They don't even try to conceal this objective. Andrew Tabler from the Washington Institute states this agenda quite plainly. "The outcome of defeating ISIS will likely be a formally partitioned Syria: Assad in the west, a Sunni center and Kurds in the northeast." He then states the breakup of Syria will break up the Syrian-Iran alliance. These war planners believe that all the bloodshed is worth it; that includes a few beheaded US journalists. Now Kerry is claiming that Syria didn't uphold the chemical weapons bargain, just as Bush accused Saddam of doing the same.

A year ago when we were facing a similar attack on Syria I said that the US would not attack while Syria still had chemical weapons and that they would try to disarm Syria first... Almost exactly a month after the chemical weapons were removed, the US began attacking Syrian soil, just as I had predicted.

Now Kerry's timely declaration that Syria did not uphold the chemical weapons deal, it sounds like an excuse to attack the Syrian army as well as ISIS. Eventually a cornered cat retaliates though, and one wonders what Russia's reaction will be... It is wise to remember the breakdown of the League of Nations was what led to World War 2. Are we now witnessing the breakdown of the United Nations? To all those patriots who love their country and sanity, I implore you to re-energize the sleeping antiwar movement, stop this mess before it ends us all. WE are the resistance. [That's right, Mimi. WE are the War on Terrorism! On state terrorism, the only real terror: the rats and moles chewing at the vitals of our republic.]

Articles:

Growth of ISIL: a Planned Decision

By Mimi al-Laham (Syrian Girl Partisan), Nov. 12, 2014
Source: http://sputniknews.com/analysis/20141109/1013195499.html

Those who have never been to Syria may find it hard to imagine that three years ago extremist groups, such as Al Qaeda and ISIL had no presence there. The idea of public beheadings on Syrian streets was unthinkable.

It is easier still to forget, that only four years ago, Libya had the highest Human Development Index of any country in Africa, that there was no Al Qaeda or ISIL in Iraq a decade ago, and that Afghanistan was a secular modern developed country with a capital that three decades ago was named 'the jewel of Asia'.

It may be more comforting for the average westerner to imagine that these Middle Eastern nations were always barbaric backwaters in constant need of western intervention. But it is western intervention in these nations that has caused the rise of Al Qaeda and ISIL.

A Responsibility to Protect NATO Interests

Claims that interventions by the USA in foreign nations are motivated by a humanitarian concern for civilian lives and democracy are readily contradicted by facts. Last year the State Department backed a coup against a democratically elected president of Ukraine and subsequently backed his replacement in bombing civilian areas in east Ukraine.

In the mission to overthrow the Syrian government, the USA has allied itself with undemocratic Gulf monarchies, including Saudi Arabia, one of the most repressive governments in the world. And over a period of months a US aerial bombardment of Syria has already resulted in dozens of civilian deaths.[149]

The so called 'moderate rebels' that NATO and some Gulf states have been supporting to overthrow the Syrian government, have made it clear they are not fighting for democracy.[150] The US administration is forced to use the word 'moderate' as opposed to 'secular' to describe them, as there are no secular insurgent groups.

They are all shades of Islamist, arguably moderate only in comparison to Al Qaeda and ISIL, with whom they are often allied. Jamaal Ma'arouf, the leader of the US sanctioned militia group Syrian Revolutionary Front (SRF), recently admitted to the Independent[151] that his groups frequently fight alongside the Al Qaeda group Jabhat Al Nusra. In the last few days a large number of SRF members defected[152] to Jabhat Al Nusra, taking US-provided weapons with them.

The real objective of the US directed intervention in Syria is not the forcible installation of democracy, nor the protection of human rights, but the destruction of the country. Syria does not kowtow to US hegemony, and has sought to have independent control over its own resources. It is one of the few countries in the Middle East that does not house military bases nor hold any loans from the IMF. Damascus opposes the US ally in the region, Israel, which occupies a part of Syria's territory. This has placed it on the so-called 'axis of evil' list of countries to be attacked, alongside Iraq and Libya.

The gulf Arab states who back regime change in Syria — Saudi Arabia, Qatar, the United Arab Emirates along with NATO-member Turkey — have been openly supporting extremist groups such as the Al Qaeda factions Jabhat Al Nusra and Ahrar Al Sham since the start of the crisis. US Vice President Joe Biden admitted this[153] in a question-answer session at Harvard, while denying any US approval or involvement in this support. In reality these proxy states served to provide the USA with plausible (?) deniability in its backing of extremist groups. The growth of ISIL thus is not an unintended consequence of incompetent US policy makers, but is part of a well-planned decision to overthrow secular nationalist governments in the Middle East by using extremist groups.

ISIS Protecting US Oil interests

As well as overthrowing defiant governments, ISIL provides the USA and its allies with a justification for war that is far more palatable to their own people than supporting democracy, or controlling weapons of mass destruction: fighting

---

[149] http://www.abc.net.au/news/2014-10-23/us-led-air-strikes-kill-553-people-in-syria-monitor-says/5837166

[150] http://www.reuters.com/article/2013/05/29/us-syria-crisis-violations-idUSBRE94S1AO20130529

[151] http://www.independent.co.uk/news/world/middle-east/i-am-not-fighting-againstalqaida-itsnot-our-problem-says-wests-last-hope-in-syria-9233424.html

[152] http://www.dailystar.com.lb/News/Middle-East/2014/Nov-03/276318-nusra-front-sweeps-aside-us-backed-rebels.ashx#axzz3HzSI5Sxz

[153] http://rt.com/news/192880-biden-isis-us-allies/

terrorism. However, the US does not intend to defeat ISIL with the aerial bombardments of Syria and Iraq.

If they were indeed serious about defeating ISIL, they would not be turning a blind eye to Turkey's long-standing and continued policy of allowing ISIL to cross its borders[154] into Syria. They would prevent the Gulf states, Saudi Arabia and Qatar, from discreetly providing ISIS with billions in funding. They would not be undermining the Syrian army by continuing to openly back other insurgent groups, whilst knowing the Syrian army is the only force on the ground that stands a chance of repelling ISIL. Far from weakening ISIL, US involvement has boosted ISIL recruitment.[155] It has given the organisation the legitimacy it desires. ISIL is able to appear to be fighting the USA in the eyes of the Islamists it wants to recruit.

The USA's real objective in creating the anti-ISIS coalition is to create perpetual instability in Syria. Former Pentagon Chief Leon Panetta said[156] that the war on ISIS could go on for 30 years. Long-term instability would prevent the Syrian state from constructing the Syria-Iraq-Iran Pipeline, an agreement signed instead of a proposed Qatari pipeline agreement. The US-backed Qatari plan to run a gas pipeline from Qatar's North field, through Saudi Arabia, Jordan, Syria and on to Turkey to supply European markets would have sidelined Russia. This in turn would give the USA and its allies a monopoly over the European energy market and grant them greater leverage in foreign policy. Isolating Russia and China from influences in the Middle East, Europe, and the Mediterranean is yet another objective in the US establishment's grand strategy. The USA is no stranger to backing extremists in order to isolate Russia; after all they created Al Qaeda to fight the Soviet Union in Afghanistan.

It's no coincidence that ISIL is in control of all the oil rich areas in Iraq and Syria; they have provided the USA with the perfect excuse to target Syrian oil and gas infrastructure. Whilst the US has been bombing ISIL targets in Kobane, ISIL has been able to overrun the Al Sha'ar gas field. It's difficult to believe that ISIL could advance if it is facing the might of the US military and has no state backer.

The only region where the USA may be interested in defeating ISIL is the designated Kurdish areas. The US fights ISIL harder in Iraq's Irbil and Syria's Kobane than anywhere else. The USA also prefers to arm Kurdish and sectarian militias over State actors, as this will help dissolve borders and balkanise the Middle East, a policy coined by former U.S. Secretary of State Condoleeza Rice as the "project for a new Middle East." The nation state *per se* is an obstacle to absolute US control over world resources and trade.

The interests of the US establishment do not align with the interests of the American people. Its policy of supporting instability has not only hurt Christians and Muslims in the Middle East, but has led to the rise of extremist ideologies in Europe and beyond. Many of the fighters now hail from Britain and pose a grave threat to the British public upon their return... Young Syrian soldiers are

---

[154] http://www.al-monitor.com/pulse/originals/2014/06/turkey-isis-border-close.html

[155] http://www.dailymail.co.uk/news/article-2760644/ISIS-signs-6-000-new-recruits-American-airstrikes-began-France-says-start-calling-group-derogatory-Daesh-cutthroats.html

[156] http://english.alarabiya.net/en/News/middle-east/2014/10/06/Ex-Pentagon-chief-predicts-30-year-ISIS-war.html

sacrificing their lives to keep the streets of Syria and the world safe from ISIL. It is time to support, or at the least, stop undermining their fight.

Why Russia Is Seriously Fighting Terrorism and the US Isn't

By Maram Susli, Oct. 20, 2015, in *Near Eastern Outlook*

In the few days that Russia has been fighting terrorism, it has achieved more than the US coalition has in years. According to the New York Times, Russian fighter jets are conducting nearly as many strikes in a typical day as the American-led coalition has been carrying out each month this year, a number which includes strikes conducted in Iraq – as well as Syria.

Even though the US has been bombing ISIS for over a year, ISIS has only grown more powerful and gained more ground in Syria. A few months ago ISIS took over the ancient city of Palmyra, a UNESCO world heritage-listed site...

The US government acknowledged ISIS cannot be defeated without ground troops, yet they have refused to work with the Syrian military...

ISIS Serves US Geopolitical Interests, Threatens Russia's

The US's main objective in Syria is not their expressed goal of 'fighting ISIS'. Their goals are regime change, isolating Russian influence, balkanization of Syria and Iraq, and the creation of failed states... Hillary Clinton herself recently stated that 'removing Assad is the top priority". The presence of ISIS and other terrorist groups serves these interests.

The US sees the Syrian state as one of the last spheres of Russian influence beyond the borders of the former Soviet Union and a threat to the US's Israeli ally in the region. The US has a history of using terrorism to topple governments friendly to Russia. Al Qaeda itself was born of the US effort to topple the Soviet-friendly government of Afghanistan. The dismemberment of Russian-friendly Serbia and the creation of Kosovo was done via the same means.

ISIS was a direct result of the US's war on Iraq and it was only established in Libya and Syria due to overt US-backed regime change efforts in those countries. Although Libya and Iraq did not have relations with Russia as strong as Syria's, Russia was still their main weapons supplier... After Russia entered the war in Syria, Saudi clerics and the Muslim Brotherhood – both US state assets – declared 'jihad' on Russia.

The former Defense Intelligence Agency (DIA) Chief Michael Flynn said in an interview that he believed the US had made a willful decision to allow ISIS to grow in Syria... The Washington Post reports:

"...the CIA has since 2013 trained some 10,000 rebels to fight Assad's forces. Those groups have made significant progress against strongholds of the Alawites, Assad's sect."[157] This shows that the US aim in Syria is regime change and it demonstrates their readiness to spawn terrorist groups to that end.

---

[157] http://bigstory.ap.org/article/1fb971e360c44a8fa7fd361bbc117681/pentagon-change-training-program-syrian-rebels. Funny how 9 days after Putin's offensive against ISIS they throw in the towel, so if they weren't trying to build up ISIS what were they trying to do?

Russia Has More to Gain by Truly Fighting Terrorism

On the other hand, Russia has clear geopolitical interests behind defending the Syrian state against terrorism. Syria has been an ally of Russia for decades and it hosts Russia's only Mediterranean naval base. Russian Foreign Minister Lavrov stated that Russia is entering Syria to prevent 'another Libyan scenario...'

Terrorism poses far greater risks to Russia's national security than it does to the US.

The US Seeks Only to Contain ISIS

...the US objective is not to defeat ISIS, but to contain them within Syria and Iraq's borders indefinitely. This was admitted by a member of the current US government and Democratic Party Representative, Adam Smith, who stated to CNN:

"...we need to find partners that we can work with in Syria to help us contain ISIS. So it is a difficult problem to figure out the best strategy. I agree, they have safe haven there in parts of Syria and that will have to be part of the strategy for containing ISIS."

Chairman of the U.S. House Intelligence Committee Representative, Devin Nunes, told CBS news: *"I think we are containing ISIS within the borders of Iraq and Syria. Outside of that we're not doing much."*

US President, Barack Obama, himself stated that he would like to like to: *"...continue to shrink ISIL's sphere of influence, its effectiveness, its financing, its military capabilities to the point where it is a manageable problem."*

... the Brooking Institute think-tank stated: *"Should we defeat ISIS? Rather than defeat, containing their activities within failed or near-failing states is the best option for the foreseeable future."* [In other words, stop the Iran-Iraq-Syria pipeline for good.]

The US is Not Actually Bombing ISIS

The US bombing of ISIS has been mostly nominal, an exercise in perception management. Although the US military makes regular claims to have bombed specific targets, rarely is video evidence of the bombings published. On the other hand the Russian military regularly releases video of most of its strikes on Russia Today...

Leaked documents show that the US had forbidden its fighter pilots from targeting a long list of ISIS training camps, camps which turn out thousands of fighters a month. Award winning journalist, Robert Fisk, told the Australian program Lateline that the US could have bombed a convoy of ISIS militants who were taking over Palmyra, but instead allowed them to take over a Syrian military post and the ancient City which they have now begun to destroy... When the US has dropped bombs on ISIS run territory, they have used it as an opportunity to destroy Syria's oil infrastructure.

The US Has 'Forgotten' its War with al Qaeda, Now Protects It

Perhaps the most ironic development of Russia's involvement in Syria's fight against terror, is the anger expressed by the US government and its media at Russia's bombing of Al Qaeda (Jabhat Al Nusra) targets.

Former US National Security Adviser, Zbigniew Brzezinski, the man largely responsible for the creation of Al Qaeda, expressed on Twitter his frustration that Russia was targeting Al Qaeda as well as ISIS.

Pro-NATO media have all but forgotten the US's war with Al Qaeda and in the last year avoided any mention of Al Qaeda's existence in Syria, preferring to concentrate on ISIS instead. As of 2015, the Google news engine reveals 219 million hits for ISIS and only 3 million hits for Al Qaeda. In keeping with this trend, Pro-NATO media has avoided bringing to light the fact Russia is bombing Al Qaeda...

The US is Continuing to Fund and Arm Terrorists

Former Ambassador to Syria, Robert Ford, admitted to McClatchy News that the rebels supported Al Qaeda.

This month, footage filmed by the Iraqi military of an oil refinery that had been captured by ISIS, shows US supply crates full of food and weapons delivered to Islamic State militants by parachute drop. In 2014, footage of another US supply drop to ISIS in Kobane Syria also emerged online. Only a few days ago the US airdropped 50 tons of ammunition into Hasake region of Syria, an area partly run by ISIS. Most of the weaponry used by ISIS is US made. In January this year, an Iraqi MP Majid al-Ghraoui publically accused the US of supplying ISIS with weapons through airdrops...

The US has been backed into a corner and in doing so, has exposed itself and its allies as the source of terrorism, not champions truly fighting it.

Maram Susli, also known as "Syrian Girl," is a commentator especially for the online magazine "New. This article first appeared here: http://journal-neo.org/2015/10/20/why-russia-is-serious-about-fighting-terrorism-and-the-us-isn-t/

US Involvement in Turkey's Shoot Down of the Russian Jet

By Maram Susli, Dec. 1, 2015, in *Near Eastern Outlook*

In the wake of Turkey's shoot down of the Russian Su-24, the Russian Foreign Minister Sergei Lavrov called the attack a planned provocation. He went further on to suggest the US had given Turkey permission to shoot down the jet. He explained that countries using US manufactured weapons must ask the US for permission before using them in operations. The aircraft used to shoot down the Su-24 was a US-made F-16. Indeed, there is evidence to suggest that not only did the US give Turkey permission, but that it was moving the strings behind the entire operation.

Two Russian aircraft were attacked that day, but the second was a far less publicised incident. A Russian helicopter was destroyed by the CIA-backed FSA, using US-provided Anti-Tank TOW missiles. The helicopter was on a rescue mission to find the missing Su-24 pilots, and the attack resulted in the death of a Russian Marine... But instead of apologizing to Russia, US state department spokesman Mark Toner defended the actions of the FSA. He also defended the actions of the Turkmen insurgents who shot at the parachuting Russian pilots, a war crime under the first Geneva Convention...

On November 3rd, the US deployed F-15 fighter Jets to Turkey which are specifically designed for air-to-air combat. Since ISIS has no planes, the target could only have been Russian aircrafts. Most significantly, on October 21st, the

US and Russia signed a deconfliction protocol, in order to 'avoid clashes in Syria's skies'. This entailed giving the US information about where and when Russia will conduct sorties. Russian president Putin suggested this information was passed on to Turkey by the US and used to shoot down the Sukhoi-24.

During the months leading up to the attack, US War hawks were increasingly calling for a direct confrontation with Russia, an act that could lead to a third world War. Several US Presidential candidates, including Hillary Clinton, were effectively calling for a shoot down of a Russian jet. Some of the more direct comments included,

Chris Christie: "My first phone call would be to Vladimir, and I'd say to him, listen, we're enforcing this no-fly zone," adding that he would shoot down Russian warplanes that violate the no-fly zone...

The spokesman for the Zionist Israeli lobbying group AIPAC, Senator John McCain, suggested arming Al Qaeda-linked rebels with anti-aircraft weapons to shoot down a Russian jet, an idea which he himself admits was "what we did in Afghanistan many years ago"– the policy which resulted in the birth of Al Qaeda and the rise of the Taliban. Indeed, Qatar had been making an effort towards this end. Documents leaked by Russian hackers 'Cyber Berkut", revealed that Qatar was negotiating with Ukraine to purchase anti-air weapons to help ISIS shoot down a Russian Jet over Syria...

In an Op-ed for the Financial times Brzezinski suggested that Obama should retaliate if Russia continues to attack U.S. assets in Syria, i.e. the Al Qaeda-linked rebels. Brzezinski has experience using Al Qaeda as an asset, having been one of the masterminds behind its creation in Afghanistan...

Instead of risking a direct conflict with two nuclear powers, Turkey was used as a proxy...

On October 8, NATO made a statement that it would defend Turkey against Russia, after a Russian jet briefly passed through Turkish airspace on its way to bomb targets in Syria... On November 12th, EU countries committed to pay Turkey 3 billion dollars ["for refugees"]. Interestingly this is the same amount Turkey is estimated to lose as a result of Russian sanctions put in place in the wake of the attack.

http://journal-neo.org/2015/12/01/us-involvement-in-turkey-s-shoot-down-of-the-russian-jet/

It's the Military-Monetary-Media Complex

by John-Paul Leonard

"Now the reason we only see the FSA side of the story is obvious: the whole operation was tailor-made FOR the MEDIA – the warmongers of yellow journalism. Just another part of the US military-industrial complex."[158]

In the post-industrial casino economy, Eisenhower's famous saying about the "military-industrial complex" is due for an update. In fact, the media have been the key to getting us into war since at least 1898.[159] Truth has always been "the first casualty in war," indeed before it, in the propaganda which sells war.

Mobilizing international opinion against a target regime is mentioned in Gene Sharp's catalog of color revolution tactics, but it's even better suited to gaining support for military aggression. It was the key to conquer Libya and Syria.

The shock troops of Color Revolution are the activists, whether on the street or in global social media. In Syria, starting around 2011, these agitators kept very busy spinning rumors and fake photos and videos. A favorite trick was to disseminate photos from some other place and time, and tag them as proof of atrocities by the Assad regime against civilians. A photoshopped image, placing a family in the ruins of Homs, was labeled as an Assad onslaught on Aleppo. A gruesome video of a Mexican gangland slaying, a beheading with a chainsaw, was propagated as "an atrocity of the Assad regime." One asks, if they had any real evidence of war crimes, why would they risk damaging their case by using fakes?

A very interesting example is the YouTube clip "Syrian Rebels Execute 16 Prisoners in Douma."

> 'Free Syrian Army' fighters in Douma cut the throats of 16 men accused of being government supporters. The evidence for this comes from two separate activist videos. One shows the victims prior to their deaths. They have been captured by insurgents who claim they are 'Shabiha' and policemen.
>
> Another video, also posted by opposition activists but purporting to show the victims of a massacre by pro-government militia, shows the bodies of the very same men earlier seen in the custody of Syrian rebels. They are seen handcuffed and their throats have been cut. [They can be clearly recognized from the first video by their clothing and appearance.] The fact that the dead men were in fact 'Free Syrian Army' prisoners proves that not only did the Syrian rebels kill 16 unarmed men, they also attempted to blame the atrocity on government forces.[160]

Many of these "activist" posters are anonymous, or linked to Western regimes or NGO's. The US taxpayer has been funding shills and trolls to conduct a smear campaign in the dirty war on Syria.

---

[158] *op. cit.* "The Big Lie & Dirty War on Syria: the Foreign Subversive Army Massacres its Human Shields in Daraya," https://www.youtube.com/watch?v=_6YAOJ35yMk Sept. 7, 2012
[159] On this note, I've published *Propaganda for War: How the US was Conditioned to Fight the Great War of 1914-1918* and *1000 Americans: The Real Rulers of the U.S.A.* about media concentration in the 1930's.
[160] https://www.youtube.com/watch?v=Wy_XmN1NoY0, Aug. 23, 2012.

The next step in laundering the lies is for the corrupt mass media to trumpet them over their high-decibel systems. Somewhere tucked away below the headlines of outrage there is often a discreet disclaimer, giving the source as an unconfirmed activist report. In other words, a biased, unfounded attack, that should never be published in the first place without checking the facts.

During the height of the psychological warfare offensive against Syria, there was such a rapid-fire stream of these planted stories that it was very difficult for anyone to track and debunk all of them. Retractions of false rumors were too little and too late, or mostly non-existent.

Sources like SANA, the Syrian Arab News Agency, were totally ignored. During 2012 and 2013 it was often impossible to even access the SANA website.

Western journalists traveling to Syria were almost always embedded with the FSA "rebel" forces, and reported the news from that angle. They showed only contempt for the Syrian viewpoint. This attitude can be seen clearly in the *Der Spiegel* interview of President Assad in the section, "Statements by Statesmen."

Human Beings as Notoriously Unreliable Witnesses

Human judgment is flawed, a good reason why a system of justice needs to be based on due process, and give a hearing to all sides of a story. War propaganda of course is one-sided, and tries to whip up fear, haste and hatred to overwhelm rational debate and decision making.

Why do our media fall in line with this when we supposedly have a free press? There is little or no state censorship, true, but there are limitations to freedom, too. Corporations insist that democracy hang its hat outside the workplace door.

Dependence on a paycheck is as effective a stick and carrot as any. So we have a mercenary army not only in the killing fields of Syria, but occupying the media production line as well. Perhaps not always willingly. When the satirist Jonathan Pie uploaded a video clip of a TV reporter blowing his top and telling the real news, it went viral.

There is the force of conformity, too. Many media people involved in relaying war propaganda appear to act as a herd, expressing group attitudes, along with personal ambition and lack of scruples.

Unfortunately, this description would fit almost any group, including the worst ones, like crime gangs or death squads.

Unfortunately also, it's human nature to readily believe what fits our preconceptions, and to ignore what we'd rather not believe. This tendency reached an extreme with media attitudes towards Libya and Syria.

Just Tell Us What We Want to Hear:
Only False Witnesses Need Apply

Unverified and incompetent sources were avidly believed until (or even after) they turned out to be fakes, like the blog of "Gay Girl in Damascus" or videos of Danny the Syrian. The media relied greatly on "experts" and "authorities" with no credentials at all – Twitter activists like the self-taught "weapons expert" Brown Moses Higgins, the untaught "chemical weapons expert" Dan Kaszeta, or the opposition "war casualties statistics bureau," in the person of the grandly named Syrian Observatory for Human Rights (SOHR). This Observatory was not fitted out with telescopes, it is just one guy with a phone in his family flat in London, far from the scene, and with no particular qualifications other than being an anti-Assad activist – not even a high school diploma.

"Gay Girl in Damascus" was a blog relating a tale of oppression by the Assad regime, which received huge publicity. It turned out that it was a 40-year old male American traveler and professional student at the University of Edinburgh, with no visible means of support. The lesbian angle got attention. One accusation against Gaddafi was the lurid claim that his troops were given Viagra to help them rape civilians! This was taken seriously by the kangaroos at the International Criminal Court, yet no first-hand evidence was ever found.

The BBC and CNN gave a lot of attention to

> English speaking opposition activists on the ground in Syria, most prominently British-Syrian dual national Danny Dayem or "Syrian Danny." Dayem claimed to have aspirations to join the Free Syrian Army, and often called for the implementation of a no fly zone, pleading for the United States, Israel, and NATO to conduct airstrikes against Syrian air bases.[161] Dayem's credibility plummeted when footage leaked of him staging sounds of gunfire and acting relaxed off camera, before going into character for a hysterical "casualty report" during an interview with Anderson Cooper of *CNN*... Given a chance to explain this on the air, Dayem nervously blurted, "I don't know how they got it, this is all private, we should have, this has all been deleted, we have to delete all this stuff."

Cooper just let him slide, ignoring this blatant admission of fakery. [162]

Information from qualified journalists who didn't chime in with the mainstream message was ignored, such as the very valuable dispatch below, by the editor of a German newsmonthly in July 2012. It is excerpted here, and well worth reading in its entirety online.[163]

Dispatch from Damascus

According to the mainstream Western media, a 'civil war' is raging in Syria. Campaigning groups like the SOHR make extravagant claims about huge numbers of casualties (they claim that around 20,000 people have already died) at the hands of the Syrian state security forces. Independent journalists, it is alleged, are not allowed to report directly from Syria, and the regime does not permit free press activities...

I arrived in Damascus on 12 July with a journalist visa... I took the land route from Beirut to Damascus, although a lot of people had told me the route wasn't safe, because Free Syrian Army (FSA) rebels had declared that they controlled around 85% of Syria. But when I crossed the Lebanese-Syrian border, I witnessed the normal border traffic – no masses of refugees, no panic, no fights...

There was no evidence of war on the streets of Damascus. I walked through the city, speaking to people... The answer was always the same – the international media completely distort what is happening. They singled out the Qatar-based TV station Al-Jazeera [affiliated with MI6] for particular criticism.

---

[161] "Syria: Life Under Fire," CNN, February 12, 2012

[162] *Subverting Syria*, p. 56

[163] "Dispatch from Damascus," Manuel Ochsenreiter, Quarterly Review, July 2012, http://www.quarterly-review.org/dispatch-from-damascus-guest-article-by-manuel-ochsenreiter/

On 16 July, I went to the old Christian village of Maalula, around an hour's drive from Damascus... one of the very last places where one can encounter people speaking Aramaic, the language spoken by Jesus... They all expressed the belief that President Bashar would lead the country out of the crisis...

I returned to Damascus via the city of al Tel, which the FSA had occupied briefly until the Syrian army re-took the city. One could still see the traces of the rebel forces and their supporters – notably graffiti on walls celebrating not freedom or democracy, but rather extremist Muslim preachers. There were also threats daubed on shops – "Go on strike or burn!" – painted by rebels seeking to force the shop owners to go on strike to place pressure on the government. Western policymakers have a woefully wrong notion of Syria's "Arab Spring". There is little or no liberal, progressive opposition; even the FSA is an assembly of different militia groups, including jihadis, mercenaries and criminals.

On 15 July, the rebels launched what they called "Damascus Volcano", their military assault on the capital, claiming it would be a decisive operation... In most of the city the only things which burned were the coals on the hubble-bubble pipes of café customers. The war was confined to a few districts, like Al-Midan... I took the opportunity to visit the military hospital of Damascus, where every day around fifteen Syrian soldiers die from their injuries – this makes about 450 soldiers a month, in the Damascus area alone...

An interview with a 34 year old Syrian Army captain who had been lucky enough to survive a rebel attack was especially memorable... He recollected, "I told my comrades to kill me before I fell into the hands of the enemy... They torture us to death – they cut off our hands and cut our throats if they capture us alive."

He assured me also that the rebels are not Syrians, but come from many countries, especially Libya, the Gulf States, Iraq, Afghanistan and Pakistan – jihadis and mercenaries who kill for petrodollars... Before I left the hospital, he showed me a picture of his two daughters and told me fervently that he was fighting for their freedom...

The rebels had attacked the hospital several times, but the UN, Amnesty International or Human Rights Watch seemed uninterested in these violations of the conventions of war.

As the fighting continued, the whole city became nervous. Shop owners closed their doors early in the afternoon; they wanted to be certain of getting back to their families. Some took their money and things of value with them. They were worried that their shops might be looted and plundered – by the rebels, not by the army – if the fighting reached the city centre...

I went to al-Midan, where the fighting had been very intense... I was brought in an armoured vehicle to the fighting zone at the edge of al-Midan... Soldiers were firing from cover at a building where rebel snipers were holed up... The dead bodies of rebels lay in the street. The face of at least one was obviously non-Arab; it seemed he had come from Afghanistan...

A small transport vehicle came along the street, loaded with the rebels' arms and equipment. The driver showed me what they had found in the FSA control centre – huge amounts of ammunition, automatic guns, machine guns, and Syrian Army uniforms, used to discredit the state and confuse civilians...

I met Foreign Ministry spokesman Dr. Jihad Makdissi on a day when he was dealing with what Al-Jazeera was calling the "Massacre of Tremseh". Al Jazeera had claimed that the regime had slaughtered more than 200 civilians in the village, but later on it emerged that there had been a fight between the army and the FSA. Dr. Makdissi, who studied in Britain and speaks fluent English, repeated patiently over and over again in press conferences the facts – the security forces had killed 37 rebel fighters and two civilians in an attack on the village, which the rebels had been using as a base to launch attacks on other areas... government forces had not used planes, helicopters, tanks or artillery.

I left Damascus on 21 July, to head back to Lebanon. I planned to go by car again. Several Syrians warned me that the journey would be dangerous, and that the border with Lebanon would be thronged by refugees. But when I asked them the sources of their 'information', they were always Al Jazeera and Al Arabia TV-news... sure enough, once again the highway to the border was calm, without much traffic...

A final surprise came at the Lebanese side of the border. There I saw for the first time the black-white-green rebel flag waving in the wind. Immediately beyond the Lebanese border station were a dozen Western TV teams, waiting for the 'refugees'. Some of them were paying interviewees in dollars for short interviews; and the wilder the story, the better they seemed to like it. It seems that reality doesn't mean all that much when the Western media talk about Syria.

Blame the Victim: the Clockwork Massacres. Houla and Tremseh

The daily feed of accusations that "the dictator Assad" was killing his own people did build up an enemy image, but to galvanize the "international community" into military intervention, something really shocking was needed.

Thus began a series of attempts to manufacture world outrage by staging fake massacres. Rebels filmed military and civilian casualties from their own attacks as evidence of war crimes by the army.

In each case, the media jumped to hasty conclusions based on "unverified activist reports." Each time, before the UN investigators could arrive, world "leaders" were calling for action against Syria.

Cutthroat Treachery in Houla

On May 25, 2012 there was one such stage-managed massacre of civilians in a village in the region of Houla, close to the Lebanese border. As in other such incidents, this one was timed a few days before a UN Security Council meeting on Syria, which might result in a green light for airstrikes against "the regime."

The Houla killings fit the Iraqi pattern of an ethnic cleansing operation by death squads. It seemed clear that the Alawites in the village had been attacked by "Sunni rebels," and this is how the *Frankfurter Allgemeine Zeitung* reported it, noting that "Those killed were almost exclusively from families belonging to Houla's Alawi and Shia minorities. Over 90% of Houla's population is Sunni."[164]

The rest of the Western media bought the claims that the victims were killed by Assad's artillery. A video was represented as a tank shelling a house, when on closer inspection, it shows a rebel shooting an RPG.[165] BBC News published the photo showing "body bags of murdered children," which was from Iraq nine years earlier (see image on next page). Then photo and video evidence of the victims,

---

[164] "Report: Rebels Responsible for Houla Massacre," John Rosenthal, *National Review*, June 10, 2012, http://axisoflogic.com/artman/publish/Article_64609.shtml

[165] "Syrian Houla Massacres: Divide & Conquer Strategy Exposed," Syrian Girl, May 28, 2012, https://www.youtube.com/watch?v=ngUJsfr5rrA

Frames from Progressive Press Hit on Youtube, "The Foreign Subversive Army Massacres its Human Shields in Daraya"

On Aug. 25, 2012 NATO-backed jihadists committed a major massacre in the Damascus suburb of Daraya. As with Houla, the mainstream media (MSM) rushed to blame the "Assad regime." On Aug. 27, Progressive Press blog "The Big Lie & Dirty War Against Syria" headlined, "MSM Close Ranks around Daraya False Flag Coverup," analyzing the evidence that the FSA were the perpetrators. On Aug. 28, a secret NATO teleconference decided on a strike against Syria, basing on the media hysteria. On Aug. 29, the first Western journalist to visit the scene, Robert Fisk, confirmed that the victims were killed before the Army came in to restore order.

Standard operating procedure: Self-styled activists (may be assets of US intel) post fake evidence to corporate media, who stir up world opinion. USA then takes actions against target nation, which are never retracted, even if media errors are. As I noted in *The War on Freedom*, this is how the US goes to war almost every time, through a coordinated campaign by the industrial-military-media complex. In our video clip we give examples of what the MSM do and do not show:

The BBC presented this "activist photo" as piles of children's bodies slain by Bashar al-Assad. In fact it shows victims of US war crimes against Iraq.

Syria massacre in Houla condemned as outrage grows

27 May 2012

PHOTO FROM ACTIVIST

This image - which cannot be independently verified - is believed to show the bodies of children in Houla awaiting burial

NEWS MIDDLE EAST

Home | UK | Africa | Asia | Europe | Latin America | Mid-East | US

The able-bodied Syrian people – 14 million out of a total population of 22 million nationwide – get out to rally behind their government, and to decry foreign intervention. The MSM suppress this news, and cover only their pet NATO-backed "protesters."

—John-Paul Leonard

also supplied by the opposition, showed great numbers of the dead were children with slit throats – a practice typical of Al Qaida in Iraq.

In fact, before striking the village, the massed rebels first attacked an army unit that had been stationed there to protect the area after earlier rebel attacks.

The media "sources" then changed their story and blamed the Shabiha, "regime paramilitaries." Even the UN tended to accept this version (according to MSM mouthpiece Wikipedia, where majority rule favors the opposition narrative). There were reports that some attackers tried to impersonate the Shabiha, such as by writing "I am Shia" on their foreheads, perhaps a trick learned earlier in Iraq or Libya, or in training supplied by the US.

Syria has universal military service, joining all ethnic groups together. They are not mercenaries, not Black Berets or Special Forces, they are the boy next door. Indeed, the Syrian Army may be the most respected institution in the country.

Thierry Meyssan noted that

> the Syrian Catholic news agency Vox Clamantis immediately issued a testimony formally accusing the opposition. Five days later, the Russian news channel Rossiya 24 aired a very detailed 45-minute report, which remains to date the most comprehensive public inquiry...
>
> The Free "Syrian" Army launched a very large-scale operation to reinforce its control over the region...

Certain families viewed as regime collaborators were murdered first.

> With only one of the Army's bases having fallen, the assailants changed strategy. They transformed a military defeat into a communication operation, attacking the al-Watani hospital and setting fire to it. They took corpses from the hospital morgue and transported them along with those of other victims to the mosque, where the bodies were filmed....
>
> This was the video evidence presented as a regime massacre.
>
> The existence of the "Shabbihas" is a myth... there is no structure or organized group that could be termed as a pro-government militia.[166]

The Shabiha myth is an attempt at role reversal. The "rebel" death squads claim they are the army protecting the village, and the army are the death squads.

The Houla attacks were timed just before a visit to Syria by the UN's Kofi Annan and served to jettison the UN peace plan. In reaction, Western nations expelled Syrian diplomats, and already on June 1, the United Nations Human Rights Council voted to condemn Syria.

The Massacre... er... Battle of Tremseh

Another battle between the army and the "terrorists" that was hawked as a massacre took place at the village of Tremseh on July 12, 2012. The Syrian Army says it acted on a complaint by villagers and carried out an operation against

---

[166] Meyssan, "The Houla affair highlights Western intelligence gap in Syria," June 5, 2012, http://www.voltairenet.org/The-Houla-affair-highlights . For a follow-up on Houla, see Adam Larson, "Syria : One Year After the Houla Massacre. New Report on Official vs. Real Truth," May 18, 2013, http://www.globalresearch.ca/syria-one-year-after-the-houla-massacre-new-report-on-official-vs-real-truth/5335562

terrorists occupying several houses, who had also ambushed an army convoy. "Activists" all the way up the line to the US State Dep't and Ban-kee Moon at the UN immediately jumped on this to medialize it as a kind of Guernica *cum* Lidice *cum* Nurnberg war crimes trial. Two days later, though, UN investigators essentially admitted the Syrian government version. The casualties were almost all fighters, not civilians.[167]

The BBC blandly quoted the Syrian news agency SANA:

> The bloodthirsty media in collaboration with gangs of armed terrorists massacred residents of Tremseh village... to sway public opinion against Syria and its people and provoke international intervention on the eve of a UN Security Council meeting.[168]

Was the BBC amused at being styled "bloodthirsty?" But this was the pattern: each time a great hue and cry was raised just in time to try and push through a UN resolution against Syria, which would let the bloodshed flow in rivers.

Activists confabulated an absurd story of a massacre to go along with the battle: "It appears that Alawite militiamen (Shabiha) from surrounding villages descended on Turaymisah after its rebel defenders pulled out, and started killing the people."[169] The claim that "rebel defenders" who had just stormed the village were protecting it from its old neighbors for peaceful generations, is clumsy propaganda.

Daraya: The Foreign Subversive Army Massacres its Human Shields

Damascus Suburbs, Aug. 25, 2012

Not having the desired effect, did the terror scriptwriters decide an escalation was needed? Here is how the Associated Press served up the next big atrocity to the world's newspapers:[170]

> **Evidence mounts of new massacre in Syria after rebels claim death toll of 300 to 600 people**
>
> According to activists' accounts, government forces retook the Damascus suburb of Daraya from rebel control three days ago and have since gone on killing spree
>
> This citizen journalism image provided by Shaam News Network SNN, taken on Sunday, Aug. 26, 2012, purports to show people killed by shabiha, pro-government militiamen, in a makeshift morgue in Daraya, Syria.
>
> Video footage posted by activists showed lineups of corpses, many of them men with gunshot wounds to their heads.
>
> The gruesome images appeared to expose the lengths to which the regime of authoritarian President Bashar Assad was willing to go to put down the rebellion that first broke out in March last year.
>
> The video footage and death toll were impossible to independently verify.

[167] http://www.nytimes.com/2012/07/15/world/middleeast/details-of-a-battle-challenge-reports-of-a-syrian-massacre.html?_r=0
[168] http://www.bbc.com/news/world-middle-east-18823303
[169] https://en.wikipedia.org/wiki/Battle_of_Tremseh
[170] http://www.nydailynews.com/news/world/evidence-mounts-new-massacre-syria-rebels-claim-death-toll-300-600-people-article-1.1145020

"Daraya, a city of dignity, has paid a heavy price for demanding freedom," the Local Coordination Committees <u>activist</u> group said in a statement, adding that the Assad regime targeted residents with executions and revenge killings "regardless of whether they were men, women or children."

"Local Coordination Committees" seem to be more of a virtual network created on line and in line with the Unconventional Warfare scenario of revolutionary organizations, with only a very sketchy presence on the ground.

Let's just compare their claims with what Robert Fisk found when he was the first Western journalist to visit the scene a couple days later:[171]

Inside Daraya - how a failed prisoner swap turned into a massacre.

The massacre town of Daraya is a place of ghosts and questions. It echoed to the roar of mortar explosions and the crackle of gunfire yesterday, its few returning citizens talking of death and assault, of **foreign 'terrorists'**, its cemetery of slaughter haunted by **snipers**. But the men and women to whom we could talk, two of whom had lost their loved ones on Daraya's day of infamy four days ago, told a story quite different from the popular version that has gone round the world: theirs was a tale of **hostage-taking by the Free Syria Army** and desperate prisoner-exchange negotiations between the armed opponents of the regime and the Syrian army, before Bashar al-Assad's government decided to storm into the town and seize it back from rebel control...

When we arrived in the company of Syrian troops ... snipers opened fire at the soldiers, hitting the back of the ancient armoured vehicle in which we made our escape. Yet we could talk to civilians out of earshot of Syrian officials – in two cases in the security of their own homes – and their narrative of last Saturday's mass killing of 245 men, women and children suggested that the atrocities were far more widespread than supposed...

Leena said that she was travelling through the town in a car and saw at least ten male bodies lying on the road near her home... She said Syrian troops had not yet entered Daraya...

Another man said... "One of the dead was a postman – they included him because he was a government worker."

The home of Amer Sheikh Rajab, a fork-lift truck driver, had been taken over, he said, by gunmen as a base for 'Free Army' forces, the phrase the civilians used for the rebels. They had smashed the family crockery and burned carpets and beds.

The saddest account of all: "We had already seen the pictures on the television of the massacre – the western channels said it was the Syrian army, the state television said it was the 'Free Army' – but we were short of food and Mum and Dad drove into the town. Then we got a call from their mobile and it was my Mum who just said: 'We are dead.' She was not. She was wounded in the chest and arm. My Dad was dead..."

Dead or alive, in a Syrian war zone, ordinary people have access to both Western and Syrian media. In America, Land of the Free, we have easy access to... Western media.

---

[171] http://www.independent.co.uk/voices/commentators/fisk/robert-fisk-inside-daraya-how-a-failed-prisoner-swap-turned-into-a-massacre-8084727.html

The subtitle of my Daraya video is "The FSA Massacres its Human Shields." Here is one reason:

> Another Syrian TV channel caught pro-FSA TV channel Al Arabiya saying this in their report on Daraya: "The Free Army takes cover in a populated neighborhood... its members take cover among residents while awaiting what they call 'Zero Hour.'" But hiding among civilians in military terminology is taking them as human shields. That's a war crime under the Geneva conventions. He who takes a civilian as a human shield knows that the other side cares for that civilian and cares for his safety. The Syrian Arab Army is doing its best to protect the Syrian people.[172]

Moreover, Fisk mentions the FSA were taking hostages. One man interviewed on Syrian TV below speaks of men who were held in a room and executed. Same pattern as in Houla and Tremseh: bodies of battle dead and massacre victims are piled up in the mosque, dead bodies are filmed, "activists" upload it to Al Jazeera, and the corrupt Western media go raving mad.

They gobbled up the "activist" video clip of the dead, but never once registered Syrian TV's coverage, which included interviews with citizens days before Fisk got there. Here are some captions from my video in the link below (I hope you may find time to watch it).[173]

> Man: "Just please relieve us from these gangs."
>
> Woman with tearful voice: "They were all men with weapons, they expelled us from our houses, yelling that the Army is coming to kill us. But when the army found us, God protect them, they brought us a car and are taking us to our homes."
>
> Man, exasperated: "We don't dare go out. Please get rid of these gangs. Our children are on the streets, we don't know where. Some children hiding in basements, they're not eating, they're not able to use the toilets. Just get rid of these gangs!"
>
> Man, holding back tears, "I don't know where is my family. Our women where are they? They sent us inside a room, when we heard sounds of bullets, and when we tried to return to the shelter, the women were crying loud, when we went upstairs, we saw all of the men were dead."
>
> Reporter: A mother tried to shield her children with her own body, but in vain, all were slain.
>
> Syrian Army Soldier: They're killing women and children in cold blood, let all the world see.

As the death count rose, finally the army had to come in to drive out the terrorists. But they were well-trained, and had a plan ready – to turn military defeat into a "communications victory." Was this training part of the non-lethal aid from the US State Dep't.?

The FSA was led by veteran Libyan death squads, such as Liwaa al-Umma, which was trained by US or Qatari special forces during the Libyan war, and the

---

[172] "The Big Lie & Dirty War on Syria: the Foreign Subversive Army Massacres its Human Shields in Daraya," https://www.youtube.com/watch?v=_6YAOJ35yMk Sept. 7, 2012
[173] Ibid. I put a major effort into this high quality video on the Daraya Massacre:

LIFG, which is on the State Dep't. list of terrorist groups.[174] "CIA-fostered terrorist groups include the Libyan Islamic Fighting Group (LIFG), which was created in Afghanistan with Libyan militants previously armed and trained by the CIA to overthrow Muammar Gaddafi in the early 1980's. After several failed attempts to seize Libya by force, these fighters filtered back into Afghanistan to fight the occupying US."[175] So behind the FSA public relations image of "democracy activists" were these trained killers.

Liwaa al Umma - Libyan Islamic Fighting Group in Syria.

The next day, the "activist informers" had turned the story inside out; now it was the government troops making house-to-house raids on the town (but Fisk told us the massacre occurred *before* the army came). *The Guardian* gobbled that up too and headlined, "If opposition group figures are correct, Saturday's action would be worst single atrocity by regime forces in 17-month civil war."

As in Houla, terror brigades mass forces to occupy a town. They kill people deemed to be pro-regime. They line up those dead bodies and their own in the mosque, then call it a massacre by the regime and call for intervention.

The media could easily have realized the people support the Syrian army a year earlier, and that the FSA are just death squads and snipers, too, if they'd picked up on Webster Tarpley's reports from Damascus, which played on RT. If they'd wanted to. RT also reported:

> The timing of the "massacre" reports is of no coincidence, believes Middle East expert and radio show host Kevin Barrett. They come as the UN Security Council is scheduled to hold ministerial meeting on the humanitarian impact of the conflict on August 30. "We really need to resist this intense psychological warfare

---

[174] See "Fall of the Arab Spring" in the section, "Who Needs a Clash of Civilizations," citing Pepe Escobar, and http://landdestroyer.blogspot.com/2012/08/uk-sends-5-million-to-listed-terrorists.html , Tony Cartalucci, Aug. 12, 2012

[175] *Subverting Syria*, p. 74-75

campaign which is mainly based on lies and distortions that's being waged by the Western countries... They don't want to bring peace to Syria. They want to break Syria up and make it a nonviable state," he argued.[176]

The *Guardian* ran interference for the escalation by the West. Because of vetoes by Russia and China,

> Western officials say they have largely given up on security council diplomacy and are stepping up their assistance to the fragmented opposition, though they say that assistance stops short of weapons. Saudi Arabia and Qatar are reported to be shipping arms to rebel groups, however, as the conflict continues to escalate.[177]

The war party did get their payoff from Daraya. On August 28, NATO held a secret teleconference with member and affiliated states, and got a unanimous decision in favor of a strike against Syria.[178]

The BBC has a timeline of "Syria's bloodiest days," which it almost always blames on "regime forces," while quoting "Syrian state news" saying "armed terrorist gangs" kidnapped residents, "killed them and then filmed the bodies to discredit Syrian forces."[179]

For instance, in Al-Bayda and Baniyas in May, 2013, Human Rights Watch is cited alleging that victims were executed *after* the army drove out the rebels. The open source forum, A Closer Look on Syria (ACLOS) says it was the other way around, and notes manipulation and staging of bodies for photographs.[180]

ACLOS is a very interesting and commendable effort. It says, "Wikipedia uses 'reliable secondary sources' and rejects primary sources. Evidence has shown that on geopolitical issues, 'reliability' in Wikipedia terms correlates inversely with the facts and what primary sources tell... ACLOS relies only on primary sources. Secondary sources are utilized only as much as primary sources can be extracted from them – or where the information provided is non-controversial."

In other words, primary source means it is based on reality and free speech, while Wikipedia and the entire Western geopolitical media sphere is based on opinion, oligarchical censorship and ulterior motives. The secondary source shibboleth elevates the herd behavior of sheep above the power of reason.

Back to the "activists," reliable or not, who are the "primary and first source" of the photos so eagerly accepted by the MSM, the mainstream media – they are the first to make photos, because they were there committing the crimes. Possibly even cross-dressed in Syrian army uniforms. The DoD's UW manual briefly discusses what tactics of "deception" are allowable under the laws of war, and what is "treachery" or inadmissible, such as false uniforms or false flags. So accusations of treachery cannot be admitted either; they will be ignored, rejected out of hand or dismissed as conspiracy theories.

---

[176] https://www.rt.com/news/daraya-massacre-reports-syria-590/

[177] http://www.theguardian.com/world/2012/aug/26/syrian-regime-accused-daraya-massacre,

[178] Gordon Duff, "NATO Secretly Authorizes Syrian Attack," Press TV, http://www.eurasiareview.com/30082012-nato-secretly-authorizes-syrian-attack-oped/

[179] http://www.bbc.com/news/world-middle-east-18255521

[180] Adam Larson, June 5, 2014, http://www.globalresearch.ca/media-disinformation-and-coverup-of-atrocities-committed-by-us-sponsored-syria-rebels/5350325 ; http://acloserlookonsyria.shoutwiki.com/wiki/Baniyas_massacre

Poison Fog:
The Ghouta CW Massacre and the Big Push for War on Syria

At least a year before the August 2013 attacks in the Damascus suburb of East Ghouta, US drumbeating about Syrian chemical weapons (CW) had bloggers warning of a CW false flag op – among them, Syrian Girl Partisan:[181]

> In the last few days a photo emerged of the insurgents unpacking boxes of gas masks... some of the gas masks are in the US style M42A1 and not in the Russian style, which means they could have only come from outside of Syria...

> Some time ago the BlogSpot Land Destroyer actually posted images of the insurgents donning the gas masks, and even RT reported about the potential for a chemical weapons false flag operation.

> In the last month there has been a lot of news and accusation coming out of the mainstream media, claiming that Syria might use chemical weapons against its own people... the Israeli Ambassador to the UN Ron Prosor demanded that the Syrian government lock down its chemical weapons and said, "We should not pretend that a regime that cuts the throats of children today will not be prepared to gas them tomorrow..." clearly a sign that they are planning some sort of false flag event. This is in order to create a *casus belli* for an attack on Syria by NATO powers, in the same way that WMDs were used in Iraq. There have also been some claims that NATO and Israel are afraid of the chemical weapons getting into the "wrong hands" and hence must act in order to stop this from happening.

These warnings proved all too accurate.

On August 20, 2012, Obama answered a question about US military intervention in Syria by saying, "We have been very clear to the Assad regime, but also to other players on the ground, that a red line for us is we start seeing a whole bunch of chemical weapons moving around or being utilized." In April 2013, a spokesman self-righteously announced that even a "transfer of chemical weapons to terrorist groups is a red line..."[182] As if the US would not be involved, but it might come in handy for a pretext to intervene sometime.

Hardly sooner said than done. The Al-Qaida gang, "Jabhat al Nusra, were reported to have seized a chemical factory near Aleppo in December 2012."

In March, Syrian Ambassador to the UN Bashar al Ja'afari reported that armed terrorist groups had fired a rocket on the town of Khan al Assal, west of Aleppo. "A thick cloud of smoke had left unconscious anyone who had inhaled it." It killed 25 people and injured 110 soldiers and civilians, who were hospitalized. Syria immediately asked the UN to investigate.

In May, 2013, Turkish police also arrested an Al Nusra cell with 2 kg. of sarin in Adana, Turkey, not far from Aleppo.[183]

---

[181] "Chemical Weapons False Flag Against Syria, Update," Aug. 3, 2012, https://www.youtube.com/watch?v=DbMdll58lis

[182] https://www.washingtonpost.com/news/fact-checker/wp/2013/09/06/president-obama-and-the-red-line-on-syrias-chemical-weapons/

[183] http://www.globalresearch.ca/chemical-fabrications-east-ghouta-and-syrias-missing-children/5442334

The Crisis[184]

In Damascus, before dawn on August 21, 2013, it is a year to the day since Obama drew his red line. Videos and commentaries from Syrian opposition sources are pouring in through the world media, claiming the Syrian government has just attacked civilians with poison gas in the rebel-held Damascus suburb of East Ghouta. Hours later, the US claims it has proof from intercepted phone calls that the Syrian Defence Ministry was behind the attack. Obama and his cabinet are calling allied leaders to mobilize a coalition for a lightning Libya-style bombing campaign.

The next day, *Russia Today* headlines, "Russia suggests Syria 'chemical attack' was 'planned provocation' by rebels."[185] On Aug. 23, the US Navy already starts moving a task force into position to strike Syria.[186]

In the week that follows, tension mounts as Syria becomes the top story. The mass media are showing horror footage of dead and dying children from Ghouta. Secretary of State Kerry (the Bonesman Democrat who ran against Bonesman Bush), keeps the media on message: all evidence points to the use of chemical weapons; THUS a war crime by the "Assad regime," mandating a military intervention under the "responsibility to protect" doctrine. War drums drown out any dissenting note that the US-backed rebels could have been the attackers, excepting a few prominent voices like Vladimir Putin and Rand Paul.

The juggernaut that brought us the Afghan, Iraq and Libya wars seems to be well on its way in record time. Yet surprisingly, online polls and constituent e-mails to Congress are running as high as 90% against any Syria strike. Only a minority of these ordinary Americans suspect a false flag. Most are saying we can't afford to be the world's policeman, or going in there will only make things worse – we will be helping our sworn enemies, Al Qaeda. Some Congressmen are openly unimpressed by the thin evidence presented by the White House.

Another glitch in the war script comes on Aug. 29, when the British Parliament votes down the government's motion for war, thanks largely to the new Labour leader Ed Miliband. It's this august body's first "No War" vote since 1782, when they declined to pursue the counterinsurgency against the breakaway American colonies.

For once, a vote could be called historic without hyperbole. The US is left with no allies, and the lesson is not lost on Obama. On Aug. 31 he decides to submit his war plan for Congressional approval, a Constitutional requirement observed largely in the breach. Now it has become a battle for US public opinion.

Obama claims the military option remains on the butcher's proverbial table, regardless how Congress votes when it returns on Sept. 9, while he and his minions keeps twisting their arms as hard as possible. The chips are down for the war party, and Israel drops for a moment its disguise of disinterest, as AIPAC cranks up an assault on Congress.[187]

---

[184] This section and the next two comprise the bulk of my unfinished e-book, *Fabrication of a Provocation*, published Sept.-Oct. 2013

[185] http://rt.com/news/russia-syria-chemical-attack-801/

[186] http://thinkprogress.org/security/2013/08/28/2539341/syria-chemical-weapons-saga/

[187] http://www.presstv.ir/detail/2013/09/06/322396/aipac-set-to-drag-us-into-war-on-syria/

On Sept. 9, Assad is interviewed on CNN, and in London, Kerry remarks that if Assad turns over the chemical weapons in the next week (*sic*), he could avoid an American attack. The State Department, hell-bent on "limited strikes," then backtracks, but the idea is picked up by the Russians.

The rest of September involves the hammering out of a plan between Russia and the US for the disarming of Syria's chemical weapons. By the end of the month, the headlines are about the Tea Party defunding and shutting down the government – ill winds for a new war.

Have Putin and Assad snatched defeat from the jaws of victory? Syrian Girl has a good argument, that Syria's chemical weapons are its only strategic deterrent. They make the world safer by diminishing the risk of a first strike by Israel. Above all, they have kept Syria safe from a ground assault by the US, while defenseless Iraq and Libya were pulverized. Assad however seemed to feel the CW were as much a liability as an asset.

There is good reason to believe the US war party is secretly very pleased with the outcome, a UN resolution "much better than expected." [188] The US gave no *quid pro quo* in exchange for Syrian disarmament, such as abandoning its campaign to destroy this independent nation by unconventional warfare.

Putin and his team scored some points. Russia took a bold step by breaking the taboo and bringing false-flag discourse into the open. Putin wrote a great op-ed in the NY Times,[189] and enjoyed a surge of popularity in the US, at least until the Ukraine crisis. There was increased awareness now that the "rebels" are actually fanatical Al Qaeda terrorists, with the almost supernatural power to vindicate even George Bush, as they really do "hate us for our freedoms."

Nevertheless, this was an ordinary stick-up, a daylight robbery – "Give up your weapons or your life!" The victim Syria was first attacked with CW, then blamed for CW, then robbed of its CW, of its right to strategic deterrence against its nuclear-tipped neighbor.

Seymour Hersh Wants to Know, "Whose Sarin?"

Seymour Hersh, in the esteemed *London Review of Books*, Dec. 19, 2013.[190]

Barack Obama did not tell the whole story this autumn when he tried to make the case that Bashar al-Assad was responsible for the chemical weapons attack near Damascus on 21 August... In the months before the attack, the American intelligence agencies produced a series of highly classified reports... citing evidence that the al-Nusra Front, a jihadi group affiliated with al-Qaida, had mastered the mechanics of creating sarin and was capable of manufacturing it in quantity. When the attack occurred al-Nusra should have been a suspect, but the administration cherry-picked intelligence to justify a strike against Assad...

'Assad's government gassed to death over a thousand people,' Obama said. 'We know the Assad regime was responsible ... it is in the national security interests of the United States to respond to the Assad regime's use of chemical weapons

---

[188] http://thinkprogress.org/security/2013/09/27/2690111/why-the-un-syrian-chemical-weapons-resolution-actually-better-than-expected/

[189] http://www.nytimes.com/2013/09/12/opinion/putin-plea-for-caution-from-russia-on-syria.html

[190] http://www.lrb.co.uk/v35/n24/seymour-m-hersh/whose-sarin

through a targeted military strike... In the days leading up to August 21st, we know that Assad's chemical weapons personnel prepared for an attack near an area where they mix sarin gas. They distributed gas masks to their troops. Then they fired rockets from a regime-controlled area into 11 neighbourhoods that the regime has been trying to wipe clear of opposition forces.'...

[However, these] were not descriptions of the specific events leading up to the 21 August attack, but an account of the sequence the Syrian military *would have followed* for any chemical attack...

Already by late May... the CIA had briefed the Obama administration on al-Nusra and its work with sarin... al-Qaida in Iraq (AQI), also understood the science of producing sarin... At the time, al-Nusra was operating in areas close to Damascus, including Eastern Ghouta.

Were advisers telling Obama something he didn't already know? The precision and complexity of the Ghouta attacks suggest the technique, the personnel and the war pretext were all in the plan. The article boils down to the white hats at the CIA doing their job and tracking what the black hats were up to. As usual, Hersh deftly manages to be sensational, yet politically correct, shoring up plausible deniability, with the image of the Best in the West free press and laurels of courageous investigative journalism...

I always get excited when I read his bombshells, but on reflection they deflate and look like limited hangouts, the CIA running damage control up the flagpole. Already in March 2013, after Khan al Assal, *the world heard* the rats have poison.

In April 2014, Hersh has "The Red Line and the Rat Line," which ventures into the zone of false flags – but by Turkey. The wily devil Erdogan trying to trick us nice guys into a war! Go on. Let's see what more Hersh pulls out of the hat. Yet he's the best we have, pushing the MSM envelope as far as it will go.

Up To Their Old Tricks

"We are sure the rebels have got sarin. They would need foreigners to teach them how to fire it. Or is there a 'third force' which we don't know about? If the West needed an excuse to attack Syria, they got it right on time, in the right place, and in front of the UN inspectors." – Syrian journalist, quoted by Robert Fisk, Sept. 22, 2013.[191]

Recent history records too many such hyper-convenient excuses. If we step back 14 years, we find the uncanniest parallel is the alleged massacre of civilians by Serbian forces in the village of Račak in 1999. It unleashed NATO's apocalyptic, three-month aerial blitzkrieg which laid Serbia to waste. It was "the first massacre in history conducted before an invited audience" – OSCE inspectors were already on the scene, called in by the Serbian side for insurance, but fatally headed by a diplomatic hit man – the American officer who ran death squads as ambassador to El Salvador in the 1980's.[192]

On August 21, 2013, UN inspectors had just arrived in Damascus, Syria, on the *invitation* of the government, to investigate a smaller, earlier chemical weapons

---

[191] http://www.independent.co.uk/voices/comment/gas-missiles-were-not-sold-to-syria-8831792.html
[192] "Appointment in Račak," in *Gladio, Nato's Dagger at the Heart of Europe*, p. 438

attack in the town of Khan al Assal, which UN investigator Carla del Ponte had already identified as the work of terrorist rebels, based on witness accounts. When the new, much larger chemical weapons explosion occurred in the suburb of Ghouta in the wee hours of Aug. 21, the UN staff were staying just two miles from the scene. They were soon diverted from Khan al Assal to Ghouta, sparing the US and its anti-Syrian bloc an embarrassing report on a chemical weapons attack by their own side.

Once again, as in Serbia, the US war party immediately seized on the killings and began to gear up to bomb Syria, ready to defy the UN Security Council. And in both crises, Russia played a weak hand as well as it could to oppose US aggression.

In Yugoslavia in 1999, the US-trained rebels were called the Kosovo Liberation Army (KLA), in 2013, they were named the Free Syrian Army (FSA). The KLA's tactic at Račak was to change the clothes on their own battle dead overnight, and pass them off as civilians. The real villagers had already left to escape the fighting. In Syria, the FSA used the same tactic to produce false-flag massacre videos in Houla and many other towns. In 2013, the suburb of East Ghouta was also a ruined, largely abandoned ghost town even before the chemicals atrocity.

In 1999, hysterical KLA reports were spread over list serves and the Internet. Since 2011, the FSA and their supporters upload videos to YouTube, which are eagerly peddled by the mass media and the White House.

Just as the Kosovo false-flag massacre gave the green light for a genocidal bombing campaign, the Ghouta false flag was meant to unleash US bombers for three months on a growing list of Syrian targets.

The endgame in 1999 was splitting off an ethnic enclave, Kosovo, that became a beachhead for the US, for Al Qaida, narcotics trade, and Camp Bondsteel, the largest overseas US military base since Vietnam. Something along these lines seems to be planned now for Kurdistan.

Like the KLA, the FSA have used their civilian victims as well as their own battle dead as false flag props. They added child victims in Houla, which multiply the emotional effect of war propaganda images. Children predominate in the Ghouta videos supplied by the FSA to such an extreme that many observers have questioned their authenticity.

The foremost researcher probing these anomalies immediately after the events was Mother Agnes de la Croix, a Catholic nun and non-partisan observer based in Syria. She and her team spent many hours comparing video footage, and finding a raft of damning discrepancies, such as the video fakery presented here.

:

CAIRO, EGYPT.   GHOUTA, SYRIA.
Aug. 14, 2013   Aug. 21, 2013

Since Račak and 9/11, as the world has grown weary of war, the body counts needed to provoke a reaction have multiplied. Yet the parallels between Ghouta and Račak remain too precise to be accidental or spontaneous. Both bands of fighters were trained by the US, played on the US media, and seem to be following the same playbook for fabricating and exploiting provocations.

Indeed, terrorism expert Yossef Bodansky asks, "Did the White House Help Plan the Syrian Chemical Attack?" He writes,

> On August 13-14, 2013 [a week before the *casus belli* in Ghouta], Western-sponsored opposition forces in Turkey started advance preparations for a major and irregular military surge. Initial meetings between senior opposition military commanders and representatives of Qatari, Turkish, and US Intelligence ["Mukhabarat Amriki"] took place at the converted Turkish military garrison in Antakya, Hatay Province, used as the command center and headquarters of the Free Syrian Army (FSA) and their foreign sponsors. Very senior opposition commanders who had arrived from Istanbul briefed the regional commanders of an imminent escalation in the fighting due to **"a war-changing development"** which would, in turn, lead to a US-led bombing of Syria.

> The opposition forces had to quickly prepare their forces for exploiting the US-led bombing in order to march on Damascus and topple the Bashar al-Assad Government, the senior commanders explained. The Qatari and Turkish intelligence officials assured the Syrian regional commanders that they would be provided with plenty of weapons for the coming offensive.

> Indeed, unprecedented weapons distribution started in all opposition camps in Hatay Province on August 21-23, 2013.... The weapons were distributed from store-houses controlled by Qatari and Turkish Intelligence under the tight supervision of US Intelligence.

> Opposition officials in Hatay said that these weapon shipments were "the biggest" they had received "since the beginning of the turmoil more than two years ago."

Senior officials from both the Syrian opposition and sponsoring Arab states stressed that these weapon deliveries were specifically **in anticipation** for exploiting the impact of imminent bombing of Syria by the US and the Western allies.[193]

The clear implication is that the Ghouta massacres were orchestrated by the US as a trigger for an invasion by rebels with US air cover.

Why would Syria invite CW investigators, and then use CW while they were there? This is one of the questions asked at the open-source forum, "Who Attacked Ghouta? An analysis of all evidence relating to the chemical attack in Ghouta on August 21st 2013 - An online collaborative effort." The conclusions of this effort:

The only plausible scenario that fits the evidence is an attack by opposition forces...

Findings which are directly indicative of a rebel attack:

The attack was launched from an opposition-controlled area 2 km north of Zamalka...

The sarin was of low quality and contained impurities that indicate it was likely produced underground and not in a military plant..

A video leaked by an anonymous source associates Liwa Al-Islam (a Jihadist rebel faction) with a rocket attack that is likely related to the chemical attack...

The distance from Zamalka to the suspected Syrian army base is 9.5 km, while the UMLACA rocket's range is 2.5 km...

Two possible motives were found plausible:

Targeting Mistake...

False flag... a deliberate attack on an opposition neighborhood, in attempt to meet the US's red line for intervention.

The research also exposed the implausibility of the regime attack scenario:

To believe that the attack was carried out by the regime, one would need to assume the following:

1. The regime decided to carry out a large-scale sarin attack against a civilian population, despite (a) making steady gains against rebel positions, (b) receiving a direct threat from the US that the use of chemical weapons would trigger intervention, (c) having constantly assured their Russian allies that they will not use such weapons, (d) prior to the attack, only using non-lethal chemicals and only against military targets.

2. The regime pressed for a UN investigation of a prior chemical attack on Syrian troops, and then decided to launch the large-scale sarin attack at the time of the team's arrival, and at a nearby location.

3. To execute the attack they decided to (a) send forces into rebel-held area, where they are exposed to sniper fire from multiple directions, (b) use locally manufactured short-range rockets, instead of any of the long-range high quality chemical weapons in their arsenal, and (c) use low quality sarin.[194]

---

[193] http://southweb.org/blog/did-the-white-house-help-plan-the-syrian-chemical-attack/
[194] http://whoghouta.blogspot.com/2013/11/the-conclusion.html

The Whoghouta blog ignores the photo fakery, evidence which rules out the targeting mistake option. It also discounts the story published by Mint Press where Ghouta rebels say they are on the Saudi payroll, and complain they had been given CW without adequate training, and some of them even died from it. They alleged that the explosion occurred from mishandling the weapons. This might be a damage control leak for local consumption, as other sources say the local villagers were pointing the finger at the rebels.

Interestingly, the Mint Press piece says that "Doctors who treated the chemical weapons attack victims cautioned interviewers to be careful about asking questions regarding who, exactly, was responsible for the deadly assault." Of course, the narrative was being controlled.

The rebels also mentioned a plan to carry out a CW attack in Latakia in revenge for the attack on Ghouta.[195] This idea was soon dropped, to go along with getting bombs dropped instead, evidently.

Staged and Scripted: The Signs of Video Fakery

Fox News: I'm sure you've seen the videos that we have seen of the child gagging on the ground, of the people vomiting on the floor.

President Assad: Yeah, but no one has verified the credibility of the videos and the pictures... The only verified things are the samples that the [UN] delegation went and took; samples of blood and other things from the soil and so on.

Fox News: Which is what they say they have.

President Assad: But you cannot build a report on videos if they are not verified, especially since we lived in a world of forgery for the last two years and a half regarding Syria. We have a lot of forgery on the internet. [196]

Forgery by the US-backed opposition in Syria has indeed been too rampant to even catalogue. Faked telephone intercepts and scores of faked "activist videos" were all the evidence Obama administration could offer Congress. All the false flags and disinformation thoroughly demonized the targeted government with a build-up of rogue reports, illusory images and loose logic. Once the myth of the murderous regime was established, new accusations would be uncritically accepted.

Terrorism has always been psychological warfare. Terrorists kill and then blame the deaths on the state. Complicit pundits then casually hold the target government accountable for inflated casualty totals, when in fact most of the dead are either rebels, or killed by the rebels.

Brainwashing Western-style is heavily dependent on imagery over reason. It is a form of entertainment, employing cinematic special effects. Most of us have driven by dozens of car accidents in real life, without seeing any wrecks that burst into flame. Yet a Hollywood car crash most often disgorges a sensational fireball. That's entertainment.

---

[195] "Syrians In Ghouta Claim Saudi-Supplied Rebels Behind Chemical Attack," Dale Gavlak, Yahya Ababneh, August 29, 2013, http://www.mintpressnews.com/witnesses-of-gas-attack-say-saudis-supplied-rebels-with-chemical-weapons/168135/

[196] http://syrianfreepress.wordpress.com/2013/09/19/president-al-assads-interview-with-fox-news/

In Syria, a CNN team has been accused of being involved with rebels blowing up a pipeline for an "explosive news story" – and blaming it on Assad to boot. CNN denies this, but it's odd that one of their crew was past British Special Forces.[197] We should never forget the lies that paved the way for the genocidal war on Iraq. There was fake yellowcake at the UN, and the "anonymous" Kuwaiti ambassador's daughter in Congress, with her wild tale of Iraqi troops throwing babies out of incubators. Her fake tears moved Congress to wage war.

Assad noted this defect in his interview with Charlie Rose: "We're not like the American administration. We're not a social media administration or government. We are the government that deals with reality."

Mother Agnes and her Syria-based group ISTEAMS made a heroic effort to dissect the reality and fakery of the rebel videos which the Obama regime used to push Congress to the brink of war. They assembled a 53-page report[198] on the anomalies they found.

Taken together, the discrepancies point to a strange and disturbing conclusion: the scenes were staged, the videos are fake. Rebel psychological warfare units evidently prepared them before Aug. 21. They then uploaded them to YouTube immediately after the staging of a low-grade release of chemicals in the early hours of Aug 21, which may have claimed some real victims. Opposition NGO's then fed the hysteria about a CW massacre to the world media.

The first odd thing is the hour of the event: around 2 or 3 a.m., under cover of darkness. Any independent observers would have slept through it. By the time they awoke, the show would be all over – the Internet. Also, 25 mph winds made it an unsuitable occasion for CW. But the timing was spot on for diverting the UN investigators from Khan al-Assal.

Ghouta was already depopulated by fighting, except for rebel bands and a few of their families. Street scenes of the aftermath after daybreak show men only. Yet the footage of victims is predominantly of children – of course evoking the strongest emotions for propaganda. In an interview with a child survivor, a boy says none of his friends or neighbors were hurt, because they all left beforehand.

Women victims are scarcely seen at all, except for one view of shrouded bodies in a separate room. Were the actors strict Islamists who didn't want to show the faces of the actresses? Or were the victims kidnapped and the women raped and killed first? There were a number of mass abductions by the rebels in the weeks before the attacks.

None of the victims are ever identified in the videos. Their names are simply not known; instead, a number is written on each forehead. If rescuers went to homes to bring people out, as they claim in the videos, they would know who the patients were by where they lived. If the families came to the clinics by themselves, they would have given their names. So if they were alive when they came in, at least some of their names should be known. The rebels claim they were treating the sick. Can you imagine a clinic or a doctor not asking a patient

[197] CNN Crew Linked With Homs Bombings , March 22, 2012
https://www.youtube.com/watch?v=DfSwJi_LUWk#t=383
[198] http://progressivepress.com/dox/AgnesVids/IsteamsGhoutaSep18.pdf

their name? Is the problem that the victims were not residents of Ghouta at all, that the rebels are guilty of their deaths?

A narrator, identified as a Revolutionary Council Commander, says, "The martyrs are 865, they are all unidentified. They are numbered on their foreheads as you can see... so that if their parents come they will be able to recognize them." By numbers? And how did so many children turn up alone, without their families? Young children are not known to go out alone much at 3 a.m.

How is it possible that all 865 are unidentified? Only if they have been brought in as props or actors. If they were families sleeping in Ghouta and awakened in the chemical attack at 3 a.m., they would go to the clinic together. Any who survived, would identify their next of kin. This is really a conclusive point.

There is not a single video of a funeral, and only one shot of a grave, with only eight bodies in it. Funerals and posters in memory of the dead are a very important part of the culture in this part of the world. Why were they not filmed for their propaganda value, in Syria and abroad? Were there no relatives to hold the funeral?

There is not a single scene of a family or a mother with her child. There is only one alleged father carrying his daughter into the clinic. He is ranting an anti-Assad diatribe, and saying "she calls me father." We then see him ranting over a little boy's body, not his own son – suggesting he is a rebel actor. Ten minutes after the scene with his "dead daughter," a video is uploaded from another location with her still alive – yet the first video showed her dead on arrival.

A clip from a Cairo morgue is presented as a scene from Ghouta. US Secretary of State Kerry also presented that same famous photo of bodies in Iraq to the UN as Ghouta victims *again*, following an old error made by the BBC after an earlier false-flag massacre in Houla. (See the photo in the section on Houla.)

Scenes of children's bodies laid out on the floor are presented in different videos as scenes from different villages. However, many of the same dead children are shown in these different places at the same time!

On the next page, the same ten children are posed as dead in two different videos supposedly from two different places, Al Marj and Kafr Batna. The 11th child, the girl in yellow, is seen in a third video from yet another place, Jobar.

The same little boy is shown in different scenarios supposedly filmed in five different areas, Ain Tarma, Hammouria, Irbin, Zamalka and Jobar. The videos were uploaded only minutes apart, a little after 4 a.m. Some of the footage is shared between the videos, but differently edited. Fast footwork indeed!

The children's bodies are often shown with their shirts pulled up to show their little bare tummies, increasing the emotional effect. Many of them appear to be anesthetized rather than dead.

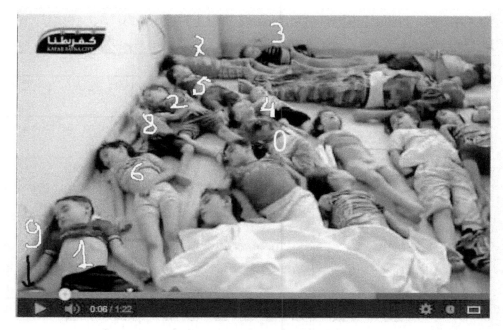

Scene from "Al Marj"

Scene from "Kafr Batna"

Assad is absolutely right in saying Kerry has no evidence. There are good reasons why it took many years for videos to be accepted as evidence in court. Even today, courts require an unedited original. What is served up by the rebels on YouTube are heavily edited pastiches with no chain of custody. Enough when you are looking for any excuse to bomb and destroy a plucky, independent little nation.

East Ghouta chemical weapons incident (August 2013): significant reports

Source/report/evidence	Method and conclusion
Carla del Ponte (UN)	Khan al Assal: Witnesses report 'rebels' used sarin gas in North Syria
Various news reports	Pre-East Ghouta: 'Rebels' (al Nusra) arrested in Turkey with sarin gas
'Syrian Rebels' and associates	1,300+ killed, including children, from Government CW shelling (however only one grave shown, with eight bodies)
Human Rights Watch	The CW used were only in possession of the Syrian Government (SG)
New York Times	Telemetry evidence links attacks to SG bases (later MIT studies force NYT to modify this claim[199])
Lloyd and Postol (MIT)	Rockets used had limited range and could not have been fired from suggested SG positions.
Gavlak and Ababneh (MINT Press)	Rebel groups admitted CW had been supplied to them by Saudis; some locals had died due to mishandling
Mother Agnes / ISTEAMS	Images were contrived, no social context, no families or women, who are the children?
John Mesler (NSNBC)	Parents identified children in photos as those kidnapped in Latakia, two weeks earlier[200]
Seymour Hersh (LRB)	Interviewed US officials. Intelligence was manipulated to blame President Assad, false claims used.
Turkish lawyers and writers group (PALJ)	Saudi backed 'rebel' group Liwa al Islam believed to be responsible.
UN Dec 2013 report on CW attacks in Syria	CW were used in East Ghouta; three of five CW attacks were 'against soldiers' or 'against soldiers and civilians'
HRC Feb 2014 report	chemical agents used in Khan-Al-Assal attack 'bore the same unique hallmarks' as those used in East Ghouta

---

[199] "Serious Questions about the Integrity of the UN Report," Subrata Ghoshroy, http://web.mit.edu/sts/Analysis%20of%20the%20UN%20Report%20on%20Syria%20CW.pdf, Sept. 26, 2013
[200] http://nsnbc.me/2014/10/10/combating-propaganda-machine-syria/

The "rescuers" and "medics" mostly look like Al Qaeda fighters, with the obligatory beards.

There is almost no indication of ambulances or other medical transport efforts, in spite of the alleged scale of the disaster. Sirens are heard only twice in the videos, an ambulance is seen only once. Scenes of arriving patients show private cars with only a single, nameless victim.

In two scenes described as rows of dead bodies, someone is giving one of the bodies an injection, or taking a blood sample. During a disaster with a great shortage of antidotes, why would they inject a dead body? Unless it is with sarin?

When ISTEAM published their report on Sept. 15th, with links to the suspect videos, YouTube quickly removed most of them... Some that could be retrieved are cached here http://www.progressivepress.com/dox/AgnesVids/

The US "intelligence community" had to be aware of these discrepancies, yet they gave their seal of approval to a whole archive of the faked videos, just as they signed off on the WMD lies for Bush's war on Iraq.

Reports Ignored Around the World

Psychology has shown that once people form an impression, they tend to deflect new information that doesn't accord with it. This principle is applied in propaganda work. Be first to the post, devil take the hindmost.

Two years after Houla, Daraya and Ghouta, Wikipedia and the media still blame "the regime." Yet a raft of studies have shown the opposite. A few of them were tabulated by Global Research, above.[201]

The article by Prof. Tim Anderson that accompanies it, "Chemical Fabrications: East Ghouta and Syria's Missing Children," is an excellent summary of the whole narrative of chemical weapons by the Syrian rebels.

The Ghouls of Ghouta

While I personally have little taste for tales of horror, the bizarre or the macabre, the facts point to some very, very weird practices in this case. I'll mention just two more YouTube videos.

The first one, "Undeniable Proof SNC & Al Farok did Chemical Weapons Attack in Syria 8/21/2013,"[202] identifies Al Farouk Brigade as the culprits, by matching photos and videos of known rebel leaders and other persons with responders, parents, doctors or victims in the Ghouta videos. One photo is labeled "Dead Men Cannot Hold Fingers Together." The subject looks like a rebel lying on the floor with one hand grasping the fingers of the other hand. The next shot is labeled, "Dead Babies Do Not Have Goose Bumps. This Baby is Alive."

Next is a government spokeswoman reporting that the Ghouta villagers say the rebels kidnapped children and men from the villages of Latakia (Alawite pro-Assad province), brought them here, put them in one place, and used chemical weapons on them. (Most people had left Ghouta, it was mostly inhabited by

---

[201] "Chemical Fabrications: East Ghouta and Syria's Missing Children," Prof. Tim Anderson, April 12, 2015, http://www.globalresearch.ca/chemical-fabrications-east-ghouta-and-syrias-missing-children/5442334

[202] https://www.youtube.com/watch?v=FdF6aSnxhDs

rebels and sympathizers. We have seen the pattern that they pick victims from the other side.) Then, footage of children and women in a truck, caption: "Alawite children and women kidnapped by terrorists: Kidnapped Shabiha, and brought to be gassed there." The rebels do have a mania for video-recording everything they do... Next a shot of a group of anti-rebel protesters who are captured and kidnapped by them prior to the attack, and then gassed: faces of filmed "shabiha" captives are matched with those of dead victims.

Then there is a monologue by a rebel in uniform with English subtitles:

> Those are trying to take out the chemicals which produce a lethal and deadly gas that I possess. We decided to harm them through their women and kids. This guy falsely quotes Quran (fight them the way they fight you). We kill their kids and women as Osama bin Laden said: "Until they cease killing our women and kids." The idea of our announcement, a couple of days ago the SAA tried to break into our region. We decided with our brothers that this weapon is powerful, effective and repelling, and the destructive one that we possess, to use it to repel. We said in the announcement, if they came close even one meter, there is no other way and everything is permitted then. We will strike them in their homes. We will turn their day into night and their night into day.

Following this is a TV reportage by Press TV in Hatay:

> Residents in the southern Turkish province of Hatay claim the chemical weapons used in an August attack in Syria's capital Damascus were used by Al-Qaida linked Al-Nusra front insurgents and not the Syrian government. Farid Maini, a Hataj resident, and an activist himself, told me those chemicals were sent to Syria from Turkey.

> Maini: "Whoever used those chemical weapons wanted to push us into war. None of us want war here. In the history of Hataj we all live peacefully side by side. Now there is Mossad, CIA, Al-Qaida, all over the place. We are worried they might also use chemical weapons against us."

> A second man, "Four months ago, Turkish security forces found a 2 kg cylinder with sarin gas after searching the homes of Syrian militants from Al Qaida and Al Nusra. They are using our borders to take the gas into Syria. The Syrian president has no reason to kill his own people."

Next is rebel selfie footage of them shooting off a mortar loaded with a blue CW canister. First voice: "Allahu Akbar... Hajji if you want it to hit the building, move it to the west 25 meters." Second voice: "I will bring just one Sarin - gas Sarin."

Then an interview with one of two Western journalists who were held hostage by the rebels. They overheard a conversation between an FSA commander and an officer from the Farouq Brigade. The journalist says, "From this conversation, it is very clear that the Assad regime is not responsible for the dissemination of this chemical weapon in the Damascus suburb."

This is the Belgian hostage Piccinin, captured by FSA together with Italian war correspondent Quirico, both of them ironically anti-Assad and pro-FSA, who overheard a Skype conversation between rebel commanders.[203]

---

[203] "Assad not Responsible for Ghouta Gas Attack, Says Freed Hostage Pierre Piccinin," Sept. 9, 2013, http://www.ibtimes.co.uk/syria-chemical-attack-assad-rebels-blame-hostage-504735

Now for the Twilight Zone video: "Syria: Rebels Caught Executing Survivor of Ghouta Chemical Massacre (2013)," by Adam Larson.[204] It's based on intensive research by Denis O'Brien, who has a legal and pharmacological background. His theory is not needed to show there was a ghoulish massacre by the opposition, as the anomalies above are enough, but it is one plausible scenario.

Because of the large number of videos uploaded by the rebels, O'Brien chose to concentrate on one site, Kafr Batna. The video concentrates on the most sensational finding: two of the corpses in the morgue are bleeding from slit throats. On one of them, his clenched hands clearly show he had still been alive. Conclusion: the victims were gassed in the basement (the "Dark Morgue"), then laid out upstairs in the "Sun Morgue" for photos and videos.[205]

O'Brien also found that the corpses are too reddish for sarin victims. Dead bodies normally turn bluish, also in death by nerve gas. Red is typical of carbon monoxide or cyanide poisoning. I confirmed this. Moreover, death by sarin is very messy – a lot of white saliva, sweat, and fecal incontinence. Pupils of the eyes shrink to "pinpoint' size. There were no such symptoms in any of the videos.

Why do it in such a weird way? There might not have been any other way. And hardly anyone would believe anything so strange were possible.

The rebels and their taskmasters were in a tight spot. Damascus had brought the UN to investigate Khan al Assal, and it was going to be clear that the rebels had used CW there. This would spoil the chances of ever getting an armed intervention based on CW. The rebels needed a big CW attack by the regime to turn the tables, and they needed it... exactly on the day the UN arrived.

Quite a challenge. The rockets must fall on a rebel-held area, to plausibly blame the regime, and to control the events. However, most residents had already fled Ghouta, and casualties from previous CW rocket attacks had only numbered a few dozen each time. They needed large numbers to trigger US intervention. Gas chambers could do that, then they could multiply the body count by remixing footage in hundreds of different videos. Using sarin in gas chambers would be risky to the operators, while carbon monoxide would be much safer to work with – and easy to produce. One rebel "doctor" allegedly remarked that patients had been hiding in basements and burning tires, and needed to be educated about that! Toxic smoke and CO in an enclosed space are deadly enough.

Finally, they needed to time it precisely when the UN came to investigate Khan al Assal, so a lot needed to be prepared in advance. Mainly victims and videos, which were uploaded very quickly, some allegedly even before the event.

Why were victims brought in only one at a time by private car? To create the impression of gathering victims (injured or dead) over a wide area? Ambulances might have taken the sick from their homes to real hospitals. There are very few scenes of arriving patients, compared to the claimed death toll. Whoghouta says all the rockets hit the village of Zamalka, but there were videos from several villages around it (Jobar, Irbin, Kafr Batna, Al Majr, Ein Tarma.) Did hundreds of people drive to neighboring villages, or was this an attempt to magnify the scope

[204] https://www.youtube.com/watch?v=IR05Bpyo7wg, June 1, 2015
[205] http://libyancivilwar.blogspot.com/2014/11/the-ghouta-massacres-sarin-myth.html

of the attacks? The UN report mentions rockets in Ein Tarma. LCC Syria claimed 600 "martyrs" (dead bodies?) were transferred from Zamalka to other towns.

The ACLOS talk page on Kafr Batna discusses O'Brien's thesis (http://acloserlookonsyria.shoutwiki.com/wiki/Talk:Alleged_Chemical_Attack, _August_21,_2013/Locations/Kafr_Batna#Denis_O.27Brien_.22Sun_Morgue.2 2_Investigation) and comes to similar conclusions.

> Yes, sarin usually kills in under 15 minutes. Most victims should be dead long before they reach the hospital. Those that do, should have a high survival rate. Yet it seems that everyone that comes to the ["rebel"] hospitals ends up dead. In Zamalka or somewhere we see several living children being treated, yet they are all later shown dead or in the morgue. A slow but unavoidable death is a symptom of chlorine gas poisoning. – Petri Krohn

The talk also noted that in the UN report, only two survivor interviews give the distance the rocket fell from their homes, and it was just 20 meters. "This suggests that the rockets didn't contain much sarin, and that it didn't spread very far." So the number of casualties should not have been so much higher than at Khan al Assal. The conclusion here is sadly similar to mine:

"A possible explanation fitting all the evidence would be something like this. The attack had two components: firing of sarin-filled rockets into Zamalka to point the finger at the regime, and a massacre of captives to generate photo-ops and outrage."

After Eastern Ghouta was finally liberated by the Syrian Army in August 2016, I asked my source for the Daraa story to go there and talk to the local people to investigate. This is what he reported.

Some witnesses told of CW bombs exploding in tunnels. One of them said he saw "forces of the Army of Islam digging the tunnel, and walk inside carrying large containers. I was nearby the tunnel during the attack, and I was hit , like many of the civilians by the toxic substances." Several witnesses said they saw the chemical rockets were launched by the Army of Islam from rebel-held orchards toward the residential areas.

One witness said that in an abandoned rebel weapons factory, they found empty white plastic bags marked "poison" and carrying the Saudi logo. This witness also said the terrorists besieged a school, not letting any children or teachers leave. Then they targeted the school with CW rockets, killing 200 children. This was the source of the photos of children without parents, taken by an Al Jazeera film team that was there. "Hundreds of children's families were outside the school fence, crying and screaming, demanding for the bodies of their children, but the Al Jazeera cameraman did not photograph them because they were cursing the militants, and accusing them of launching the chemical rockets and blowing up the toxic mines . The Syrian army was innocent of this, army troops were hurt too, because we saw the ambulances taking out Syrian army soldiers who were suffocated. The army surrounded Ghouta to help families that can escape from the militants."

Of course, the rocket attack on the school could simply be a plausible theory, and I'm not in any position to confirm these reports. It's ironic, however, that exactly one year earlier, I had predicted exactly such a maneuver.

Give Us Each Day Our Fill of Lies

The Dirty War on Syria Blog, Aug 24, 2012

A top story on Yahoo yesterday blared the headline, "Assad's War on Syria's Children." The casual viewer will assume that Assad is massacring 1000s of kids. Read it and come to find out all they have is two kids who exhibit violent behavior, after their rebel father and uncle fought back against the army instead of evacuating. Moral: terrorists make terrible parents.

Typical, twisted, Goebbelsian MSM war propaganda, from the aptly named "Daily Beast."

For that false flag the US is planning in order to get their war on Syria, I bet you their proxy insurgents the FSA Fanatic Saudi Assassins wipe out a school full of kids with chemical weapons and blame it on Assad. No war propaganda more potent than the killing of babies.

They have already recycled the phony Kuwait/Iraq incubator babies deaths tale from 1990 against Syria now.

Already on August 29, 2013 Mintpress printed a famous article by reporter Yahya Ababneh, who interviewed Ghouta residents. AP stringer Dale Gavlak helped him write the story and lost her job because of it.[206]

The U.S., Britain, and France as well as the Arab League have accused the regime of Syrian President Bashar al-Assad for carrying out the chemical weapons attack, which mainly targeted civilians. U.S. warships are stationed in the Mediterranean Sea to launch military strikes against Syria in punishment for carrying out a massive chemical weapons attack...

However, from numerous interviews with doctors, Ghouta residents, rebel fighters and their families, a different picture emerges. Many believe that certain rebels received chemical weapons via the Saudi intelligence chief, Prince Bandar bin Sultan, and were responsible for carrying out the dealing gas attack.

"My son came to me two weeks ago asking what I thought the weapons were that he had been asked to carry," said Abu Abdel-Moneim, the father of a rebel fighting to unseat Assad, who lives in Ghouta.

Abdel-Moneim said his son and 12 other rebels were killed inside of a tunnel used to store weapons provided by a Saudi militant, known as Abu Ayesha, who was leading a fighting battalion. The father described the weapons as having a "tube-like structure" while others were like a "huge gas bottle..."

"They didn't tell us what these arms were or how to use them..." "Jabhat al-Nusra militants... merely used some ordinary rebels to carry and operate this material."

Doctors who treated the chemical weapons attack victims cautioned interviewers to be careful about asking questions regarding who, exactly, was responsible for the deadly assault...

More than a dozen rebels interviewed reported that their salaries came from the Saudi government.

---

[206] http://www.mintpressnews.com/witnesses-of-gas-attack-say-saudis-supplied-rebels-with-chemical-weapons/168135/

The "Moderate Opposition," the Children from Ballouta, and the Sarin Gas Attack on Eastern Ghouta

Adapted from John Mesler, NSNBC, Oct. 10. 2014.[207] This report answers questions about the high number of children in the videos, the speed with which these were edited and uploaded from different locations with different arrangements of the same victims, and the reason some observers noted that children in the photos appear to be alive, under anesthesia.

On Aug. 4, 2013, FSA terrorists came into the peaceful Alawite farming village of Ballouta in Latakia to carry out sectarian cleansing. They went house-to-house, wiping out whole families. 220 dead bodies were counted in the hospital, greeted by the deafening silence of the "international community" and its human rights organs. The survivors fled until the army could free the village two weeks later. The FSA also kidnapped 100 small children and a few women. They were taken to a nearby place called Selma, still held by the FSA. Some of the captives were tortured. About two weeks later,

> They drugged the 100 children and arranged them in poses on the floor to appear dead. They created many videos using their captives as actors. The video was sent via cell phone to a contact person in Damascus... who later uploaded the famous Sarin Chemical attack video on YouTube.com...

> There really was sarin used in Damascus, this is proven from various investigations. However, it never involved vast numbers of people, as the first reports claimed... CNN's Fred Pleitgen could not find gas victims when he went to all the hospitals in Damascus, excepting the few Syrian soldiers in the military hospital, who had happened on gas canisters in a rebel tunnel.

Why no sarin victims in hospitals? Were the FSA "clinics" hoarding victims – and keeping a lid on talkative witnesses?

> On May 7, 2014 after 9 months of captivity, 44 of the original 100 kidnap victims were released from Selma to a hospital in Latakia. Their release was part of the deal that also released terrorists in the Old City section of Homs. However, the remaining kidnap victims continue to be held in Selma.

The parents are not talking about the incident because they hope to get their children back alive.

Of course, there were other casualties besides the 100 virtual child victims, and the CW rockets were necessary – to establish the regime attack narrative, and for survivors to show to the UN investigators for testing. But if most of the dead were killed with other gases, they would test negative for sarin. For the operation to succeed, then by no means must the investigators take blood samples from the dead. And the UN didn't take a single one.

Oksana Boyko from RT grilled UN investigator Angela Kane about this.

Kane: "A dead body can't tell how the person dies ... a living person can tell you that." Incredible. Translation: The living, under the thumb of the rebels, will tell us just what we and the rebels want. Which was not forensic autopsies.

---

[207] http://nsnbc.me/2014/10/10/combating-propaganda-machine-syria/

Failure of the Human Rights Bureaucracies

If the old colonialism was sanctified by the "White Man's Burden" and "civilizing mission," the new twist in neo-colonialism is the Humanitarian Intervention, or as Alex Jones loves to say, "Love bombs" – especially lovely when dropped under a UN Resolution on the Right to Protect Civilians.

The UN

Being financed largely by the US and its allies, the UN Human Rights Council was ready to rubber-stamp accusations against Libya and Syria.

> Unverified reports accusing Muammar Gaddafi of strafing peaceful demonstrators with fighter jets and killing more than 6,000 civilians were the basis for the Libyan Jamahiriya government's expulsion from the UN Human Rights Council shortly before the UN Security Council issued Resolution 1973, which imposed a no-fly zone on Gaddafi...[208]

A main source of the reports was Libyan "human rights activist" Dr. Soliman Bouchuiguir. He prepared a petition together with "human rights organizations" UN Watch and the National Endowment for Democracy (NED). UN Watch cherry-picks alleged abuses in countries on the US hit list, such as Venezuela. The NED is an actor in instigating color revolutions. Their petition claimed that Gaddafi was committing war crimes, and 70 more NGO's signed it.

> French investigative journalist Julien Teil interviewed Bouchuiguir in his 2011 documentary film, *"The Humanitarian War."*
>
> **Teil:** The Human Rights Council, where you gave your speech, did not investigate the information you provided before the UN Security Council used them. How do you explain the lack of investigation and testimony that led directly to a United Nations Resolution? ...
>
> **Bouchuiguir:** I think the decisive fact is that Gaddafi used the air force against his own people...
>
> **Teil:** About the number of people killed, can you give us any evidence?
>
> **Bouchuiguir:** There is no evidence.[209]

While *Al-Jazeera* and *BBC* repeated the claim that Gaddafi's air force was strafing popular demonstrations, Russia reported their satellite monitoring of Libya showed there were no such attacks.

In Syria the pattern was the same. Tony Cartalucci in *Subverting Syria*:

> The UN Human Rights Commission UNHC report late in 2011, was based entirely on "witness accounts" recorded not in Syria, but rather in Geneva... the report itself was compiled by a director of a corporate-funded US think-tank representing the collective interests of the very corporations pushing for Syrian "regime change."
>
> Organizations including Soros-funded Human Rights Watch (HRW) have likewise weighed in with reports based entirely on "witness" and "activist" accounts," [210]

---

[208] *Subverting Syria*, p. 49
[209] Ibid., p. 51
[210] http://landdestroyer.blogspot.com/2012/03/syria-game-over-for-western-propaganda.html

In the wake of the Ghouta CW attacks, activist Mother Agnes said in an interview on Russia Today: "The footage that is now being peddled as evidence had been fabricated in advance. I have studied it meticulously, and I will submit my report to the UN Human Rights Commission based in Geneva."

On Sept 11, 2013. Press TV reported, "Russia says the United Nations Human Rights Council (HRC) has confirmed that the videos and photos purporting to show the victims of a chemical attack near the Syrian capital, Damascus, were fabricated."[211]

Yet the agency never went public with the facts. In June at the UNHRC meeting in Geneva, Mother Agnes challenged them, "The report talks about 4.25 millions of internally displaced. Can we know why the 85% of those displaced move naturally to regions stabilized by the government if, as alleged in the report, the government forces are killing them and ruining their properties?"[212]

The United Nations cheated Syria outright. They came to Damascus to investigate who had fired the CW rocket on Khan al-Assal; it was clearly the FSA. Instead, they investigated Ghouta, but only the question whether CW had been used, which was obvious, and not who used it, which was what the UN was needed for, to prevent a war. This left the field open for US-globalist MSM waves to carry their side. A report from MIT also criticized the UN report on Ghouta for bias against the Syrian government.[213]

In the final UN report covering various CW incidents in Syria, under Khan al-Assal, they only said there was evidence sarin had been "used against soldiers and civilians," and noted that the US alleged the Syrian government was guilty.

The Whoghouta blog also faulted the UN final report:

> While previously there was some hope that the UN's multiple mistakes were somehow attributable to human error, this mess-up leaves us with the unavoidable distressing conclusion that someone within the UN team has been manipulating evidence. The blunt error in the Zamalka trajectory, the ridiculous analysis of the Moadamiyah "impact site", and now the loss of blood samples cannot all be honest mistakes, especially when considering all three happen to contribute to the regime-attack theory.[214]

Who might that manipulator be? The Head of Mission: "The Sellstrom Report: The United Nations' Syria Inspector Shills for NATO and Israel:"

> Instead of a non-politicized investigation and lab analysis, the UN investigation of alleged nerve-gas attacks inside Syria was led by Professor Ake Sellstrom, a man of mystery who keeps a veil of secrecy around his research and political-military relationships... his seeming objectivity and non-partisanship is based on the myth

---

[211] https://syria360.wordpress.com/2013/09/10/unhrc-confirms-chemical-weapons-attack-photos-are-fake/

[212] http://australiansforreconciliationinsyria.org/mother-agnes-mariam-un-human-rights-council-commission-of-inquiry-on-syria-7-june/

[213] Subrata Ghoshroy, op. cit.

[214] http://whoghouta.blogspot.com/2014/01/analysis-of-second-un-report.html

of Sweden's neutrality... Sweden's military-industrial complex, which includes Saab and Bofors, is anything but peace-loving and neutral.[215]

Biochemist Sellstrom heads the European CBRNE Center for major incidents with (C)hemical, (B)iological, (R)adiological, (N)uclear and (E)xplosive substances] at Sweden's Umea University. It gets major EU funding for the war on terror. Umea and CBRNE are "deeply involved in joint research with Technion (Israel Institute of Technology), the Haifa-based university that provides state-of-art technology to the Israel Defense Force (IDF) and its intelligence agencies."

Searchable text versions of the two UN reports are here: http://progressivepress.com/dox/UNGhouta/

Tony Cartalucci noted (in *Subverting Syria*, p. 49):

> Syrian Non-Governmental Organizations (NGOs) that provided the United Nations with its official casualty rates were financially supported through organizations such as the National Endowment for Democracy and other institutions that receive funding directly from the US Congress and State Department.

Human Rights Watch, a Member of the Soros Group

As noted above, HRW has made statements based on rumors, fakes and third-hand hearsay from the SOHR[216] kitchen, supporting the terrorists and assailing the government in Syria. Nevertheless, to maintain its own credibility,

> in March 2012 HRW issued a report on "Syria: Armed Opposition Groups Committing Abuses," detailing a systematic campaign of kidnapping, torture, and mass murder.... The findings of (and reactions to) the Human Rights Watch report were muted, with most media outlets electing to downplay, spin, or obfuscate the war crimes ... which implicated NATO, led by the US, UK, France, and Turkey, as well as their proxy "Arab League," in backing torturers, kidnappers, and mass murderers in their campaign to topple the Syrian government.

> By early April 2012, the "Friends of Syria" group met in neighboring Turkey to devise a method to rearm and redeploy militant rebel fighters, while demanding Syrian troops be withdrawn from cities recaptured from rebel forces.[217]

Amnesty International

Syrian Girl Partisan, "Amnesty International Killing Syrians," June 22, 2012, https://www.youtube.com/watch?v=ubUGoXQoCcY

Amnesty International is not the neutral, anti-war, human rights organization that it claims to be, but it is the opposite. It is a tool of war for the US Empire...

George Soros is the man behind the operation. He funds Amnesty along with many other NGOs that promote color revolutions and humanitarian interventions, and one of those NGOs is called Avaaz. [*Guardian* headline,

---

[215] Yoichi Shimatsu, Sept. 18, 2013, http://www.globalresearch.ca/the-sellstrom-report-the-united-nations-syria-inspector-shills-for-nato-and-israel/5350287 The author is a science journalist who led a team of investigative reporters during the Tokyo subway sarin gassing in 1995.

[216] http://journal-neo.org/2015/12/12/the-syrian-observatory-for-human-rights-is-a-tool-of-western-propaganda/

[217] *Subverting Syria*, p. 24

"Avaaz faces questions over role at centre of Syrian protest movement...[218]] Avaaz has been providing logistical support to the insurgents in Syria for the last 15 months. So by giving money to Amnesty International, you're directly funding George Soros, who's directly funding Syria's insurgency. Soros... said, "We are with the drones and Special Forces of the US and why they are attacking Syria."

Also, the new executive director of Amnesty International is Suzanne Nossel, who's an advocate of humanitarian intervention, i.e. wars. Is there anything more Orwellian than the word "humanitarian war?" She has worked under Hillary Clinton, Susan Rice, and the infamous Madeleine Albright. She was involved in a leading role with subversive U.S. foreign policy regarding Libya, Iran, Syria and the Ivory Coast.

So the organization Amnesty International, their vice[219] is becoming more and more overt. A scandal arose this year when Amnesty International's advertising clearly took sides with NATO in Afghanistan. "Keep the Progress Going" was the slogan, and it painted NATO as humanitarian occupiers, and the war in Afghanistan as a war for women's rights, as opposed to a war for opium and oil pipeline control.

Over the last year, Amnesty has been running an extravagant disinformation campaign against Syria. Well-meaning people are giving money to what they think is helping civilian lives, when in fact they're giving money to help with the destruction of a nation...

Amnesty International has been caught lying numerous times, and yet people still view them as angels that could do no wrong, could never lie. They helped spread the baby incubators story during the first Gulf war, and in Libya they promoted the ethnic cleansing of black migrant workers, by spreading the lie that Gaddafi was employing sub-Saharan Africans as mercenaries. Then after all the killing was over, Amnesty International admitted that they had no evidence that black mercenaries were being used by Gaddafi's forces.

Amnesty International claim that the Syrian government butchered to death 18 year old Zainab al-Hosni, but this story fell flat on its face when Zainab turned up alive and well in Syria. [Screenshot from *The Guardian*, Oct. 5, 2011, "Syria attacks 'media fabrications' by showing 'beheaded' woman alive on TV."] Amnesty have continued spreading disinformation about the Houla massacre, taking the US government lie, contrary to eye-witness accounts and the report by the German newspaper FAZ.

While Saudi Arabian troops commit crimes against unarmed Bahrain protesters, Amnesty chooses to concentrate on stopping only one side of the violence in Syria: the Syrian government military. Amnesty has been asking their followers to pressure Russia to stop arming Syria, but they never ask their

---

[218] http://www.theguardian.com/world/2012/mar/02/avaaz-activist-group-syria "Avaaz is only five years old, but has exploded to become the globe's largest and most powerful online activist network." Avaaz co-founder Ricken Patel, "You can raise more money online faster than any other model. You can mobilise people offline in the streets and protests faster." An Unconventional Warfare unit in cyberspace.

[219] This might be an allusion to Vice News, another Soros-funded "alternative" agit-prop engine, which embeds itself with US-backed insurgencies to sell their viewpoint. With its bold and slick style, Vice News took the lead in purveying propaganda for the Kiev putsch.

followers to pressure the US and Qatar to hold money and arms shipments to insurgents.

This is the kind of image they have been using to advertise the Syrian insurgency on their Facebook page [woman protester in FSA flag face paint with poster, "We want freedom"], but here is the reality [photo of terror brigade with ISIS black flags]. I think Amnesty International needs a new name. I've come up with "Travesty International," I've also heard "Shamnesty International" and "Am Nasty International." If you can come up with a name for them that better suits their <u>true</u> identity, please post it in the comments below.

Doctors Within Borders

John Mesler: Doctors Without Borders (MSF) never saw even one patient with gas symptoms [in Ghouta]. They claimed to have had a phone call from a man claiming to be a doctor and he had seen 300 patients. But, MSF later admitted they had no staff or facilities inside Syria. I had confirmed that fact earlier, when I contacted MSF via email for help with the refugees I was working with. MSF first replied to my request by asking me for money. Then after replying to that, and restating my original purpose to help refugees inside Syria, they said they did not have any staff or facilities inside Syria, but were in Arsal, Lebanon. Arsal, Lebanon is a rest and recuperation station for FSA.[220]

Some documented CW attacks by extremist groups in Syria

December 2013. UN reports concluded that "rebels" used CW on Syrian soldiers on March 19, August 24 and August 25, 2013.[221]

2013-2014. Debate involving MIT scientist Theodore Postol, Seymour Hersh, and FSA blogger Eliot "Brown Moses" Higgins.[222] Conclusion: Postol showed that the rockets used in Eastern Ghouta were made in a machine shop and not of a type used by the Syrian Army. They did not have the range to be fired from Syrian Army positions.

In April and May of 2014, according to Wikipedia, over 20 chemical weapons attacks occurred, originating from areas controlled by "Syrian opposition."[223]

August 2015, mustard gas was used in a battle between ISIS and another rebel group in a town north of Aleppo, Reuters reported.[224]

August 2015, US-supported terror-rebels launched toxic gas shells on the Old Town of Aleppo, according to RT and Mint Press.[225]

---

[220] *op. cit.* http://nsnbc.me/2014/10/10/combating-propaganda-machine-syria/

[221] http://www.globalresearch.ca/syria-un-mission-report-confirms-that-opposition-rebels-used-chemical-weapons-against-civilians-and-government-forces/5363139

[222] http://www.mintpressnews.com/the-failed-pretext-for-war-seymour-hersh-eliot-higgins-mit-professors-on-sarin-gas-attack/188597/

[223] https://en.wikipedia.org/wiki/Use_of_chemical_weapons_in_the_Syrian_civil_war

[224] http://uk.reuters.com/article/uk-mideast-crisis-syria-chemicalweapons-idUKKCN0SU2Q920151106

[225] http://www.mintpressnews.com/shocking-beheading-moderate-rebels-allegedly-unleash-chemical-weapons-syria/219168/

World Markets for the ISIS Brand: Paris

It's a Drill Wind that Blows No Good

By John-Paul Leonard

A sensational massacre took place in Paris on Friday, Nov. 13th, 2015, killing scores of people. Black-masked hit men carried out the shootings, and the carnage was claimed for ISIS by a spokesman.

However, the rehearsing of the Paris attacks in official drills just before they occurred is a tell-tale signature of state-sponsored false-flag terrorism, paralleling closely the pattern seen in the London 7/7 attacks (see *Terror on the Tube*), as well as the 46 Drills of 9/11 (See *9/11 Synthetic Terror* 5th ed.), or the Utoya Island massacre in Norway (see *Gladio: NATO's Dagger at the Heart of Europe*).

***

The preparatory drills came to light in interviews on French TV; translations follow.[226]

> More footage has come to light where Parisian officials are openly admitting that an exercise was being conducted the day of the Paris attacks. The first clip is the chief of emergency services for the city of Paris. (SAMU), Dr. Pierre Carli.
>
> Carli: "That evening had in fact started that morning because we were doing an exercise with the exact same scenario as the one that happened that night."
>
> TV Reporter: "Hang on. That morning you had a drill of real-world conditions in case of an attack? You couldn't imagine that same evening it would happen for real. So that helped you a lot."

Another clip from the day before. Dr. Pierre Carli on France 5 TV, Nov 16, 2015.

> Reporter 1: "That same morning, the SAMU was running a multi-site attack exercise."
>
> Carli: This is something that, when we mention it now, it seems unreal. A simulation of essentially what happened that night, regardless of where or when it was going to happen.
>
> Reporter 2. What does that mean? They knew and warned you about a shooting?

The next clip is from 11/15/15 and features Patrick Pelloux, the survivor of the Charlie Hebdo attacks who also reported a contemporaneous drill "coincidence" in that atrocity.

> Pelloux: We were conducting an exercise with the SAMUs for this exact type of attack.
>
> Reporter: What a coincidence!
>
> Pelloux: Yes, a chilling coincidence.

JE SUIS
CI A LIE

Select Viewer Comments

"That public officials openly confess to the existence of drills they were involved in, that simulated exactly what subsequently took place, suggests that

---

[226] STFNews.com, Video by Panamza, English translation
https://www.youtube.com/watch?v=AUb721gXB5s

they were ignorant of the black ops people (non-public, deep-state operatives) who pushed the drill(s) over the line, with their foreign or locally recruited patsies, over the line into real world attacks. No wonder they say it was a "coincidence" and approvingly state they were helped in the rescue operations by being well prepared. They need not be complicit at all - so naive are their remarks it shows only that the deep state has failed, unlike in the USA, to make sure all public officials are silenced in advance. It's a pattern you can recognize almost anywhere - novices are less practiced in the art of public deception (public relations). – Des Carne"

"+Des Carne: Witness Describes Paris Attackers: 'They Looked Like Soldiers Carrying Out a Military Operation' — No Masks, White, Clean-Shaven, Muscular, Calm, Haven't Shouted Anything.

Times of Israel Edits Article, Scrubs Out History of Paris Jewish Community Being Warned of Attack. – Mabelle Vonk"

***

The first commenter above notes that "black ops people pushed the drills over the line." This is shorthand for the description given by Tarpley in *9/11 Synthetic Terror*: "the method of conduiting covert operations through a military or security bureaucracy, under the cover of a sanctioned drill plan which has been redirected through inserted changes." The drill allows the planners to organize lethal assets at the scene; it is then switched live; but only a few participants – the planners and the hit men – are in the know.

Because of the drills, we can conclude attacks were executed by the secret police – the deep state, French Gladio, NATO, Israeli Mossad, CIA etc. Outsiders like ISIS would not have the credentials to organize a drill, although they might be brought in as extras. That ISIS took credit for the attacks is part of the programme, they are puppets who want to show off their power. Al Qaida elements might have participated as shooters or patsies (who took care to bring their passports along, whether real or fake), but the drills inescapably betray the signature of state-supported false-flag terrorism (against the people – that's us – we who are unfortunately seen by the power elite as *Untermenschen,* and their eternal internal enemy).

The motive: Same as the Charlie Hebdo false flag. Strategy of tension, foment Islamophobia, prop up Zionism, stoke opposition to the flow of refugees from Muslim countries – who could change the electoral demographics and become a large enough minority to oppose Zionist candidates – foster an enemy image and rally the herd around the leader, increase popular support for the government (Hollande's support peaked after the attacks.)

Here I reproduce highlights of a very cogent article on the

Paris Shooting: 10 Ways it Looks Like a False Flag Op[227]

The Paris shooting of November 2015 which just occurred on Friday 13th November bears many of the telltale signs of a false flag operation. Now more than 48 hours later, we have some clues that the New World Order manipulators are up to their old tricks again – which are getting very predictable by now. Here are 10

---

[227] activistpost.com, November 16, 2015; http://tinyurl.com/on8cxnv

signs that the Paris shooting is yet another false flag attack designed to scare the common citizen (in France and everywhere), demonize Islam, provide "reason" for Governments at G20 and around the world to waste more money and take more liberty fighting terrorism, provide justification for the French Government to increase surveillance, and provide France and NATO with an excuse to escalate violence against Syria.

Paris Shooting False Flag Sign #1: Drills on Same Day. (see above)

False Flag Sign #2: Terrorist Passport Magically Found

Stuart Hooper of 21st Century Wire also reports that many mainstream media outlets (AFP, RT, Reuters, ITV, Sky News, AP, Fox News and Sputnik) have been claiming that a Syrian passport was magically found at one of the scenes of the Paris attacks, either on or near the shooter's body. Remember the terrorist passport on 9/11 that somehow managed to survive heat and fire that could supposedly burn steel, and landed unscathed on the streets below? Remember too the "lost ID" of one of the terrorists in the Charlie Hebdo getaway car? The false flag script is showing signs of predictability …

False Flag Sign #3: Terrorists Already Known to French Authorities

It turns out that some of the terrorists were already known to French security agencies, as the Daily Mail reports...

One the hallmarks of a false flag operation is the way it is "allowed" to happen. People in high places have the power to direct, control and call off people in lower positions in accordance with the overall plan. Were certain known terrorists allowed to gain entry to France?[228]

This is also typical for patsies, who are often recruited among petty criminals, perhaps as part of a plea bargain, to participate in "anti-terrorist" drills. They can also be ordinary citizens working part time for the secret police. This appears to be the fate of the four "Lads from Leeds" in London on 7/7/2005 (Kollerstrom, *Terror on the Tube*), and the Tsarnaev brothers at the Boston Marathon massacre.

False Flag Sign #4: Terrorist Declares he is from ISIS

As Brandon Turbeville reported, one of the Paris shooters just blurted out "I am from ISIS", giving us a short and concise soundbite which tells us everything we need to know about the killers. Is it just a coincidence that the Israeli Mossad intelligence front SITE (which have been busted before releasing "ISIS" material that was actually generated by Israel) were the ones to let us all know that ISIS is claiming responsibility for the job?

And, if it is really is ISIS, we know what this means: the controllers are now using ISIS in Western nations to further their goals. Bernie Suarez puts it best:

Realize that as soon as they suggested that the attackers claimed they were killing "for ISIS", given what we all know about ISIS, this constitutes 100% proof that the

---

[228] More on the ability of "Europe's most wanted terrorist" Abaaoud to travel back and forth between Syria and France – evidently as a protected intelligence asset, in "Decoding the Paris Attacks: ISIS Blowback or French-Israeli False Flag?" Brandon Martinez, Nov. 28, 2015, http://martinezperspective.com/

CIA and the West was involved because they are the ones who created, trained, funded and run ISIS.

False Flag Sign #5: Terrorist States Reason for the Shooting

Conveniently, we are also told in reports that one or some of the shooters screamed, "This is for Syria!", meaning they were killing innocent French people because of France's involvement in aggressively attacking Syria, alongside the US, Britain, Israel, Turkey and other Gulf states. If the shooters really are from ISIS, why not attack Russia, since Russia has been actively bombing and obliterating ISIS stations?

Was the motive for ISIS attacks in France and the USA to drum up support for military intervention in Syria, to keep Russia from picking up the pieces?

False Flag Sign #6 and 7: Shooting Occurs Right Before G20 Summit and Paris UN Climate Change Summit

The 7/7 London Tube bombings occurred during the G8 Summit in Scotland. The 2015 G20 summit took place in Turkey, and Syria was high on the agenda. The Climate summit was a huge confab of leaders from all over the world. They would be influenced by the Strategy of Tension by visiting Paris on the heels of the massacre.

False Flag Sign #8: Charlie Hebdo Precedent

This was the false flag attack on the offices of an obscure Islamophobic "humor" magazine, in Paris in January 2015. It was quickly followed by an orchestrated worldwide orgy of self-righteousness, under the famous *"Je suis Charlie"* banner. (The book on it is the anthology *We Are NOT Charlie Hebdo! Free Thinkers Question the French 9/11*, edited by Kevin Barrett.)

False Flag Sign #9: Numerology

"The date of 11/13/15... is numerologically significant, as is the fact the Paris shooting took place on Friday 13th." In *Terror on the Tube* it's noted that one reason they use Illuministic numerology is to signal to initiates that it's "their" operation. The pseudo-mystical element could also help shield them from natural guilt feelings about their crimes.

False Flag Sign #10: A Long List of Beneficiaries

There is a long list of beneficiaries who stand to gain something from this horrendous Paris attack, such as the French Government, G20, Islamophobes, Zionist Israel and the New World Order manipulators... French militarists and NATO who have been wanting to attack Syria will now have the perfect excuse to increase their military presence there.

About the author of this web source:

Makia Freeman is the editor of alternative news / independent media site The Freedom Articles and senior researcher at ToolsForFreedom.com, writing on many aspects of truth and freedom, from exposing aspects of the worldwide conspiracy to suggesting solutions for how humanity can create a new system of peace and abundance.

Shooters and Patsies – Drama Without a Protagonist

In the 13 November 2015 Paris Attack, one of the targets was the café La Belle Equipe.

A witness, Mr Admo, 26, described the shooter.

"He was white, clean shaven and had dark hair neatly trimmed.

"He was dressed all in black accept for a red scarf.

"The shooter was aged about 35 and had an extremely muscular build, which you could tell from the size of his arms...

"The driver had ... a machine gun rested on the roof of the car. He stood there ... acting as a lookout.

"I would describe him as tall, with dark hair and also quite muscular.

"They looked like soldiers or mercenaries and carried the whole thing out like a military operation."

We were told that Samy Amimour was one of the November 2015 Paris Attack shooters at the Bataclan theatre.

It now emerges that Samy trained at the police shooting club in Paris.

Police officers taught Samy how to use a semi-automatic handgun, using 38 Special and 22 Long Rifle ammunition.

Patsies Salah Abdeslam and his brother Ibrahim were "regular guys who enjoyed a laugh," played cards and talked about football, but "never Islam or anything jihadist." The brothers opened a bar which served alcohol. Ibrahim Abdeslam would openly drink alcohol, contrary to Islamic rules.

In 2015, the authorities served the bar with a notice saying they would shut it down in August due to alleged drug use ... The brothers quickly sold the bar, in late September 2015.

Did they strike a plea bargain so they could avoid jail and sell the bar – in turn for doing undercover police work. Easy to set up a "police informant" as a patsy. They have to keep the job a secret, even from their wives, and they can be sent to the scene for the sting.

Ibrahim's widow said he never went to the mosque, he was not opposed to the West, he was a jobless layabout who smoked cannabis 'all day every day', and he had spent time in prison. He lived in Brussel's Molenbeek district, where the CIA reportedly recruits its patsies. On 13 November, Ibrahim 'blew himself up' outside the Comptoir Voltaire cafe in Paris...

One witness who was in the road in front of the Bataclan concert hall before the attack and saw at least one of the assassins told BMFTV that he wasn't hooded: 'I saw a guy, quite small, white, European looking.

Some reported hearing at least two of the terrorists at the Bataclan Theatre speaking perfect French.

A witness present at the Bataclan Theatre told Reuters that the attackers all had brown hair.[229]

So we have two disparate groups here: one, the shooters who are executing the operation – white, macho professional commandos, or death squads. And two, the fall guys, the patsies, marginal characters, easy-going, ethnically Muslim, but who never step inside a mosque.

---

[229] http://aanirfan.blogspot.com/2015/11/paris-attack-like-mumbai-attack-and.html

Simply missing or mythical are the figures the headlines are screaming about: bands of trained militants, fanatical Islamist gunmen. You just can't rely on what you read in the papers.

> One of the guns used in the attacks comes from a Florida arms dealer which was involved in the CIA's Iran-Contra operation...

> Witnesses reported that two cars linked to the attacks had Belgian license plates.[230]

An interesting detail: Brussels, the Belgian capital, is home to NATO, the EU, corruption and pedophilia scandals. Paris was the original headquarters of NATO, but the CIA, NATO, and their Gladio death squads made one failed assassination attempt too many against Charles DeGaulle. Furious, he took France out of NATO and sent them packing in the 1960's. They moved up the road to Brussels, Belgium, which became the new heart of darkness on the continent for their dirty war against democracy.[231]

Gladio, the word for the short sword the Roman gladiators carried, is the code name for the Italian branch of "NATO's secret armies." Ostensibly instituted as "stay behind" units that would fight against a Soviet invasion, their real mission was – and still is, very much alive and kicking – to protect elite interests by defeating social forces struggling to gain a larger slice of the pie for the common people, when it can't be done by the usual methods. The Italian Gladio branch was co-founded by right-wing politician Francesco Cossiga, who was President during the murder of the Christian Democratic leader Aldo Moro, the most famous and best-documented Gladio hit.[232]

Webster Tarpley's first book was one requested by an Italian parliamentarian in 1978 to investigate the Moro slaying: *Chi ha ucciso (Who killed) Aldo Moro*.

> The main finding was that Moro had been killed by NATO intelligence, using the Red Brigades as tool and camouflage at the same time. The cause of the assassination was Moro's determination to give Italy a stable government by bringing the Italian Communist Party into the cabinet and the parliamentary majority.[233]

So Moro's murder was claimed by the "Red Brigades," a leftist faction, which had been infiltrated by Gladio provocateurs. Strange, how Communist extremists allegedly killed the best friend of the Communist Party, how alleged Islamists in Paris targeted ordinary Tunisians. This is beyond the art of judo, of using the adversary's strength against him.

> Recently Cossiga gave advice to the current Italian Minister of the Interior Robert Maroni about how to deal with protestors... "Maroni should do what I did when I was Minister of the Interior. University students? ... infiltrate them with agents provocateurs ... and let the agents provocateurs devastate shops, set fire to cars and put cities to the sword for ten days. Then, having won the sympathy of the public ... the police should pitilessly beat up the protesters and send them all to hospital."[234]

---

[230] Ibid.

[231] Richard Cottrell, *Gladio, NATO'S Dagger at the Heart of Europe: The Pentagon-Nazi-Mafia Terror Axis*, p. 145

[232] Ibid., p. 8.

[233] Tarpley, *9/11 Synthetic Terror: Made in USA*, 5th ed., p. 30

[234] http://aanirfan.blogspot.com/2015/11/paris-attack-like-mumbai-attack-and.html

This is what worked against the Red Brigades. But infiltrating such groups of hot-headed activists is slow and complicated, especially when there are none around. Accordingly, the more modern method is to fake it. This is what was done in the Kennedy assassination; it is what Lee Harvey Oswald meant when he protested his innocence with, "I'm just a patsy." Famous last words. Nowadays the patsies are killed before they get a chance to make such embarrassing remarks to the cameras. (Richard Cottrell, the author of *Gladio*, links the JFK assassination with Gladio's transformation into a terrorist organization under Lyman Lemnitzer.)

In Paris, the Charlie Hebdo and Friday the 13th attacks were escalations of the murders of innocent victims – including the patsies – in the south of France three years ago:

> The attacks which stunned France in March 2012 dramatised once again the unease and anxiety of the French at the rising numbers of Muslim immigrants. They were ruthlessly exploited by incumbent president Nicholas Sarkozy to provide high-octane fuel for his flagging re-election campaign...

> As the hunt for the killers began, Sarkozy switched to the replacement line that the authorities 'knew' who they were looking for. The new suspect: a feeble-minded, 32-year-old small-time crook of Algerian origins called Mohammed Merah. In no time at all he was provided with a full identikit, as an Al Qaeda activist picked up by US forces in Afghanistan and expelled back to France. The media dutifully churned out the claim that he was allied with a terrorist cell in Morocco that had been planning attacks to disrupt the election campaign. Never mind the report in The Guardian that a witness saw the gunman had clear green eyes, when Merah's eyes are brown — nor that the ex-director of French intelligence revealed that Merah had been an informant for the agency.

> Merah was hunted down to his apartment in a quiet quarter of Toulouse. The place was surrounded by a huge force of police, special forces, reporters and television cameras. Merah allegedly shot and slightly wounded one officer, before his senses snapped and he jumped out of his apartment window to his death, guns blazing. The important fact is that Toulouse and Merah between them became the French election campaign...

> Toulouse counted as the classic Gladio outing. A masked man on a motor scooter, aiming with precision and skill. Targets selected to raise maximum racial tensions. Attacks on Jews in a country with a difficult history of anti-Semitism, perfectly timed in the throes of the presidential elections. [Sarkozy himself is Jewish.] The branding of the usual Gladio patsy, a drifter hearing voices in his head, well-known to police and intelligence services, easily marketed as the lone rogue gunman, who jumps from a window to his death. Vintage tactics copied straight from the Strategy of Tension playbook. Sarkozy, the friend of NATO who brought France back into the alliance, was well informed when he blurted that the authorities knew who they were searching for.[235]

Let's review the parallels here that can be applied to the self-styled "Islamic State" in Iraq and Syria.

---

[235] *Gladio*, p. 423

- Like the Red Brigades membership, ISIS is tasked with triggering a devastating backlash against the cause it supposedly holds dear, Islam and its nation states.

- In the Near East as in Paris, death squads and snipers initiated the shooting. They were used to ignite both the Syrian and Iraqi insurgencies. Of course, there is also a core of Islamists, the Muslim Brotherhood in Syria, and some deeply rooted fundamentalist extremists in eastern Libya, and the usual mix of fools, criminals and desperadoes ready to join for money. Part of the well-paid job of these mercenaries will be to play-act the role of jihadist.

- Both Gladio and ISIS are artificial creations. Gangs of killers can't survive long under a functioning police system, without support in high places or from foreign powers.

Sectarianism also had to be imported to the Near East. Syrian and Iraqi society were not divided on sectarian lines before the war. Nor were the Afghans ever a people given to religious manias;[236] Islamism was fostered when the US supported the mujahideen against the Taraki regime. The Taliban, whom the US Army is still fighting, were created by Pakistan's secret services, the ISI – with US funding[237] – and the ISI director is appointed by the CIA.[238]

So Afghanistan has been torn by war since 1979, that's 36 years as of this writing. Evidently, the US has some reason for wanting to hang around the neighborhood.

Wayne Madsen notes in this volume, "The USA's real objective in creating the anti-ISIS coalition is to create perpetual instability in Syria. Former Pentagon Chief Leon Panetta said[239] that the war on ISIS could go on for 30 years."

That was before Mr. Putin decided to try and put an end to it, but they haven't given up.

Why would the US unleash "ISIS" on Syria and also on itself? There is an enormous difference in the dosage of terrorism in Syria vs. Paris or California. Massive, overwhelming terrorist attacks can destroy the state. Pinpricks only destroy freedom. They make the people weaker and the state stronger, turn it towards a police and surveillance state - which suits the powers that be just fine.

Not only that, but the actual victims are often people that the deep state wants to eliminate. The wannabe-communist Red Brigades were steered to murder the left-leaning Italian leader Aldo Moro, rather than a fascist one, in the most famous Gladio assassination of them all. In Paris on Friday the 13th, November 2015, a hipster quarter was targeted. In Norway in 2011, a youth camp for future socialist leaders was decimated. In San Bernardino, a few weeks after Paris, "ISIS" didn't strike, say, a police station or an army recruiting post. It was a social

---

[236] As can be seen from prewar video footage: *Afghanistan Before the Wars* (Eric Siegel, 1972, 2003) or *Bitter Lake* (Adam Curtis, 2015).

[237] https://www.mtholyoke.edu/~amjad20s/classweb2/page2.html

[238] For more on US sponsorship of the Taliban, see the entry on Afghanistan in "Islamic Fundamentalism" below, in the chapter "Who Needs a Clash of Civilizations?"

[239] http://english.alarabiya.net/en/News/middle-east/2014/10/06/Ex-Pentagon-chief-predicts-30-year-ISIS-war.html

services center for the disabled – at a site that conducts SWAT drills regularly...[240]

There are too many such incidents to even keep track of, but the pattern repeats, because they are being mass produced. This is the strategy of *tension* – and of *repetition* – two of the main forces applied in conditioning or manipulating opinion and behavior.

***

Cologne de Paris

A few disjointed thoughts on the events in Cologne, by The Saker, Jan. 11, 2016

First, the figures are staggering: according to Russian sources there have been over 700 hundred assaults in Cologne, 40% of which were sexual (the rest being "regular" assaults, robberies, battery, etc.). There is mounting evidence that this was a coordinated attack organized through the social media. [Social media? What's up, another Soros network?]...

Innocent people on both sides are suffering because of events unleashed by their common enemy – the AngloZionist plutocracy which runs the Empire. As long as this crucial fact remains unspeakable and, therefore, unspoken, the crisis will continue and the victims will continue to attack each other instead of turning against their common enemy. This is why no matter how hard it will be to defend this position, I will always personally be a proponent of an alliance between Europeans and immigrants, against those who seek to destroy the European continent, the Maghreb and the Mashriq. The Wahabi crazies in Syria, the immigrant thugs in Cologne, the Kosovar Mafia, the neo-Nazis in Germany (and the Ukraine), the Turkish "Grey Wolves" – they are all tools in the hands of the same master who simply seeks to divide and rule. The good news is that all these forces are always composed of a minority of thugs, and that always leaves at least the possibility of uniting the decent and honest people in defense of their common interests.

http://thesaker.is/a-few-disjointed-thoughts-on-the-events-in-cologne/

Andrew Korybko shares this view; in his "2016 Trends Forecast, mega analysis" he writes,[241]

> The "Refugee" Crisis: This US-designed and Turkish-assisted operation aims to demographically plant the seeds for long-term identity conflict in key EU states, most of all Germany, so that Color Revolution-like social conditions can be manufactured upon demand as a form of 'bottom-up' pressure against any forthcoming uncompliant administrations.

Historically, there has long been tension with the large Turkish minority in Germany. Turkish guest workers came to Germany to make up for the labor shortages caused by the decimation of the able-bodied male population in WWII.

---

[240] https://www.intellihub.com/false-flag-formula-15-ways-detect-false-flag-operation/
[241] http://thesaker.is/2016-trends-forecast-by-andrew-korybko/

What Is Our Oil Doing Under Their Soil?

CNN: Why the War in Iraq was Fought for Big Oil

Story highlights: Opening up Iraq to foreign oil companies was main goal of Iraq War. Plans for Western oil exploration in Iraq were drawn up years before 2003 invasion. Bush administration pressured Iraqi government to pass law allowing foreign firms in. Defense Secretary Chuck Hagel in 2007: "People say we're not fighting for oil. Of course we are."

By Antonia Juhasz, Special to CNN, Mon. April 15, 2013

Yes, the Iraq War was a war for oil, and it was a war with winners: Big Oil.

It has been 10 years since Operation Iraqi Freedom's bombs first landed in Baghdad. And while most of the U.S.-led coalition forces have long since gone, Western oil companies are only getting started.

Before the 2003 invasion, Iraq's domestic oil industry was fully nationalized and closed to Western oil companies. A decade of war later, it is largely privatized and utterly dominated by foreign firms.

From ExxonMobil and Chevron to BP and Shell, the West's largest oil companies have set up shop in Iraq. So have a slew of American oil service companies, including Halliburton, the Texas-based firm Dick Cheney ran before becoming George W. Bush's running mate in 2000.

The war is the one and only reason for this long sought and newly acquired access.

Oil was not the only goal of the Iraq War, but it was certainly the central one, as top U.S. military and political figures have attested to in the years following the invasion.

"Of course it's about oil; we can't really deny that," said Gen. John Abizaid, former head of U.S. Central Command and Military Operations in Iraq, in 2007. Former Federal Reserve Chairman Alan Greenspan agreed... Then-Sen. and now Defense Secretary Chuck Hagel said the same in 2007: "People say we're not fighting for oil. Of course we are."

For the first time in about 30 years, Western oil companies are exploring for and producing oil in Iraq from some of the world's largest oil fields and reaping enormous profit... the benefits are not finding their way through Iraq's economy or society.

These outcomes were by design, the result of a decade of U.S. government and oil company pressure. In 1998, Kenneth Derr, then CEO of Chevron, said, "Iraq possesses huge reserves of oil and gas-reserves I'd love Chevron to have access to." Today it does.

In 2000, Big Oil, including Exxon, Chevron, BP and Shell, spent more money to get fellow oilmen Bush and Cheney into office than they had spent on any previous election...

Planning for a military invasion was soon under way. Bush's first Treasury secretary, Paul O'Neill, said in 2004, "Already by February (2001), the talk was mostly about logistics. Not the why (to invade Iraq), but the how and how quickly."...

Here's how they did it.

The State Department Future of Iraq Project's Oil and Energy Working Group met from February 2002 to April 2003 and agreed that Iraq "should be opened to international oil companies as quickly as possible after the war."...

Ibrahim Bahr al-Uloum – who was appointed Iraq's oil minister by the U.S. occupation government in September 2003 – was part of the group... For the next decade, former and current executives of western oil companies acted first as administrators of Iraq's oil ministry and then as "advisers" to the Iraqi government.

Before the invasion, there were just two things standing in the way of Western oil companies operating in Iraq: Saddam Hussein and the nation's legal system. The invasion dealt handily with Hussein...

This Iraq Hydrocarbons Law, partially drafted by the Western oil industry, would lock the nation into private foreign investment under the most corporate-friendly terms...

But due to enormous public opposition and a recalcitrant parliament, the central Iraqi government has failed to pass the Hydrocarbons Law... the oil companies settled on a different track.

Bypassing parliament, the firms started signing contracts that provide all of the access and most of the favorable treatment the Hydrocarbons Law would provide – and the Bush administration helped draft the model contracts.

Upon leaving office, Bush and Obama administration officials have even worked for oil companies as advisers on their Iraq endeavors. For example, former U.S. Ambassador to Iraq Zalmay Khalilzad's company, CMX-Gryphon, "provides international oil companies and multinationals with unparalleled access, insight and knowledge on Iraq."

The new contracts lack the security a new legal structure would grant, and Iraqi lawmakers have argued that they run contrary to existing law, which requires government control, operation and ownership of Iraq's oil sector.

But the contracts do achieve the key goal of the Cheney energy task force: all but privatizing the Iraqi oil sector and opening it to private foreign companies.

They also provide exceptionally long contract terms and high ownership stakes and eliminate requirements that Iraq's oil stay in Iraq, that companies invest earnings in the local economy or hire a majority of local workers.

Iraq's oil production has increased by more than 40% in the past five years to 3 million barrels of oil a day (still below the 1979 high of 3.5 million set by Iraq's state-owned companies), but a full 80% of this is being exported out of the country while Iraqis struggle to meet basic energy consumption needs...

Basic services such as water and electricity remain luxuries, while 25% of the population lives in poverty... The oil and gas sectors today account directly for less than 2% of total employment, as foreign companies rely instead on imported labor.

In just the last few weeks, more than 1,000 people have protested at ExxonMobil and Russia Lukoil's super-giant West Qurna oil field, demanding jobs and payment for private land that has been lost or damaged by oil operations. The Iraqi military was called in to respond.

Fed up with the firms, a leading coalition of Iraqi civil society groups and trade unions, including oil workers, declared on February 15 that international oil companies have "taken the place of foreign troops in compromising Iraqi sovereignty" and should "set a timetable for withdrawal.".…

The Iraq War was a war for oil, and it was a war with losers: the Iraqi people and all those who spilled and lost blood so that Big Oil could come out ahead.

***

PNAC Clique Rush to Steal Golan Heights Oil[242]

By F. William Engdahl

What do Dick Cheney, James Woolsey, Bill Richardson, Jacob Lord Rothschild, Rupert Murdoch, Larry Summers and Michael Steinhardt have in common? They all are members of the Strategic Advisory Board of a Newark, New Jersey-based oil and gas group with the name, Genie Energy. It's quite a collection of names.

Dick Cheney, George W. Bush's VP and handler, was CEO of the world's largest oilfield services company, Halliburton… James Woolsey, a neo-con, former CIA Director, chairman of the neo-con think-tank, Foundation for Defense of Democracies, member of the pro-Likud Washington Institute for Near East Policy (WINEP), a member of the infamous Project for a New American Century (PNAC), along with Cheney, Rumsfeld and other Bush era neo-cons. Bill Richardson, former US Secretary of Energy. Rupert Murdoch, owner of major US and UK media including the *Wall Street Journal*, financier of the neo-con *Weekly Standard* of Bill Kristol, who founded the PNAC. Larry Summers was US Treasury Secretary and drafted the laws that deregulated US banks out from the 1933 Glass-Steagall Act, in effect opening the floodgates to the US financial crisis of 2007-2015. Michael Steinhardt the hedge fund speculator, is a philanthropic friend of Israel, of Marc Rich and a board member of Woolsey's neo-con Foundation for the Defense of Democracies. And Jacob Lord Rothschild is a former business partner of convicted Russian oil oligarch, Mikhail Khodorkovsky. Before his arrest Khodorkovsky secretly transferred his shares in Yukos Oil to Rothschild. Rothschild is a part-owner of Genie Energy, which in 2013 was granted exclusive oil and gas exploration rights to a 153-square mile radius in the southern part of the Golan Heights by the Netanyahu government. In short, it's quite an eye-popping board.

Golan Heights and International law

The Israeli government gave the concession to Genie in the disputed Golan Heights in 2013 when the US-led destabilization of the Syrian Assad regime was in full force. Conveniently, Israel also began building fortifications at that time to seal off the illegally-occupied Golan Heights from Syria, knowing there was little Assad or Syria could do to stop it. In 2013, as Genie Energy began moving into Golan Heights, Israeli military engineers overhauled the forty-five mile border fence with Syria, replacing it with a steel barricade that includes barbed wire, touch sensors, motion detectors, infrared cameras, and ground radar, putting it on par with the Wall Israel has constructed in the West Bank.

[242] F. Wm. Engdahl, Oct. 26, 2015, "Genies and Genocide: Syria, Israel, Russia and Much Oil," http://journal-neo.org/2015/10/26/genies-and-genocide-syria-israel-russia-and-much-oil-2/

Now, as Damascus fights for its life, apparently, Genie has discovered a huge oil field precisely there.

The Golan Heights, however, are illegally occupied by Israel. In 1981, Israel passed the Golan Heights Law, imposing Israeli "laws, jurisdiction and administration" to the Golan Heights. In response the UN Security Council passed Resolution 242 which declared Israel must withdraw from all lands occupied in the 1967 war with Syria, including the Golan Heights.

Again in 2008 a plenary session of the UN General Assembly passed a resolution 161–1 [against the Israeli occupation]. Israel was the only nation to vote against....

Genie Claims Huge Discovery

On October 8, into the second week of Russian airstrikes against ISIS and other so-called "moderate" terrorists at the request of the Assad government, Yuval Bartov, chief geologist from Genie Energy's Israeli subsidiary, Afek Oil & Gas, told Israel's Channel 2 TV that his company had found a major oil reservoir on the Golan Heights: "We've found an oil stratum 350 meters thick in the southern Golan Heights. On average worldwide, strata are 20 to 30 meters thick, and this is 10 times as large as that, so we are talking about significant quantities."

This oil find has now made the Golan Heights a strategic "prize" that clearly has the Netanyahu government more determined than ever to sow chaos and disorder in Damascus and use that to de facto create an Israeli irreversible occupation of Golan and its oil. A minister in the Netanyahu coalition government, Naftali Bennett, Minister of Education and Minister of Diaspora Affairs and leader of the right-wing religious party, The Jewish Home, has made a proposal that Israel settle 100,000 new Israeli settlers across the Golan in five years... a growing chorus in Tel Aviv is arguing that Netanyahu demand American recognition of Israel's 1981 annexation of the Golan.

Energy war has been a significant component of US, Israeli, Qatari, Turkish, and Saudi, strategy against Syria's Assad regime... .

In 2009 the government of Qatar, today home to the Muslim Brotherhood and a major funder of ISIS in Syria and Iraq, met with Bashar al-Assad in Damascus.

Qatar proposed to Bashar that Syria join in an agreement to allow a transit gas pipeline from Qatar's huge North Field in the Persian Gulf adjacent to Iran's huge South Pars gas field. The Qatari pipeline would have gone through Saudi Arabia, Jordan, Syria and on to Turkey to supply European markets. Most crucially, it would bypass Russia. An Agence France-Presse report claimed Assad's rationale was "to protect the interests of his Russian ally, which is Europe's top supplier of natural gas." In 2010 Assad instead joined talks with Iran and Iraq for an alternative $10 billion pipeline plan that would also potentially allow Iran to supply gas to Europe from its South Pars field in the Iranian waters of the Persian Gulf. The three countries signed a Memorandum of Understanding in July 2012 – just as Syria's civil war was spreading to Damascus and Aleppo.

F. William Engdahl is a strategic risk consultant and lecturer, with a degree in politics from Princeton University. He is a best-selling author on oil and geopolitics, with books like *A Century of War* and *Full Spectrum Dominance*, and frequent articles at New Eastern Outlook http://journal-neo.org/author/william-engdahl/.

Raqqa's Rockefellers: How ISIS Oil Flows to Israel[243]
By staff writers at Al-Araby al-Jadeed, Nov. 26, 2015

Oil produced from fields under the control of the Islamic State group is at the heart of a new investigation by al-Araby al-Jadeed. The black gold is extracted, transported and sold, providing the armed group with a vital financial lifeline.

But who buys it? Who finances the murderous brutality that has taken over swathes of Iraq and Syria? How does it get from the ground to the petrol tank, and who profits along the way?

The Islamic State group uses millions of dollars in oil revenues to expand and manage vast areas under its control, home to around five million civilians.

IS sells Iraqi and Syrian oil for a very low price to Kurdish and Turkish smuggling networks and mafias, who label it and sell it on as barrels from the Kurdistan Regional Government.

It is then most frequently transported from Turkey to Israel... IS is heavily dependent on its oil revenues... IS is producing an average of 30,000 barrels a day from the Iraqi and Syrian oil fields it controls... IS' profit is $15 to $18 a barrel. The group currently makes $19 million on average each month...

"After the oil is extracted and loaded, the oil tankers leave Nineveh province [in Iraq] and head north to the city of Zakho, 88km north of Mosul," the colonel said. Zakho is a Kurdish city in Iraqi Kurdistan, right on the border with Turkey.

"After IS oil lorries arrive in Zakho - normally 70 to 100 of them at a time - they are met by oil smuggling mafias..."

Once in Turkey... the oil is delivered to a person who goes by the aliases of Dr Farid, Hajji Farid and Uncle Farid... an Israeli-Greek dual national ... Farid owns a licensed import-export business that he uses to broker deals between the smuggling mafias that buy IS oil and the three oil companies that export the oil to Israel...

In August, the *Financial Times* reported that Israel obtained up to 75 percent of its oil supplies from Iraqi Kurdistan... It exports the oil to Mediterranean countries.

"Israel has in one way or another become the main marketer of IS oil. Without them, most IS-produced oil would have remained going between Iraq, Syria and Turkey. Even the three companies would not receive the oil if they did not have a buyer in Israel," said a European official at an international oil company.

***

Wikipedia on "Petroleum industry in Iraq" and "Oil Reserves in Libya"

Iraq was the world's 12th largest oil producer in 2009, and has the world's fifth largest proven petroleum reserves after Venezuela, Saudi Arabia, Canada, and Iran. Just a fraction of Iraq's known fields are in development, and Iraq may be one of the few places left where vast reserves, proven and unknown, have barely been exploited... Oil reserves in Libya are the largest in Africa and among the ten largest globally with 46.4 billion barrels as of 2010.

---

[243] http://www.alaraby.co.uk/english/features/2015/11/26/raqqas-rockefellers-how-islamic-state-oil-flows-to-israel

Who Needs a Clash of Civilizations?

The short answer, ladies and gentlemen, is, You don't, and I don't. Who does? Zionists, oilmen, banksters and their puppet politicos. Plus the arms industry, of course.

There may not be many differences between these groups. The oil industry is part of the same clique sharing the same legacy as Wall Street or the City of London, while the puppets in Washington or the media are their errand boys. They all have the same credo: There is no god but money, which is the Arabic inscription, adapted from the ISIS flag, on the cover of this book.

Yet it is the Zionist neocons who are the hardliners pushing for this clash, and for a very transparent reason. The agenda of Zionist expansion needs to harness the immense power of the West as a hammer to pound the majority populations of the Near East, and make them subservient to tiny Israel. Phenomena like ISIS or the 9/11 terror attacks have led to US interventions in favor of the Zionist agenda. They also have given rise to a sharp increase in Islamophobia,[244] which further reduces the already tiny Arab-American voice against Zionism in US politics. Hostility towards Arabs and Muslims discourages immigration and encourages emigration – also a kind of ethnic cleansing. Abby Martin reports that the year 2015 set records for hate crimes against Muslims in the US and Europe, due to the two Paris attacks. Obama is quoted, "an extremist ideology has spread within some Muslim communities. It's a real problem that Muslims must confront without excuse." Aahh, collective guilt. Finance and train psychopaths to smear Islam, then blame the victims. What about all the other shootings by non-Muslims: ordinary law-abiding Americans are responsible?

***

Islamic Fundamentalism:

Fostered by US Foreign Policy

Excerpted from *9/11 Synthetic Terror*, Ch. XVI
By Webster Griffin Tarpley

Again and again, terrorist groups with US-UK backing have intervened against progressive nationalists in the Arab world...

US policy, like that of the British Empire earlier, objectively favors the growth of Islamic fundamentalism...

For centuries, the British had cultivated the smaller ethnic groups of the Ottoman Empire with a view to inciting them to rebel against the Ottoman Sultan:

---

[244] http://www.soundvision.com/article/islamophobia-statistics-usa-2011, Sept. 8, 2011. Neocons Daniel Pipes and John Ashcroft have spoken in favor of detention camps for American Muslims. One study found that 50% of Arab-Americans suffer from depression, apparently due to a hostile environment. See also Abby Martin, "A Deeper Look at Islamophobia in the US Empire," interview with Dr. Deepa Kumar, http://www.washingtonsblog.com/2016/01/islamophobia-derives-empires-interest-controlling-middle-east.html

thus, the British began working with the Serbs around the time of the American Revolution; they helped the Greeks to become independent after the Napoleonic wars. Under Lord Palmerston in the 1830s and 1840s, the British introduced the idea of a homeland for the Jews in Palestine...

During these years the British Arab Bureau and the British Indian Office carefully profiled the Arab psychology and ideology. Their starting point was that the Arabs would inevitably become hostile to British colonialism, and that nothing could be done to prevent this. However, these British orientalists also concluded that it might well be possible to provide synthetic ideologies for the inevitable Arab revolt which would help to make it self-isolating, abortive, and impotent. An obvious way to do this was to make the revolt not specifically anti-British, but anti-western and anti-European in general, lest the Arabs be able to ally with Russia or Germany to eject the UK. The Islamic tradition offered the raw material for the fabrication of a synthetic ideology of Arab rejection of the west to which today's more fantastic ideologues of the Arab and Islamic worlds are much indebted...

Despite neocon blathering about democracy, and Bush's so-called Middle East initiative, the US never had any serious plans for democracy in Iraq. To begin with, the US itself cannot seriously be described as a democracy; the US is currently an oligarchy in Plato's precise definition of a "constitution teeming with many evils...based on a property qualification... wherein the rich hold office and the poor man is excluded," a system favoring "the member of a ruling class – oligarchy." (*Republic* 544c, 550c, 545a) Sure enough, the regime created by the US in Iraq in the spring of 2003 was an ... oligarchy, composed of twenty-five handpicked puppet oligarchs with a weak revolving presidency. Such arrangements have been perpetuated after the alleged restoration of Iraqi sovereignty. US interference in post-communist Russia favored oligarchical domination through the Yeltsin coterie in a similar way...

The open secret of the post-1945 world is that the US and the other NATO states have systematically and implacably opposed the reasonable alternative of modernizing secular nationalism among the Arab and Islamic states, while favoring the fundamentalist alternative, the more benighted the better. Modernizing secular nationalists are by far the most effective adversaries of the imperialists – they have the potential to score real political, diplomatic and cultural gains for their countries. Theocratic reactionaries are easier to isolate, since their appeal is more circumscribed. In practice, Washington and London have always fostered the rise of fundamentalists, while attempting to eliminate modernizing nationalists...

Iraq – When the British seized control of Iraq in 1919, they installed a reactionary monarchy of the Hashemites. In 1958, the puppet monarch King Faisal was assassinated. General **Kassem** became prime minister and instituted a program of modernizing reforms, including the progressive constitution of 1959. The 1959 Iraqi constitution and other Kassem-era legislation made literacy compulsory, abolished slavery, and guaranteed equal rights for women. The impact of these reforms was permanent. To cite only one example, during the mid-1970s the Iraqi Ambassador to Rome was a highly intelligent woman, Selima Bakir. As any Iraqi nationalist would, Kassem assumed the position that Kuwait was an integral part of Iraq. In this he was correct since Kuwait had been illegally detached from the Ottoman Empire by the British in 1899 to prevent the

German-sponsored Berlin to Baghdad railway from ever reaching the head of the Gulf. **In 1962 the British fomented a revolt of the Kurds under the Barzani clan**, and Kassem was assassinated in 1963. After Kassem was assassinated by the CIA and replaced by then CIA asset Saddam Hussein, the chance for successful development in Iraq was severely limited. The positive features of Iraq during the Saddam Hussein years were largely inherited from the Kassem era.

Pakistan – The great opportunity for modernization in Pakistan came under **Ali Bhutto** in the mid-1970s. Bhutto was determined to advance his country to the leading edge of modern technology with a peaceful nuclear energy program in the Eisenhower Atoms for Peace tradition. He was soon confronted by Kissinger, who threatened to make a terrible example of him unless he desisted from his ambitious development plans. Shortly thereafter, Bhutto was overthrown by the US-supported coup of General Zia ul Haq. Bhutto was framed up on various charges and hanged by the new regime in accordance with Kissinger's earlier threats. Bhutto's wife and children later took refuge in West Germany. Fundamentalist tendencies have grown in the era following the death of Bhutto.

Kosovo – When the Federal Republic of Yugoslavia began to break up in 1991, the ethnic Albanian Muslim population of the province of Kosovo under the leadership of the secular nationalist LDK party responded by a highly effective non-violent self-organizing process, which allowed them to defy the Serb occupiers for most of the rest of the 1990s. Using the tools of passive resistance, the Kosovars created their own parallel government, including their own school system, their own separate elections, their own public health system, and their own parallel system of economic enterprises. The leader of this magnificent effort was Ibrahim **Rugova**, who made pilgrimage after pilgrimage to Washington during the 1990s, always sporting the Parisian red silk scarf which was his trademark. But the US was never willing to lift a finger for Rugova and the eminently reasonable LDK... In 1997,... as the Albanian state collapsed, its weapons depots were looted, and many of these weapons soon found their way across the border into Kosovo. This engendered the Kosovo Liberation Army (KLA), a very dubious outfit composed of narcotics smugglers, Islamic fundamentalists from Kosovo and abroad, and out-and-out terrorists...

This time the US, in the person of Madeleine Albright, became the direct sponsor of the terrorist KLA. Starting in March, 1999, the US and NATO waged a criminal 78-day bombing campaign against Serbia, one of the great acts of international vandalism in then late twentieth century – all in support of KLA-related demands. As for Rugova and the LDK, they were trampled..., and the US depended more and more on the KLA.

Afghanistan... the CIA always supported the most benighted, the most reactionary, the most opium-mongering factions – especially their favorite, Gulbuddin Hekmatyar.

The CIA was looking for forces of absolute self-isolating negativity, incapable of getting along with Iran or anyone else. In the decade of war that followed (December 1979- February 1989), Afghanistan was economically and demographically destroyed...

In his first spring in office, Bush offered a large grant to the Taliban. This caused columnist Robert Scheer to comment: "Enslave your girls and women, harbor anti-US terrorists, destroy every vestige of civilization in your homeland, and the Bush administration will embrace you. That's the message sent with the recent gift of $43 million to the Taliban rulers of Afghanistan. The gift...makes the US the main sponsor of the Taliban." ("Bush's Faustian Deal with the Taliban," *Los Angeles Times*, May 22, 2001)...

This list could go on and on. In Bangladesh, Kissinger persecuted Sheikh Mujibur Rahman of the Awami League, the leading nationalist force on the scene after independence in the early 1970s. In Lebanon, Kissinger did everything possible to destroy the 1943 multi-sectarian constitution and set off a civil war...

The flip side of this pattern is the brutal treatment meted out to those in Europe who have wanted to make development deals with the Arab states on the obvious basis of mutual advantage. A celebrated case is that of the elimination of Enrico Mattei, the president of the Italian state oil company, ENI, as we saw in Ch. II. The German banker Juergen Ponto was interested in financing development projects in the Arab world and in Africa; he was eliminated by the Baader-Meinhof gang in 1977. It is evident that the Baader-Meinhof was acting as a false-flag operation for CIA and MI-6. There were some thirty attempts to assassinate French President Charles de Gaulle. There were many motivations for this, but a prominent one was the pro-Arab diplomacy of the French government.

Given the implacable US and NATO persecution of progressive Arab nationalist leaders, this breed has tended to disappear entirely from the scene. With the remaining choices narrowed to reactionary monarchies, such as the Saudis, repressive dictatorships, such as that typified by Hafez Assad, or experiments with Islamic fundamentalism, it is not surprising that many young Arabs regard the fundamentalists as the viable option...

Historical parallels to the seizure of energy resources in Libya and Iraq
by Stewart Halsey Ross

Source: *Global Predator: US Wars for Empire.*

In 1903, the U.S. fomented a revolution in the Panama Department of Colombia that led to the establishment of a new nation that would be an American doormat: the Republic of Panama. The U.S. sent a gunboat to prevent Colombia from sending military forces to put down the artificial insurgency and immediately recognized the new government by sending in troops to protect its "new interests." At the end of the year, Phillipe Bunau-Varilla, a French citizen not authorized to sign treaties without approval of the Panamanians, nevertheless signed the Hay-Bunai-Varilla Treaty which granted the U.S. rights to a ten-mile-wide strip of land running from the Atlantic to the Pacific coast. It also gave the U.S. the right to build and administer—in perpetuity—the Panama Canal. T.R. was not bashful. To anyone who asked him, he said: "I took the Canal and let Congress debate.

The Panama Canal takeover was the first of some sixty armed American interventions in the first thirty years of the 20th century. Here is a sampling: Cuba, 1898-1902; Cuba turned into a "protectorate" under the Platt Amendment, 1901; Dominican Republic, 1905-1941, financial supervision, with troops sent in 1913 and 1917-1924; Haiti, 1914-1941, military occupation to "restore order," with Marines shooting over 2,000 Haitians who resisted "pacification"; Nicaragua, 1909-1910 and 1911-1925, financial supervision and large-scale military operations in 1927—plus Coolidge's "private war" and occupation until 1933; Mexico, 1914, bombardment and capture of Veracruz.(Ross 14)

The author lists all sixty in a short "History of Interventions by U.S. Armed Forces in the Western Hemisphere, 1806-1933." (Ross 292-298

Fall of the Arab Spring: NATO's Islamist Extremist Allies

by Christopher L. Brennan

Excerpts from *Fall of the Arab Spring: From Revolution to Destruction*, by Christopher L. Brennan, 2015, pp. 177-185

It is self-evident that the rebel forces staging an uprising against Qaddafi were not defenseless civilians, but an armed force. More paradoxically for US officialdom's propaganda narrative, they were armed forces allied to al-Qaeda – putatively the targets and enemies of the US in its so-called "War on Terror." Despite the paradox, this was no aberration in policy. Author Peter Dale Scott explains in *Asia-Pacific Journal*, "al-Qaeda was a covert U.S. ally" in interventions in the Balkans and Libya "rather than its foe..."[245]

There have been other interventions in which Americans have used al-Qaeda as a resource to increase their influence, for example Azerbaijan in 1993. There a pro-Moscow president was ousted after large numbers of Arab and other foreign mujahedin veterans were secretly imported from Afghanistan, on an airline hastily organized by three former veterans of the CIA's airline Air America... This was an ad hoc marriage of convenience: the *mujahedin* got to defend Muslims against Russian influence in the enclave of Nagorno-Karabakh, while the Americans got a new president who opened up the oilfields of Baku to western oil companies.

The pattern of U.S. collaboration with Muslim fundamentalists against more secular enemies is not new. It dates back to at least 1953, when the CIA recruited right-wing mullahs to overthrow Prime Minister Mossadeq in Iran, and also began to cooperate with the Sunni Muslim Brotherhood...

In the late 1990s a plot to assassinate Qaddafi involving al-Qaeda was revealed by British MI-5 agent David Shayler. In *The Forbidden Truth,* Shayler and a group of authors report that the British intelligence agency MI6 paid al-Qaeda the equivalent of $160,000 to help fund an assassination attempt against Qaddafi...[246]

The West Point study explained,

> The vast majority of Libyan fighters that included their hometown in the Sinjar Records resided in the country's northeast, particularly the coastal cities of Darnah

---

[245] Peter Dale Scott, "Bosnia, Kosovo, and Now Libya: The Human Costs of Washington's On-Going Collusion with Terrorists," Asia-Pacific Journal, http://japanfocus.org/site/make_pdf/3578

[246] See History Commons, "1996: British Intelligence and Al-Qaeda Allegedly Cooperate in Plot to Assassinate Libyan Leader" http://www.historycommons.org/context.jsp?item=a96libya#a96libya

60.2% (52) and Benghazi 23.9% (21). Both Darnah and Benghazi have long been associated with Islamic militancy in Libya, in particular for an uprising by Islamist organizations in the mid-1990s. The Libyan government blamed the uprising on 'infiltrators from the Sudan and Egypt' and one group—the Libyan Fighting Group (jama-ah al-libiyah al-muqatilah)—claimed to have Afghan veterans in its ranks. The Libyan uprisings became extraordinarily violent.

As al-Jazeera let slip, this Islamist extremist group, also referred to as Libyan Islamic Fighting Group (LIFG), was the leading edge in initiating the February 2011 rebellion against Qaddafi. [They were later to infiltrate Syria with the assistance of NATO powers USA and Turkey, becoming the leading edge in the Syrian insurrection as well.]

This group, providing an institutional basis for the rebellion, was a branch of al-Qaeda. On November 3, 2007 LIFG merged with al-Qaeda to form its North African branch, Al-Qaeda in Islamic Maghreb or AQIM. A 2008 statement attributed to al-Qaeda chief Ayman Zawahiri confirmed this merger...[247]

When Tripoli finally fell to the NATO-Qatari and rebel forces, the de facto emir and founder of LIFG, Abdel-Hakim Belhaj, emerged as the military dictator of Tripoli. Belhaj led the highly trained "Tripoli Brigade" which stormed Qaddafi's fortress of Bab-al-Aziziyah. As explained by Pepe Escobar of the *Asia Times*, "the so-called Tripoli Brigade [was] trained in secret for two months by US Special Forces. This turned out to be the rebels' most effective militia in six months of tribal/civil war."[248] Being the most battle-hardened warriors, many key rebel leaders were of this same coloration: "Hardly by accident, all the top military rebel commanders are LIFG..."[249]

In a revelatory study released in 2014 by the center-right Accuracy in Media group, it was reported the US willingly facilitated a large shipment of weapons to al-Qaeda in Libya to combat Qaddafi... As reported by the UK *Daily Mail*, this US support provided an estimated $500 million in weapons to al-Qaeda militants...

The Citizens Commission on Benghazi, a self-selected group of former top military officers, CIA insiders and think-tankers, declared... "these weapons that came into Benghazi were permitted to enter by our armed forces who were blockading the approaches from air and sea... The intelligence community was part of that, the Department of State was part of that..." The weapons were intended for Gaddafi but allowed by the U.S. to flow to his Islamist opposition.

In sum, what was speciously framed as a pro-democracy protest in Libya was yet another violent uprising against Qaddafi, supported by al-Qaeda mercenaries and fanatics...

---

[247] "Libya releases scores of prisoners," Al-Jazeera, April 09, 2008, http://www.aljazeera.com/news/africa/2008/04/200861502740131239.html
[248] Pepe Escobar, "How al-Qaeda got to rule in Tripoli," Asia Times, August 30, 2011, http://www.atimes.com/atimes/Middle_East/MH30Ak01.html
[249] Ibid.

NATO's direct intervention in Libya was framed under the pretext of protecting civilians. In the aftermath of UNSC Resolution 1973, no such actions to protect civilians were carried out. The opposite occurred. NATO proceeded with a ruthless bombing campaign to topple Qaddafi's regime and any allied resistance completely. NATO acted as the Air Force for rebel fighters. Brushing aside the enumerated restrictions of the UN mandate, NATO and Qatar provided weapons, Special Forces on the ground to direct anti-Qaddafi rebels and mercenaries, carried out targeted assassinations, bombed civilian population centers and vital infrastructure that had no military utility. These actions contradicted both the spirit and letter of UNSC Resolution 1973, itself of dubious legality...

NATO carpet-bombed Tripoli to pave the way for the rebel seizure of control, causing at least 7,000 deaths... By contrast, a HRW report states that of 949 people wounded in the rebellion's start only 30 were civilian women or children... meaning that Qaddafi's forces focused narrowly on combatants." The hysterically hyped humanitarian catastrophe and Rwanda-style genocide supposedly imminent in Libya and Benghazi—short of a NATO military intervention —was a sham —until it was inflicted by NATO itself, and its terrorist troops who carried out massacres in Tripoli and Sirte with NATO air support.

A Word on Wahhabism

Britain and the Rise of Wahhabism and the House of Saud[250]
By Dr. Abdullah Mohammad Sindi

I. Introduction:

One of the most rigid and reactionary sects in all of Islam today is Wahhabism [self-styled as "Salafism"]. It is the official and dominant sect in Saudi Arabia... Wahhabism and Saudi Arabia's ruling House of Saud have been intimately and permanently intertwined since the births. Wahhabism created the Saudi monarchy, and the House of Saud spread Wahhabism. One could not have existed without the other. Wahhabism gives the House of Saud legitimacy, and the House of Saud protects and promotes Wahhabism.

Unlike Islam in other Muslim countries, Wahhabism treats women as third class citizens, imposes the veil on them, and denies them basic human rights.

Wahhabism is highly self-centered and extremely intolerant of progressive ideologies, other religions, and other Islamic sects such as Shiism and Sufism. It despises Arab Nationalism with a great deal of passion, yet it promotes "Saudi" nationalism. Wahhabism considers itself to be the only correct way in all of Islam, and any Muslim who opposes it as heretic or non-believer.

---

[250] Excerpted from http://www.liveleak.com/view?i=b47_1372845684

II. The Birth of Wahhabism

Wahhabism was born in the middle of the 18th century in the sleepy desert-village of Dir'iyyah located in the Arabian Peninsula's central region of Najd. The Wahhabi sect derives its name from the name of its founder Mohammad Ibn Abdul-Wahhab (1703-92).Born in the Najdi small desert-village of Uyayna, Ibn Abdul-Wahhab was a zealot preacher who married a total of 20 wives (no more than 4 at a time) and had 18 children.[251] Before becoming a preacher, however, Ibn Abdul-Wahhab traveled extensively for years for business, pleasure, and education to Hejaz,   Egypt, Syria, Iraq, Iran, and India.

Although Ibn Abdul-Wahhab is considered to be the father of Wahhabism, it was actually the British who initially impregnated him with the ideas of Wahhabism and made him its leader for their own sinister purposes to destroy Islam and the Muslim Ottoman Empire. The intricate details of this intriguing British conspiracy, are to be found in the memoirs of its master spy, titled "Confessions of a British Spy" from which the following two paragraphs are drawn.[252]...

While in Basra, Iraq young Ibn Abdul-Wahhab fell under the influence and control of a British undercover spy nicknamed "Hempher" who was one of many spies sent by London to Muslim lands in order to destabilize the Ottoman Empire and create conflicts among Muslims. Hempher, who pretended to be Muslim, went by the name of "Mohammad" and cunningly established a long-term intimate friendship with Ibn Abdul-Wahhab. Hempher, who showered Ibn Abdul-Wahhab with money and gifts, completely brainwashed him by convincing him that most Muslims should be killed because they had "dangerously violated" the basic tenets of Islam by becoming "heretics" and "polytheists". Hempher also fabricated for him a wild dream in which he supposedly "saw" Prophet Mohammad "kissing" Ibn Abdul-Wahhab between the eyes, telling him you are the "greatest", and asking him to be his "deputy" to save Islam from "heresies" and "superstitions". Upon hearing Hempher's dream, Ibn Abdul-Wahhab was wild with joy and became more determined than ever to assume the responsibility of establishing a new Islamic sect to "purify" and "reform" Islam.

In his memoirs Hempher described Ibn Abdul-Wahhab as "extremely unstable", "extremely rude", "morally depraved", "nervous", "arrogant", and "ignorant". The British, who viewed Ibn Abdul-Wahhab as a "typical fool", also arranged for him to have Nikah Mut'a ("marriage for pure sex") with two British female undercover spies. The first was a Christian woman, the other was Jewish.

III. The First Saudi-Wahhabi State: 1744-1818

After returning to Najd from his trips, Ibn Abdul-Wahhab began to preach his wild ideas in Uyayna. However, because of his rigid preaching, he was thrown out of his birthplace. He then went to preach in nearby Dir'iyyah where his dear friend Hempher and other undercover British spies joined him.

---

[251] Alexei Vassiliev, Ta'reekh Al-Arabiya Al-Saudiya [History of Saudi Arabia], Translated from Russian to Arabic by Khairi al-Dhamin and Jalal al-Maashta (Moscow: Dar Attagaddom, 1986), p. 108

[252] "Confessions of a British Spy", http://www.ummah.net/Al_adaab/spy1-7.html

Although many people opposed Ibn Abdul-Wahhab's rigid teachings and actions, including his own father and brother Sulaiman, who were both religious scholars, British undercover spies and money succeeded in cajoling an insignificant Dir'iyyah sheik, Mohammad al-Saud, to support him. In 1744, al-Saud joined forces with Ibn Abdul-Wahhab by forging a political, religious, and marital alliance. With this union between them and their families, which is still in existence today, Wahhabism as a religious and political movement was born.

Ignorant people, not by means of knowledge or persuasion, but by pure violence, bloodshed, and terror, spread Wahhabism in the Arabian Peninsula. As a result of the 1744 Saudi-Wahhabi alliance, a small Bedouin army was established with the help of British undercover spies who provided it with money and weapons. In time this army grew into a major menace, that eventually terrorized the entire Arabian Peninsula up to Damascus, and caused one of the worst episodes of *Fitnah* ("violent civil strife") in the history of Islam. In the process, this army was able to viciously conquer most of the Arabian Peninsula, to create the first Saudi-Wahhabi State.

For example, to fight what they considered Muslim "polytheists" and "heretics", the Saudis-Wahhabis shocked the entire Muslim world in 1801 by brutally destroying and defacing the sacred tomb of the martyr Hussein Bin Ali (Prophet Mohammad's grandson) in Karbala, Iraq, a particularly holy shrine to Shiite Muslims. They also mercilessly slaughtered over 4,000 people in Karbala and stole anything that was not nailed down. It took over 4,000 camels to carry the huge loot.[253] They attacked and desecrated Prophet Mohammad's Mosque, opened his grave, and sold and distributed its valuable relics and expensive jewels.

These Saudi-Wahhabi terrorist acts and blasphemous crimes aroused the deep anger of Muslims around the world including the Ottoman Caliph in Istanbul. As the official ruler of the Arabian Peninsula and the guardian of Islam's holiest mosques, Caliph Mahmud II ordered an Egyptian force to be sent to the Arabian Peninsula to punish the Saudi-Wahhabi clan. In 1818, an army led by Ibraheem Pasha (son of Egypt's ruler) destroyed the Saudis-Wahhabis and razed their desert capital of Dir'iyyah to the ground. The Wahhabi Imam Abdullah al-Saud and two of his followers were sent to Istanbul in chains where they were publicly beheaded. The rest of the Saudi-Wahhabi clan was held in captivity in Cairo.

IV. The Second Saudi-Wahhabi State: 1843-1891

Although the fanatically violent Wahhabism was destroyed in 1818, it was soon revived with the help of British colonialism. After the execution of the Wahhabi Imam Abdullah al-Saud in Turkey, the remnants of the Saudi-Wahhabi clan looked at their Arab and Muslim brothers as their real enemies, and to Britain and the West in general as their true friends. Accordingly, when Britain colonized Bahrain in 1820 and began to look for ways and means to expand its colonization in the area, the Wahhabi House of Saud found it a great opportunity to quickly seek British protection and help. In 1843 the Wahhabi Imam Faisal Ibn Turki al-Saud escaped from captivity in Cairo and returned to the Najdi town of Riyadh...[254]

---

[253] Vassiliev, Ta'reekh, p. 117.

[254] Gary Troeller, *The Birth of Saudi Arabia: Britain and the Rise of the House of Sa'ud* (London: Frank Cass, 1976), pp. 15-16.

the British sent Colonel Lewis Pelly in 1865 to Riyadh to establish an official British treaty with the Wahhabi House of Saud. To impress Pelly with his Wahhabi fanaticism and violence, Imam Faisal said that the major difference in the Wahhabi strategy between political and religious wars was that in the latter there would be no compromise, for "we kill everybody".[255]

In 1866 the Wahhabi House of Saud treacherously signed a "friendship" treaty with Britain, a power hated by all Muslims because of its colonial atrocities in the Muslim world. The treaty was similar to the many infamous unequal treaties imposed by Britain on other Arab puppets on the Arab Gulf (also known as the Persian Gulf). In exchange for British help, money, and weapons, the Wahhabi House of Saud agreed to collaborate with Britain's colonial authorities in the area...

Among those who were extremely outraged at the Wahhabi House of Saud was the patriotic al-Rasheed clan of Hail in central Arabia. In 1891 the Turkish-supported al-Rasheeds attacked Riyadh and destroyed the Saudi-Wahhabi clan. However, some members of the Wahhabi House of Saud managed to escape; among them was Imam Abdul-Rahman al-Saud and his teenager lad Abdulaziz. Both quickly fled to British-controlled Kuwait seeking British protection and help.

V. The Third Saudi-Wahhabi State (Saudi Arabia): 1902-?

Because Britain's colonial strategy in the Arabian Peninsula at the beginning of the 20th century was quickly gearing towards the final and complete destruction of the Muslim Ottoman Empire and its allies in Najd, al-Rasheed clan, the British decided to swiftly support the new Wahhabi Imam Abdulaziz. Fortified with British support, money, and weapons, the new Wahhabi Imam was able in 1902 to capture Riyadh. One of his first savage acts after capturing Riyadh was to terrorize its inhabitants by spiking the heads of the falling al-Rasheeds at the edge of the city. He and his fanatical Wahhabi followers also burned over (1,200) people to death.[256]

Known in the West as "Ibn Saud", the Wahhabi Imam Abdulaziz was well loved by his British masters. Many British officials and emissaries in the Arab Gulf area frequently met or interacted with him, and generously supported him with money, weapons, and advisors... With British weapons, money, and advisors, Imam Abdulaziz was able to gradually conquer most of the Arabian Peninsula in a ruthless manner under the banner of Wahhabism to create the Third Saudi-Wahhabi State, known today as Saudi Arabia.

In creating Saudi Arabia, the Wahhabi Imam Abdulaziz and his fanatical Wahhabi soldiers of God committed horrible massacres especially in Islam's holy land of Hejaz from which they brutally expelled its noble Shareef ruling class, the direct descendants of Prophet Mohammad. In Turabah in May 1919 they waged a sneak attack in the dead of the night on the Hejazi army and viciously massacred over 6,000 of its men. Again, in August 1924 the fanatical Saudis-Wahhabis barbarically broke into people's houses in the Hejazi city of Taif, threatened them, and stole their money at gunpoint. They decapitated boys and old men, and were

---

[255] Quoted in Robert Lacey, *The Kingdom: Arabia and the House of Saud* (New York: Harcourt Brace Jovanovich, 1981), p. 145

[256] Said K. Aburish, *The Rise, Corruption and the Coming Fall of the House of Saud* (New York: St. Martin's Press, 1995), p. 14.

amused by the horrified women who were screaming and weeping... They destroyed many of Makkah's beautiful tombs, ornamental mosques, and shrines that had stood for centuries reflecting the glorious Islamic past and the great history of the holy city. In addition, the ignorant invaders barbarically destroyed any physical traces of Prophet Mohammad's historical monuments and sights in the holy city as well as all other historical buildings or physical structures that could in any way be traced to his disciples "in order not to be worshiped as holy spots".[257]

Imam Abdulaziz's Wahhabi soldiers of God savagely bombarded Islam's second holiest city of Madinah. To the horror of all Muslims around the world, their British-made bombs and shells fell on Prophet Mohammad's tomb...

During the 30 years of creating Saudi Arabia (1902-32), the fanatical Saudis-Wahhabis brutally killed and wounded over 400,000 Arabs throughout the Arabian Peninsula; and carried out over 40,000 public executions and 350,000 public amputations, respectively 1% and 7% of the then estimated population of 4 million. In addition, the Saudi-Wahhabi terror forced more than one million inhabitants of the Arabian Peninsula to flee for their lives to other parts of the Arab world, never to return.[258]

Unlike a century earlier when the Egyptian Ibraheem Pasha under Ottoman orders punished the Saudi-Wahhabi warriors for their crimes against Hejaz's holy cities and inhabitants, this time the Arab and Muslim worlds were under the brutal control of Western colonial powers. Accordingly, the fanatical Saudis-Wahhabis escaped punishment and found protection and safety in Britain's power and friendship.

After establishing his British-made Wahhabi State, Imam Abdulaziz became a brutal dictator who took control of everything personally. He destroyed Hejaz's free press, political parties, constitution, and all of its governmental apparatuses. The Wahhabi Imam then brazenly named the whole country after his own family, calling it the Kingdom of "Saudi" Arabia. Besides being a dictator, King Abdulaziz was well known for his insatiable sexual appetite. In addition to his innumerable concubines, the "pious" Wahhabi Imam married about 300 wives; some of them were only a one-night stand... Abdulaziz encouraged the practice of slavery by personally owning hundreds of slaves for himself as well as for his family members. However, to avoid international embarrassment, Wahhabism and the House of Saud were finally forced to abolish slavery in 1962. [at least officially... but in practice not so much]...

All of Imam/King Abdulaziz's sons who assumed power after his death in 1953 (Saud, Faisal, Khalid and Fahad) became brutal dictators like him and continued to rely heavily on the enemies of Islam and Arabs in the West for protection. And ever since the US replaced Britain during World War II as the dominant power in the Arab world, the Wahhabi House of Saud has shamelessly turned Saudi Arabia (the holy land of Islam) over to Islam's foes to make it into a virtual American colony.

... with Saudi Arabia's immense oil wealth at its disposal, Wahhabism has been able in recent decades not only to mute most of its critics, but also to dramatically improve its own image throughout the Muslim world. Hence, Wahhabism has now

---

[257] A. Sindi, *The Arabs and the West: The Contributions and the Inflictions*
[258] Aburish, *The Rise*, p. 27.

been presented as a "reformist movement" that re-established the "purity" of Islam. Even the name "Wahhabism" itself has been dropped in favor of new more suitable names such as "Salafi movement" ("noble tradition") and "Muwahhedoon" ("unitarians"). Furthermore, the Wahhabi founder himself, Mohammad Ibn Abdul-Wahhab, has been presented as a "great man" of immense character and knowledge, a man who single-handedly "saved" Islam from "superstitions"...

VI. Prophet Mohammad's Sayings ("Hadiths"):

The Prophet was recorded as saying, "There (in Najd) is the place of earthquakes and afflictions and from there comes out the side of the head of Satan..."[259]

VII. Conclusion:

It is very clear from the historical record that without British help neither Wahhabism nor the House of Saud would be in existence today. Wahhabism is a British-inspired fundamentalist movement in Islam. Through its defense of the House of Saud, the US also supports Wahhabism directly and indirectly...

Wahhabism is violent, right wing, ultraconservative, rigid, extremist, reactionary, sexist, and intolerant. Its bloody historical record is well documented... Wahhabi leaders have openly supported and defended all of the House of Saud's unpopular domestic and foreign policies including allowing the US to occupy the land of Islam and Arabs, as well as to destroy Arabs and Muslims in Afghanistan and Iraq.

Indeed, the two families of the House of Saud and the Wahhabi House could not be separated because they are interwoven by bloodline and marriage since 1744...Wahhabism's intimate association with and support of the House of Saud, which is widely recognized to be one of the most brutal, corrupt, undemocratic, and feudal ruling classes in the entire world, makes its boastful claim of representing "the best form of Islam" the target of Muslim ridicule and derision. Today many educated Arabs and Muslims feel that Wahhabism gives Islam a bad name, and represents a reactionary shackle that prevents Arabs and Muslims from advancement. Certainly many Muslim Sunni scholars in the last 250 years both conservative and liberal, all across the Muslim world from Morocco to Indonesia, as well other Muslim sects such as the Shiite and Sufi, have all rejected Wahhabism since its birth as a horrible deformation of Islam.

The author, Dr. Abdullah Mohammad Sindi was born in Mecca, Arabia in 1944. He studied in France and Belgium, did his BA and MA at California State University, Sacramento, and his Ph.D. at the University of Southern California. He has taught as a professor of International Relations at King Abdulaziz University in Jeddah, Arabia, at the University of California, and at other California universities. He is the author of many articles both in Arabic and English, and a book, *The Arabs and the West: The Contributions and the Inflictions*.

Mohamed Ali Pasha, Patriarch of Arab Nationalism

Ibrahim Pasha, who destroyed the Saudi-Wahhabi counter-gang in 1818, was a son of Mohamed Ali Pasha, a leader of the cut of Napoleon or Lincoln. Ali Pasha

---

[259] Mohammad Muhsin Khan, Sahih al-Bukhari: Arabic-English (al-Medinah al-Munauwara: Islamic University-Dar al-Fikr, n.d.), Vol. 9, p.166.

was an Albanian tax-collector and army officer who saw the decline of the Ottoman empire, "the weak man of Europe," and the need for the Arabs to modernize, industrialize, educate, and build a nation state, economic independence and military power. His Wikipedia entry is a fascinating read. Ali Pasha set up tariffs to protect Egyptian industry, nationalized landownings and increased the wages of workers four-fold. He conquered Sudan, Syria and Crete, and was well on the way to take Turkey and unite the Arab world as a progressive force. But Europe wanted to pick apart the Ottoman Empire as it declined. In 1840 the British and Austrian navies forced Ali Pasha to renounce Syria, Crete, the Hijaz (Arabia) and the tariffs that were the key to industrialization. This was at the height of mercantilism, during the Opium War, when England forced China to let in drugs, and pay in silver. ("Free trade," as in today's WTO and TPP.) None of Ali Pasha's descendents were as gifted, and Egypt drifted until Nasser overthrew the dynasty. Now ISIS is used to caricature the "Caliphate," or empire of Islam, to make it an epithet. The sole superpower requires vassals, not rivals. Ali Pasha's dream empire would be a great civilization in its own right, sharing Arabia's fabulous oil wealth with the region's enormous human resources. Wouldn't a multipolar world be a livelier, safer and healthier place to live? – JPL.

Saudi Wahhabism[260]

By Haytham A. K. Radwan

Since the eighteenth century, and in conjunction with the Wahhabi religious establishment, Saudi Arabia became the centre for a new brand of religious imperialism based on sectarian movements...

Islam itself as a faith is not a threat to international security, it is Saudi Islam that is a threat... American politicians, journalists, and ideologists have ignored the truth that the threat is coming from Saudi Islam – a tactic to avoid any damage to the relations with the House of Saud and to keep economic and political interests alive.

As a result, the Saudi-US relationship and the Saudi-Wahhabi expansionist policy not only transform Muslim world politics, but also world politics...

It was actually the British who initially provided the Saudis with the ideas of Wahhabism and made them its leaders for their own purposes to destroy the Muslim Ottoman Empire...

Wahhabism itself is nothing more than an extension of Western imperialism.

The Plot to Create a Puppet Caliphate

ISIS ARE NOT SUNNIS. THEY ARE A BRITISH AND SALAFI PLOT TO CREATE NEO-CALIPHATE[261]

In 1932, again with British support, the Saud clan seized control of Arabia, which they proceeded to name after themselves, and of al Haramain, the sacred precincts of Mecca and Medina, thus donning the very false pretense of being defenders of Sunni Islam. In 1933, they signed away oil concessions to the Rockefellers' Standard Oil, remaining the chief source of petroleum to that company, which has now evolved into ExxonMobil, the

---

[260] http://www.intifada-palestine.com/2011/11/saudi-wahhabism-and-conspiracies/
[261] https://www.facebook.com/timeman786/posts/858017427568192

world's third largest company by revenue, and the second largest publicly traded company by market capitalization.

The extraordinary Saudi wealth was a key factor in their support for the spread of Wahhabism, as well as the related Salafi movement, which have since essentially become one. Salafism began in the last eighteenth century, headed by a notorious imposter and British agent by the name of Jamal ud Din al Afghani. Afghani was not only the Grand Master of the Freemasons of Egypt, but also purportedly a leading figure of the Hermetic Brotherhood of Luxor, which played a pivotal role in the rise of the European Occult Revival, leading to the Theosophical Society of H. P. Blavatsky, considered the godmother of the New Age movement, and of the Golden Dawn and then eventually the Ordo Templi Orientis (OTO) of Aleister Crowley. Afghani was also an original source of the Masonic teachings of the wayward Nation of Islam in the US.

Like the Wahhabis, the focus of the Salafi mission was to call for a re-opening of the Doors of Ijtihad, and Afghani's leading disciple Mohammed Abduh, was installed by the British as Mufti at the prestigious university of al Azhar, where he proceeded to use that pretence re-write the laws of Islam to suit the purposes of his sponsors. In Afghani's own words, as cited in Elie Kedourie, *Afghani and Abduh: An Essay on Religious Unbelief and Political Activism in Modern Islam*:

> We do not cut off the head of religion except with the sword of religion. Therefore, if you were to see us now, you would see ascetics and worshipers, kneeling and genuflecting, never disobeying God's commands and doing all that they are ordered to do.

Afghani's British handler, Wilfred Scawen Blunt, was the first to propose the establishment of a British controlled "Caliphate" (leader of the entire Muslim community) to replace the Ottoman Empire. In 1881, when Blunt visited Abdul Qadir al Jazairi, a Freemason and Algerian hero residing in exile in Damascus, he decided that he was the most promising candidate for Caliphate, an opinion shared by Afghani and Abduh.

The idea of a neo-caliphate was later actively pursued by T. E. Lawrence, aka "Lawrence of Arabia," who managed the Arab Revolt against the Ottoman Empire on behalf of the British at the end of WWII. The ostensible aim of the Arab Revolt was autonomy for the Arab peoples of the Ottoman Empire, creating a single unified Arab state from Syria to Yemen, under a puppet Caliphate, where Hussein would be proclaimed "King of all the Arabs."

The plan to create a neo-Caliphate was devised by London's Middle East team, which included foreign secretary Lord Curzon, Robert Cecil and his cousin Arthur Balfour, and also Mark Sykes and David George Hogarth, the chief of the Arab Bureau. They were joined by Winston Churchill and Arnold Toynbee, who was head of the Round Tablers' Royal Institute for International Affairs (RIIA), the sister organization of the Rockefellers' CFR. Outlining the policy was Lawrence:

> **If the Sultan of Turkey were to disappear, then the Caliphate by common consent of Islam would fall to the family of the prophet, the present representative of which is Hussein, the Sharif of Mecca. Hussein's activities seem beneficial to us, because it marches with our immediate aims, the breakup of the Islamic bloc and the disruption of the Ottoman Empire, and because the states he would set up would be as harmless to ourselves as Turkey was. If properly handled the Arab States would remain in a state of**

political mosaic, a tissue of jealous principalities incapable of cohesion, and yet always ready to combine against an outside force.[262]

The ISIS' handlers (Mossad, CIA, MI5 or all of the above) have learned a lot over the years. They made a mistake in choosing bin Laden who was an engineer by education and profession, and therefore failed to convince the Islamic world of his qualifications to set himself up as a leader or to interpret the nuances of Jihad. Similarly, when Mullah Omar, the leader of the Taliban, finally gained control over the country of Afghanistan, he diffused the enthusiasm of large swaths of the Muslim world's would-be radicals, who had merely been watching for the outcome, by instead only declaring himself "Amir ul Mumineen," or "Commander of the Faithful."

But now the situation seems to be interpreted as being more timely by ISI's hidden manipulators. It's been well advertised that not only did ISIS' leader, Abu Bakr al-Baghdadi, who has now dared to declare himself "Caliph" of the world's Muslims, earn a master's degree and a PhD in Islamic studies from the Islamic University of Baghdad, but he is also a descendant of the Prophet Mohammed, a supposed prerequisite for that office.

The re-establishment of a Caliph over the world of Islam is the universal aspiration of the Muslims. Every Muslim despairs at the ravages of Western Imperialism, as well as its blind sponsorship of rapacious Zionism. But that makes them especially manipulable by their enemies, who dare to prop up false oppositions, or Pied Pipers like al Baghdadi.

But they've made one colossal mistake: they have mistakenly claimed that ISIS is a "Sunni organization." Since the absence of true Sunni authority, with the fall of the Ottoman Empire in 1924, the Saudis have taken advantage of the vacuum to fund their aberrant interpretations, and succeeded to a great extent in fooling the world that Wahhabism and Salafism are merely reform trends within Sunnism. And for the most part, many Muslims are convinced. But the problem with the Muslims today is they are prone to extremism and lapses mistakenly identified as "Shariah" precisely for the reason that they have been estranged from their true Islamic legal tradition, which is found in following the Maddhabs.

Once they recognize that truth, they will no longer be suspectible to imposters like ISIS. But more dangerously still, they will have rediscovered their true heritage, which made them incorruptible and an indomitable force in the past.

Saudi 'Tsunami of Money' to Pakistan for 24,000 Madrassas[263]

About 24,000 'madrassas' in Pakistan are funded by Saudi, Arabia which has unleashed a "tsunami of money" to "export intolerance", a top American senator has said, adding that the US needs to end its effective acquiescence to the Saudi sponsorship of radical Islamism.

Senator Chris Murphy (D-CT) said Pakistan is the best example of where money coming from Saudi Arabia is funneled to religious schools that nurture hatred and terrorism.

---

[262] Wikipedia, The McMahon–Hussein Correspondence

[263] http://www.scoopwhoop.com/Tsunami-of-money-from-S-Arabia-funding-24000-Pak-madrassas/ . The story was found only on Indian sources on the Web. India is concerned about extremism in Pakistan, while US-global media "cover" such news by covering it up. The focus on Pakistan could also be directed against Afghanistan and Russia.

"In 1956, there were 244 madrassas in Pakistan. Today, there are 24,000. These schools are multiplying all over the globe. These schools, by and large, don't teach violence. They aren't the minor leagues for al-Qaeda or ISIS. But they do teach a version of Islam that leads very nicely into an anti-Shia, anti-Western militancy. Those 24,000 religious schools in Pakistan – thousands of them are funded with money that originates in Saudi Arabia," Murphy said in an address yesterday to the Council on Foreign Relations, a top American think-tank.

According to some estimates, since the 1960s, the Saudis have funneled over $100 billion into funding schools and mosques all over the world with the mission of spreading puritanical Wahhabi Islam. As a point of comparison, researchers estimate that the former Soviet Union spent about $7 billion exporting its communist ideology from 1920-1991.

"Less-well-funded governments and other strains of Islam can hardly keep up with the tsunami of money behind this export of intolerance," Murphy said.

"The uncomfortable truth is for all the positive aspects of our alliance with Saudi Arabia, there is another side to Saudi Arabia that we can no longer afford to ignore, as our fight against Islamic extremism becomes more focused and more complicated," he said.

"The United States should suspend supporting Saudi Arabia's military campaign in Yemen, at the very least until we get assurances that this campaign does not distract from the fight against IS and al-Qaeda, and until we make some progress on the Saudi export of Wahhabism," he said.

Murphy demanded that Congress should not sign off on any more US military sales to Saudi Arabia until similar assurances are granted. He said that the political alliance between the House of Saud - Saudi Arabia's ruling royal family - and orthodox Wahhabi clerics is as old as the nation, resulting in billions funnelled to and through the Wahhabi movement.

The vicious terrorist groups that Americans know by name are Sunni in derivation, and greatly influenced by Wahhabi and Salafist teachings, Murphy said, adding that leaders of both Democratic and Republican parties should avoid the extremes of this debate, and enter into a real conversation about how America can help the moderate voices within Islam win out over those who sow seeds of extremism.

***

I am like a man who has lighted a fire, and all the creeping things
have rushed to burn themselves in it.
– Saying of the Prophet[264]

Justice and fairness, not religion or atheism,
Are needful for the protection of the State.
–Hakim Jami[265]

---

[264] In *Caravan of Dreams*, by Idries Shah
[265] In *The Way of the Sufi*, by Idries Shah

The Yinon Plan: Balkanization for Greater Israel

The Zionist doctrine of Herzl and Netanyahu envisions a Greater Israel, an empire reaching from the Nile to the Euphrates. The ultimate aim is for a World Empire, eclipsing even the USA. [266]

The Yinon Plan was a continuation of Britain's colonial design in the Middle East... Israeli strategists viewed Iraq as their biggest strategic challenge from an Arab state. This is why Iraq was outlined as the centerpiece to the balkanization of the Middle East and the Arab World. In Iraq, on the basis of the concepts of the Yinon Plan, Israeli strategists have called for the division of Iraq into a Kurdish state and two Arab states, one for Shiite Muslims and the other for Sunni Muslims. The first step towards establishing this was a war between Iraq and Iran, which the Yinon Plan discusses...

The Yinon Plan calls for a divided Lebanon, Egypt, and Syria. The partitioning of Iran, Turkey, Somalia, and Pakistan also all fall into line with these views. The Yinon Plan also calls for dissolution in North Africa and forecasts it as starting from Egypt and then spilling over into Sudan, Libya, and the rest of the region... [Sudan was split into two parts in 2011.]

Israel must 1) become an imperial regional power, and 2) must effect the division of the whole area into small states by the dissolution of all existing Arab states...

What they want and what they are planning for is not an Arab world, but a world of Arab fragments that is ready to succumb to Israeli hegemony...

Contrasted with the detailed and unambiguous Zionist strategy elucidated in this document, Arab and Palestinian strategy, unfortunately, suffers from ambiguity and incoherence...

The idea that all the Arab states should be broken down, by Israel, into small units, occurs again and again in Israeli strategic thinking...

The strong connection with Neo-Conservative thought in the USA is very prominent... the real aim of the author, and of the present Israeli establishment is clear: To make an Imperial Israel into a world power. In other words, the aim of Sharon is to deceive the Americans after he has deceived all the rest.

---

[266] Chossudovsky, Michel; Shahak, Israel, and Nazemroaya, Mahdi Darius in "'Greater Israel': The Zionist Plan for the Middle East," Nov. 7, 2015, http://www.globalresearch.ca/greater-israel-the-zionist-plan-for-the-middle-east/5324815. See also: Yinon's CV at Wikileaks.org.

Israeli Colonel Leading ISIL Terrorists Captured in Iraq[267]

Iran reported the capture of an Israeli colonel by Iraqi forces, who "participated in the Takfiri ISIL group's terrorist operations... Several ISIL militants arrested in the last one year had already confessed that Israeli agents from Mossad and other Israeli espionage and intelligence bodies were present in the first wave of ISIL attacks on Iraq and capture of Mosul in Summer 2014."

In July, Iraqi forces also shot down an ISIS drone that was made in Israel.

Kremlin Accuses Mossad of Training ISIS

A senior aide to Russian President Vladimir Putin, Alexander Prokhanov, told Iran's *Press TV* that Israel's spy agency, the Mossad, is training ISIS takfiri terrorists operating in Iraq and Syria, probably including training in espionage. ISIS recently launched an attack against Russia in Chechnya.[268]

"ISIL is a tool in the hands of the United States," he said.

Wags have noted that the initials ISIS also stand for Israeli Secret Intelligence Agency, which happens to be the long name for Mossad in English.

Bring 'em on

Five hundred Al Qaida extremists wounded in the Syrian war are being treated in an Israeli hospital before going back to fight against Assad (and so they claim also against Daesh, i.e. against themselves – Lo, they have attained to the Greater *Jihad*, the struggle against one's self! Much like their Caliph, Barack Obama.)[269]

Israel prefers ISIS over Iran

Israel's Defense Minister Moshe Ya'alon declared he'd rather see Syria fall to ISIS than to any Iran-backed group. He said ISIS "is not a threat for us," and that the region is at the "height of the clash of civilizations." The *Washington Post* report noted, "Israel has largely avoided any involvement in the fight against the Islamic State but has struck Hezbollah inside Syria."[270]

New UN Report Reveals Collaboration Between Israel and Syrian Rebels

"A report from the UN Disengagement Observer Force (UNDOF) reveals that Israel has been working closely with Syrian rebels in the Golan Heights." Aside from medical care for ISIS and Al Qaida fighters, UN observers saw Israelis deliver supplies to them, and set up a crossing point for them into Israel.[271]

---

[267] "Israeli Colonel Leading ISIL Terrorists Captured in Iraq," Oct. 22, 2015, http://en.farsnews.com/newstext.aspx?nn=13940730000210

[268] "Mossad training ISIL terrorists: Russia," Dec. 7, 2015, http://edition.presstv.ir/detail/389121.html

[269] Thierry Meyssan, "More than 500 jihadists cared for at the Ziv Medical Centre," Nov. 24, 2015, http://www.voltairenet.org/article189411.html

[270] https://www.washingtonpost.com/news/worldviews/wp/2016/01/19/israeli-defense-minister-if-i-had-to-choose-between-iran-and-isis-id-choose-isis/731453261570143/

[271] http://chicagopost.net/world-news/alarming-evidence-suggests-isis-is-now-a-us-israel-proxy-army/2/ citing the Jerusalem Post.

Mapmakers Eagerly Carving Up the Middle East

Decline of the Ottoman Empire, 1807-1923

Perfidious Albion. In the Levant, Britain took what belonged not to her, but to Turkey, and promised it to conflicting parties, the Arabs, Jews and French.

The Arab Revolt against the Turks was made famous by "Lawrence of Arabia," the British agent who was instrumental in inciting it. Britain promised rulership of all the Arab lands of the Ottomans to the leader of the revolt, Sharif Hussein of Mecca, for joining in the war against Turkey. With the Ottoman defeat in 1918, Arab troops led by Sharif's son Faisal entered Damascus.

The Arabs quickly set up local governments all over Syria, and were hoping for the single Arab state stretching from the Turkish border to Yemen, which the British had promised them. But French troops quickly landed, occupied Lebanon and dissolved the popular Arab governments, in line with the secret Franco-British Sykes-Picot Agreement. France got Syria, Britain got Iraq, Palestine came under "international" control.

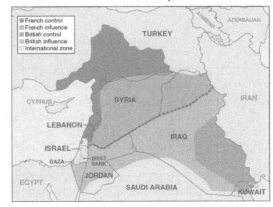

"Sykes and Picot never consulted local inhabitants or political leaders in the Middle East. In fact, the world learned of the plan only after the new, communist government in Russia published the text in party newspapers." – *Stars and Stripes*, "Sykes-Picot Agreement: Line in the sand still shapes Middle East."

France divided Syria into six parts, but the occupation and division was bitterly opposed by the population, and it took three years to crush the insurgency. A few years later, the British betrayed Sharif Hussein by helping the Wahhabi Saudis oust him and take over the Arabian peninsula. In 1937 France gave Alexandretta (Hatay) to Turkey in reward for staying out of WWII.

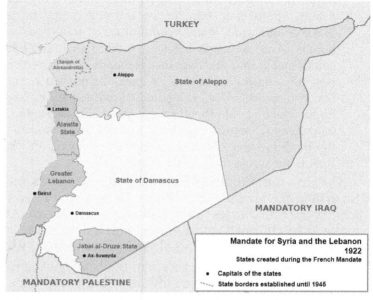

Above, the French Mandate Map of Syria (Wikipedia)

At right, the Bernard Lewis Plan. Lewis (born 1916) is an influential Anglo-American Jewish "Orientalist" historian of the Near East, Islam, and its interaction with the West. He argues that Muslims have no real grievances, only an irrational rage against the West.

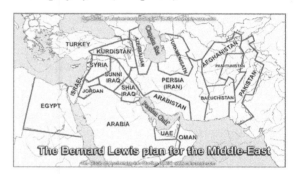

Below, the Wright Plan, New York Times *Opinion page, Sept. 28, 2013.*
Accompanying text on next page.

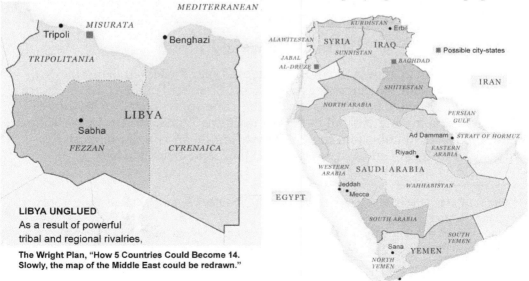

LIBYA UNGLUED
As a result of powerful tribal and regional rivalries,

The Wright Plan, "How 5 Countries Could Become 14.
Slowly, the map of the Middle East could be redrawn."

Syria: the trigger? Sectarian and ethnic rivalries could break it into at least three pieces. Spillover to Iraq: In the simplest of several possibilities, northern Kurds join Syrian Kurds. Many central areas of Iraq, dominated by Sunnis, join Syria's Sunnis. And the south becomes Shiitestan. It's not likely to be so clean. Libya could break into its two historic parts — Tripolitania and Cyrenaica — and possibly a third Fezzan state. Yemen, the poorest Arab country could break (again) into two pieces following a potential referendum in South Yemen on independence. South Yemen could then become part of Saudi Arabia. Saudi Arabia faces its own (suppressed) internal divisions. It could break into the five regions that preceded the modern state... Robin Wright is the author of "Rock the Casbah: Rage and Rebellion Across the Islamic World." [272]

The Ottoman Empire crested with the conquests and administration of Sultan Suleyman the Magnficent, Caliph of Islam, who ruled from 1520 to 1566. He gained huge territories in the Balkans, North Africa, Arabia and the Levant, making the empire a world power, with a flourishing culture, a population of 20 to 30 million, and command of the Mediterranean, Black Sea and Red Sea.

It was all downhill from there. In the heyday of European colonialism, France took the Maghreb, Italy got Libya, the Balkans became independent or fell to Austria, Russia regained ancestral lands around the Black Sea, Egypt became a British "protectorate."

By 1914, all that was left for the feeding frenzy was the Levant, Iraq and Arabia. Turkey's alliance with rising power Germany led to defeat in WWI, bringing these core domains under the control of Britain, France and the Zionist movement. Since then, their final balkanization has been a recurring theme. First the British-Zionist Balfour Declaration giving Palestine over for Jewish settlement, and the Sykes-Picot plan fragmenting the Ottoman legacy. Kamal Ataturk was able to block a Franco-British plan to split up Turkey itself. In more recent decades, as the Peters plan in "Unmasking ISIS" shows, the US now runs the Franco-British-Zionist jigsaw. ISIS is just the latest cutting blade for the perennial colonial Sykes-Picot-Lewis-Yinon-Peters-Juppé-Wright plan.

The tragedy of the Arab world has been the inability to keep a winning streak going after the successes of a great leader. Arab nationalism tries to overcome this by creating modern nation states. Neo-colonialism wants the Arabs backward and disorganized, so it encourages tribalism and atavistic distortions of Islam.

Islamophobia and Empire[273]

Abby Martin: 2015 was the most dangerous year for Muslims in America, setting records for hate crime against them... Members of the community are saying the climate of hate is worse now than after 9/11. To take a look at Islamophobia in America and its roots in empire, I talked to Dr. Deepa Kumar, author of Islamophobia and the Politics of Empire and professor of Media Studies at Rutgers University ["one very smart and articulate lady."]

[272] http://www.nytimes.com/interactive/2013/09/29/sunday-review/how-5-countries-could-become-14.html

[273] http://www.washingtonsblog.com/2016/01/islamophobia-derives-empires-interest-controlling-middle-east.html

Prof. Deepa: It has been a horrible year for Muslims not just in the United States but around the world. Because if you see the two events that book end 2015 it is the horrific Charlie Hebdo attacks in France and the Paris attacks later on towards the end of the year, and then San Bernardino... hate crimes against Muslims and "those who look Muslim" have skyrocketed... France or the United States and so on saying, these people are a fifth column, they don't belong here... What these attacks have done it's legitimized this. But what it's also legitimized is the very security apparatus. After the Paris attacks the French police carries out more than 2,000 raids on Muslims, both citizens as well as immigrants, arrest hundreds of Muslims, and it legitimizes these activities by the state to keep us safe.

Abby: How do you define Islamophobia?

Prof. Deepa: It's a form of cultural racism. That is based on turbans, or people wearing hijabs... There's an assumption that is made that these people all have a certain behavior that... when they practice Islam they are programmed to be violent, they are programmed to be misogynistic, if you're a woman you're programmed to be subservient, you're programmed to be a terrorist and so on...

Abby: Another talking point that I hear used pretty often by people like Bill Maher and Sam Harris. 17% of Muslims in France support ISIS...[274]

Prof. Deepa: Islam is practiced by 1.5 billion people... they're just as different a group and non-homogenous a group as those in the west... One myth that gets peddled again and again is that Muslim women are just so horribly oppressed all over the world. Well that's not true... Muslim women just like every other woman in the world do face... things like inability to get good jobs... Women in the US face the same sort of situation. However conditions vary widely across Muslim majority countries. In Saudi Arabia a woman can't drive, but in Bangladesh women have been elected to heads of state, not once but twice...

That diversity is simply not acknowledged by the likes of Sam Harris and the new atheists and all the rest of it. If anything, what they do is that they use the clash of civilizations argument. They somehow hold up this mantle of the west as being this place of enlightened values, and then say that they want to critique all religions. But if you look at their work, the work of the new atheists, the sharpest knife is dug into Islam. That's true of Hitchens, it's true of Dawkins, Sam Harris and so on. So they actually have an agenda, but they hide behind objectivity as a way to spout Islamophobia as academic, as research...

Prof. Deepa: the legal system in the United States refuses to acknowledge racism... In my discussions with lawyers and friends and colleagues who are lawyers, what they've told me is that in cases that they've prosecuted there are just ridiculous things that are brought up as "evidence" to show that somebody is radicalized. What is this evidence? That they had a copy of the Quran in their pocket. That means this person must have been getting ready to commit a violent crime. That's ridiculous. That's Islamophobic, that's cultural racism. It's the idea I mentioned earlier that somehow Islam is this virus that programs people to go out and do murderous things...

---

[274] An international poll showed extremely low support for ISIS in all Muslim majority countries surveyed, with 100% "strongly against" in Lebanon. http://www.pewresearch.org/fact-tank/2015/11/17/in-nations-with-significant-muslim-populations-much-disdain-for-isis/

I was following the sort of coverage of San Bernardino versus the Planned Parenthood shooting, and the differences could not be clearer in terms of how perpetrators of gun violence are treated. So Planned Parenthood happens, the religion of Robert Dear barely mentioned... even though we know he's an evangelical Christian... a great admirer of this group called the Army of God, which is this right wing fundamentalist anti-abortion group that's committed murders and violence, and so he calls them heroes. So we know he's at least in part driven by this kind of Christian fundamentalist ideology, but that doesn't become part of the story. Because the reason Robert Dear did this is because there's something wrong with him. There's something in his head that's wrong, because we won't associate his action with the actions of white Christians overall. We won't call on white Christians to apologize for the actions of Robert Dear.

San Bernardino happens and yes these people are religious, they are fundamentalists and so on. Now, however, even President Obama says, well, there's an extremist ideology that is spreading through Muslim communities and all Muslims have to take responsibility for it. Why? Why are Muslims any more responsible for the actions of the San Bernardino shooters than Christians for Robert Dear? You see the double standards, right? And so straight away of course the story is entirely about Islam, it's about the virus of Islam, it's about how Islam makes people do all sorts of violent things, and the war on terror becomes the way in which the story is spun. So, you know, one [tongue in] cheeky way of looking at it is to say, "They actually carried out what is a tradition that's as American as apple pie, which is shootings." That really is so endemic to American society in a way that it's not to other societies, and we might see this as a sign of their "integration". But in fact of course othering has become so much a part of media coverage, so much the common sense ideology... that present their violence as somehow being tied to terrorism, as tied to Islam. Whereas our violence, people like Robert Dear and so on, those are just isolated individuals.

Abby: The clash of civilizations of course is the ideology that Islam is destined to clash with the West, that our cultures are just intrinsically separate, and they can't ever co-exist...

Prof. Deepa: In particular Bernard Lewis would write an essay titled "Roots of Muslim Rage," in which he argues that politics has nothing to do with why people in the Middle East may be angry with the United States, or may have grievances with Europe, western Europe. Colonialism has nothing to do with it; the formation of Israel has nothing to do with it. He says that there's an irrational rage that has spanned 14 centuries which characterizes this inevitable clash. First of all that's not true. It is not at all the clear case that the East and West have always clashed. There have been various periods of cooperation right through history which I don't have the time to get into but it's in my book. But it becomes a convenient way in which to define the politics in the post-Cold War era. So one enemy is gone that justifies US imperialism and US reach all over the world. What is it going to be substituted by?[275]

And Samuel Huntington actually the political scientist would pick up this term clash of civilizations, and his theory of what politics would be characterized by in

---

[275] See the "Three World Wars" plan in *The Money Power* by Carr and Knuth. WWI, Germany vs. Britain, result: Soviet Communis. WWII: Fascism vs. Zionism. WWIII: Zionism vs. Islam.

the post-Cold War world is the following: Conflict is not going to be political, conflict is going to be cultural. And Mahmood Mamdani, who has written this book called "Good Muslim, Bad Muslim," says that what that does is it very conveniently displaces all the political stuff onto the cultural terrain, and now we don't have to talk about occupation, we don't have to talk about war, we don't have to talk about drone strikes, which is what we see in the era of the war on terror, we'll just call it the clash of cultures. You know these people they like to wear hijabs, that's why we don't get along with them and so on. Never mind that every democratic movement that's existed in the Middle East has been squashed by the US government in order to keep oil flowing, in order to keep alive the dictators who are the allies of the US, and so forth. All those political grievances get sidelined and instead culture becomes the focus, and I think that's an extremely problematic way to look at what is fundamentally a political issue.

Abby: So what are the roots of Islamophobia and how is it related to Empire maintaining itself?

Prof. Deepa: So all empires, at least most empires, rely on some form of othering in order to justify wars, in order to justify taxation, in order to justify conscription and so on. This is not just true of American imperialism, and I will talk about American imperialism. But I want to actually start all the way with antiquity with the Roman Empire...

So when the Romans went about conquering people... one of the first things they would do is try to inculcate them in Roman values, Roman lifestyle, Roman culture, Roman architecture and so on, and when the people accepted these cultural values of Rome, they became Romans. So in this large empire, everybody was considered Roman, but for people who were not as easily conquered, who resisted and who wouldn't come on the Roman fold just as easily, there was a term invented for them. They were called barbarians, and the Romans invented this very interesting hierarchy, this kind of typology, which was the following. It said all human beings have two elements that define them; one is the physical body, the other is the mind... And what they would argue is that Romans, not all Romans, elite Romans are driven by the mind. The mind controls the body. They are rational, they are intelligent, in that sense they're closer to God, whereas the barbarians are closer to animals, because the body controls the mind, and therefore they are inferior, and therefore it's justified we go off and kill them and make them slaves, or one of the routine forms of entertainment in Rome is that the barbarians would be brought to these amphitheaters and killed.

Now let's move to the United States. There are a lot of similarities but also some differences. The US takes over the reins of the Middle East from France and Britain in the post-war period. NSC 68, which is the secret policy document written in 1950, would lay out quite clearly why militarism is going to be the key way the US is going to fill the vacuum left behind by the collapse of the European empire, the rise of the Soviet Union, and how the world has now become a battle field, and militarily that's how the US is going to assert its hegemony...

In the Middle East it has many geostrategic interests, rivalry with the Soviet Union, but oil certainly is a part of this story. Daniel Yergin tells us that part of what he calls the post-war petroleum order is about creating a certain arrangement between oil producing states, and states to which oil will flow, so that cheap oil would be available... anyone who disrupted this post-war petroleum order was necessarily an enemy. They were either hand in glove with the Soviet Union or they were just barbaric people who lived in the deserts and so on who needed to be taken out, and so that's the mythology.

These ideas don't just exist in ether, in Hollywood films or in novels and so on for no reason. They're systematically reproduced in academia, in think tanks, they're used by political figures, they're reproduced in the media and so on as a way to justify US policy. Of course at first it's about demonizing the Arabs, but then it turns into the demonization of the Muslim.

Abby: Donald Trump shocked the world by his declaration of a ban on Muslims entering this country if he were to be president.

Prof. Deepa: Donald Trump is basically stating out loud and making explicit what actually has been US policy for the last few decades. That is, if you look at the mass deportation of immigrants under Obama you know it's huge. Over two million people have been deported, but you don't talk about that... When Trump says let's prevent Muslims from coming in or let's create a registry and a database to document all Muslims, you don't say that if you're a respectable politician, but in practice we've been doing that. Over the last 20 some years there's been an attempt to systematically collect information on various groups of Middle Easterners. In fact going all the way back to the late 70s on Iranians.

For people like Trump who represent the class of the 1%, bashing immigrants has been staple, because if you look at the same period of time, we've seen a massive growth of class inequality, class polarization, the vast majority of people around the world have grown poorer, the 1% has grown phenomenally rich, there have been cuts in social services, attack on the welfare state, tuition costs of colleges have been going up, healthcare costs are going up, this is the neo-liberal system. But rather than blame the regime of the 1%, it's easy to bash immigrants, and you've seen this logic everywhere. This is not just a western European or American phenomenon. In Russia, in Australia, in India, in Myanmar, all over the world this agenda, this Islamophobic agenda has helped to deflect attention away from the structural inequality and to point fingers, to scapegoat Muslims as a way to get people to fight with each other, rather than to look at the structural problems caused by neo-liberalism. So to see Donald Trump as some sort of lone wolf who's responsible for the escalation of Islamophobia or who is otherwise corrupting a great political system I think is deeply problematic, because Donald Trump is just a part of a larger system which both Democrats and Republicans are responsible for creating.

[In San Diego's recent mayoral election, the 1% candidate Faulconer beat the 99% candidate Alvarez by turning it into a racial contest of whites vs. Hispanics.]

If we don't get to the root of what causes Islamophobia, which is empire, the national security state, the neoliberal order in which we live, and the class power that sustains all of this... then we're not going to do away with Islamophobia... We need to come together across national lines and build a global movement that can take on the regime of the 1%, one that prioritizes the interests of the 99%.

Closing Argument: We Are ISIS

by Ken O'Keefe[276]

Ken O'Keefe is a pro-Palestine activist, and former US Marine and Gulf War veteran. In January 2003 he instigated and led the human shield action to Iraq to try to stop the war. He was also on board the flotilla that tried to break the blockade of Gaza in 2010.

Ken O'Keefe: This is an edited transcript of my appearance on Press TV shortly after the 11/13/15 Paris attacks.[277]

I really think it necessary at this point to spread the understanding that WE, the West and all of our puppet governments, are in very real terms, the so-called "ISIS." We created this monster, we use it to foster more insane policies in the Middle East, to demonize Muslims, to take away more rights from the people ... and it serves one agenda above all others, the Greater Israel Project.

I say WE are responsible because WE have not done all that we are capable of to stop it, when we do it will stop, and the truth is the most powerful weapon WE have. We need to spread this truth further and further and use the mainstream media's incessant lies against them to wake up more people. These false flags are exposing the powers that be and their agents more and more; in a tactical sense these are great opportunities for humanity, so let us keep exposing the truth on every level and also start pushing for war crimes charges for mass media as well as military and government "officials." It may seem impossible to think this could happen right now, but it will if we make it so and the transformation to a better world can occur much, much faster than people currently realize...

And I hope it's even more of a wake-up call for us to realize that WE ARE ISIS... Let us remember that before the United States invaded Iraq there was no al-Qaeda in Iraq. Look at it today. Let us also remember that when Qaddafi was in power in Libya there was very little al-Qaeda. And now look at it. It's an absolute basket case, full of these operatives...

I believe that it is beyond any doubt that not only is the United States providing the financial, political, and military cover for these terrorists, through our proxies, but we've also provided the training for these people in Jordan. And Turkey, another of our best friends, has been shuttling these psychopaths into Syria for a long time now. So the idea that the West is actually fighting a war against ISIS is beyond ridiculous. So what we really need to do is start realizing that we *are* ISIS. And the reason our corrupt, treasonous governments are carrying out these policies is that they do not represent us. They represent the bankers. And the bankers make a hell of a lot of money off of war. And more importantly, as long as we're all fighting each other, as long as we're all not trusting each other, as long as we're all being played as pawns, over and over, then they can maintain this tyrannical system of never-ending war.

---

[276] Excerpted from *ANOTHER French False Flag? Bloody Tracks from Paris to San Bernardino*, edited by Kevin Barrett, 2016
[277] Press TV: Former US Marine Ken O'Keefe on Paris False Flag
https://www.youtube.com/watch?v=_vmSHXF-vX8

So this is really a wake-up call. What has happened in Paris is us. We are responsible through our corrupt governments...

PressTV: Some of the events we've been talking about, in terms of Islamophobia, more policies against Muslims... maybe this is what the intent is behind these attacks...

Indeed, that is the case. And it's just more of the same now, isn't it? I'm a non-Muslim, and I'm angry at the way Muslims have been portrayed around the world. I have lived in Muslim lands, and I have experienced some of the greatest hospitality and generosity that you will ever experience. And yet Muslims in general are being associated with this monstrosity known as ISIS—which again I say is Israeli Secret Intelligence Service. And also, before that, al-Qaeda, the al-Nusra Front. All of these are intended to smear Islam as a whole, all 1.8 billion on this planet, to associate them with this sort of madness, when in fact it is us in the West who are creating this stuff, funding it, protecting it. In fact, America has been providing air cover to these psychopaths in Syria and Iraq... It is really disgusting that people have been conned into thinking that Muslims have anything to do with this.

And let us hearken back to the original incident which has caused this madness known as the war on terror. "The So-Called Hijackers and Osama Bin Laden" is one of the greatest fairy stories ever created. The idea that this man in a cave in Afghanistan on dialysis masterminded this incredible operation against the United States with 19 so-called hijackers wielding box cutters, Mohamed Atta among them, snorting cocaine and hanging out with strippers in Florida, that these people are responsible for this event, in defiance of the greatest military machine in the history of mankind, never mind all of the evidence that has come forward that makes the official version of 9/11 beyond ridiculous ... Muslims did not carry out 9/11. In fact, those who blame the Muslims, primarily the Jewish-supremacist-Zionist-controlled media of America, and the government that is controlled by these Jewish-supremacist Zionists—all of them parrot the same ridiculous tired old line that Muslims were responsible. This is an agenda that is intended to create a clash of civilizations. Those who are collaborating in this agenda need to be held accountable for war crimes and crimes against humanity. And I'm including not just the politicians and the military, but those in the media who have perpetuated these lies...

PressTV: There has been a piece of breaking news, a message from Assad to Hollande: "France suffered the brutality of terrorism that has plagued Syria for more than five years." That's quite telling in terms of what Syria has experienced. Your reaction?

It is truly incredible that we listen to anyone, whether it is François Hollande or Obama or any of these other puppets, as if anything they say has any merit whatsoever. There is no moral authority at all in the West. These people are an embarrassment to all of us who have a functioning brain and a heart. These people are traitors. Whether they come from France or whether they come from Britain or America. And everything they say is to be taken as complete and total rubbish. The idea that France and the West are not directly responsible for the mayhem that has been occurring in Syria is, again, beyond ridiculous. We know for a fact how we've been funding and supporting the supposedly "moderate rebels." There is no such thing. Recently a US general admitted that there might be four or five of these people in Syria.

The entire policy is intended to create havoc in the Middle East. And it is extremely important that people around the world begin to comprehend that these policies that are being carried out in the Middle East are actually not failures. I'm getting sick of hearing so-called experts talking about geopolitics and how America is failing to learn from its mistakes and all of this nonsense. These are not mistakes! These are intentional polices to wreak havoc, to sow the seeds of sectarian hatred. Again, let me cite the fact that before we took Saddam Hussein out in Iraq there was no al-Qaeda in Iraq. Before we played this game in Libya there was no such thing as ISIS and all of this madness that's going on in Libya today... Every country that we, the West, touch in the Middle East is full of these monsters.

***

WE... are the human race. What is the root meaning of the word race. It is exactly that – a root.

We are all of one root. The human race is like one body. If one limb feels pain, the whole body is ill.

Divide and conquer is an illusion. We are living in one house. When there is disturbance in one room, how can there be peace in any room.

The refugee problems in Europe and North America are telling us something. You can't just fire and forget and throw problems over the fence. They don't go away that way. They are still there, getting worse. And they come back.

So maybe you can build walls and live in a gated community. But this is just a nice word for a prison. A real estate sales word for a luxury prison, but it still fills the bill. Walls keep people out, and they keep people in. Walls can't let you wander safe and free in the wide garden of the world.

Why can't we have a world of fair play and caring for each other? Instead of arrogance, greed and hatred. What makes us so bad?

Why can't we see that contentment comes from within. That buying a lot of toys, strutting and lording it over others, never brought happiness.

How many millenia have moral philosophers and religious teachers racked their brains trying to explain these simple facts to the idiotic human race.

Of course people are smart enough to understand the words. In fact we are too smart. We think we can outsmart the rules of life, and get away with it.

Our pride is our prison. – JPL

***

Hillary's critics may be thinking more about the depths of her corruption than about the outrages of her war crimes, but corruption is a big factor driving unjust wars, too. It's also a major motive behind the surveillance state, mining data for illicit profit as well as political reasons.

Appendices

DIA Memo on Extremist Threat in Syria and Iraq

Here is the full declassified text of the memo referred to by more than one author in this book – the Defense Intelligence Agency (DIA) finding of August 2012 that the Syrian insurgency is dominated by Al Qaeda extremists and other terrorist elements.[278]

Highlights of this assessment were explained on CBS TV's program "Reality Check with Ben Swann" after the Paris massacre on Nov. 13, 2015:[279]

France is tonight a police state, and there is concern over ISIS infiltrating Syrian refugees. And of course the big question: How can the world rid itself of the Islamic State? Now before you listen to one more politician tell you what we need to do, you need to know what politicians knew about ISIS three years ago, and the actions they took anyway. This is a reality check you won't see anywhere else... [footage from Obama speech on "war on ISIS"]

There is no doubt the US and its allies must stop ISIS. After the Paris attacks that left 129 dead and more than 350 people injured, and an entire nation in lockdown, there is no doubt that ISIS has to be stopped. Now shortly after the Paris attacks, ISIS fighters recorded this new video, claiming they will soon strike the United States, including Washington DC.

But look, there's no question that ISIS is a serious threat to people everywhere – especially to people in Iraq and in Syria who have been decimated by that terror group. In Syria alone nine million people have been displace or fled the country, which makes what I'm about to share with you so infuriating.

Seven pages of this secret Pentagon document were leaked earlier this year, and put online by the organization Judicial Watch.

The report is from 2012, and specifically it explains the dangers of what the US government is doing in Syria at the time. Remember, in 2012 ISIS as we know them today did not exist.

Page three of those linked pages state three facts about the situation in Syria:

A. Internally events are taking a clear sectarian direction.

B. The Salafists, the Muslim Brotherhood and AQI or Al-Qaida in Iraq are the major forces driving the insurgency in Syria, and

C. the West, Gulf countries and Turkey, they support the opposition, while Russia, China and Iran support the regime.

So to be clear: our Department of Defense in 2012 state that the Russians, Chinese and Iran were supporting the Assad regime, and the US and Gulf partners like Qatar and Saudi Arabia were supporting the opposition to Bashar al-Assad. But the DoD also made it clear that the major forces driving that opposition were the Muslim Brotherhood, Al-Qaida in Iraq and something called the Salafists. Stay with me because if you don't know the term Salafist, that movement is an ultra-

---

[278] Source: https://www.judicialwatch.org/wp-content/uploads/2015/05/Pg.-291-Pgs.-287-293-JW-v-DOD-and-State-14-812-DOD-Release-2015-04-10-final-version11.pdf

[279] https://www.youtube.com/watch?v=Z1aDciHCejA

conservative orthodox movement within Sunni Islam. The doctrine is summed up as taking a fundamentalist approach to Islam. Sound familiar? Salafism is the same belief system as Wahhabism, from which ISIS draws their radical violent merciless beliefs.

So now let's go back to that document, because after reading page 5 in Section 8C where the Department of Defense warns this: "**If the situation unravels there is a possibility of establishing a declared or undeclared Salafist principality in eastern Syria, and this is exactly what the supporting powers to the opposition want** in order to isolate the Syrian regime, which is considered the strategic depth of the Shia expansion (Iraq and Iran)."

So what you need to know is that according to this DOD report, opposition forces, the US, the Saudis, Jordan, Qatar, and more, they wanted a Salafist or fundamental Islamic group to take over eastern Syria in order to isolate and overthrow the Syrian President Bashar al-Assad's regime.

It was a plan to overthrow Assad, but three years later, Assad is still in power, and now the most violent radical terror group in the modern world is entrenched in parts of Syria and Iraq, while exporting terror to Europe.

So here's the real question: Why would we as the American public believe any politician who claims they have a plan for what to do with ISIS when not one leader has ever acknowledged our role in the creation of that very problem.

The "smoking gun" memo itself:

CLASSIFICATION: SECRET ENVELOPE
(b)(3):10 USC § 424
ZNY SSSSS HEADER R 0SQ839Z AUG 12
RHEFHLC/DEPT OF HOMELAND SECURITY WASHINGTON DC
RHMFISS/DEPT OF HOMELAND SECURITY WASHINGTON DC
RUEHC/DEPT OF STATE WASHINGTON DC/
RHEFDIA/DIA WASHINGTON DC
RUZDFBI/FBI WASHINGTON DC
RHMFISS/FBI WASHINGTON DC
RHMFISS/HQ USSQCQM MACDILL AFB FL
RUEKJCS/JOINT STAFF WASHINGTON DC/
RUGIAAA/NGA NAVY YARD WASHINGTON DC
RUEKJCS/SECDEF WASHINGTON DC/
RUEHC/SECSTATE WASHINGTON DC
CEN MACDILL AFB FL//
CEN MACDILL AFB FL// MACDILL AFB FL/[
RUMICEA/USCENTCOMf
RUMICEA/USCENTCOMj
RUZCISR/USCENTCOMf
BT
14-L-0552/DIA/ 291

CONTROLS ~~S E C R E T//NOFORN~~ SECTION 1 OF 3 QQQQ

THIS IS A COMBINED MESSAGE

BODY

 DEPARTMENT OF DEFENSE INFORMATION REPORT, NOT FINALLY EVALUATED INTELLIGENCE.

COUNTRY: (U) IRAQ (IRQ).

14-L-0552/DIA/ 288

(bX3):10 USC §424

THE GENERAL SITUATION:

A. INTERNALLY, EVENTS ARE TAKING A CLEAR SECTARIAN DIRECTION.

B. THE SALAFIST, THE MUSLIM BROTHERHOOD, AND AQI ARE THE MAJOR FORCES DRIVING THE INSURGENCY IN SYRIA.

C. THE WEST, GULF COUNTRIES, AND TURKEY SUPPORT THE OPPOSITION; WHILE RUSSIA, CHINA. AND IRAN SUPPORT THE REGIME.

(bX1) Sec 14(c).(bX1) Sec 1 4(d)

E. THE REGIME'S PRIORITY IS TO CONCENTRATE ITS PRESENCE IN AREAS ALONG THE COAST (TARTUS, AND LATAKIA); HOWEVER, IT HAS NOT ABANDONED HOMS BECAUSE IT CONTROLS THE MAJOR TRANSPORTATION ROUTES IN SYRIA.

THE REGIME DECREASED ITS CONCENTRATION IN AREAS ADJACENT TO THE IRAQI BORDERS (AL HASAKA AND DER ZOR).

3. (C) AL QAEDA - IRAQ (AQI):

A. AQI IS FAMILIAR WITH SYRIA. AQI TRAINED IN SYRIA AND THEN INFILTRATED INTO IRAQ.

B. AQI SUPPORTED THE SYRIAN OPPOSITION FROM THE BEGINNING, BOTH IDEOLOGICALLY AND THROUGH THE MEDIA. AQI DECLARED ITS OPPOSITION OF ASSAD'S GOVERNMENT BECAUSE IT CONSIDERED IT A SECTARIAN REGIME TARGETING SUNNIS.

C. AQI CONDUCTED A NUMBER OF OPERATIONS IN SEVERAL SYRIAN CITIES UNDER THE NAME OF JAISH AL NUSRA (VICTORIOUS ARMY), ONE OF ITS AFFILIATES.

D. AQI, THROUGH THE SPOKESMAN OF THE ISLAMIC STATE OF IRAQ (ISI), ABU MUHAMMAD AL ADNANI, DECLARED THE SYRIAN REGIME AS THE SPEARHEAD OF WHAT HE IS NAMING JIBHA AL RUWAFDH (FOREFRONT OF THE SHIITES) BECAUSE OF ITS (THE SYRIAN REGIME) DECLARATION OF WAR ON THE SUNNIS.

ADDITIONALLY, HE IS CALLING ON THE SUNNIS IN IRAQ, ESPECIALLY THE TRIBES IN THE BORDER REGIONS (BETWEEN IRAQ AND SYRIA), TO WAGE WAR AGAINST THE SYRIAN REGIME, REGARDING SYRIA AS AN INFIDEL REGIME FOR ITS SUPPORT TO THE INFIDEL PARTY HEZBOLLAH, AND OTHER REGIMES HE CONSIDERS DISSENTERS LIKE IRAN AND IRAQ.

E. AQI CONSIDERS THE SUNNI ISSUE IN IRAQ TO BE FATEFULLY CONNECTED TO THE SUNNI ARABS AND MUSLIMS.

4. (C) THE BORDERS:

A. THE BORDERS BETWEEN SYRIA AND IRAQ STRETCH APPROXIMATELY 600KM WITH COMPLEX TERRAIN CONSISTING OF A VAST DESERT, MOUNTAIN RANGES (SINJAR MOUNTAINS), JOINT RIVERS (FLOWING ON BOTH SIDES), AND AGRICULTURAL LANDS.

B. IRAQ DIRECTLY NEIGHBORS THE SYRIAN PROVINCES OF HASAKA AND DER ZOR, AS WELL AS (SYRIAN) CITIES ADJACENT TO THE IRAQI BORDER.

C. THE LAND ON BOTH SIDES BETWEEN IRAQ AND SYRIA IS A VAST DESERT PUNCTUATED BY VALLEYS, AND IT LACKS TRANSPORTATION ROUTES, WITH THE EXCEPTION OF THE INTERNATIONAL HIGHWAY AND SOME MAJOR CITIES.

5. (C) THE POPULATION LIVING ON THE BORDER:

A. THE POPULATION LIVING ON THE BORDER HAS A SOCIAL-TRIBAL STYLE, WHICH IS BOUND BY STRONG TRIBAL AND FAMILIAL MARITAL TIES.

B. THEIR SECTARIAN AFFILIATION UNITES THE TWO SIDES WHEN EVENTS HAPPEN IN THE REGION.

C. AQI HAD MAJOR POCKETS AND BASES ON BOTH SIDES OF THE BORDER TO FACILITATE THE FLOW OF MATERIEL AND RECRUITS.

D. THERE WAS A REGRESSION OF AQI IN THE WESTERN PROVINCES OF IRAQ DURING THE YEARS OF 2009 AND 2010; HOWEVER, AFTER THE RISE OF THE INSURGENCY IN SYRIA, THE RELIGIOUS AND TRIBAL POWERS IN THE REGIONS BEGAN TO SYMPATHIZE WITH THE SECTARIAN UPRISING. THIS (SYMPATHY) APPEARED IN FRIDAY PRAYER SERMONS, WHICH CALLED FOR VOLUNTEERS TO SUPPORT THE SUNNI'S IN SYRIA.

6. (C) THE SITUATION ON THE IRAQI AND SYRIAN BORDER:

A. THREE BORDER BDES ARE SUFFICIENT TO CONTROL THE BORDERS DURING PEACE TIME FOR OBSERVATION DUTIES AND TO PREVENT SMUGGLING AND INFILTRATION.

(b)(1) Sec. 1. 4 (c)

C. IN PREVIOUS YEARS A MAJORITY OF AQI FIGHTERS ENTERED IRAQ PRIMARILY VIA THE SYRIAN BORDER.

7. (C) THE FUTURE ASSUMPTIONS OF THE CRISIS:

A. THE REGIME WILL SURVIVE AND HAVE CONTROL OVER SYRIAN TERRITORY.

B. DEVELOPMENT OF THE CURRENT EVENTS INTO PROXY WAR: WITH SUPPORT FROM RUSSIA, CHINA, AND IRAN, THE REGIME IS CONTROLLING THE AREAS OF INFLUENCE ALONG COASTAL. TERRITORIES (TARTUS AND LATAKIA), AND IS FIERCELY DEFENDING HOMS, WHICH IS CONSIDERED TIIE PRIMARY TRANSPORTATION ROUTE IN SYRIA. ON THE OTHER HAND, OPPOSITION FORCES ARE TRYING TO CONTROL THE EASTERN AREAS (HASAKA AND DER ZOR), ADJACENT TO THE WESTERN IRAQI PROVINCES (MOSUL AND ANBAR), IN ADDITION TO NEIGHBORING TURKISH BORDERS. WESTERN COUNTRIES, **THE GULF STATES AND TURKEY ARE SUPPORTING THESE EFFORTS.** THIS HYPOTHESIS IS MOST LIKELY IN

ACCORDANCE WITH THE DATA FROM RECENT EVENTS, WHICH WILL HELP PREPARE SAFE HAVENS UNDER INTERNATIONAL SHELTERING, SIMILAR TO WHAT TRANSPIRED IN LIBYA WHEN BENGHAZI WAS CHOSEN AS THE COMMAND CENTER OF THE TEMPORARY GOVERNMENT.

8. (C) THE EFFECTS ON IRAQ:

A. SYRIAN REGIME BORDER FORCES RETREATED FROM THE BORDER AND THE OPPOSITION FORCES (SYRIAN FREE ARMY) TOOK OVER THE POSTS AND RAISED THEIR FLAG. THE IRAQI BORDER GUARD FORCES ARE FACING A BORDER WITH SYRIA THAT IS NOT GUARDED BY OFFICIAL ELEMENTS WHICH PRESENTS A DANGEROUS AND SERIOUS THREAT.

B. THE OPPOSITION FORCES WILL TRY TO USE THE IRAQI TERRITORY AS A SAFE HAVEN FOR ITS FORCES TAKING ADVANTAGE OF THE SYMPATHY OF THE IRAQI BORDER POPULATION, MEANWHILE TRYING TO RECRUIT FIGHTERS AND TRAIN THEM ON THE IRAQI SIDE, IN ADDITION TO HARBORING REFUGEES (SYRIA).

C. IF THE SITUATION UNRAVELS THERE IS THE **POSSIBILITY OF ESTABLISHING A DECLARED OR UNDECLARED SALAFIST PRINCIPALITY IN EASTERN SYRIA (HASAKA AND DER ZOR), AND THIS IS EXACTLY WHAT THE SUPPORTING POWERS TO THE OPPOSITION WANT, IN ORDER TO ISOLATE THE SYRIAN REGIME,** WHICH IS CONSIDERED THE STRATEGIC DEPTH OF THE SHIA EXPANSION (IRAQ AND IRAN).

D. THE DETERIORATION OF THE SITUATION HAS DIRE CONSEQUENCES ON THE IRAQI SITUATION AND ARE AS FOLLOWS;

-1. THIS CREATES THE IDEAL ATMOSPHERE FOR **AQI TO RETURN TO ITS OLD POCKETS IN MOSUL AND RAMADI** AND WILL PROVIDE A RENEWED MOMENTUM UNDER THE PRESUMPTION OF UNIFYING THE JIHAD AMONG SUNNI IRAQ AND SYRIA, AND THE REST OF THE SUNNIS IN THE ARAB WORLD AGAINST WHAT IT CONSIDERS ONE ENEMY, THE DISSENTERS. **ISI COULD ALSO DECLARE AN ISLAMIC STATE THROUGH ITS UNION WITH OTHER TERRORIST ORGANIZATIONS IN IRAQ AND SYRIA, WHICH WILL CREATE GRAVE DANGER IN REGARDS TO UNIFYING IRAQ** AND THE PROTECTION OF ITS TERRITORY.

(b)(1) Sec. 1. 4 (c)

-3. THE RENEWING FACILITATION OF TERRORIST ELEMENTS FROM ALL OVER THE ARAB WORLD ENTERING INTO IRAQI ARENA.

(bX1) Sec 1 4 (c).(bX3)'10 USC § 424.(bX3) 50 USC § 3024(i)

(bX3): 10 USC § 424

(bK3) 10 USC § 424

14-L-0552/DIA/ 292

BT

#3497

NNNN

CLASSIFICATION: ~~SECRET~~

(b)(3):10 USC § 424

Plain Text of Unconventional Warfare Graphics

Figure 2-2: Structure of an insurgency or resistance movement: Underground Activities

(A pyramid in ascending chronological order)

Large-Scale Guerrilla Actions

Minor Guerrilla Actions

Increased Political Violence and Sabotage

Intense Sapping of Morale (Government, Administration, Police, and Military)

Increased Underground Activities to Demonstrate Strength of Resistance Organization and Weakness of Government

Overt and Covert Pressures Against Government (Strikes, Riots and Disorder)

Intensification of Propaganda. Psychological Preparation of Population for Rebellion

Expansion of Front Organizations

Establishment of National Front Organizations and Liberation Movements; Appeal to Foreign Sympathizers

Spreading of Subversive Organizations Into All Sectors of Life of a Country

Penetration Into Labor Unions. Student and National Organizations, and all Parts of Society

Recruitment and Training of Resistance Cadres

Infiltration of Foreign Organizers and Advisors and Foreign Propaganda. Material. Money. Weapons, and Equipment

Increased Agitation. Unrest, and Disaffection: Infiltration of Administration. Police. Military, and National Organizations Boycotts. Slowdowns, and Strikes

Agitation; Creation of Favorable Public Opinion (Advocating National Cause); Creation of Distrust of Established Institution

Creation of Atmosphere of Wider Discontent Through Propaganda and Political and Psychological Efforts to Discredit the Government

Dissatisfaction With Political, Economic, Social, Administrative, and Other Conditions; National Aspiration (Independence) or Desire for Ideological and Other Changes

Figure 1-3. Phases of unconventional warfare

PHASE 1. Preparation. Resistance and external sponsors conduct psychological preparation to unify population against established government or occupying power and prepare population to accept U.S. support.

PHASE II. Initial Contact. USG agencies coordinate with allied government-in-exile or resistance leadership for desired U.S. support.

PHASE III. Infiltration. SF [special forces] team infiltrates operational area, establishes communications with its base, and contacts resistance organization.

PHASE IV. Organization. SF team organizes, trains, and equips resistance cadre. Emphasis is on developing infrastructure.

PHASE V. Buildup. SF team assists cadre with expansion into an effective resistance organization. Limited combat operations may be conducted, but emphasis remains on development.

PHASE VI. UW forces conduct combat operations until linkup with conventional forces or end of hostilities.

PHASE VII. UW forces revert to national control, shifting to regular forces or demobilizing.

News and Notes

Dec. 29, 2015. Today's top story is the Iraqi army has retaken the city of Ramadi from ISIS. And it's reported by Iran's Fars News Agency that an Iraqi commander is accusing the US of rescuing and evacuating the ISIS leaders who were trapped there.

If it's true, the US has not repented, it is not giving up its "assets." Who will be the lucky recipient of these "special forces" next?

Earlier this year, an Iraqi commander had complained that the US let ISIS take Ramadi in the first place...

And a Pakistani newspaper reported that the leader of Daish / ISIS in Pakistan confessed to "getting funding – routed through America – to run the organisation in Pakistan and recruit young people to fight in Syria."[280]

***

August 1, 2015. Ukraine and NATO member Turkey announced the creation of an "International Islamist Brigade" composed of Al-Qaïda and Daesh combatants, and stationed in Kherson (Ukraine). This Brigade proposes to fight Russia in Crimea.[281]

We have not been told which fundamental tenet of Islam commands believers to take up arms for Kiev against Crimea. Probably because the fighters are not "jihadists" at all, but petrodollar mercenaries.

Quotable: "America is using ISIS in three ways: to attack its enemies in the Middle East, to serve as a pretext for U.S. military intervention abroad, and at home to foment a manufactured domestic threat, used to justify the unprecedented expansion of invasive domestic surveillance." – Garikai Chengu[282]

***

The wave of refugees trying to reach safety in Europe finally focused the West's attention on the problem they created. A photo of a young Syrian boy who drowned when a refugee boat capsized went viral in social networks. This wave of concern may have opened the door for Putin's offensive against ISIS.

Westerners are concerned not only about the welfare of the victims of violence, but also about increased violence in their own countries, from terrorists disguised as refugees, or other difficulties in integrating the new people.

As noted in the opening, the godfather of ISIS in Iraq was the same ambassador who was a principal in the creation of death squads in Honduras and El Salvador. Ironically, the US now has a problem with refugees fleeing gang violence in... Honduras, El Salvador and Guatemala. It is fueled partly by the so-called "War on Drugs," which is as duplicitous as the "War on Terror:" it's really the War *For* Drugs and the War *Of* Terror. Corruption made El Salvador the world capital of murder in 2015. In Honduras, the US supported a military coup

---

[280] http://www.zerohedge.com/news/2015-12-29/proof-us-directly-supporting-isis
[281] "The CSTO arrives in Iraq and Syria," Sept. 21, 2015, Thierry Meyssan, http://www.voltairenet.org/article188763.html. Kherson is the Ukrainian province bordering Crimea.
[282] http://www.globalresearch.ca/america-created-al-qaeda-and-the-isis-terror-group/5402881

against elected president Zelaya in 2009. He was trying to raise the minimum wage, which would not be tolerated by the Dole and United Fruit companies – nor Hillary Clinton's State Dep't. As noted by John Perkins, author of *Economic Hit Man* and *Hoodwinked*,

> Chiquita (United Fruit) and the CIA had toppled Guatemala's democratically-elected president Jacobo Arbenz in 1954... Haiti's president Jean-Bertrand Aristide had been ousted by the CIA in 2004 because he proposed a minimum wage increase, like Zelaya's... I was told by a Panamanian bank vice president, "Every multinational knows that if Honduras raises its hourly rate, the rest of Latin America and the Caribbean will have to follow. Haiti and Honduras have always set the bottom line for minimum wages. The big companies are determined to stop what they call a 'leftist revolt' in this hemisphere. In throwing out Zelaya they are sending frightening messages to all the other presidents who are trying to raise the living standards of their people."[283]

> The US Department of State had prior knowledge of the coup. The Department of State and the US Congress funded and advised the actors and organisations in Honduras that participated in the coup. The Pentagon trained, schooled, commanded, funded and armed the Honduran armed forces that perpetrated the coup and that continue to repress the people of Honduras by force.[284]

One might be tempted to feel that all this mayhem and misery is a hidden price we pay to get cheap bananas and not so cheap gasoline. To be sure, Big Fruit and Big Oil would like us to feel that way. But productive labor wages are a tiny percentage of the retail price, and it would be naive to believe that those who deny a fair break to the common people in one region would be generous in another. Those ill-gotten riches go to fuel corruption in the US: less visible, yet of astronomical proportions, compared to the take in poorer nations.[285]

In Guatemala, the US installed as president a general who had been in charge of the death squads, Otto Perez Molina. When, like ex-CIA asset Saddam, he tried to forge an independent policy, he was toppled in a color revolution coup. In 2015, the US embassy

> used the fight against corruption to topple Perez. Officially, the International Commission against Impunity in Guatemala (CICIG) leads the fight under United Nations auspices. In reality, the Commission is controlled by the US State Department and the Central Intelligence Agency, that do their best to clear the way for a "new generation" of US henchmen into Guatemalan politics.[286]

President Kennedy, who set up an Alliance for Progress for Latin America in 1961, was of course assassinated.

***

---

[283] http://www.globalresearch.ca/honduras-military-coup-engineered-by-two-us-companies/14862

[284] http://www.globalresearch.ca/washington-behind-the-honduras-coup-here-is-the-evidence/14390

[285] http://www.zerohedge.com/news/2016-01-06/how-corrupt-american-government

[286] Ibid.

The Sting of the Serpent

"Serpents, thirst, heat, and sand ... Libya alone can present a multitude of woes that it would beseem men to fly from." Lucan, Pharsalia[287]

The path to hell is paved with good intentions, as in, save a snake and die. In January, 2011, two months before the onslaught on Libya, the UN Human Right Council (UNHRC) presented a positive annual report on Libya's human rights record. Gaddafi, who was co-sponsor of the Al-Gaddafi International Prize for Human Rights, may have been nominated to receive a human rights prize himself. Was he led to believe he would be rewarded for freeing dangerous prisoners?

Gaddafi's son Saif al-Islam Gaddafi, who had a PhD from the London School of Economics, handled many of Libya's relations with Western countries, and also attempts to negotiate with extremists. He and the Gaddafi International Charity and Development Foundation invited a team from the International Centre for Political Violence and Terrorism Research (ICPVTR), based at a university in Singapore. "ICPVTR conducts research, training, and outreach programs aimed at reducing the threat of politically motivated violence." Their optimistically titled report, "Combating Terrorism in Libya Through Dialogue and Reintegration,"[288] tells the story behind the amnesty of 214 Islamist terrorists by Gaddafi the younger in March 2010. "It was Saif Gaddafi's fraternal, friendly qualities that touched the hearts of the LIFG" (the Libyan Islamic Fighting Group, who brought ISIS-style terror to Syria).

To gain their freedom, the LIFG compiled a 417-page volume, "Corrective Studies on the Concepts of Jihad, Accountability and Passing Judgment on Others." In it, the LIFG leaders blithely admit that "violence is a result of being extreme and ignorant of the major tenets of Islam," which prohibits extremism.

Among those freed was the LIFG, including its leader, Abdelhakim Belhaj. Releasing him was suicide. Under his command, the resurrected LIFG or "Tripoli Brigade" stormed Gaddafi's compound and seized power, with Belhaj as "Emir of Tripoli." They then went on to lead the death squad insurrection in Syria. Muammar Gaddafi was murdered, and his son is in prison. Belhaj, who is now the leader of ISIS in Libya, has sentenced his idealistic benefactor to death.

There is a parallel in this tragic tale to the Assads, strongman father Hafez and eye doctor son Bashar. The younger Assad also studied in the UK, and is more the nice guy reformer type, who made some concessions to the West. His reward too was treachery. Syria lifted controls on social media in February 2011; in March, the "insurgency" was unleashed, which they still cannot control.

A brief look at the idealistic ICPVTR website did not seem to indicate they had learned much from the fiasco, nor that their research topics include state sponsorship or mercenary motives as causes of terrorism.

The story does show how little Islamic belief has to do with "Islamist" terrorism.

---

[287] Cited by Webster Tarpley in "The CIA's Libya Rebels: The Same Terrorists who Killed US, NATO Troops in Iraq," March 24, 2011, http://tarpley.net/2011/03/24/the-cia%E2%80%99s-libya-rebels-the-same-terrorists-who-killed-us-nato-troops-in-iraq/

[288] http://mai68.org/spip/IMG/pdf/RSIS_Libya.pdf , cited in Pepe Escobar, *op. cit.*

~~~

"All truth passes through three stages. First, it is ridiculed. Second, it is violently opposed. Third, it is accepted as being self-evident." – Arthur Schopenhauer.

Lies may pass through these stages in reverse. First, they are accepted as self-evident. Second, they are violently opposed. Finally, they are ridiculed.

This book aims to help overcome the first stage by concentrating on the second, with an occasional resort to the comic relief of the third – the best place to be.

~~~

The idea for this book came to me on a visit to Barnes & Noble in summer 2015. The current events shelves were dominated by best-selling ISIS titles displayed face out. Clearly, the hot topic – and all from an MSM or neocon viewpoint. Even alternative blogs rarely saw past the "Oops, blowback, shot ourselves in the foot" position. Those who did were evidently inundated with so many issues that no one had time to write that book. One way to get it done was as an anthology by a team effort, the way Kevin Barrett did *We are NOT Charlie Hebdo*. Two consistent writers on the "ISIS on purpose" theme were George Washington's Blog and Wayne Madsen, and they kindly provided the foundation for the book.

My earlier effort to expose these war crimes in a book was *Subverting Syria* with Tony Cartalucci in 2012:

The cover images display the tactical progression of "soft warfare." First, introduce gangs of terrorists, calling them "freedom fighters." Second, the bandits spread chaos with attacks, such as this car bombing. Third, after cynically pinning their own atrocities on the Syrian government and spreading this Big Lie worldwide through the corporate-controlled media, they call for intervention by NATO... Finally, a proud, prosperous and independent nation is pummeled into submission by American weapons of mass destruction. [Photo of the bombed out city center of Sirte in Libya.] The images form a letter L, for LIBYA.

Entry from The Dirty War on Syria blog, Oct. 29th, 2012.

In an important entry to his Landdestroyer blog on Oct. 24th, Tony Cartalucci underscores a point that is often overlooked. The present crisis in nothing new under the sun – the Baathist government is a hereditary enemy of Islamist extremism. Hafez Assad's reputation as a brutal dictator is attributable in large part to the bloody suppression of the Moslem Brotherhood in the city of Hama in 1982. Constant Islamist pressure to overthrow the secular state forced the Syrian government to adopt authoritarian controls. "Hafez Assad's 'brutality' was aimed at sectarian extremists - fanatics that would later form the foundation of Al Qaeda and serve as a force of violence and destabilization throughout the world."

British and American imperialists have been fostering Islamist extremism for over two centuries, since the founding of the Wahhabi-Saudi partnership, as has been documented by David Livingstone in *Terrorism and the Illuminati* and by Webster G. Tarpley in *9/11 Synthetic Terror*. It is a potent mixture, with Arabia's oil wealth financing reactionary propaganda and ignorance. These dragon's seeds have raised a potentially immense new Mongol horde of ruthless, fanatical jihadis that might overwhelm any progressive or secular state in the region.

But why would the neo-liberal, materialist-atheist USUK foster "religious" extremist Al-Qaeda? For the very same reason the banksters financed the Nazis, the Bolsheviks and the Japanese militarists: the Countergang strategy. Before seeking a war pretext with a powerful rival nation, first infiltrate it with a countergang who hijack it and poison it with an extremist ideology. Then, when your alliance is victorious in your great war with your mad stooges, their moral defeat will be so great that the once proud rival nations become vassals who can never raise their heads from mortal shame again.

This presupposes familiarity with the work of historian Antony Sutton. A research fellow at the Hoover Institution at Stanford University for 15 years, he was forced out after publishing a book saying the West built the Soviet Union. He went on to write books on Wall Street financing both Hitler and the Bolsheviks.

The Countergang is an extremely useful concept that should be much, much better known. See Webster Tarpley's *9/11 Synthetic Terror* (5th ed., p. 313):

The US-UK occupation of Iraq was using terrorist counter-gangs and agents provocateurs in a bid to isolate and demonize the national resistance. These techniques had been refined by UK Colonel Frank Kitson in Kenya during the early 1950s Mau Mau era, as shown in Kitson's book on low intensity warfare.

It was Kitson who coined the immensely useful term counter-gang... If you want to discredit a clandestine organization, then set up your own false-flag group under the same name, and have them commit unspeakable atrocities in the name of the target group... We may assume that a large part of the beheadings and other spectacular atrocities coming out of Iraq were in fact perpetrated by US-UK-Mossad, acting through these obvious counter-gangs.

Or, "Webster Tarpley explains the Origins of Fake Terrorism," https://www.youtube.com/watch?v=L2gMqH_6QVI , 5:01.

Treachery, the Ninth Circle of Dante's Inferno

Dante condemned those guilty of betrayal and treachery to the deepest layer of Hell, along with Satan himself. What more heinous or treacherous crime is there than massacring innocents and blaming their protectors, in order to spark a genocide? For this, new infrastructure is needed: a still deeper tenth circle.

Good News and Bad

In Conclusion, my fellow Americans.
First the Good News.
ISIS is Ours. No Worries!
Now for the Bad News.
The *USA* isn't ours any more. "Our" government does what it damn pleases.
What a terrible swap - US for ISIS. We sure got the short end of this bargain.
Worse than Manhattan for a string of beads.

Progressive Press Books

Six by Webster Griffin Tarpley

9/11 Synthetic Terror: Made in USA — by a network of moles, patsies, killers, corrupt politicians and media. The authoritative account of 9/11. "Strongest of the 770+ books I have reviewed" – R. Steele. 5th ed., 569 pp, $19.95.
In Spanish: ***11-S Falso Terrorismo***. 408 pp, $19.95.

George Bush: The Unauthorized Biography Vivid X-ray of the oligarchy dominating U.S. politics, with a full narrative of GWHB's long list of crimes. How Skull-and-Bonesmen Bush and Brown Bros Harriman made fortunes building up Hitler's war machine. Bush Sr is linked to Iran-Contra, Watergate, and genocide in Iraq after luring Saddam Hussein to attack Kuwait. 700 pp, $19.95.

Just Too Weird: *Bishop Romney and the Mormon Putsch Against America: Polygamy, Theocracy and Subversion.* Mormonism exposed as part of the British-neocon financier plot to take back the colonies. 284 pp, $16.95.

Barack H. Obama: the Unauthorized Biography The abject corruption of a Wall Street lackey, and a richly detailed profile of the finance oligarchy. 595 pp, $19.95.

Obama – The Postmodern Coup: Making of a Manchurian Candidate. The Obama puppet's advisors are radical reactionaries. This study distills decades of astute political insight and analysis. 320 pp, $15.95.

Surviving the Cataclysm, ***Your Guide through the Greatest Financial Crisis in Human History***, by W.G. Tarpley. The unwinding of the hedge funds and derivatives bubble, and with them, life as we knew it in the USA. Richly detailed history of the financier oligarchy, how they plunder our nation. Plus, How to cope with the crisis. 668 pp, $25.

Five by F. Wm. Engdahl

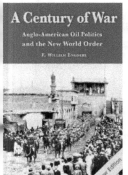

A Century of War: Anglo-American Oil Politics and the New World Order. The classic exposé; the empire controls the oil to control the world. 352 pp, $25.

Full Spectrum Dominance: Totalitarian Democracy in the New World Order. They are out for total control: land, sea, air, space, cyberspace, media, money, movements. 258 pp, $23.95.

Gods of Money: Wall Street and the Death of the American Century. The banksters stop at nothing: setting world wars, plunging our world in chaos and corruption. 390 pp, $24.95.

Seeds of Destruction: The Hidden Agenda of Genetic Manipulation. A corporate gang is out for complete control of the world by patenting our food. Inside the corporate boardrooms and science labs, a world of greed, intrigue, corruption and coercion. 340 pp, $25.95.

Target China: How Washington and Wall Street Plan to Cage the Asian Dragon. The secret war on many fronts to thwart the Chinese challenge. 256 pp, $24.95.

Three by Michel Chossudovsky

Towards a World War III Scenario: The Dangers of Nuclear War. The Pentagon is preparing a first-strike nuclear attack on Iran. 103 pp, $15.95.

The Global Economic Crisis: The Great Depression of the XXI Century, by Prof. Chossudovsky, with a dozen other experts. 416 pp, $25.95.

The Globalization of Poverty and the New World Order. Brilliant analysis how corporatism feeds on poverty, destroying the environment, apartheid, racism, sexism, and ethnic strife. 401 pp, $27.95.

Two by Henry Makow

Illuminati: Cult that Hijacked the World tackles taboos like Zionism, British Empire, Holocaust. How international bankers stole a monopoly on government credit, and took over the world. They run it all: wars, schools, media. 249 pp, $19.95. ***Illuminati 2: Deception & Seduction***, more hidden history. 285 pp, $19.95

History

Two by George Seldes, the great muckraking journalist, whistleblower on the plutocrats who keep the media in lockstep, and finance fascism. ***1,000 Americans Who Rule the USA*** (1947, 324 pp, $18.95) Media concentration is not new! ***Facts and Fascism*** (1943, 292 pp, $15.95) How our native corporatist élite aimed for a fascist victory in WW2.

Two by Prof. Donald Gibson. ***Battling Wall Street: The Kennedy Presidency.*** JFK: a martyr who strove mightily for social and economic justice. 208 pp, $14.95. ***The Kennedy Assassination Cover-Up.*** JFK was murdered by the moneyed elite, not the CIA or Mafia. 375 pp, $19.95.

Two by Stewart H. Ross. ***Global Predator: US Wars for Empire.*** A damning account of the atrocities committed by US armed forces over two centuries. ***Propaganda for War: How the US was Conditioned to Fight the Great War*** Propaganda by Britain and her agents like Teddy Roosevelt sucked the USA into the war to smash the old world order. 350 pp and $18.95 each.

Fall of the Arab Spring: from Revolution to Destruction. Protests as cover for destabilization. 205 pp, $14.95.

Enemies by Design: Inventing the War on Terrorism. A century of imperialism in the Middle East. Biography of Osama bin Ladeen; Zionization of America; PNAC, Afghanistan, Palestine, Iraq. 416 pp, $17.95.

The Iraq Lie: How the White House Sold the War, by former Congressman Joseph M. Hoeffel. Bush Lied about WMD — and went ahead with war. $14.95

The Nazi Hydra in America: Suppressed History of a Century by Glen Yeadon. US plutocrats launched Hitler, then recouped Nazi assets to erect today's police state. Fascists won WWII because they ran both sides. "The story is shocking and sobering, and deserves to be widely read." – Howard Zinn. 700 pp, $19.95.

Inside the Gestapo: Hitler's Shadow over the World. Intimate, fascinating Nazi defector's tale of ruthlessness, intrigue, and geopolitics. 287 pp, $17.95.

Sunk: The Story of the Japanese Submarine Fleet, 1941-1945. The bravery of doomed men in a lost cause, against impossible odds. 300 pp, $15.95.

Terrorism and the Illuminati, A 3000-Year History. "Islamic" terrorists are tentacles of western imperialism. 332 pp, $16.95.

Troublesome Country. Throughout its history the US has failed to live up to our guiding democratic creed. 146 pp, $12.95.

Psychology: Brainwashing

The Rape of the Mind: The Psychology of Thought Control, Menticide and Brainwashing. Conditioning in open and closed societies; tools to defend against torture or social pressure. Classic by Dr Joost Meerloo, survivor of Nazism and McCarthyism. 320 pp, $16.95.

The Telescreen: An Empirical Study of the Destruction of Consciousness, by Prof. Jeffrey Grupp. How mass media brainwash us with consumerism and war propaganda. Fake history, news, issues, and reality steal our souls. 199 pp, $14.95. Also by Grupp: ***Telementation: Cosmic Feeling and the Law of Attraction***. Deep feeling is our secret nature and key to self-realization. 124 pp, $12.95.

Conspiracy, NWO

Corporatism: the Secret Government of the New World Order by Prof. Jeffrey Grupp. Corporations control all world resources. Their New World Order is the "prison planet" that Hitler aimed for. 408 pp, $16.95.

Descent into Slavery. How the banksters took over America and the world. The Founding Fathers, Rothschilds, the Crown and the City, world wars, globalization. 310 pp, $16. Also by Des Griffin: ***Fourth Reich of the Rich***, 316 pp, $16.

Dope Inc.: Britain's Opium War against the United States. "The Book that Drove Kissinger Crazy." Underground Classic, new edition. 320 pp, $12.95.

Ecology, Ideology and Power by Prof. Donald Gibson. Ulterior motives of the reactionary elite pushing population and resource control. 162 pp., $14.95

Final Warning: A History of the New World Order by D. A. Rivera. Classic, in-depth research into the Great Conspiracy: the Fed, the Trilateral Commission, the CFR, and the Illuminati. 360 pp, $14.95.

How the World Really Works by A.B. Jones. Crash course in conspiracy. Digests of 11 classics like *Tragedy and Hope, Creature from Jekyll Island*. 336 pp, $15.

Killing us Softly: *the Global Depopulation Policy* by Kevin Galalae, 146 pp., color. The Why and How of the covert, indirect war on the people. $15.95.

The Money Power: Empire of the City and Pawns in the Game. Two classic geopolitics books in one. The illuminist Three World Wars conspiracy: to divide us on ethnic and political lines to conquer humanity. 320 pp, $16.95

The Triumph of Consciousness. The real Global Warming and Greening agenda: more hegemony by the NWO. 347 pp, $14.95.

Conspiracy: False Flag Operations

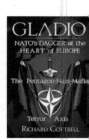

9/11 on Trial: *The W T C Collapse.* 20 proofs the World Trade Center was destroyed by controlled demolition. 192 pp, $12.95.

Gladio, NATO's Dagger at the Heart of Europe: *The Pentagon-Mafia-Nazi Terror Axis.* The blood-red thread of terror by NATO death squads in Europe, from WW2 to the present. 490 pp, $25.

Conspiracies, Conspiracy Theories and the Secrets of 9/11, German best-seller explores conspiracy in history, before tackling competing theories on 9/11. 274 pp, $14.95.

Grand Deceptions: Zionist Intrigues. The Neocon World Order, from Herzl, to the world wars, Bolshevism, 9/11, Al-Qaeda, and media tyranny. 177 pp., $13.95.

In Search of the Truth: *An Exposure of the Conspiracy,* by Azar Mirza-Beg. A portrait of our times, society and religion, and the threat we face. 208 pp, $17.

JFK-911: 50 Years of Deep State, by Laurent Guyénot. The Greater Israel strategy behind the JFK and 9/11 murders. 238 pp, $15.95.

Subverting Syria: *How CIA Contra Gangs and NGO's Manufacture, Mislabel and Market Mass Murder.* Syrian "uprising" is a cynical US plot using faked news, provocateurs, opportunists, mercenaries, and Wahhabi fanatics. 116 pp, $10.00.

Terror on the Tube: Behind the Veil of 7/7, an Investigation, by Nick Kollerstrom. The glaring evidence that all four Muslim scapegoats were completely innocent. 7/7 clinched the assault on our rights. 3rd ed, 322 pp, $17.77.

The War on Freedom. The seminal exposé of 9/11. "Far and away the best and most balanced analysis of September 11th." – Gore Vidal. 400 pp, $16.95.

Truth Jihad: *My Epic Struggle Against the 9/11 Big Lie.* Kevin Barrett's profound and humorous autobiographical testament. 224 pp, $9.95.

Coming Soon

A Prisoner's Diary, by Hussain Mohammed Al-Amily
The New World Order in Action: *from the Middle East through Greece to Ukraine,* by Takis Fotopoulos.

E-Books
9/11 Synthetic Terror; Barack Obama Unauthorized Biography;
Gladio; Grand Deceptions; In Search of the Truth; ISIS IS US; Iraq Lie;
JFK-911; Just Too Weird; Killing Us Softly; Fall of the Arab Spring;
Nazi Hydra; Subverting Syria; Surviving the Cataclysm; Target: China.

Author Biographies

"George Washington" – the pen name for the head writer at Washington's Blog – is a busy professional, a former adjunct professor, an American and a family man. He is post-partisan ... believing that neither the Republican nor Democratic parties represent the interests of the people as opposed to the big banks, major corporations, and the military-industrial complex. He strives to provide real-time, well-researched and actionable information.

Wayne Madsen is an American journalist, television news commentator, online editor of Wayne Madsen Report.com, investigative journalist and author specializing in intelligence and international affairs. Throughout Wayne's career he has uncovered many explosive stories, reporting from places like Washington, Iraq, Israel, the Congo, Rwanda, Pakistan, Hong Kong, Libya, Thailand, Cambodia, London, Paris, Venezuela. He has interviewed famous people and heads of state. Wayne has written for many daily, weekly, and monthly publications, and has been a television commentator on many programs, including *60 Minutes, Russia Today, Press TV*. He has authored ten books.

"Syrian Girl Partisan" became an activist on Twitter, Facebook and YouTube to protest and expose the dirty war on her country, Syria, gaining a great following in social media. Her intelligence, political acumen and rare beauty would make her a Superstar if she toed the mainstream party line. As a graduate student in chemistry, she played an important role in exposing the lies about the chemical weapon rocket attacks in Ghouta, Damascus in 2013. Syrian Girl also goes by the name of Mimi al-Laham and Maram Susli. She is a regular columnist at New Eastern Outlook.

John-Paul Leonard works as publisher at Progressive Press. He has a BA in Political Science from UCLA and a Masters in Finance from UC Berkeley. After a business career that took him for 18 years to Europe, East and West, he returned to the US and took over the family publishing business. In 2001 he wrote on international politics for Media Monitors Network, leading to the first 9/11 truth book in English, *The War on Freedom* (2002). In 2012 and 2013 he kept up blogs on the the dirty wars on Syria and Ukraine. Deeply shocked by the destruction of Libya and Syria, J-P saw the need for a book exposing the method behind this madness, *ISIS IS US* (2016).

Cartoonist's draft sketch for "ISIS is Us"–
Hillary Clinton, John McCain, Netanyahu, Erdogan, Bandar "Bush" and François Hollande.
Clinton is featured rather than Obama. As Secretary of State, influenced by Sarkozy, she led the
drive to destroy Libya and Syria, against the advice of Obama's top military advisers.

Hillary's leaked emails exposed her and Sarkozy's machinations against Gaddafi: "admissions of rebel war crimes, special ops trainers inside Libya from nearly the start of protests, Al Qaeda embedded in the U.S. backed opposition, Western nations jockeying for access to Libyan oil, the nefarious origins of the absurd Viagra mass rape claim, and concern over Gaddafi's" African gold dinar plan threatening the role of the CFA, the French African franc – according to *The Levant Report*, "New Hillary Emails Reveal Propaganda, Executions, Coveting Libyan Oil and Gold."